Bizarreries and Fantasies of Granduille

Bizarreries and Fantasies of Granduille

266 Illustrations from
UN AUTRE MONDE and LES ANIMAUX

Introduction and Commentary by
Stanley Appelbaum

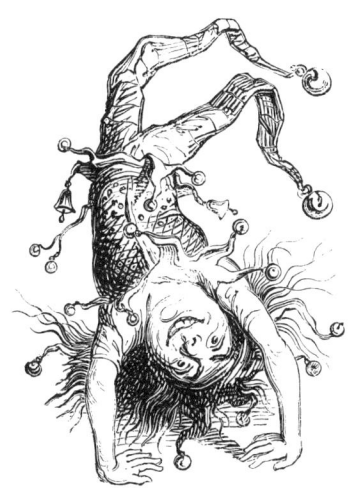

DOVER PUBLICATIONS, INC.
NEW YORK

Published in Canada by General Publishing Company, Ltd., 30 Lesmill Road, Don Mills, Toronto,
Ontario.
Published in the United Kingdom by Constable
and Company, Ltd., 10 Orange Street, London WC 2.

Bizarreries and Fantasies of Grandville is a new
work, first published by Dover Publications, Inc., in
1974. It contains 266 illustrations by Grandville
reproduced from the first editions of the following
works:
   Scènes de la vie privée et publique des animaux,
J. Hetzel et Paulin, Paris, 1842.
   Un Autre Monde, H. Fournier, Paris, 1844.
   The selection and the text, all prepared specially
for the present edition, are by Stanley Appelbaum.

International Standard Book Number: 0-486-22991-2
Library of Congress Catalog Card Number: 73-76962

Manufactured in the United States of America
Dover Publications, Inc.
180 Varick Street
New York, N.Y. 10014

Contents

Introduction

One of the magical eras in the history of French book illustration was the Thirties and Forties of the nineteenth century. A much broader segment of the population than ever before was able and eager to acquire sumptuous illustrated volumes, and this public, in its rage for pictures, called for numerous freshly illustrated editions of old classics and demanded illustrations in new novels and travel accounts. Moreover, enterprising publishers concocted a variety of books that existed primarily for the sake of the illustrations.

Meanwhile, the very nature of the illustrated book was changing. The sedate rectangular eighteenth-century frontispiece and full-page plates, engraved on copper, were giving way to a riot of images of all shapes cavorting over the pages and onto the binding, to a profusion of pictures closely integrated with the letterpress text. Unceasing experiments with fanciful borders (sometimes printed in a variety of colors), with unusual vignettes, initials, headpieces and tailpieces, gave the French book greater visual interest than at any time since the early sixteenth century. No doubt the Romantics' infatuation for the Middle Ages was at least partially responsible for this return to the pictorial richness of illuminated manuscripts and early printed books. Yet it was a contemporary advance in technique that made this return possible.

Lithography, though also enjoying a peak period in the Thirties and Forties, was little used for book illustration. Steel engraving was employed more extensively, with some notably fine results, but this technique, too, worked best for isolated plates or discreet vignettes. The specific marvels of Romantic book illustration were made possible by the adoption of the "white-line" wood engraving (the end of the plank worked with the burin) popularized by Thomas Bewick in England late in the eighteenth century. This technique combined enormous flexibility with perfect compatibility of picture and type from the point of view of both printer and viewer.

Fortunately, just at this time France was blessed with a number of artists who rose nobly to the occasion. Daumier, Gavarni, Töpffer (a Swiss), Gigoux, Nanteuil and Lami were just a few of those who provided lively and imaginative drawings for the industrious workshops of the professional wood engravers. But it was Grandville, though he came to book illustration relatively late in his career, who created the most extraordinary elements of this varied production.

II

The artist, whose real name was Jean-Ignace-Isidore Gérard, was born in Nancy on September 15, 1803, into a family connected with the theater and the arts. His grandparents, whose professional name of Grandville he later adopted, had been actors at the court of Lorraine. His father, the younger of two brothers who were painters of miniatures, imparted his craft to the sickly but talented boy. Several critics have traced the mature Grandville's finicky draftsmanship and crowded compositions to this early training. It is clear from later events that he also learned lithography.

When Grandville was a young man, the artist Mansion, a prosperous relation on a visit to Nancy, admired his work and encouraged him to try his fortunes in Paris. Various writers give Grandville's age on his arrival in Paris as anywhere between seventeen and twenty-three; the more advanced age makes better sense when compared with the known dates of his early work. His first piece printed is said to have been a lithograph, "The Cherry Vendor," in 1824, published in Nancy; the first firm date for his Paris productions seems to be 1826.

These 1826 pieces, also lithographs, were costume studies after sketches by the noted costumier Hippolyte Lecomte. Grandville had quickly renewed contact with theatrical circles, since an older cousin of his was a stage manager at the Opéra-Comique. This backstage experience not only secured him some immediate assignments; it was to form a lasting thematic element in his art. Throughout the remainder of the Twenties and into the Thirties, Grandville produced many small series of lithographs, some humorous (like *The Beverages of Man* and *The Sundays of a Parisian Bourgeois*), others quite tame (like *Every Age Has Its Pleasures*). Two of these series stand out and deserve further mention.

In 1830 there was the set of nine lithos, *A Trip to Eternity*, a modern Dance of Death in which a fatal skeleton appears abruptly before people of varied ranks and occupations, all in contemporary dress. The immediate inspiration for this excellently drawn series was most probably the similar one done by Rowlandson in 1814–16. Though prized today, Grandville's Dance of Death was not nearly as successful at the time as the series of seventy lithographs he issued in 1829 under the title *The Metamorphoses of the Day* (see Fig. B). These instantly established his fame and determined much of his future activity.

The "metamorphoses" were the satirical human-animal combinations to which Grandville was to recur so often, and with which his name is still most closely linked: full bodies of animals in human clothes, human bodies with animal heads, or even further variations. These hybrids should not be misunderstood as childish simplifications or perversions of animal behavior in the manner of *The Living Desert*. They are concerned exclusively with human behavior, and the animals are used emblematically to represent the personality traits (greed, cowardice, etc.) traditionally associated with them in fables, bestiaries, folk sayings and other popular lore. This does not preclude loving attention on the part of the artist to the physical characteristics, and even the real habits, of the animals depicted. Many critics, finding Grandville's animals stiff and contrived, have accused him of merely pillaging the plates of Buffon, and indeed, there is evidence that he sometimes used printed models; but closer and fuller examination of his work (together with well-attested reminiscences of his friends) make it absolutely clear that he loved animals and knew them well at first hand.

What may be called the second phase of Grandville's career (and here again, the most important work is lithographic, although he now supplied only the preliminary drawings) began in 1830, when Charles X was ousted and succeeded by the "Citizen King," Louis-Philippe. Restrictions on journalists were considerably eased, but it was still not hard for a liberal to run afoul of the government. Grandville's services were enlisted for France's first journal of caricature, *La Silhouette*, which lasted only till January 1831, then for Charles Philipon's new magazine *La Caricature*, the illustrious model for the later *Punch* in England and for many other similar ventures. Grandville, later joined on the staff by Honoré Daumier, five years his junior, contributed scathing cartoons to *La Caricature* from its beginnings and throughout its stormy existence, which was ended by the unusually repressive laws of September 1835 passed after an attempt on the king's life. The contributors to *La Caricature* considered Louis-Philippe to have betrayed the ideals of the Revolution of 1830, and Grandville's cartoons attacked the regime's support of capital, the officious censors, the ultra-conservative National Guard and other features odious to the liberals. At the same time, Grandville pilloried many foibles of social life, often using animal characters. In many of his cartoons he was developing bold techniques of pictorial narrative and expressive distortion which were to reappear in some of his best book illustrations.

Philipon also edited *Le Charivari*, similar to *La Caricature*, but milder and thus able to weather the tempest that destroyed his other magazine. Grandville contributed to it on and off from its inception late in 1832 until 1835. He also sent nonpolitical humorous drawings, which appeared as woodcuts, to *L'Illustration* and several other periodicals in the Thirties and Forties. A particular favorite of his, apparently, was *Le Magasin pittoresque*, edited by Edouard Charton. This journal published some of Grandville's most exquisite and intriguing pieces: his famous animated music; a soliloquy, with many small drawings of the speaker's changing expressions, that prefigures Jules Feiffer; a picture of a shaving machine that is a direct ancestor of the feeding machine in *Modern Times;* several charming insect scenes equal to the best in *Les Animaux;* and (at the very end of the artist's life) two of his highly esteemed dreamlike gradual-transformation pictures. Yet despite his frequent contributions to periodicals after 1835, this year marked the last decisive turning point in his career. Outspoken political cartoons were no longer a possible source of income for Grandville, who had married a cousin from Nancy, Marguerite-Henriette Fischer, in 1833.

III

Book commissions were welcome to the artist, since the illustrated volumes of the time were literally crammed with pictures. Some of Grandville's book work was for collective albums but many books were illustrated by him alone. Only highlights of his tremendous unceasing activity can be mentioned here (it is estimated that between 1827 and 1847 he produced about 3000 of his complex and fastidious drawings for all sorts of publications).

His first major illustrated book was a new edition of the song lyrics of Béranger. Two publications of 1838 tapped different aspects of his talent. A *Gulliver's Travels* brought his love of the fantastic into play, while a *Fables of La Fontaine* was a logical (and well-executed) assignment for the man who made his reputation with the

Metamorphoses of the Day. Grandville was also to illustrate the work of the later and lesser French fabulists Lavalette and Florian (publications of 1841 and 1842). His *Robinson Crusoe* illustrations appeared in 1840. The end of that year saw the beginning of a vast undertaking, the first book specifically conceived as a vehicle for Grandville's genius.

This was one of the two works represented in this volume: *Scènes de la vie privée et publique des animaux* (Scenes of the Private and Public Life of the Animals), a title which seems to allude to the division of Balzac's *Comédie humaine* into various *Scènes de la vie*. An alternate title, used in early stages of publication and then for the much altered economical republication of 1866, was *Les Animaux peints par eux-mêmes et dessinés par un autre* (The Animals Painted by Themselves and Drawn by Another), which is a clear allusion to the celebrated and much imitated collection of essays and drawings that began publication in 1840, *Les Français peints par eux-mêmes* (Grandville contributed several items to this). Finally, the subtitle of the animal book, which clearly states its import, is *Etudes de mœurs contemporaines* (Studies of Contemporary Manners). Throughout the present volume this book will be referred to as *Les Animaux*.

The guiding spirit of the book was its energetic young publisher, Pierre-Jules Hetzel (born 1814), who was still working in partnership with the older man Paulin, the publisher of the 1835 edition of *Gil Blas* that had consolidated the triumph of wood engraving as a medium for book illustration. During 1839 and most of 1840, Hetzel, who enjoyed Grandville's animal drawings best of all his work, planned *Les Animaux* as a spotlight for Grandville and a stepping-stone to independence for himself. He created the literary framework and wrote a great deal of the text under the pseudonym P.-J. Stahl (at first the incognito mystified almost everyone; he was to use it for his original writing all his life). He hired the finest wood engravers and sought out many of the most prestigious writers in Paris. Four of the stories (in general, the best) are signed by Balzac, who probably also assisted Hetzel with some of his. Balzac surely wrote the one signed by George Sand, who consented to the use of her name (perhaps Hetzel wanted to avoid the appearance of a plethora of Balzac). This was Balzac's first contact with Hetzel, who was to publish a grand illustrated edition of the *Comédie humaine*. Other distinguished contributors were the poet and playwright Alfred de Musset, who was offered his choice among thirty-five animal subjects; his brother, Paul de Musset; Jules Janin, novelist and dramatic critic of the *Journal des Débats* for forty-one years; Charles Nodier, librarian of the Bibliothèque de l'Arsenal, where his literary salon harbored the great Romantics, and author of numerous tales of dream and fantasy; his talented daughter Marie Mennessier-Nodier; and Louis Viardot, co-founder of the important *Revue indépendante*, director of the Théâtre Italien and husband of the opera singer Pauline Garcia. The other contributors were also writers of much experience. (In his further career Hetzel published some of the most significant French books of the nineteenth century, his last great author-protégé being Jules Verne.)

Like many long and elaborate books of the time, *Les Animaux* was issued in short installments bound in colorful paper wrappers. Its hundred installments appeared between November 1840 and December 1842. The stories were commissioned and written (with Grandville in mind) gradually during that entire period, the artist executing the illustrations as the text was supplied to him. The bound books (two volumes) were dated 1842. It is clear from the book's subtitle and preface that it was conceived as a satire of government and society (contemporary readers thought they recognized specific human individuals in some of the animal portraits, but Hetzel always denied such an intention). Another claim of the preface, that this was the first time in literary history that animals were allowed to speak for themselves, is not true; Cervantes and Hoffmann, to name just two well-known writers, had used this device earlier. The success of *Les Animaux* with the public is revealed by an incident mentioned in Balzac's correspondence with Hetzel: statuettes of some of the animal characters were being manufactured and sold without proper authorization. Synopses of each of the stories appear on page 86, together with brief annotations that may give the present-day non-French reader a better idea of how Grandville expected his drawings to be understood.

It was only natural for some of Grandville's numerous illustrations for *Les Animaux* to repeat elements from previous work. For instance, the *Metamorphoses* had already included the owl-and-bat combination, snakes hissing in a theater, ravens as medical students and monkeys as painters.

IV

During these years of achievement, Grandville was pursued by family griefs that affected him severely; contemporaries describe him as gray and stooped at forty. Two of his three children by Marguerite Fischer died at the age of four, and she herself died in July 1842. From all accounts his life with her had not been happy, though he respected her and adored his children. She had been overbearing and dictatorial, even in matters of art, and is said to have made curl papers out of drawings by her husband that failed to meet her approval. Certainly his work is deeply tinged with misogyny. Marguerite apparently insisted, while on her deathbed, that her husband marry again and even appointed her successor, a Mlle. Lhuillier, whom Grandville did marry in 1843 (it seems they had corresponded during Marguerite's lifetime).

One of Grandville's finest jobs of illustration appeared in an 1843 book, *Les petites misères de la vie humaine* (The Petty Sorrows of Human Life). It was in the following year that the publisher-printer Henri Fournier, who had commissioned Grandville's illustrations for La Fontaine, brought out the book (also represented in this volume) that has contributed most to Grandville's enduring fame in the twentieth century.

This was *Un Autre Monde* (Another World), issued in thirty-six installments. In this case the text was written to accommodate already existing (but unpublished) Grandville drawings. Naturally, Grandville did a few more to illustrate specific characters and incidents invented by the writer of the frame story, but the primacy of the illustrations is a basic factor in the evaluation of the book: the text is generally a lame, hotchpotch attempt to group and interpret pictures that were conceived independently. The author of the words was Taxile Delord, a writer on many topics and editor-in-chief of *Le Charivari* from 1848 to 1858. Delord's name appears only in an illustration near the end of the book. Grandville appears as sole author on the title page, on which the full title appears as: *Un Autre Monde/ Transformations, visions, incarnations, ascensions, locomotions, explorations, pérégrinations, excursions, stations/ Cosmogonies, fantasmagories, rêveries, folâtreries, facéties, lubies/ Métamorphoses, zoomorphoses, lithomorphoses, métempsycoses, apothéoses et autres choses.* (*Folâtreries, facéties, lubies* = madcap ideas, gags, caprices; *et autres choses* = and other things.) The full-page plates were tinted in the orginal edition.

Un Autre Monde is the work in which Grandville's oneiric leanings receive fullest expression (leading to his adoption by the Surrealists as one of their multitude of spiritual progenitors and giving psychoanalytically minded art critics a field day). The public of 1844 was respectfully awed and disconcerted, and many people today still view the book as a random collection of whimsies and eccentricities. But it is most fruitful to regard it as an integral part of Grandville's career as a satirist and caricaturist. He continues to attack the same kinds of victims as in the past, and even with regard to the specific content and artistic devices, there is much that had appeared in his earlier works. For instance, his lithographs in *La Caricature* had already included demons, the allegorical figure of Caricature, animated canes and umbrellas, street carnivals with a weighing machine and a Punch and Judy show, very tall and very short people, and anamorphic distortions. In a way, *Un Autre Monde* is a summation of all that had gone before, Grandville's artistic testament. But it is true nevertheless that it contains a great many fresh and striking ideas, and that even the older ideas are pushed to a new imaginative extreme, are made bolder and unforgettable, lending the book incredible vigor and giving it a place unique in nineteenth-century artistic production.

Like *Les Animaux, Un Autre Monde* reflects the preoccupations and amusements of the reign of Louis-Philippe: the Anglomania in customs and costumes, the triumphs of the Romantic opera and ballet, the endless war in Algeria, the vagaries of the utopian socialists, the wild abandon of Carnival, the growth of capitalism and the birth of modern high-pressure advertising and publicity, the social inequalities and inequities, the fashionable diabolism, and much more. Strange and fanciful as the drawings are, they can make the era more real and tangible to students of history than many a dry "realistic" rendering. A synopsis and explanations of *Un Autre Monde* will be found on page 2.

V

The next two books completely illustrated by Grandville, *Cent Proverbes* (A Hundred Proverbs) in 1845 and *Jérôme Paturot* in 1846, show him at the top of his form. The last major book under his signature (though it is now believed that he contributed only part of the drawings) was *Les Fleurs animées* (The Personified Flowers), an elaboration of sections of *Un Autre Monde*, which appeared posthumously in 1847; some writers say Wagner had this book in mind when he created the Flower Maidens in *Parsifal*. Grandville was at work on *Les Etoiles animées* (The Personified Stars) at the time of his death, which occurred only a few months after the sudden death of the remaining child of his first marriage. Much has been written about the artist's melancholia, fatalism and second-sight in these last months, and the fact of his dying in a "madhouse" has led many careless authors to speak of a strain of insanity apparent throughout his *œuvre*. The truth appears to be

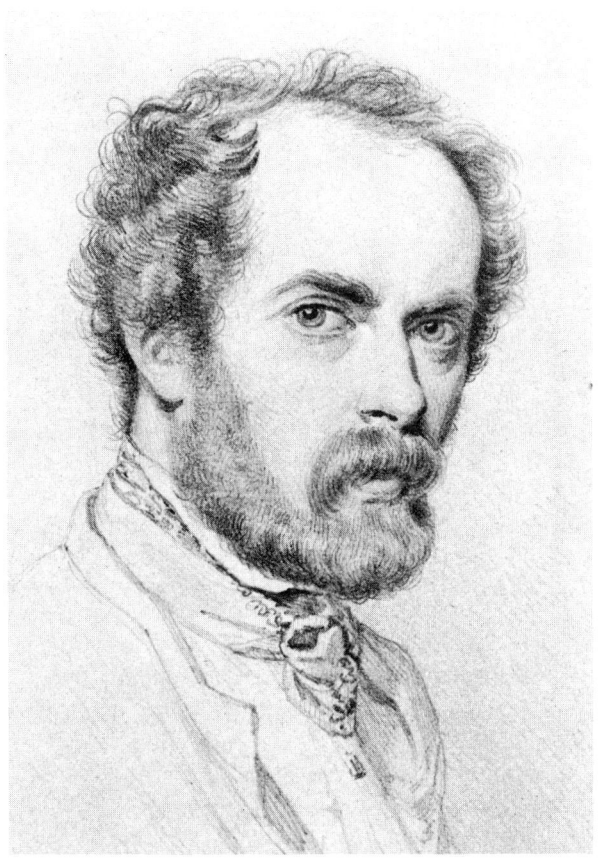

Fig. A. Self-portrait of Grandville. Pencil drawing. (Courtesy Musée des Beaux-Arts, Nancy)

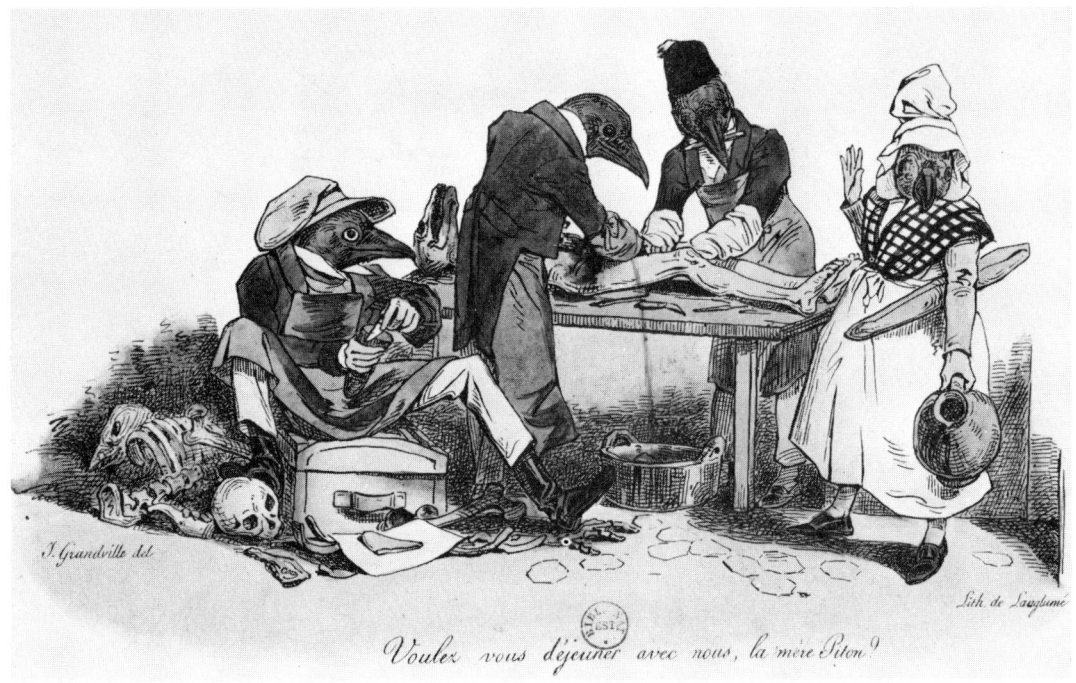

Fig. B. Ravens as medical students. Lithograph from Grandville's 1829 series *The Metamorphoses of the Day*. (Courtesy Bibliothèque Nationale, Paris)

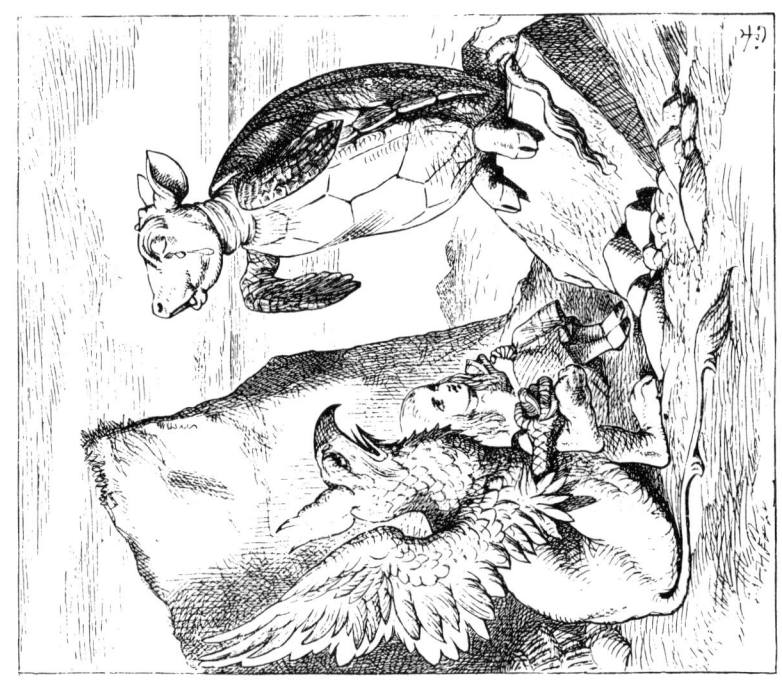

Fig. D. Illustration by John Tenniel for *Alice's Adventures in Wonderland* (1865). Compare the figure of the Mock Turtle with that of the weeping calf in illustration No. 101 in the present volume.

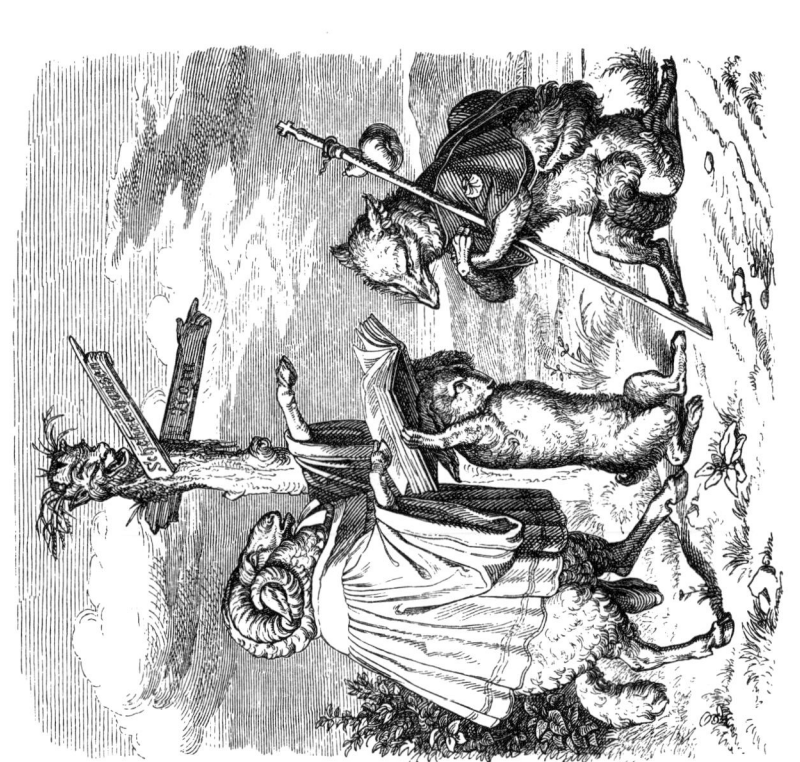

Fig. C. Illustration by Wilhelm von Kaulbach for Goethe's *Reineke Fuchs*. (The original 1846 edition had engraved illustrations; the woodcut version reproduced here from the 1857 edition makes the resemblance to Grandville even clearer.)

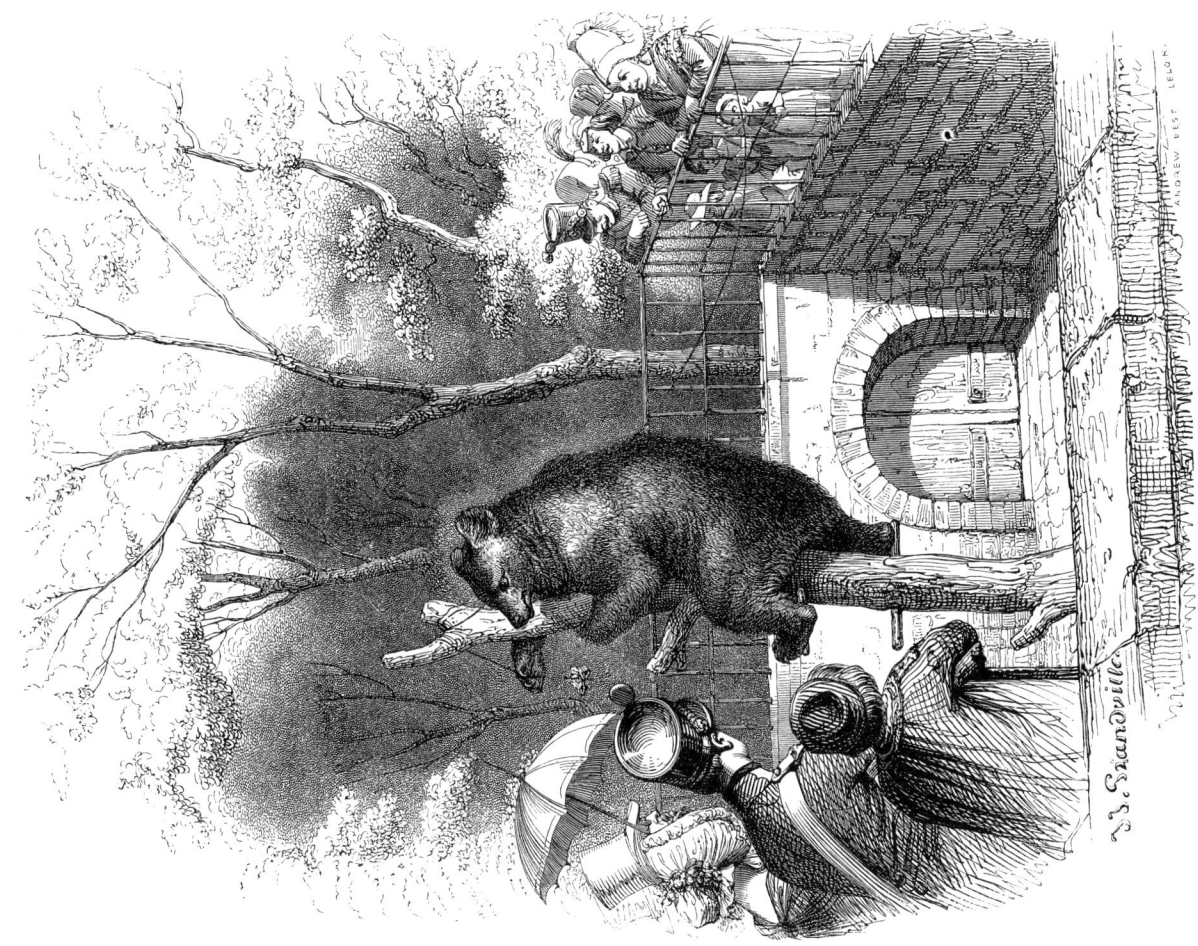

Fig. F. Illustration by Grandville for Boitard's *Le Jardin des Plantes* (1842), showing the bear-pit at that Parisian zoo. Grandville distorted this drawing when he created one of the most unusual illustrations in *Un Autre Monde* (No. 55 in the present edition).

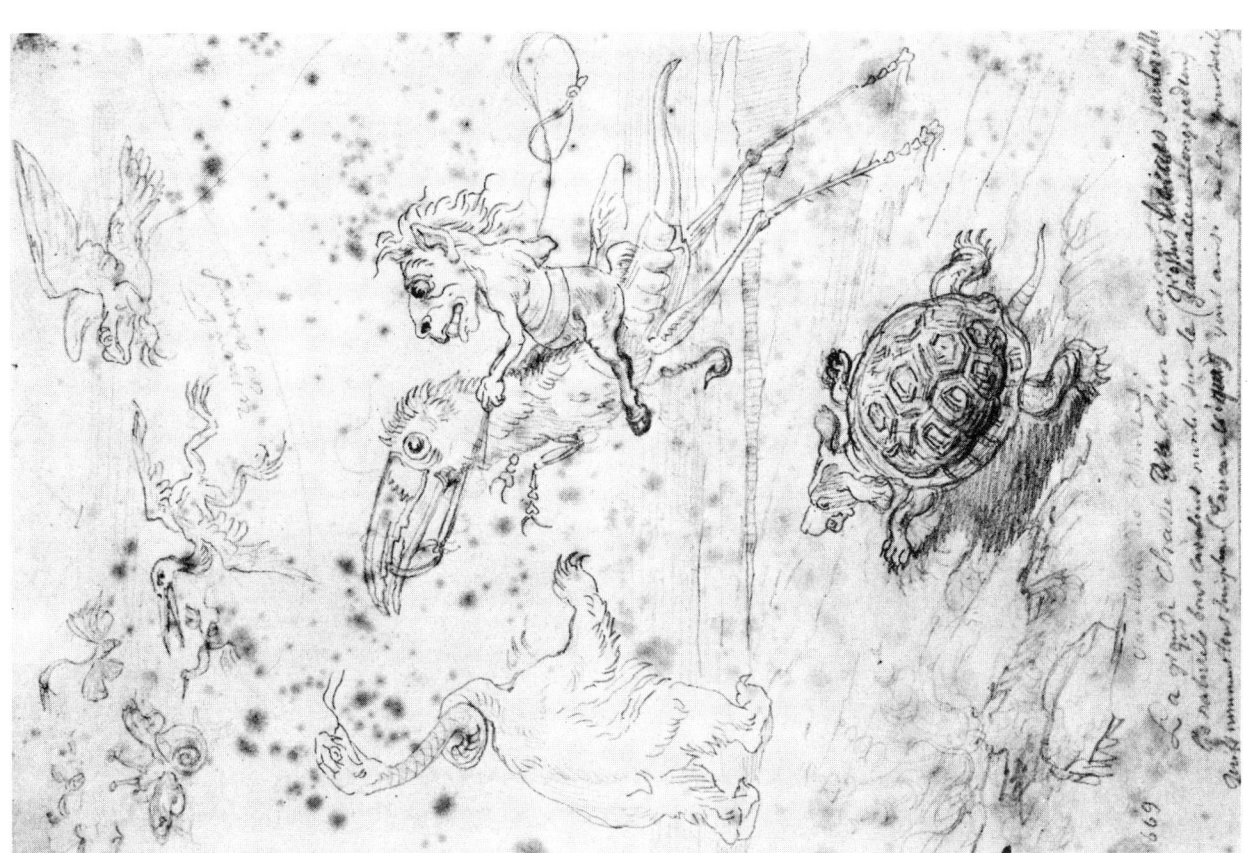

Fig. E. Grandville's preliminary drawing for an illustration in *Un Autre Monde* (No. 52 in the present volume). The woodcut process results in the reversal of the image. (Courtesy Musée des Beaux-Arts, Nancy)

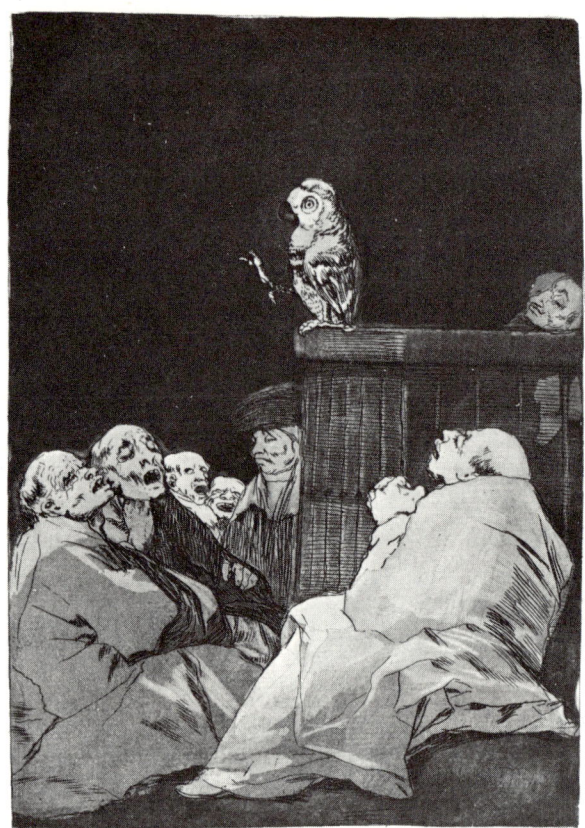

Fig. G. Plate 53 (etching with aquatint) of Goya's *Caprichos* (1799). Compare with No. 158 of the present volume. (Courtesy Museum of Fine Arts, Boston)

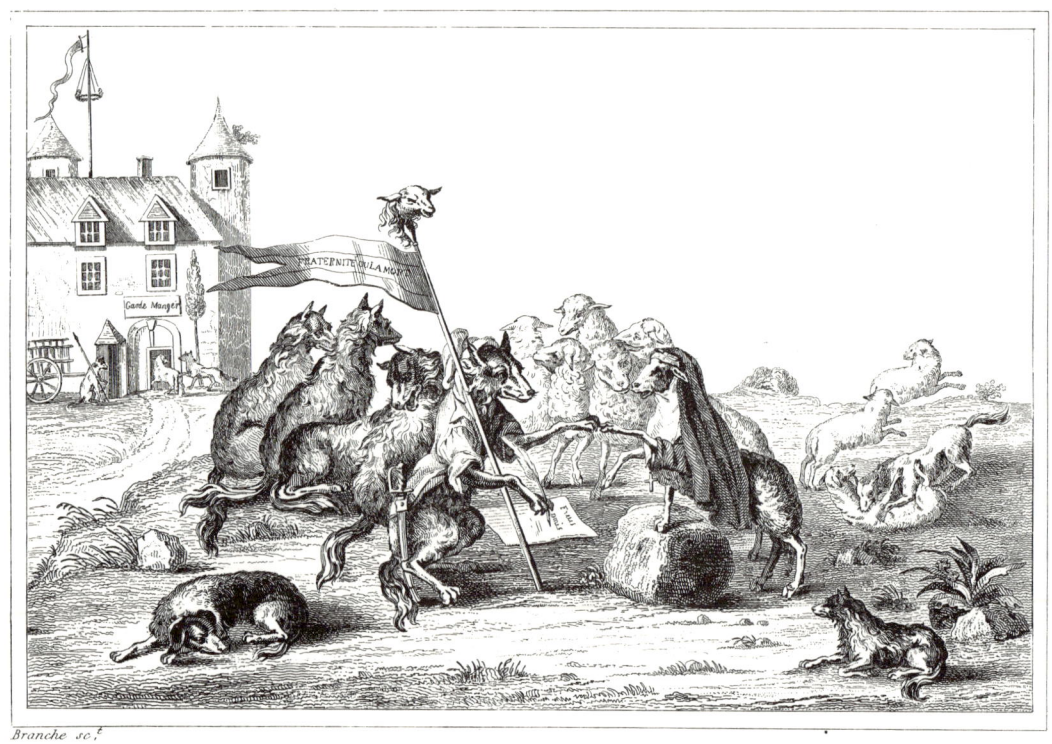

Fig. H. A French animal-subject broadside of 1794. Compare with No. 165 of the present volume. The version reproduced is from a redrawn copperplate engraving published in Augustin Challamel's *Histoire-Musée de la République Française* (1842).

that he fell victim to a septic throat ailment, very hard to diagnose, that finally caused wild delirium necessitating the patient's removal to a private clinic outside Paris. There he died three days later, on March 17, 1847. He had composed an epitaph for himself: "Here lies Grandville; he loved everything, made everything live, speak and walk, but could not make a way for himself." He was survived by his second wife and their son.

Many of Grandville's book illustrations were used again and again by the publishers in various new packages that usually clouded or cheapened their significance —not to mention the deterioration of the wood blocks. It is only the editions that appeared during his lifetime (or immediately after his death, in the case of his last works) that are of real value; these are still eagerly sought after by collectors, and command substantial prices. The illustrations in the present volume are reproduced from first editions.

VI

Despite a very few obscurities of meaning (which probably did not exist for the artist's cultured contemporaries), Grandville's art offers no difficulties to viewers today. But opinions as to its merit have always been divided. Actually his work was rather uneven, and often gives the impression that the underlying idea is superior to the somewhat stilted execution—although few critics have been as brutal as Paul de St-Victor, who wrote in 1854 that Grandville "wanted to dance on the clouds in leaden shoes" and "tried to get to heaven on a bus."

Recent writers who have had a chance to examine Grandville's preliminary drawings preserved in Nancy, throw much of the blame for the stiffness of the woodcuts on the engravers. Like other artists of the time, Grandville drew on paper; other men copied the drawings onto the blocks, which were engraved by still others. Yet it must be remembered that this was the best reproductive technique at the time, that the drawings were prepared for just that purpose—this was not a "betrayal"— and that Grandville's publishers usually hired the finest engravers available, such as the team of Andrew, Best and Leloir, whose studio preserved traditions that were in a direct line of master-pupil descent from Bewick himself. The engravers of this period, reputed to be more faithful to the original drawings than those in the second half of the century, generally signed the blocks under the image toward the lower right; these signatures show up clearly in the present volume.

Another feature of Grandville's work that estranges some people is its frequent dependence on the word. Many elements that appear in the drawings can be explained only by a pun or other word play—in French, naturally. As many of these verbal-visual puns as possible have been clarified in the commentary to this volume; it is hoped that this will add to the reader's enjoyment.

The influences on Grandville's art are many and varied. Only a few immediate sources that could easily have been known to him will be mentioned here. He was definitely familiar with the work of his great English predecessors (Rowlandson's *Dance of Death* has already been cited; there are also direct reminiscences of famous cartoons by Gillray and others in Grandville drawings). French broadside cartoons of the 1789 Revolution and First Empire are filled with human-animal hybrids used for satirical or allegorical purposes; some are extremely similar to pieces in *Les Animaux*. It is hard to say whether Goya in the *Caprichos* should be considered as a fellow-user of this anonymous political imagery or as an influence on Grandville in his own right: probably both. Social satire is a prominent feature of the countless lithographs that appeared singly or in small series throughout the early nineteenth century. In addition, there are many indications that Grandville knew and appreciated French *imagerie populaire*, with its numerous portrayals of rustic amusements, ages of man, woes of old maids, and so on. Naturally, there was cross-fertilization in the production of Grandville, Daumier, Gavarni . . . . People's memories were just as short, and their information just as defective, in that day as in ours, and many of Grandville's works stunned contemporaries on their first appearance by what was considered their unqualified novelty.

Furthermore, French literature of the eighteenth and early nineteenth centuries offers some remarkable examples of human-animal hybrids in dream situations (notably in *Les Bijoux indiscrets* by Diderot and in *La Fée aux miettes* and other stories by Charles Nodier, a contributor to *Les Animaux*), but it is impossible to say whether Grandville knew these.

The influence of Grandville outside his circle and on later artists is more difficult to estimate. No one can say how directly he affected the work of Doré, Busch, Nast, the comic-strip artists and Disney, among others, since many of his ideas have long been common property. It is said that silent film directors were fascinated by his work. Two very direct examples of his influence seem undeniable, however, though one of them has been hotly contested. The uncontested case is that of Wilhelm von Kaulbach (an artist admired by Grandville), whose illustrations for the 1846 edition of Goethe's *Reineke Fuchs* (a latterday version of the *Roman de Renart*) are modeled quite closely on Grandville's animal pieces (see Fig. C). Oddly, these drawings by Kaulbach, very different from the bulk of his rather academic output, are those esteemed most highly today by many critics.

The other case was demonstrated by Marguerite Mespoulet in 1934. Arousing clamors of "blasphemy!" she claimed that Lewis Carroll must have been familiar with at least the illustrations for *Un Autre Monde* when he wrote *Alice*, and that Tenniel subsequently based some of his drawings for Carroll on these items by Grandville. Examples: the battle of cards (No. 102 in the present volume), the weeping calf (the comment to No. 101 explains why the French calf weeps) that suggested the lachrymose Mock Turtle (there is no fundamental reason why an English Mock Turtle should cry; compare Fig. D with No. 101); the talking flowers (Nos. 59–61). She connects the picture of the Dodo presenting the thimble with a drawing of a cormorant holding a wedding ring in *Les Animaux* (not reproduced here). The ingenious reader may find other parallels.

S. A.

Bibliography

Blanc, Charles, *Grandville*, Emile Audois, Paris, 1855.

Cabanès, (Docteur), "Un grand caricaturiste visionnaire: Grandville," in *Autour de la Vie de Bohème*, Albin Michel, Paris, [1938], pp. 177–204.

Carteret, L(éopold), *Le Trésor du Bibliophile Romantique et Moderne 1801–1875*, Vol. 3: "Livres Illustrés du XIXᵉ Siècle," L. Carteret, Paris, 1927.

Catalogue Illustré des Dessins et croquis originaux exécutés à l'aquarelle, à la sépia, à la plume et au crayon par J.-J. Grandville dont la vente aura lieu après son décès à Paris, rue des Jeûneurs, 42 Salle nᵒ 3 [,] les 4 et 5 mars 1853 à une heure, Typographie de Plon Frères, Paris, 1853.

Fuchs, Eduard, *Die Karikatur der europäischen Völker*, 4th ed., 2 vols., Albert Langen, Munich, 1921.

Garcin, Laure, *J. J. Grandville, Révolutionnaire et Précurseur de l'art du mouvement*, Eric Losfeld, Paris, 1970.

Grand-Carteret, J., *Les Mœurs et la caricature en France*, Librairie Illustrée, Paris, [1888], esp. pp. 272–281.

Grandville: Das gesamte Werk, 2 vols., Rogner u. Bernhard, Munich, 1969.

Gusman, Pierre, *La Gravure sur bois en France au XIXᵉ siècle*, Albert Morancé, Paris, 1929.

J(anin), J(ules), article on Grandville in *Biographie Universelle (Michaud) Ancienne et Moderne*, C. Desplaces & M. Michaud, Paris, 1854, Vol. XVII, pp. 340–346 (offset reprint by Akademische Druck- u. Verlagsanstalt, Graz, 1967).

Lonchamp, F(rédéric)-C(harles), *Manuel du Bibliophile Français 1470–1920*, Librairie des Bibliophiles, Paris & Lausanne, 1927.

Meixmoron de Dombasle, C. de, "J.-J. Grandville," *Memoires de l'Académie de Stanislas, 1893*, 5ᵉ Serie, Tome XI (Nancy), 1894, pp. 300–339.

Mespoulet, M(arguerite), *Creators of Wonderland*, Arrow Editions, N.Y. [1934].

Münz, Ludwig, "Über die Bildsprache von Jean Ignace Isidore Gérard dit Grandville (1803–1847)," *Alte und Neue Kunst/Wiener Kunstwissenschaftliche Blätter* III, 1954, Doppelheft 3/4.

Parménie, A(ntoine), & C. Bonnier de La Chapelle, *Histoire d'un éditeur et de ses auteurs: P.-J. Hetzel (Stahl)*, Albin Michel, Paris, 1953.

Vicaire, Georges, *Manuel de l'amateur de Livres du XIXᵉ siècle 1801–1893*, 8 vols., Librairie A. Rouquette, Paris, 1894–1920.

Un autre Monde

ANOTHER WORLD

wood engravings

Synopsis of the Text
and Explanatory Notes on the Illustrations

1. Frontispiece: Caricature (*La Charge*) and Imagination (*La Fantaisie*) leave the badly battered "old world" (*ancien monde*) and move on to "another world" (*un autre monde*). They are surrounded by numerous miniaturizations of pictures that appear later in the book. The male allegorical figure, possibly a self-caricature of Grandville, is a reminiscence of the one he had drawn for the original announcement of Philipon's periodical *La Caricature*.

PREFACE
"Freedom"

A pencil (symbolizing the graphic artist) tells his desk neighbor, the plume pen (symbolizing the literary man), that he desires his freedom. No longer will he merely illustrate what the writer has set down; he will draw whatever he pleases. When he returns from his journeys into the unknown, the pen will describe his findings in words.

2. Headpiece to the Preface: The artist, half man and half fool's-cap, passes through a pencil-gateway into freedom. The picture contains some verbal-visual puns. The French idiom for "freedom" used in the text is *la clé des champs* ("the key to the open fields"). Note Grandville's initials on the key. **3.** The plume pen (writer) agrees to describe whatever the pencil (artist) draws, rather than vice versa.

CHAPTER I
"Apotheosis of Dr. Puff"

Dr. Puff, a confidence man as his name indicates [he is modeled on the figure of Robert-Macaire, which Daumier had made tremendously popular], is at the end of his rope. He decides to found a new religion [in imitation of the followers of the utopian socialists Saint-Simon and Fourier], to be called Neo-Paganism.

4. Headpiece to the first chapter: the name of the book.

CHAPTER II
"Casting Lots for the Universe"

Puff joins forces with two "co-neo-gods," Krackq [probably from English "crack," with its connotations both of "clever sportsman" and "burglar"; the word *krach*, "financial crash," may not yet have been current in French] and Hahblle [from *hâbleur*, "boastful chatterbox"]. They decide to explore the universe, gathering data to be sold to an eccentric publisher. Puff will visit the earth; Krackq, the sea; and Hahblle, the sky. As Hahblle begins to ascend in his balloon, he finds mankind small and insignificant. [A recent event that may have suggested Hahblle's adventurous flight was the celebrated eighteen-hour balloon trip from England to Germany made in 1836 by Charles Green, Robert Hollond and Monck Mason.]

5. Street acrobats and their audience as seen by Hahblle when beginning his balloon ascension.

CHAPTER III
"Steam Concert"

Puff produces a concert of metal musicians and singers —the only kind that will satisfy the public's current demand for super-virtuosity and tremendous performing forces [this was the heyday of Liszt and Berlioz, Rubini and Lablache].

6. Steam-powered metal musicians performing "The I and the Non-I, Symphony in C Major." **7.** Part of the same concert: "Air for 200 Trombones."

CHAPTER IV
"The Rhubarb and the Senna"

[The title refers to a French proverb equivalent to "You scratch my back and I'll scratch yours."] A newspaper editor, whose novels had once been praised by Puff, agrees to print Puff's own rave review of his mechanical concert.

8. Mlle. Tender [i.e., the car attached to a locomotive] hits a perfect ultra-high A during her duet with Monsieur Tunnel. **9.** A child prodigy, on a "harmonic railway," plays difficult variations on the steam harp. The inscription (imitating childish handwriting and misspellings) reads: "Barely weaned, I was 22 months old at most." **10.** An accident at the concert: an ophicleide bursts from too much harmony, peppering the listeners' ears with notes.

CHAPTER V
"The Earth Left in the Lurch"
Hahblle continues his ascension.

11. In his flight, Hahblle sees a circus bareback rider. **12.** He also sees his beloved cousin Gertrude kissing a young man in a garden.

CHAPTER VI
"As the Bird Flies and Views"
More of the same.

13. Hahblle sees street performers, with trained animals and a hurdygurdy, playing outside houses. **14.** From his height, he finds that all human glory is vanity. This, of course, is the column in the Place Vendôme, bearing the statue of Napoleon in uniform placed there in 1833 and now in the Hôtel des Invalides (the statue of Napoleon in Roman garb now on the column was placed there in 1853). Curiously, the text states that Hahblle is so high that the column seems just as tiny to him as the people around it; this is not the case in the illustration. **15.** Hahblle sees a procession of carnival masqueraders on a boulevard.

CHAPTER VII
"Carnival in a Bottle"
Puff, walking by the shore, finds a bottle with a message from Krackq, who had witnessed an undersea carnival ball.

16. Krackq's bottle making signs of distress to Puff. The label reads: "To Dr. Puff, residing on the globe. Fragile. Postpaid." **17.** The undersea carnival procession of the fatted ox. The procession of the *bœuf gras* was a standard feature of former French carnival practices; it is often portrayed in popular prints. In the present case the ox is escorted by gastronomic delights: a gamy hare (verbal-visual pun on *faisandé*, "gamy," and *faisan*, "pheasant"), a salmon-lobster, a crayfish-partridge, a snail-turtle, a chicken-pig-truffle combination, and so on. **18.** At the undersea ball, a male lamb dances with an aging female panther, a fox casts loving glances at a hen, and a partridge captivates a hound with her gaze. (In the illustrations, each animal wears as a mask the features of its partner.) **19.** At the ball, a hare attacks a lioness, a gazelle drags by his mane her lion-lover who has paid too much attention to a ballerina-greyhound, and a raven in a black domino tells jokes. **20.** Before the tolerant eyes of the police, an adolescent duck-frog performs a very free dance with an owl-mouse. .

CHAPTER VIII
"Character Masquerades and Physiological Disguises"
Krackq's message gives Puff the idea of selling "neo-carnival" costumes that will reveal the true character of the wearer.

21. At a more aristocratic undersea ball visited by Krackq, the animals masquerade as human beings rather than as other animals. **22.** Puff's new costumes—examples of the contrast between people's public images and their true characters. Translations: "Dandyism and straitened circumstances," "Grandison-Macaire" [Grandison is the hero of Samuel Richardson's novel *Sir Charles Grandison,* an exemplar of the best in manhood; Macaire is the well-known assassin from the play *L'Auberge des Adrets*], "Diplomatic bases" [ambassador's uniform above the frame], "Conviction and harlequinade," "Today's morals" [the judge is wearing the trousers and slippers of a *débardeuse* ("female longshoreman," one of the most popular carnival get-ups, associated with loose-living bohemian women), as is the seemingly pious lady to the right of him], and "Our Lady of Lorette and the Opéra" [the rue Notre-Dame de Lorette, named for the nearby church, was then inhabited by professional ladies dubbed *lorettes;* the Opéra was the site of the largest carnival ball].

CHAPTER IX
"The Kingdom of Marionettes"
On his balloon flight, Hahblle arrives in this kingdom. [His fantastic journey to various realms has literary antecedents in Lucian, Ariosto, Rabelais, Cyrano de Bergerac and Swift, among others.] Here he witnesses a ballet.

23. A "pas de crabes" in the grand Romantic ballet *The Loves of Venus,* in which the nymphs of the *corps de ballet* are mice and grasshoppers, while the Cyclopes (who perform a hammer dance) are scarab beetles. **24.** Fantastic vision of the audience's worship of the great Romantic *prime ballerine.* The *premier danseur* is just a pair of legs in tights. The *prima ballerina,* decked out in tinsel and fake finery, becomes a spinning top, eventually transformed calligraphically into the braying donkey and other animals below. Over her head on the stage are the flaming hearts of admirers, combinations of plume pens (apparently for writing *billets doux*) and (love's) arrows, and wreathes and money. At her feet are loving hearts, a reviewer swinging a censer, a bouquet, soapsuds, etc. In the audience (right to left), a pair of gloves becomes a pair of clapping hands, then pincers, then washerwomen's paddles, then bottles, then drinking glasses, then an hourglass. Grandville specialized in such multiple transformation pictures, in which objects slowly dissolve into different objects, bearing subtle nuances of meaning. **25.** A marionette ballerina. She wears the wings used by Marie Taglioni in *La Sylphide* and plays castanets like Fanny Elssler in *Le Diable boiteux* and numerous other ballets. **26.** Other marionette ballet stars.

CHAPTER X
"A Revolution in the World of Plants"
Puff, who understands the language of flowers, hears about a great conspiracy of plants to free themselves from man's dominion. But internal dissensions prevent the plotters from undermining the bases of gastronomy.

27. Conspiratorial vegetables plot revolution. **28.** Flowers and bushes awaken from their complacent slumbers. **29.** Artichokes, mushrooms and others vow to be food for man no longer. **30.** The proletarian thistle, fomenter of the revolt, harangues the gherkins. (He tells them that not only does man imprison them in jars, but uses their name—*cornichon*—to mean "fool.") **31.** Fight between two "refined" gentlemen—the sugar cane and the sugar beet. The cane, wearing a planter's hat, is using a sugar cane as a weapon. There is a pool of sugar-beet "blood" on the ground. The carrot arrives too late to halt the affray. The tobacco plant nonchalantly smokes a pipe. The objects in the left background are sugar loaves.

CHAPTER XI
"An April-Fool Journey"

This is the name of a travel book written by Puff to earn some quick money. The chapter consists of excerpts from his book, recounting things seen on the journey.

32. Fish fishing for people, using various desirable items as bait. The words on the paper read: "Gold medal to the first 10,000 subscribers." The cattails are made of coins. The underlying pun is that in French an April-fool joke is called an "April fish," *poisson d'avril*. **33.** Satire on carriages: some as low-slung as armchairs, some as tall as steeples. **34.** A dog walking his man. **35.** Fashionable people represented in public by their accoutrements. **36.** The Duchess of Sorrel with two of her English thoroughbreds, one mounted by her mechanically miniaturized groom.

CHAPTER XII
"Just As at Longchamps"

A further selection from Puff's book. [Longchamps was a neighborhood beloved for aristocratic promenades in Paris.]

37. Dandyism and women's emancipation carried to the point of near-transvestism (satire on current trends).

CHAPTER XIII
"Back in the Kingdom of Marionettes"

Hahblle's adventures continued. He meets the artists of this land.

38. Painters who turn out many pictures in record time. **39.** An academic teacher of painting and his pupils, mounted on a Raphael hobbyhorse, trace details from the old masters. In the background is a living pantograph. **40.** The expert who is to judge the pictures submitted by the artists.

CHAPTER XIV
"The Marionettes' Louvre"

Hahblle visits the art exhibition in the local Louvre.

41. A portal of the Louvre is demolished to allow a vast academic canvas to be brought in. **42.** An exhibition room. The viewers include eyes and optical instruments. Among the subjects are "The Angel of Painting imploring divine mercy for the jury," "The crossing of the Red Sea" (the long, narrow picture over the angel), a portrait of a society woman's jewels, stormy waves, and a bucolic landscape. **43.** An exhibition gallery. A visiting mole is dazzled by a painted sunrise; birds peck at a realistic orchard scene; hoofs, weapons and the like emerge from a lively battle picture. **44.** A great sculptor finishing his masterpiece, "The Finger of God." **45.** An exhibition room with licentious paintings.

CHAPTER XV
"A Conjugal Eclipse"

A puppet lets Hahblle into a secret of the skies: a solar eclipse is actually caused by the Sun and his wife the Moon kissing. A celestial judge, incensed by their marital infidelities, forces them to perform this action publicly from time to time. When the planet Venus appears in the sky, the puppet faints.

46. Astronomers on Earth, represented by their instruments, observe a solar eclipse—the Moon kissing the Sun. The words "Paris" and "Nancy" are legible on the globe. **47.** The passage of a comet across the sky. Below her is the Big Dipper. **48.** The constellations of the Zodiac, overjoyed at the eclipse, dance a sarabande. Virgo is dressed like a *débardeuse* (see No. 22); Leo is a "salon lion"; Aquarius has the garb and equipment of a contemporary Parisian water seller. **49.** The puppet faints when Venus appears.

CHAPTER XVI
"The Love Affair of a Puppet and a Star"

The puppet tells his story. He once was a Zephyr, but offended Venus, who transformed him into a human poet, and caused him to be madly in love with her. When he accosted her at the opera, she changed him into a puppet and relegated him to the planet Hahblle is visiting. When he finishes his story, he becomes a Zephyr once more.

50. Venus in an opera box, with all eyes turned toward her. **51.** Venus as evening star.

CHAPTER XVII
"An Afternoon at the Jardin des Plantes"

Krackq's bottle message, continued. Walking beneath the sea he meets a centaur who captures rare animals for the local Jardin des Plantes (zoo). Krackq visits the zoo.

52. The centaur, with his turtle-hound, in pursuit of a boa-bear. Grandville's preliminary drawing for this illustration is reproduced in Fig. E of the Introduction. **53.** Krackq visits the siren pool in the zoo. **54.** The cages of heraldic animals. Included are a French chanticleer, a lion-unicorn ("donated by Lord Goddam") and Siberian two-headed eagles donated by Kakikoff.

CHAPTER XVIII
"An Afternoon at the Jardin des Plantes, Continued"

More of the same.

55. The pit of "doublivores" (animals that eat at both ends) at the zoo. The architectural setting is actually that of the contemporary bear-pit at the Parisian Jardin des Plantes. Grandville based this drawing directly on a realistic rendering of the bear-pit he had done two years earlier for the publication *Le Jardin des Plantes: Description et mœurs des mammifères de la ménagerie et du Muséum d'Histoire Naturelle*, by Pierre Boitard (J.-J. Dubochet et Cᵉ, Paris, 1842). The latter illustration is reproduced in Fig. F of the Introduction. **56.** The bird collection at the zoo. The female visitor who is part fish refers to a celebrated phrase of Horace in his *Ars poetica*, where he compares a disconnected piece of writing to a picture of a beautiful woman's head and torso ending in a hideous fish's tail. **57.** The mineralogical collection, showing that manmade buildings and objects are based on forms occurring in nature. **58.** The marine life collection, showing that underwater plants and animals are based on forms invented by man—fans, wigs, combs, brushes, etc.

CHAPTER XIX
"The Death of an Immortelle"

Puff converses with an immortelle ("everlasting flower"), which hates its eternal loveless life and finally commits suicide by uprooting itself.

59. Flowers and fruits rejoice at the coming of spring. **60.** The entrance to a hothouse where a floral ball is being given. The guards—at the left, snapdragons (in French, *gueules-de-loup*, i.e., "wolves' mouths"); at the right, a pomegranate plant (in French, *grenadier*, which also refers to a type of soldier)—are admitting a tulip, which carries a sign, "La Fanfan" (since the eighteenth century, "Fanfan la Tulipe" has been a jocular designation for French soldiers). **61.** The rose, queen of the flowers, and her consort, the laurel, are borne in procession.

CHAPTER XX
"Aerial Locomotion"

Puff, still gathering material for travel literature, makes aerial journeys of different types.

62. Puff makes a "zigzag trip." The text states that Puff got the idea from the prospectus for a new book. This, of course, was the delightful *Voyages en zigzag*, written and illustrated by the Genevan artist Rodolphe Töpffer and published in the same year as *Un Autre Monde* (1844). Töpffer's "zigzag" is figurative, but Puff uses a real *zigzag*, that is, lazy-tongs. **63.** Puff makes a trip by kite. **64.** An undersea message from Krackq arrives by spring. **65.** Puff travels in a detached windmill.

CHAPTER XXI
"The Mysteries of Infinity"

Hahblle continues his travels through space, learning the secrets of many celestial phenomena.

66. An interplanetary bridge. Saturn's ring is a balcony. **67.** The secret of celestial mechanics: the worlds are soap bubbles blown by an old magician, who fails to notice that a female demon is insufflating love, jealousy and other woes into them. **68.** A juggler of universes, with a meteorite in the form of the Cross of the Legion of Honor. **69.** The great bellows that causes hurricanes.

CHAPTER XXII
"The Four Seasons"

Hahblle meets the beings responsible for various climatic phenomena.

70. A lightning rod seizes a thunderbolt and extinguishes it in a bucket of water. **71.** Hoarfrost and Rime, satellites of Winter, enjoying an ice at the North Pole.

CHAPTER XXIII
"The Marquesas"

Puff visits an island where the love-hungry natives are dressed like French nobles of the reign of Louis XV [France had occupied the Marquesas Islands in 1842].

(No illustrations selected.)

CHAPTER XXIV
"The High and the Low"

Puff discovers a group of islands where social distinctions are reflected in the stature of the inhabitants. He names them the Society Islands [pun on the name of the archipelago that includes Tahiti].

72–75. Scenes in the land where differences in rank are made visible by differences in size (No. 74 shows misalliances). The sign in No. 73 reads: "Public notice." **76.** Poachers of small stature. The sign reads: "Hunting law." **77.** Duel between a high and a low soldier. **78.** Local soldiers courting nursemaids. **79.** The tall inhabitants are natural-born drum majors.

CHAPTER XXV
"Young China"

Puff arrives in China, where he falls in with a group of extreme advocates of progress. [Théophile Gautier's 1833 novel *Les Jeunes-France* had satirized the excesses of the French Romantics.]

80. European figures as tumbler toys in China. Such toys in Europe are often in the form of mandarins; here the tables are turned. The figure with the knife and fork is a judge. **81.** A group of Chinese at a "French-shadow" play. In French, shadow plays are known as *ombres chinoises* ("Chinese shadows"); this is another reversal. The play they are watching is *Colin Beats His Missus*. One of the spectators is holding a copy of *Le Charivari*, the paper with which Grandville was associated.

CHAPTER XXVI
"A Day At Rheculanum"

Krackq's adventures continued. He visits Rheculanum [based on Herculanum], the capital of the land of Antiquity, where Greco-Roman and modern customs are blended. [The illustrations in this chapter, which have very little shading, parody the outline drawings of antique subjects by Flaxman and other neo-classicists.]

82. The public baths of Rheculanum. Public baths were almost as popular in the Paris of Grandville's day as in ancient Rome, and were a common subject for illustrators. The words on the wall panel are names of ancient and modern wines. **83.** The salon of an "emancipated" lady of Rheculanum. For the significance of "Lorette," see No. 22; the building in this illustration is an actual representation of the Parisian church. **84.** A performance of *Phèdre* in Rheculanum. This seventeenth-century French tragedy, Racine's masterpiece (based on *Hippolytus* by Euripides), had recently been restored to favor by the great actress Rachel, who took it upon herself to revive the French classical plays after the hostile inroads of Romanticism. In the scene portrayed, the chaste young huntsman Hippolyte (Hippolytus) is repulsing the advances of his stepmother Phèdre (Phaedra). The panels overhead depict Hippolyte's chariot and team and the sea monster which frightens the horses and causes Hippolyte's death. The musician with an eyeshade represents the blind poet Homer.

CHAPTER XXVII
"Celestial Medley: Gods, Angels, Demons"

Cupid, seeking virgins' tears as fuel for the lamp of love, visits the Christian heaven, the Moslem heaven, and Earth. He finds a supply. A few drops spill and thaw out Hahblle, who had been frozen solid at the North Pole.

85. Demons tormenting angels. The book reads: "Memoirs of the Devil." **86.** Demons mocking angels. The standard reads: "Gentleness, patience." **87.** Cupid with his cup of tears and hearts on a spit.

CHAPTER XXVIII
"The Marital Steeplechase"

Puff considers marriage, but changes his mind upon examination of the wares offered.

88. An assortment of marriageable women. The sign reads: "At the Sign of the Marriage Altar. Complete assortment of brides: widows, virtuous maidens, etc." Standing, left to right, are a bluestocking authoress, a fiery Spaniard, an aging Englishwoman with a tea caddy, a German with a dish of sauerkraut, and a more ordinary girl. Seated in front is a "good housewife" type.

CHAPTER XXIX
"The Pleasures of the Elysian Fields"

Krackq dreams that he visits the Elysian Fields and sees illustrious people of all eras. [The underlying joke is that the dead heroes in the Elysian Fields are enjoying the types of popular amusements offered on the Champs-Elysées in Paris.]

89. Voltaire and Frederick the Great weigh themselves, while Galileo and Newton play ball with a celestial sphere. **90.** Penthesilea and Brutus wait their turn while William Tell shoots at plaster tyrants. The sign reads: "Games of skill." **91.** A puppet show attended by [going round the circle counterclockwise] Cervantes, Shakespeare, Rabelais, La Fontaine, Aesop, Molière and Picard. Aesop and La Fontaine carry the ant and the grasshopper of the fable and have wolf and lamb pulltoys. Molière carries his plays like a schoolboy. Louis Benoît Picard (1769–1828) was a prolific playwright, highly acclaimed in his day. The sign reads: "Plautus. Sophocles. Greek Theater. Punch, the Conqueror." **92.** Great military figures of the past watch a play in which the exploits of French troops in Algeria are wildly exaggerated. The man with the ruff is Henri IV of France. Next to him is Tamerlane. On the cushion is Mohammed. The helmeted men in the first row are Achilles and Attila. Also mentioned in the text as spectators are Condé, Turenne, Lannes, Peter the Great and Charles XII of Sweden. **93.** Great conquerors competing for the ring on a merry-go-round. Counting heads strictly from left to right: Charlemagne, Napleon, Caesar, Alexander, Louis XIV and the Maréchal de Saxe.

CHAPTER XXX
"Krackq's Inferno"

Still dreaming, Krackq moves on to other regions of the underworld.

94. Charon's boat on the Styx filled with noted figures of fun. Seated on the gunwale are Momus, Mayeux (a hunchback who appeared in many popular satirical prints, then was adopted as a standard character by the caricaturist Traviès) and Harlequin. Standing at the far right are Falstaff and Sganarelle (a figure from Molière). The man standing behind Mayeux is Jocrisse, a foolish servant in old farces. The man standing next to Charon is Bertrand, the stupid sidekick of Robert-Macaire in Daumier's famous lithographs. To the left of him in the background is Sancho Panza. The others in the boat are also various stock clown types. On the near shore is the three-headed dog Cerberus; on the far shore, departed spirits who lack the fare for the boatride. The sign reads: "Toll 5 centimes per soul." **95.** The punishment of Tantalus interpreted as sexual longing; the myth of Sisyphus interpreted as gluttony. The pictorial motif of the belly that must be carried on a wheelbarrow goes back at least as far as the sixteenth century; its most celebrated occurrence is in the drawing "Gluttony" by Breughel the Elder. **96.** The three Fates.

CHAPTER XXXI
"The Wedding of Puff and Advertising"

After escaping the marriage-lust of a group of old maids, Puff finally weds a girl called Advertising.

97. Old maids climbing a greased pole [carnival sport] to catch Puff for a husband. Similar contests for husbands and laments of old maids are frequent subjects in French popular prints. **98.** The wedding of Puff and Advertising. The bride, Advertising (*la Réclame*), is escorted by her brother, Broadsheet (*le Canard*, literally "duck"—the English word "canard" meaning "false report" or "hoax" comes from this French term for broadsheet). Puff gives his arm to his mother-in-law, Announcement (*l'Annonce*). Note the broadsheets, pen and ink, trumpet and drum, and billposter's ladder and pastepot. The signs read: "Public notice," "Private sale," "House for rent," "Sandwichmen's signs," "Universal publicity," etc. The mayor, nude except for a wreath, boots and his sash of office, carries the torch of Hymen in his left hand and the Code (lawbook) in his right.

CHAPTER XXXII
"The Metamorphoses of Sleep"

Hahblle, rendered ecstatic by the drops of Cupid's elixir, has strange visions.

99. Hahblle's vision of his beloved Gertrude. One of Grandville's most famous "dissolves." Reading from top to bottom, a bird becomes a bow and quiver, then a sort of baluster, then a cup-and-ball game, then a flower in a vase, then the beloved woman, who fades away, leaving behind flowers and a serpent. **100.** A vision of the beloved tempted by riches. **101.** A vision of the adoration of the Golden Calf (wealth). The calf's tears refer to the French expression *pleurer comme un veau*, meaning "bawl" or "blubber," but literally "to weep like a calf." **102.** A vision of a battle of playing cards. There are some verbal-visual puns: in French, *pique* means "pike" as well as the card suit "spades"; the fallen diamonds (this suit is *carreau* in French) refer to the expression *rester sur le carreau*, "to be left dead on the battlefield." See p. xviii and Fig. D of the Introduction for the probable influence of this chapter on Lewis Carroll.

CHAPTER XXXIII
"The Best Form of Government"

Krackq returns to Earth and discusses constitutions with Puff.

103. "Today social leveling is synonymous with compression." **104.** Applying the discoveries of the phrenologists, society will eliminate crime and encourage virtue by physically altering the bumps on people's heads. **105.** Allegory of Medicine. Signs (top to bottom and left to right): "Aesculapius," "Gelatin. Bone. Madder," "Clear water," "Potion according to the formula," "Diet," "Poultice," "White mustard." **106.** Human happiness—food for the asking—in the Fourierist utopia. Charles Fourier (1772–1837) was an opponent of competition and individualism as moving forces in society. He believed in cooperative living, free from the traditional restraints imposed upon the emotions. Humanity was to be divided into groups called phalanges, each phalanx dwelling in a common building called a phalanstery, and each member occupying himself with congenial tasks. Fourier and his followers even predicted a reformation of the physical universe that would make life more comfortable for man. **107.** The new aspect of the heavens in the Fourierist utopia. Seven moons of different colors will replace the old dead moon. An aurora borealis will carry the polar ice into the ocean, which will cease to be salty and will change into lemon sherbet.

CHAPTER XXXIV
"The End of This World and the Other"

Hahblle, returning to Earth with an angelic woman who proves to be a she-devil in disguise, discusses the sorry state of the world's customs and morals with his co-neo-gods. They load animals—and Puff's sons—onto a steam ark in expectation of a new Flood. The three gods hug each other to death.

108. Hahblle's disappointment in love. **109.** Literature being reeled off and sold in chunks. On the paper: "Novel in installments, continuation of . . . ." On the retort: "Wit." On the dish: "Macaronic style." **110.** Allegory of the blood-and-thunder Romantic drama. **111.** A pump to flood a city with prospectuses and ads. **112.** Criers advertising their bargains from the housetops. Their papers read: "We pay the buyer. The only . . .," "6 for ½ centime," "100% loss," "3 for a centime," "Free," "Discount," "Unlimited credit," "Pay nothing in advance," "1 centime." **113.** The wheel of Fashion. **114.** New Year's gifts that deliver themselves. The signs read: "French Theater" and "The kisses of Judas." **115.** The animals entering the steam ark. These are direct reminiscences of characters in *Les Animaux*.

EPILOGUE

Arriving at the end of their journey, the pen and the pencil are still jealous of one another, but agree that *Un Autre Monde* is a masterpiece.

116. A punning rebus giving advice to the reader. Solution: The individual elements on the obelisk are to be read as *A-croix* (A with a cross), *mois* (month), *A* (A), *mi-lecteur* (half a reader), *neuf fées* (nine fairies), *pâque* (Passover), *homme* (man), *sept* (seven). These French sound values, read consecutively, produce the French sentence: *Ah! crois-moi, ami lecteur, ne fais pas comme cet [imbécile qui se casse la tête pour me deviner].* Which translates as: "Ah, believe me, dear reader, do not behave like this [imbecile who is breaking his head in order to solve me]." **117.** The pencil and the pen on Grandville's initials (J.-J. G.). In the shadow is the name of the author of the text, T[axile] Delord. The book tied to the top of the G is marked "Sketches."

118. Headpiece of the table of contents (at the end of the book): the title.

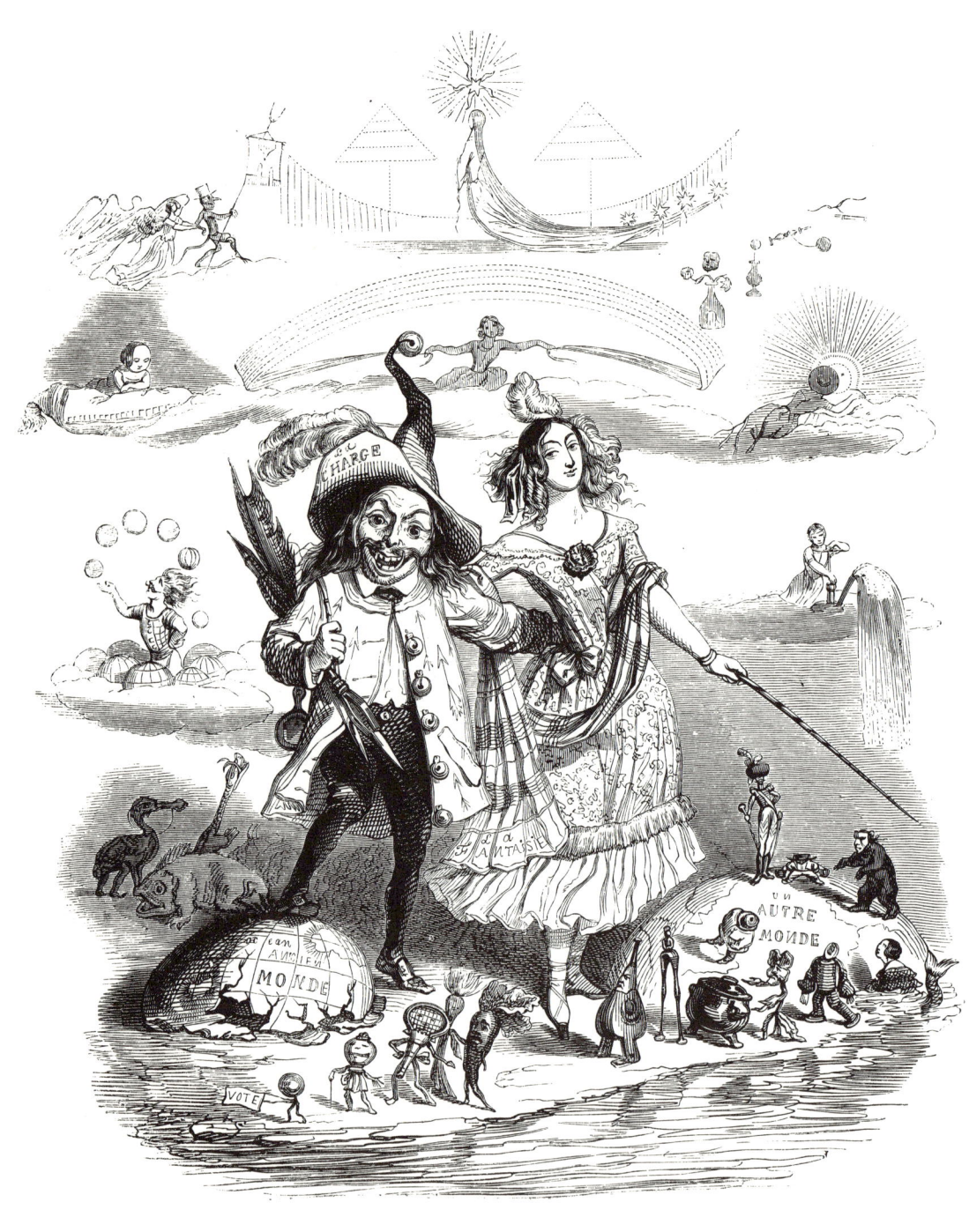

1. Frontispiece: Caricature (*La Charge*) and Imagination (*La Fantaisie*) leave the badly battered "old world" (*ancien monde*) and move on to "another world" (*un autre monde*). They are surrounded by numerous miniaturizations of pictures that appear later in the book.

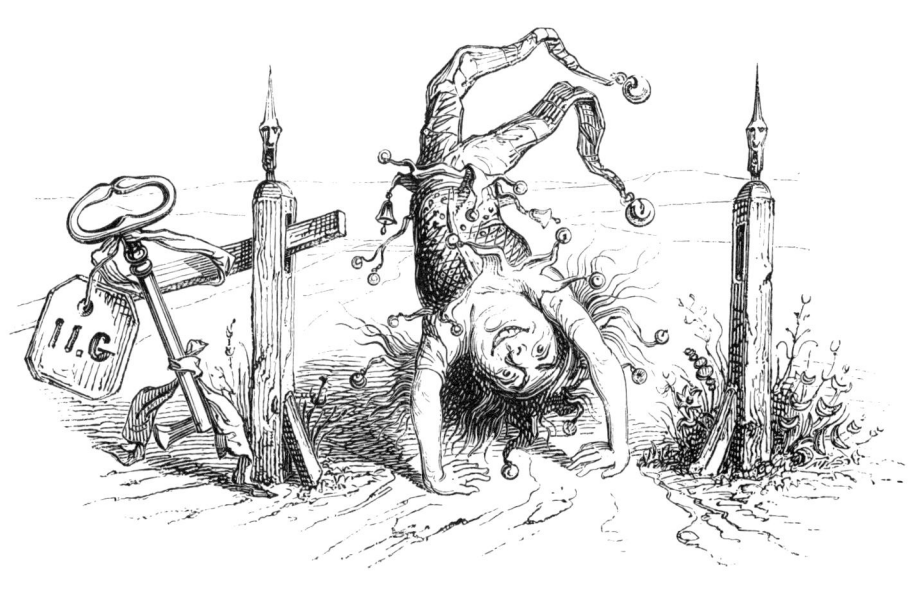

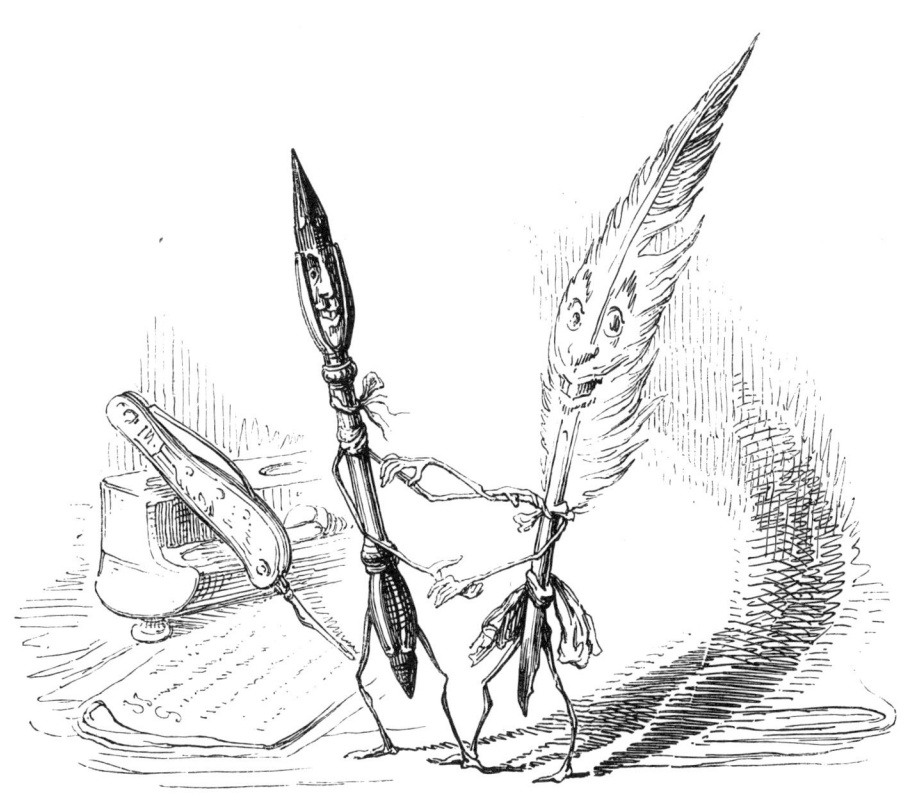

2. Headpiece to the Preface: The artist, half man and half fool's-cap, passes through a pencil-gateway into freedom. **3.** The plume pen (writer) agrees to describe whatever the pencil (artist) draws, rather than vice versa.

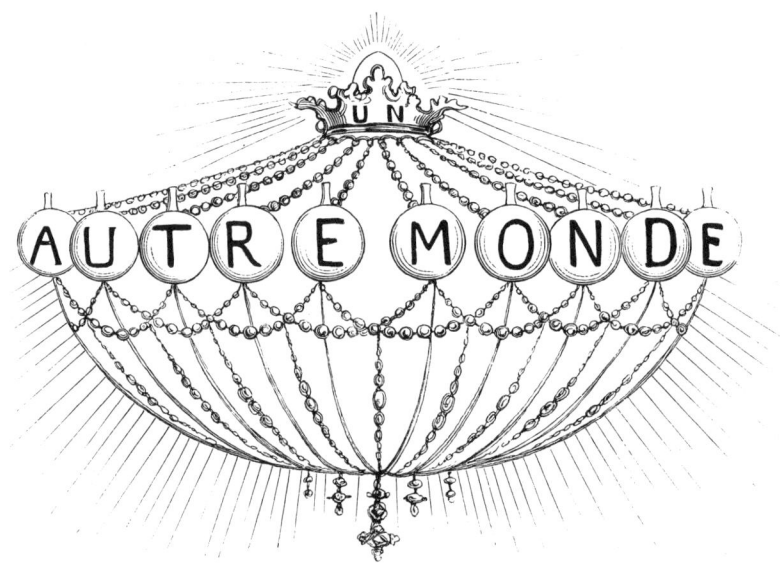

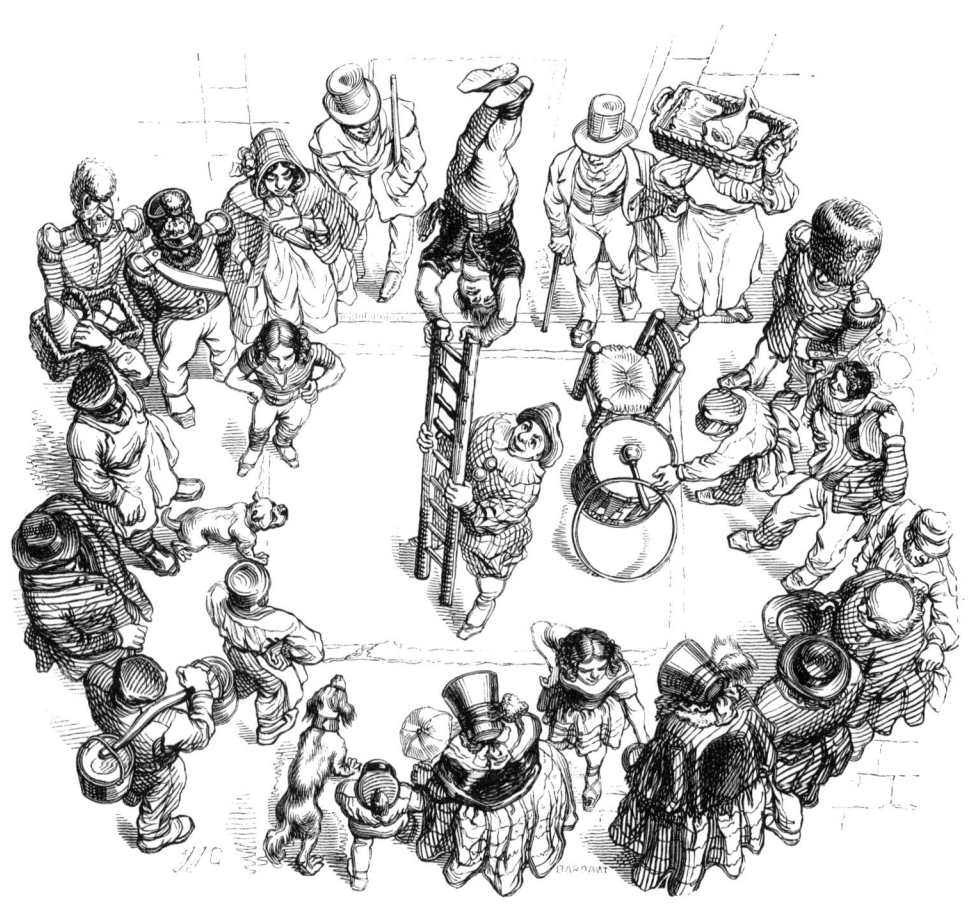

4. Headpiece to the first chapter: the name of the book. **5.** Street acrobats and their audience as seen by Hahblle when beginning his balloon ascension.

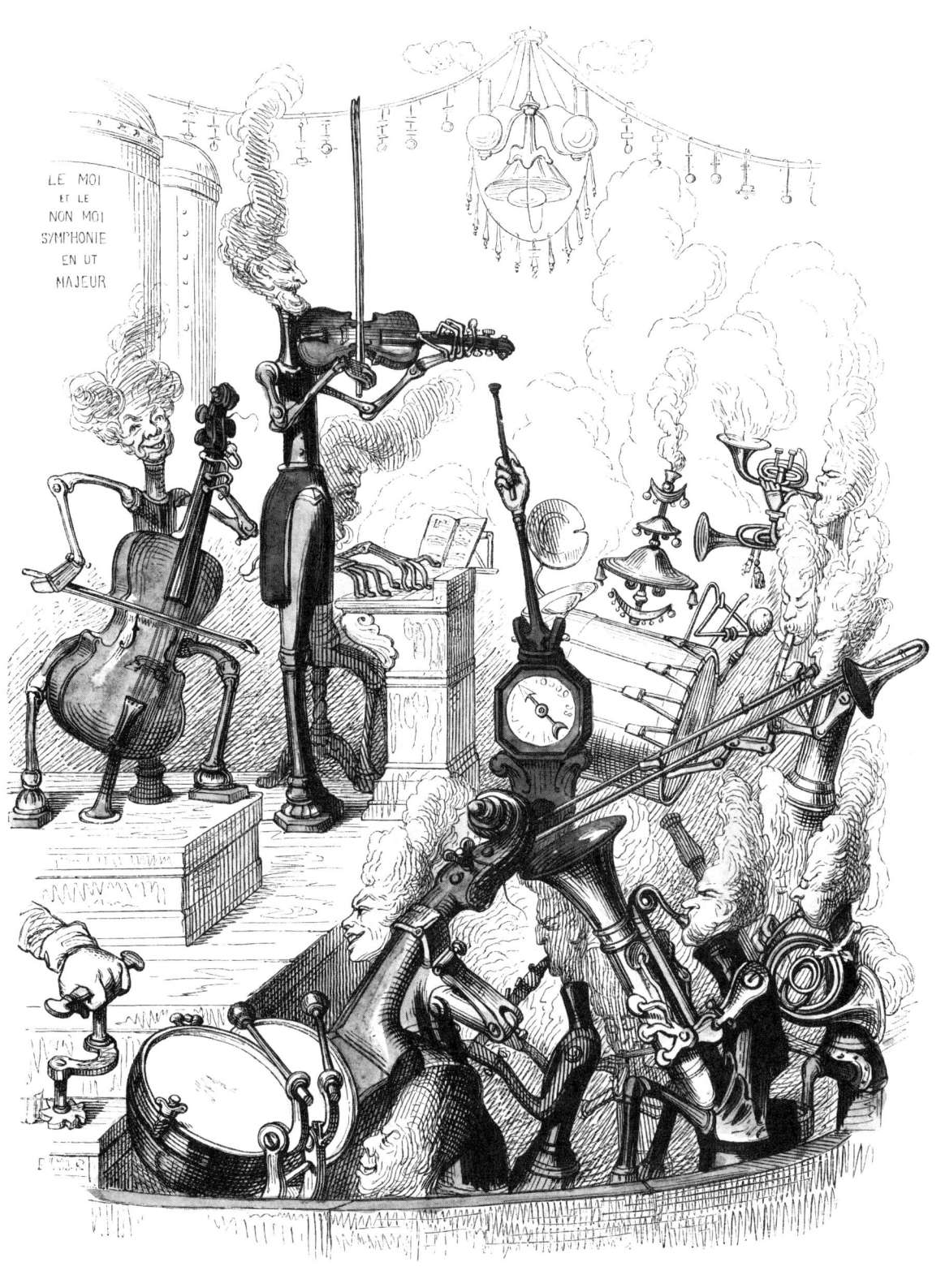

6. Steam-powered metal musicians performing "The I and the Non-I, Symphony in C Major."

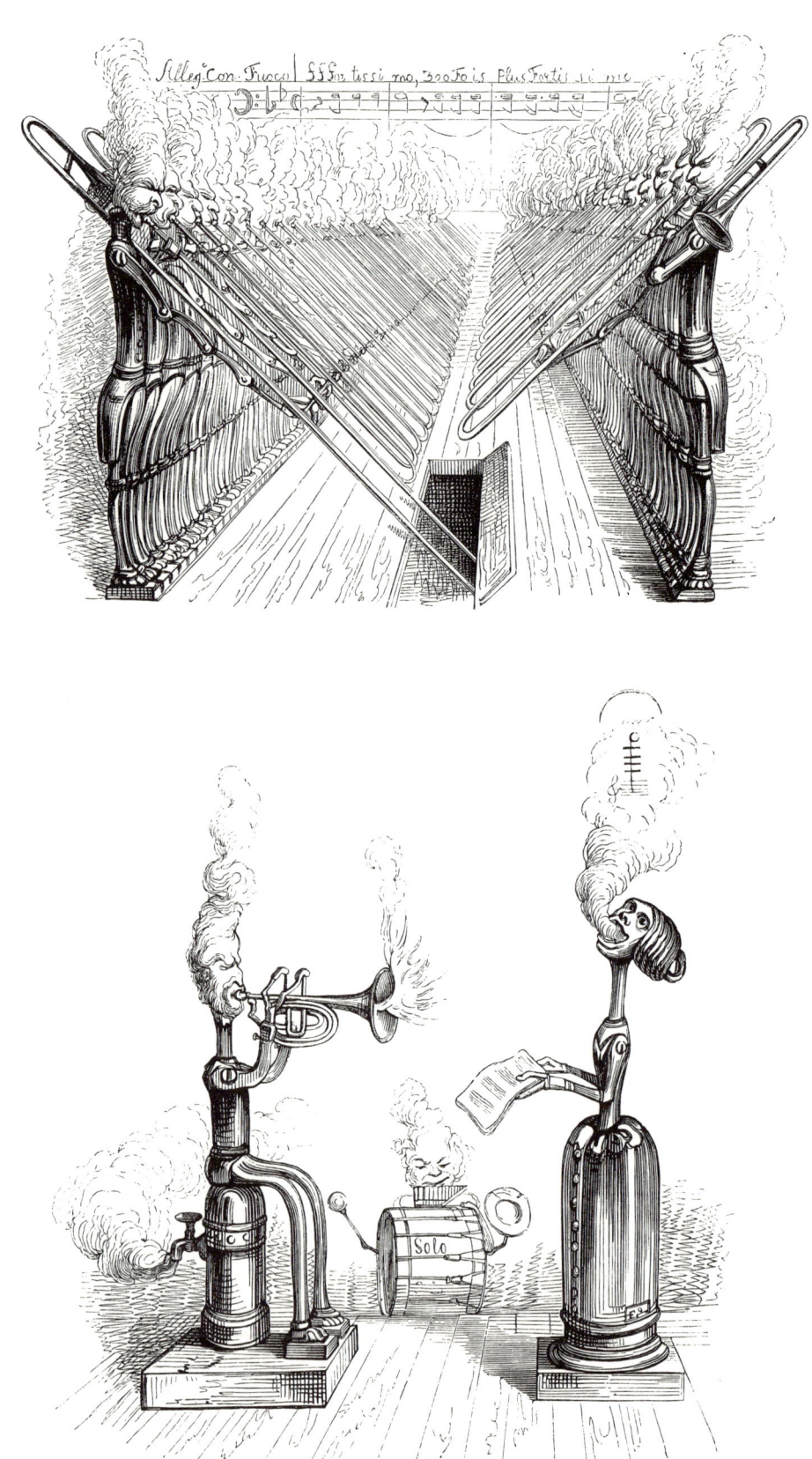

7. Part of the same concert: "Air for 200 Trombones."   **8.** Mlle. Tender [i.e., the car attached to a locomotive] hits a perfect ultra-high A during her duet with Monsieur Tunnel.

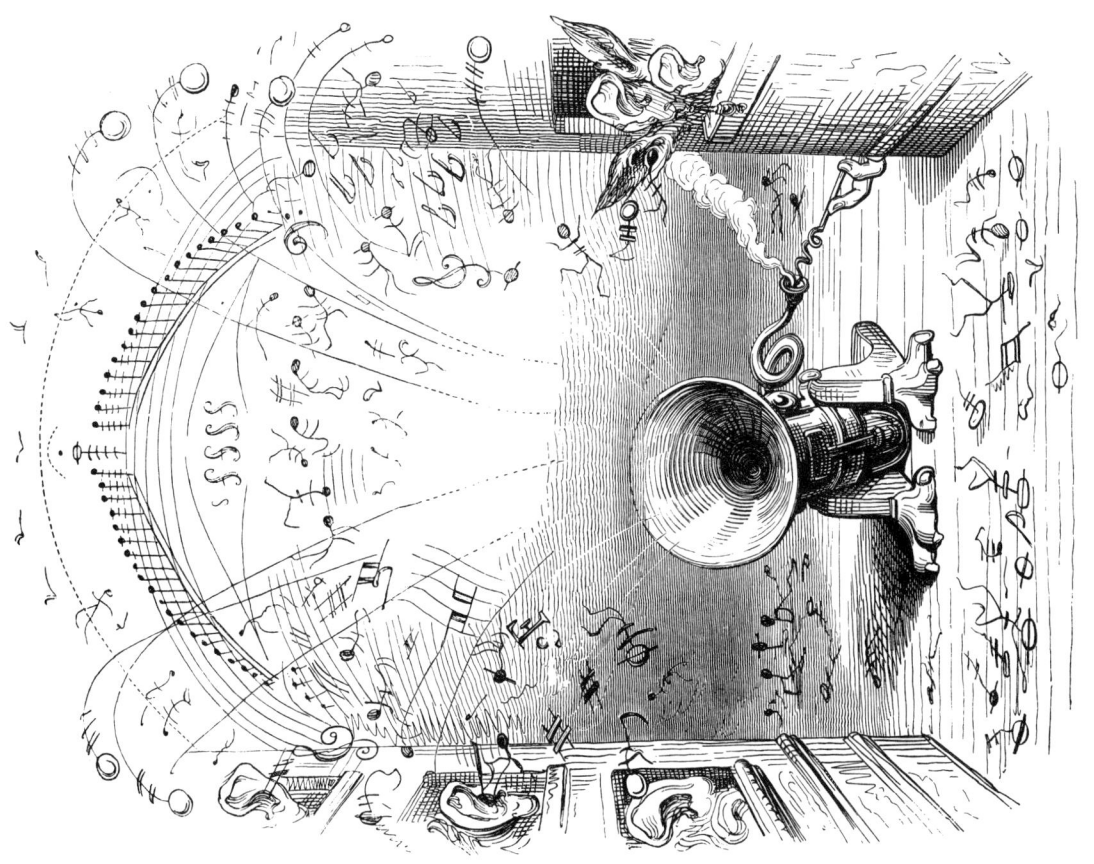

à peine au sortir de nourrice
22 mois au plus, e comptait...

10. An accident at the concert: an ophicleide bursts from too much harmony, peppering the listeners' ears with notes.

9. A child prodigy, on a "harmonic railway," plays difficult variations on the steam harp.

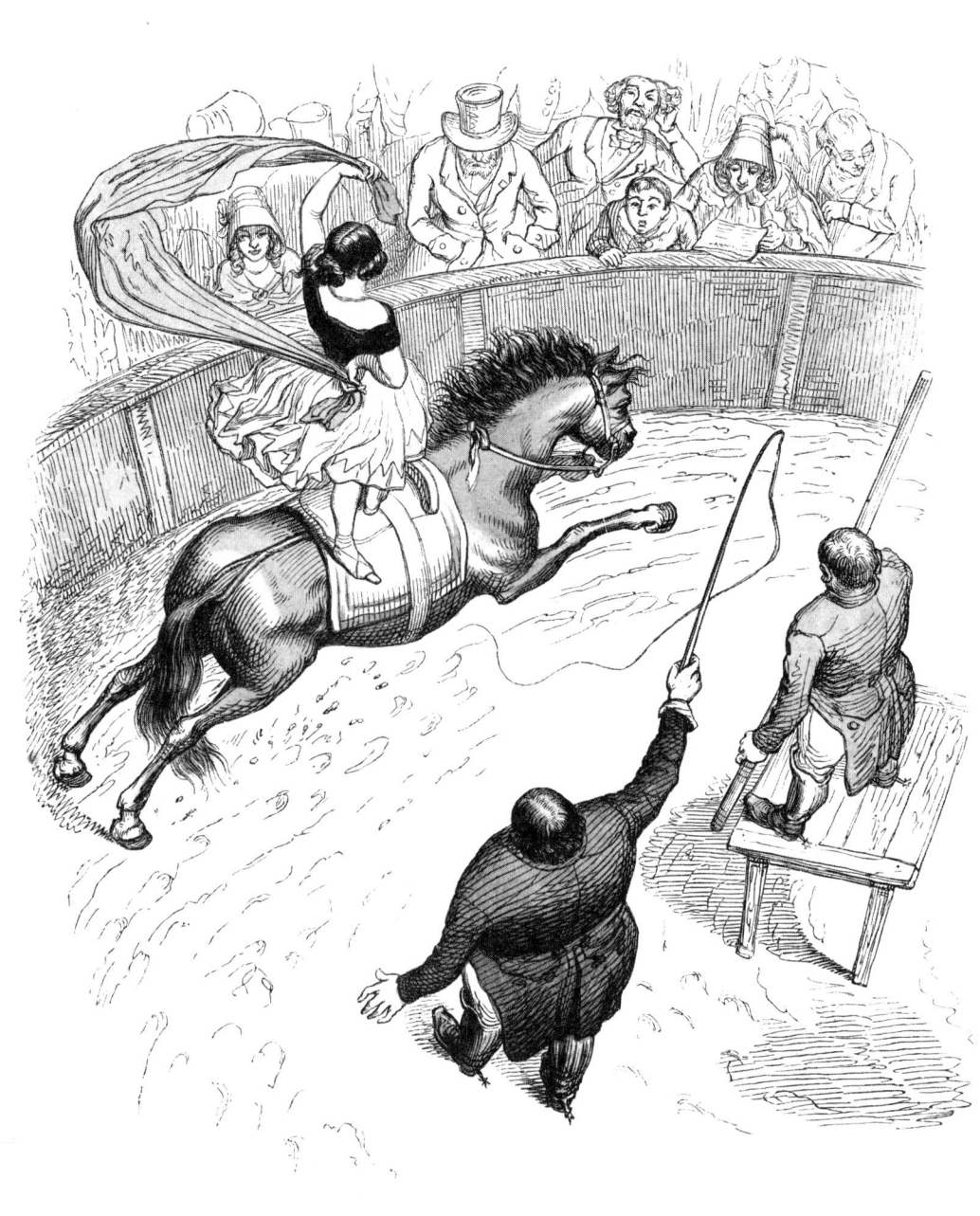

11. In his flight, Hahblle sees a circus bareback rider. **12.** He also sees his beloved cousin Gertrude kissing a young man in a garden. **13.** Hahblle sees street performers, with trained animals and a hurdygurdy, playing outside houses.

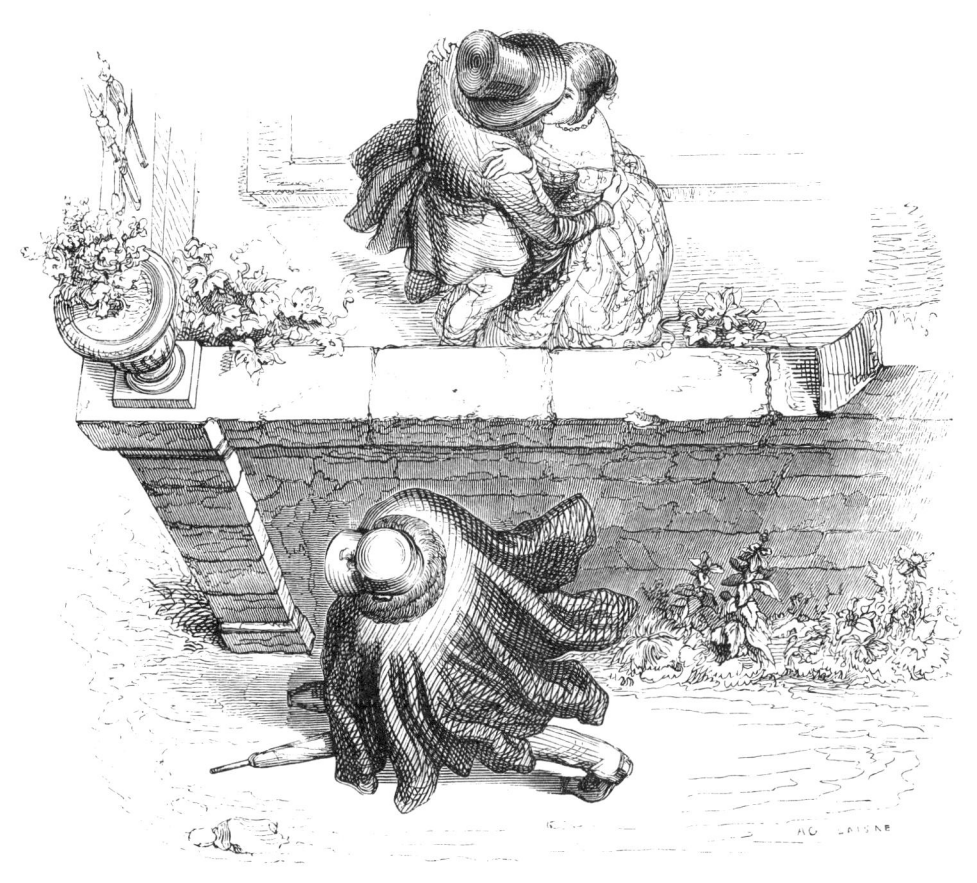

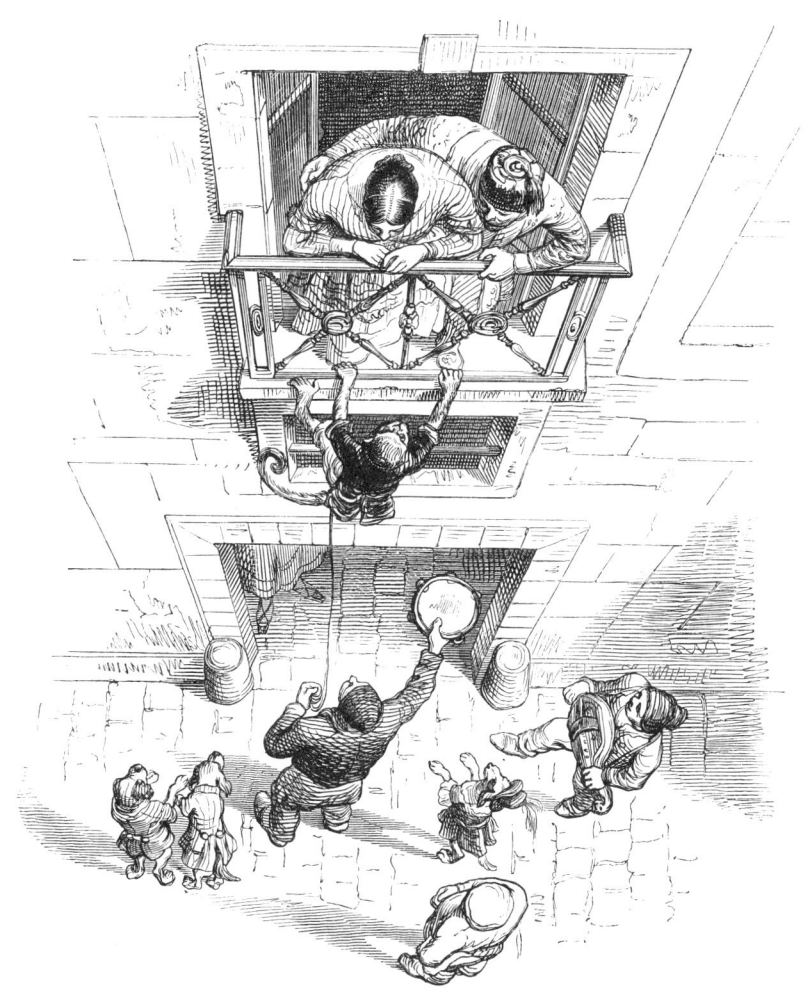

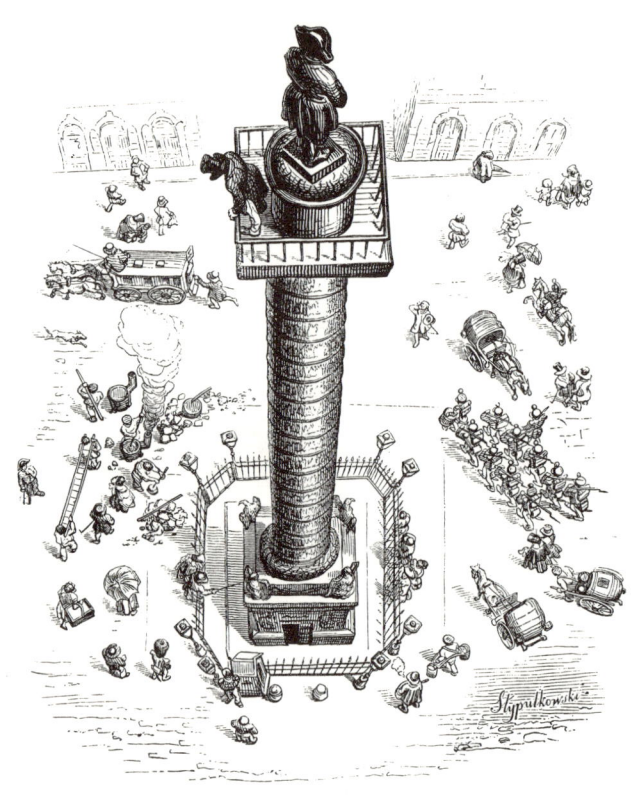

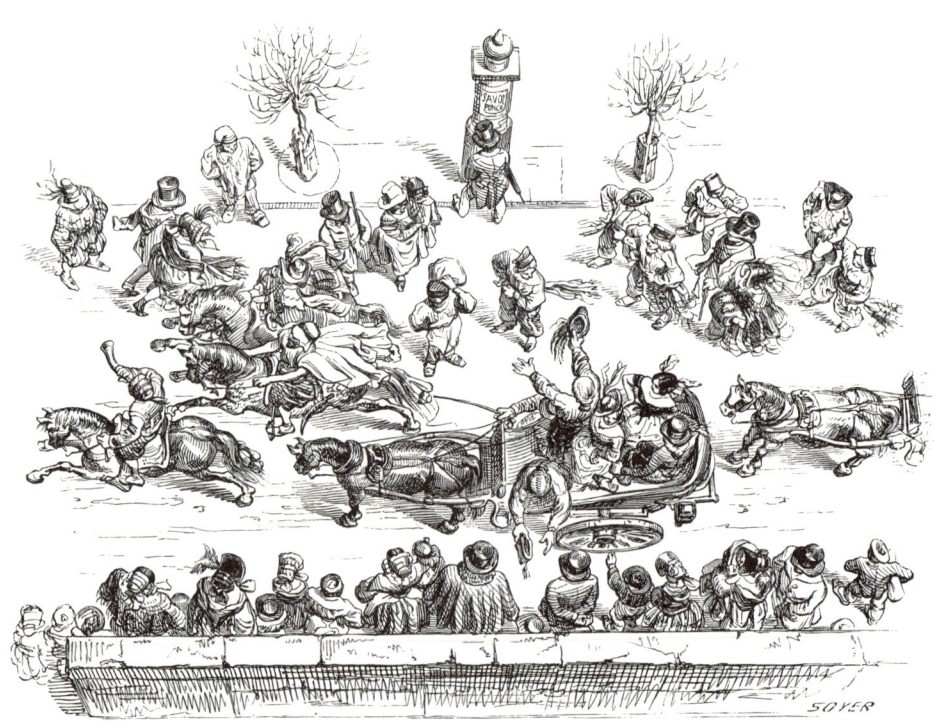

14. From his height, he finds that all human glory is vanity. **15.** Hahblle sees a procession of carnival masqueraders on a boulevard. **16.** Krackq's bottle making signs of distress to Puff. **17.** The undersea carnival procession of the fatted ox.

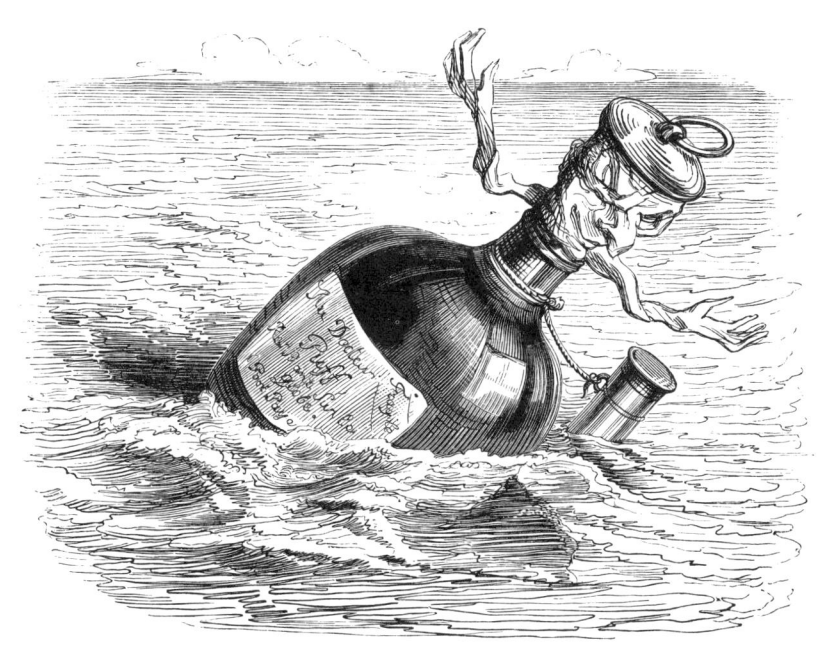

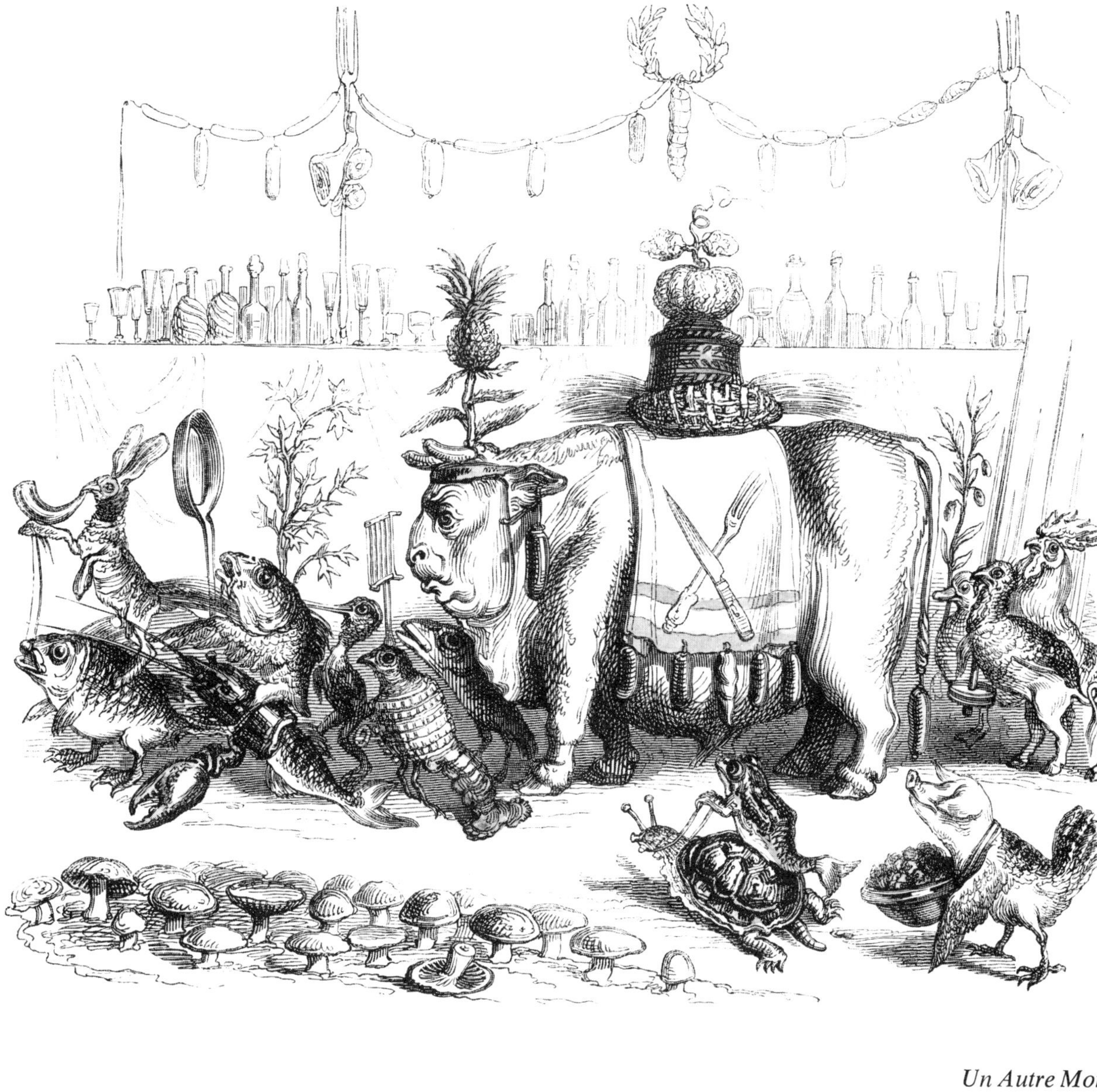

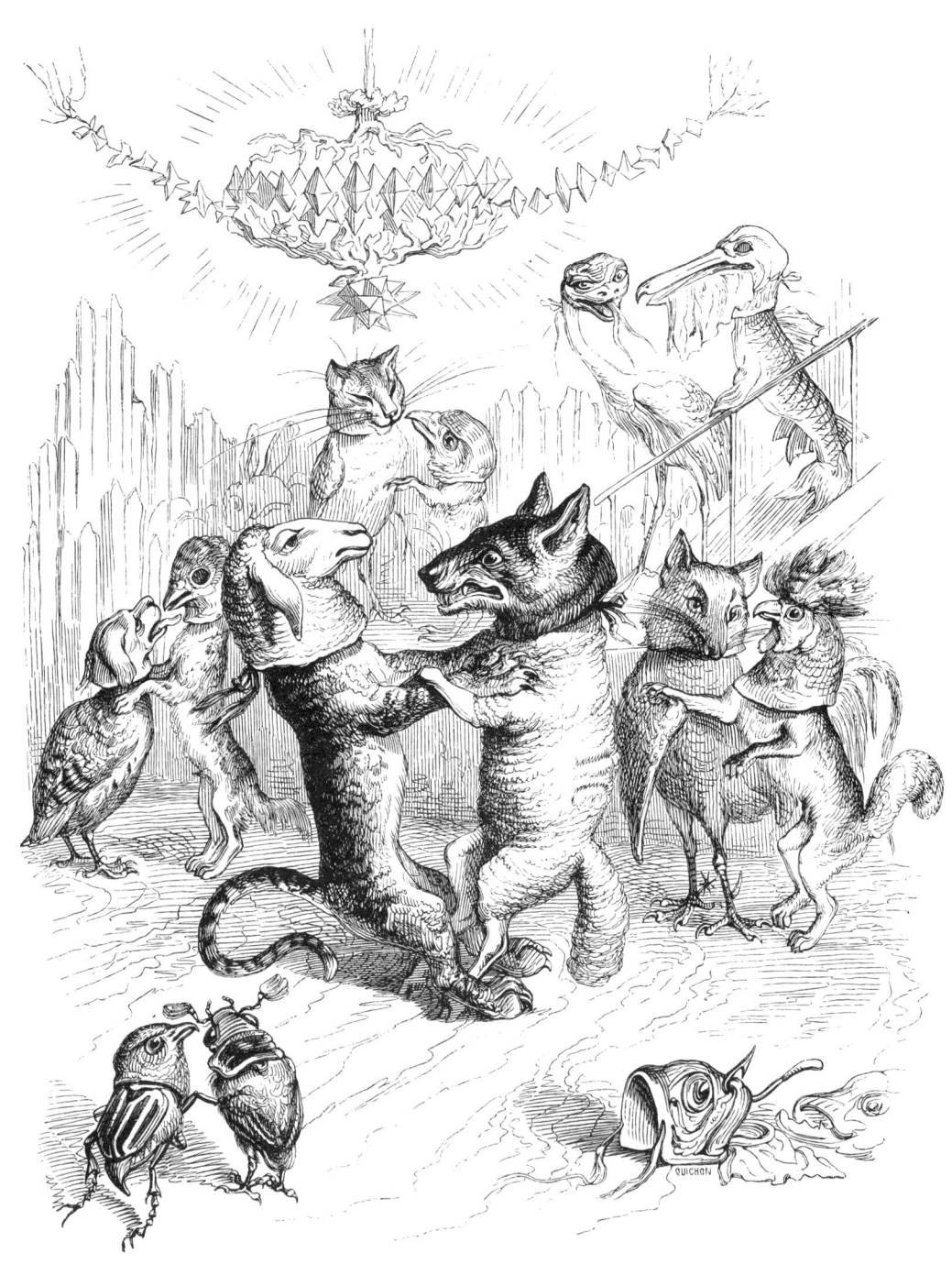

18. At the undersea ball, a male lamb dances with an aging female panther, a fox casts loving glances at a hen, and a partridge captivates a hound with her gaze. **19.** At the ball, a hare attacks a lioness, a gazelle drags by his mane her lion-lover who has paid too much attention to a ballerina-greyhound, and a raven in a black domino tells jokes. **20.** Before the tolerant eyes of the police, an adolescent duck-frog performs a very free dance with an owl-mouse.

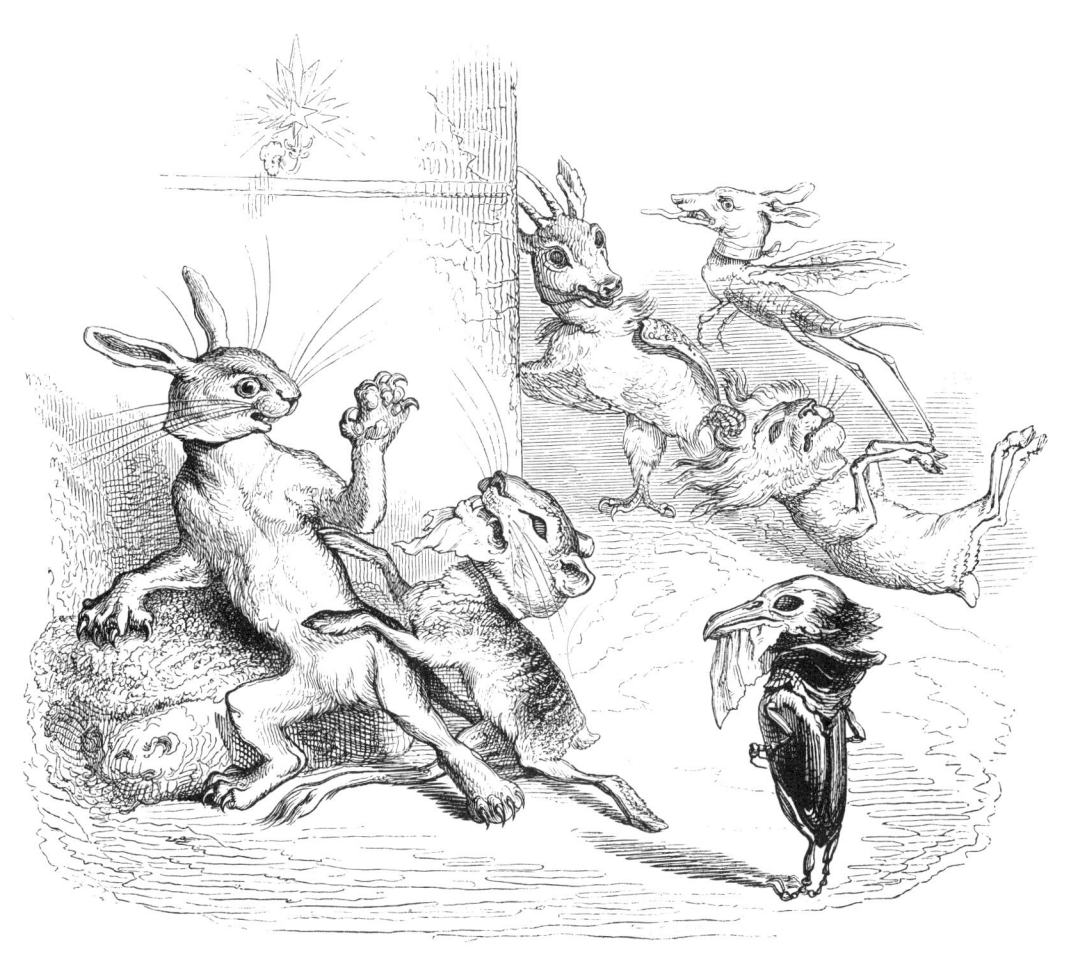

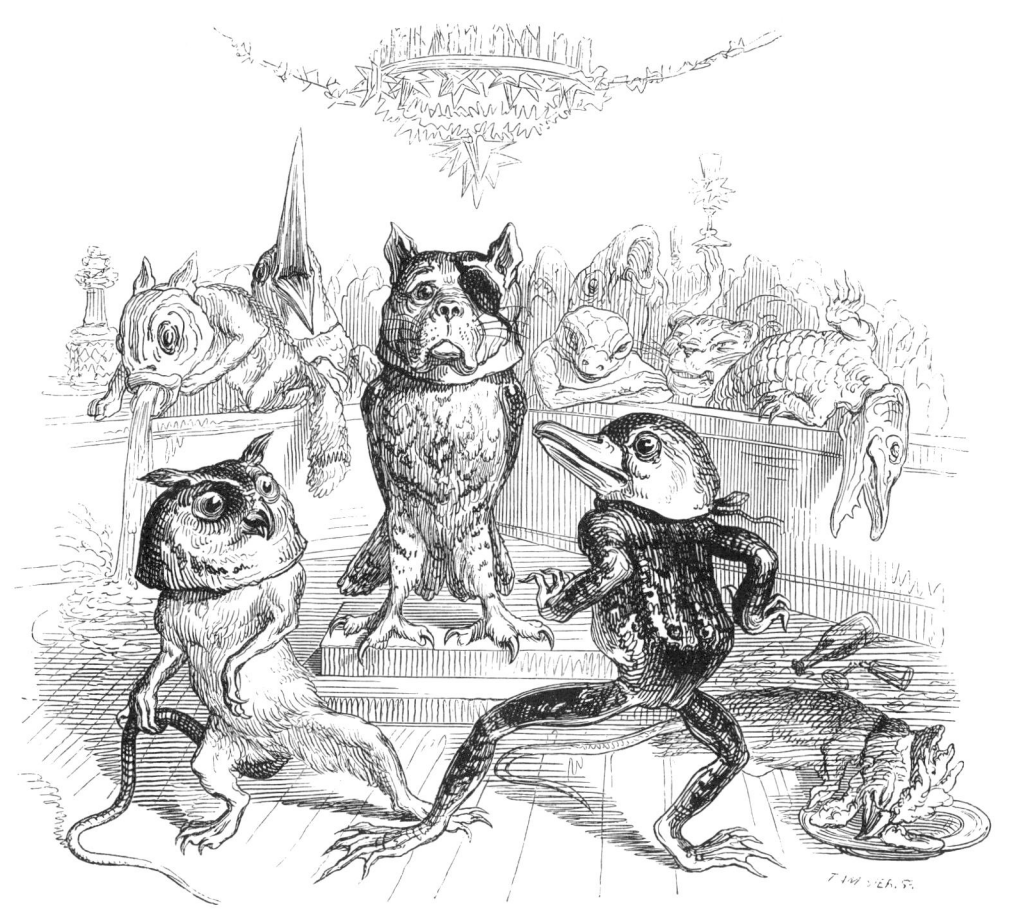

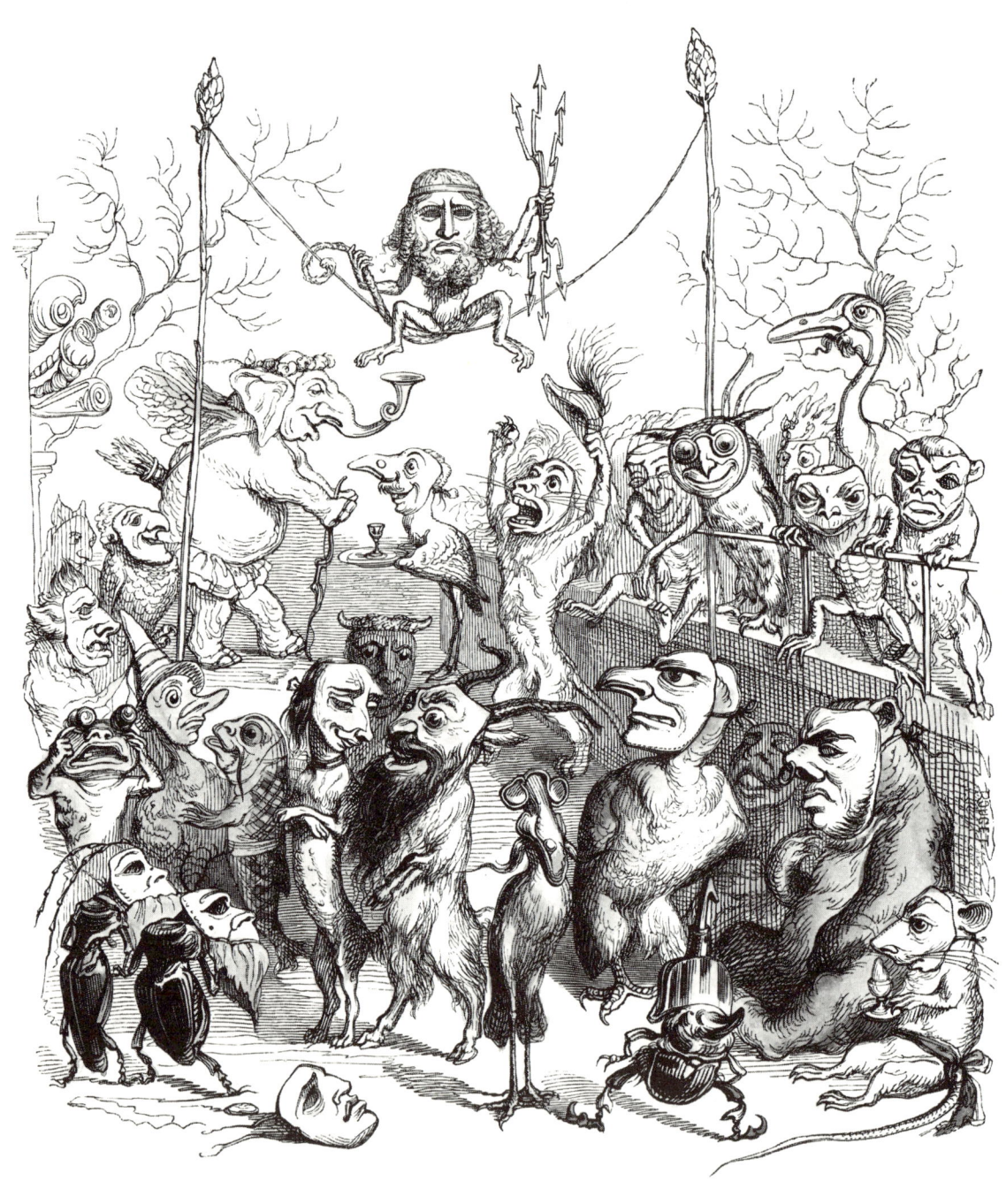

21. At a more aristocratic undersea ball visited by Krackq, the animals masquerade as human beings rather than as other animals.   **22.** Puff's new costumes—examples of the contrast between people's public images and their true characters.

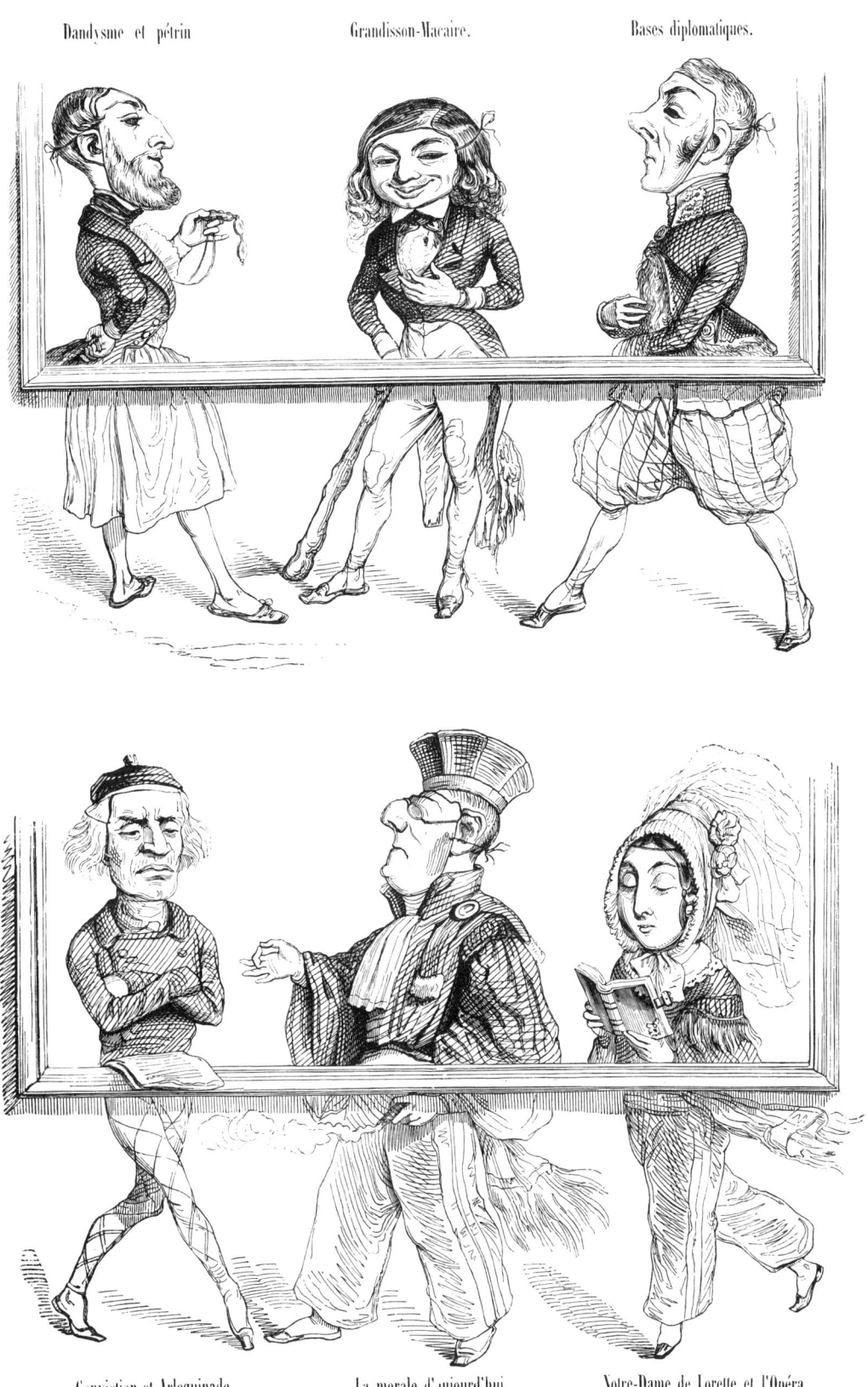

Dandysme et pétrin   Grandisson-Macaire.   Bases diplomatiques.

Conviction et Arlequinade.   La morale d'aujourd'hui.   Notre-Dame de Lorette et l'Opéra.

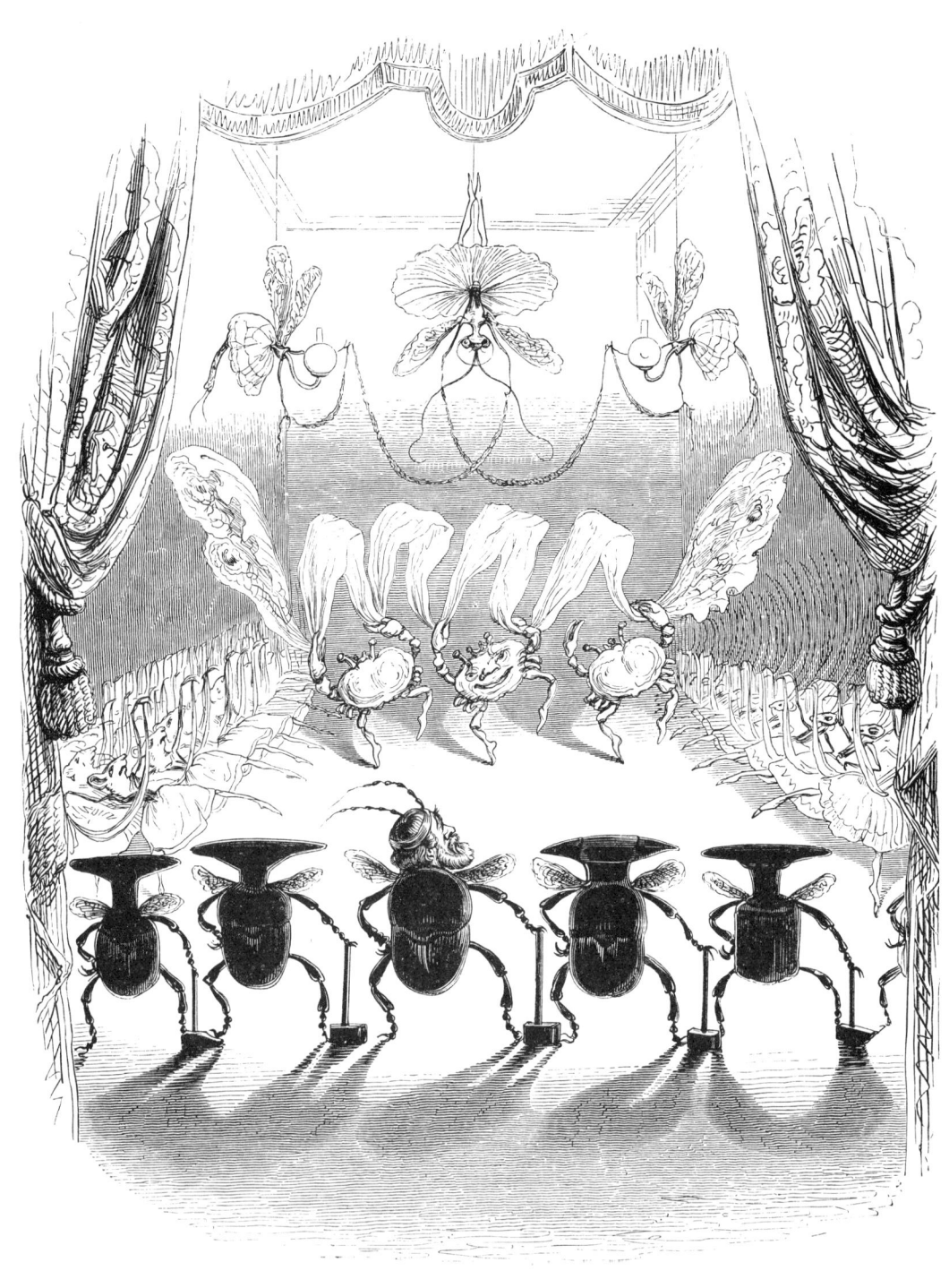

23. A "pas de crabes" in the grand Romantic ballet *The Loves of Venus*, in which the nymphs of the *corps de ballet* are mice and grasshoppers, while the Cyclopes (who perform a hammer dance) are scarab beetles.

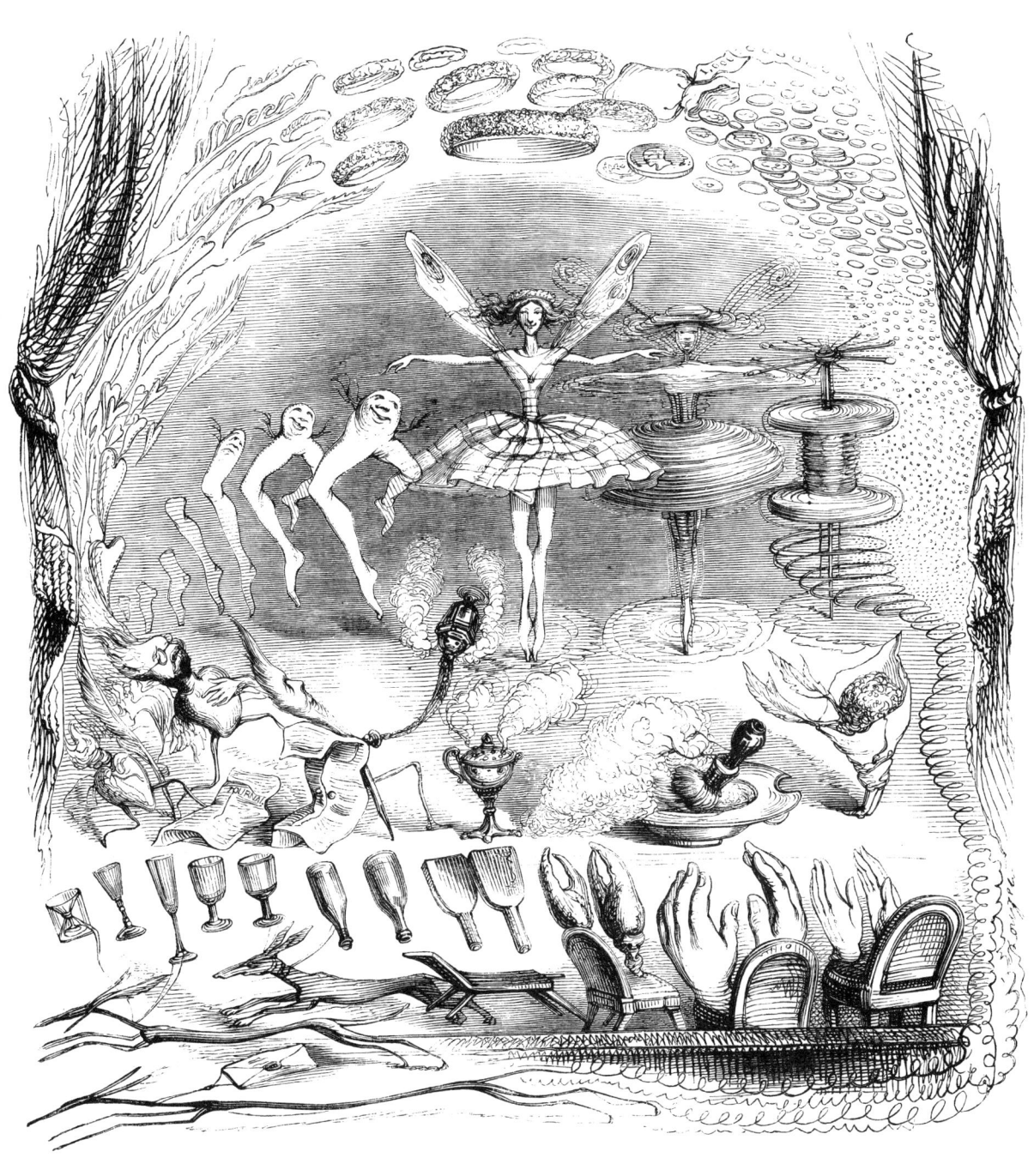

24. Fantastic vision of the audience's worship of the great Romantic *prime ballerine*.

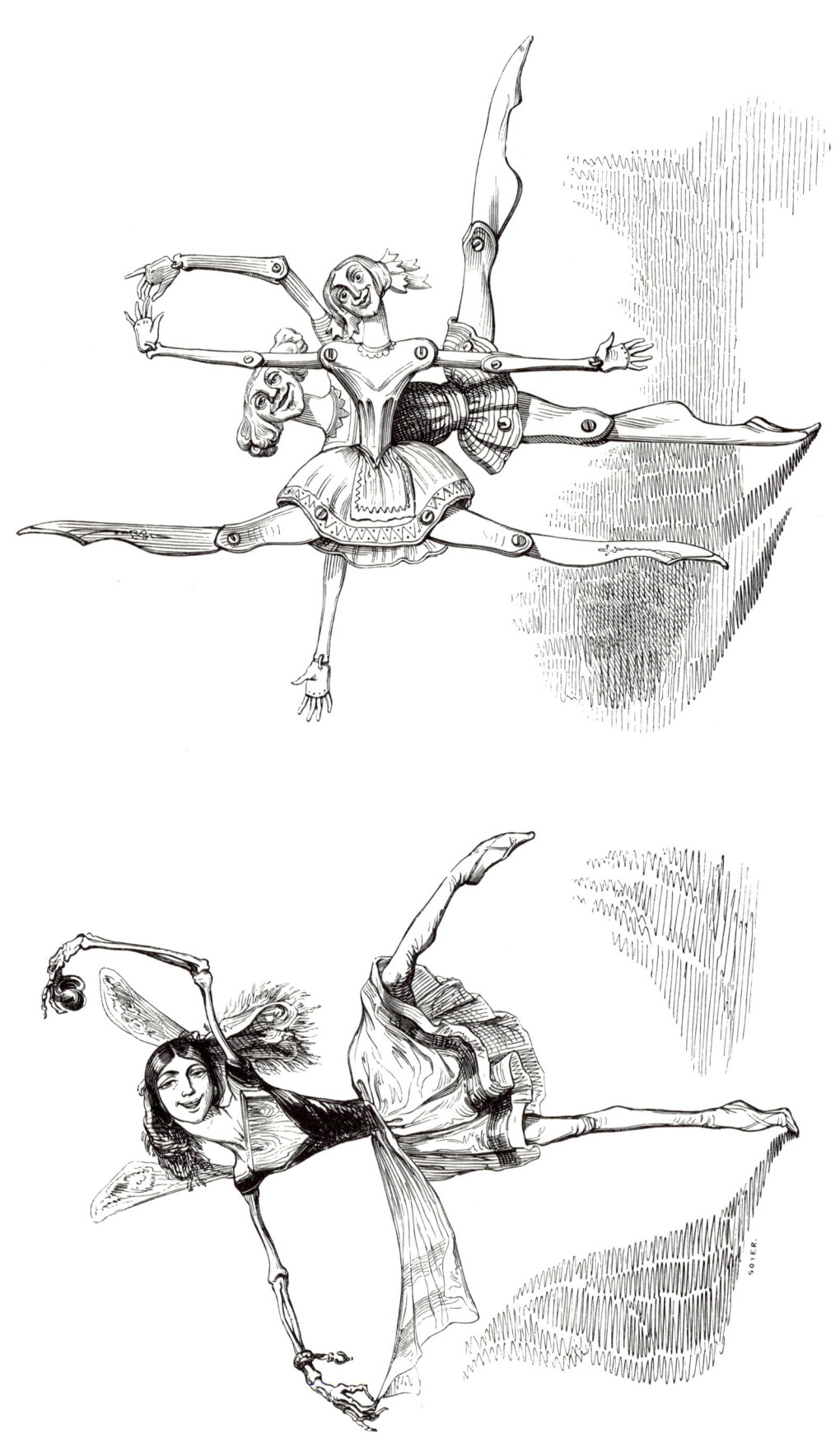

26. Other marionette ballet stars.

25. A marionette ballerina.

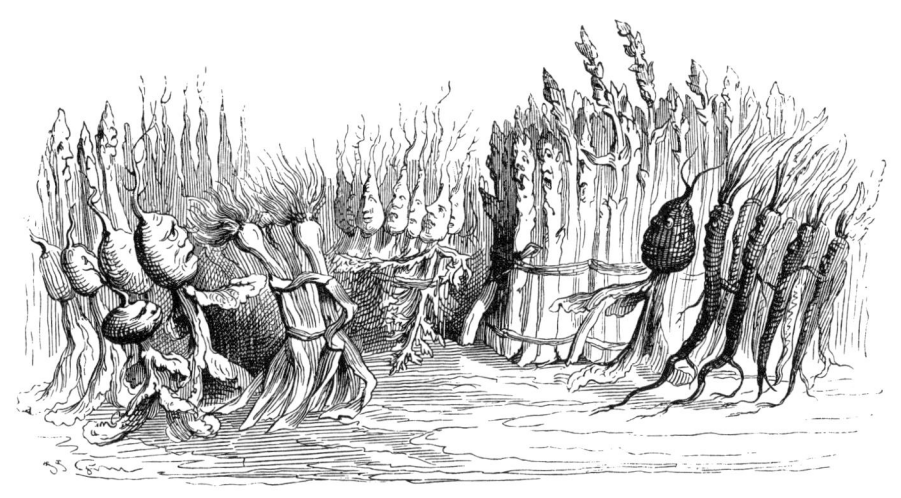

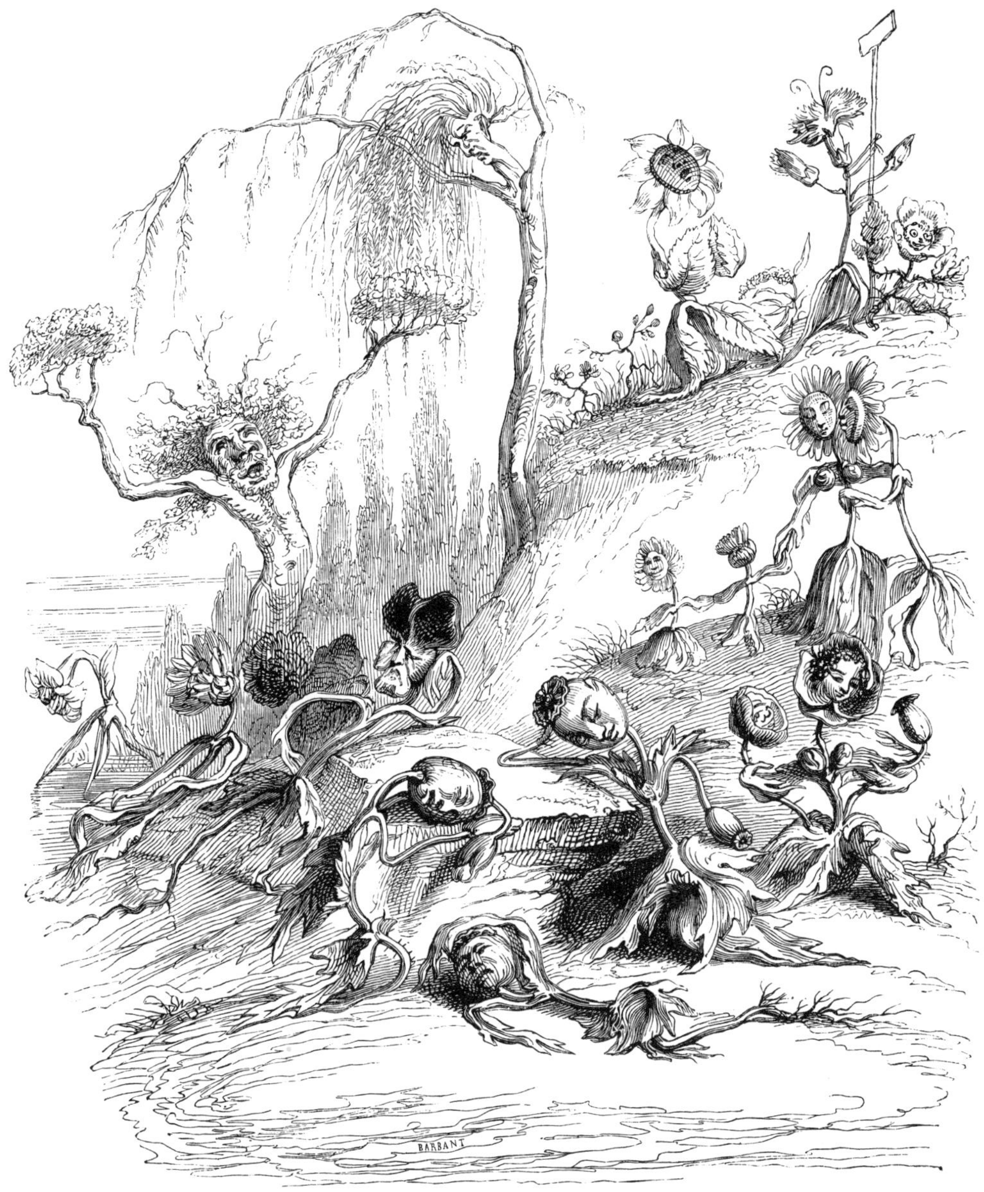

27. Conspiratorial vegetables plot revolution. **28.** Flowers and bushes awaken from their complacent slumbers.

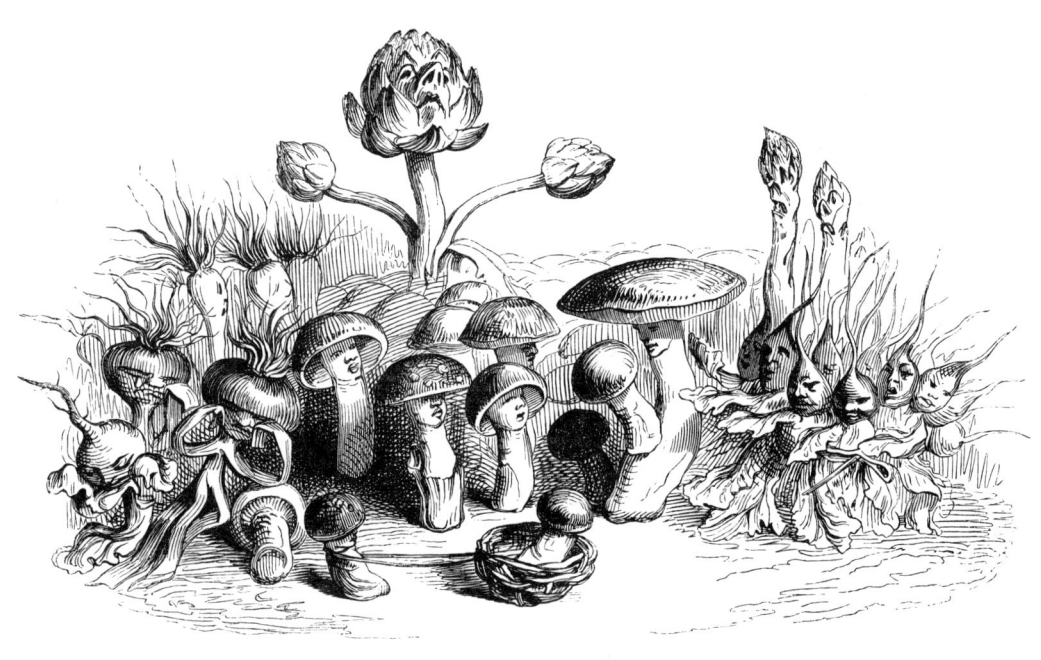

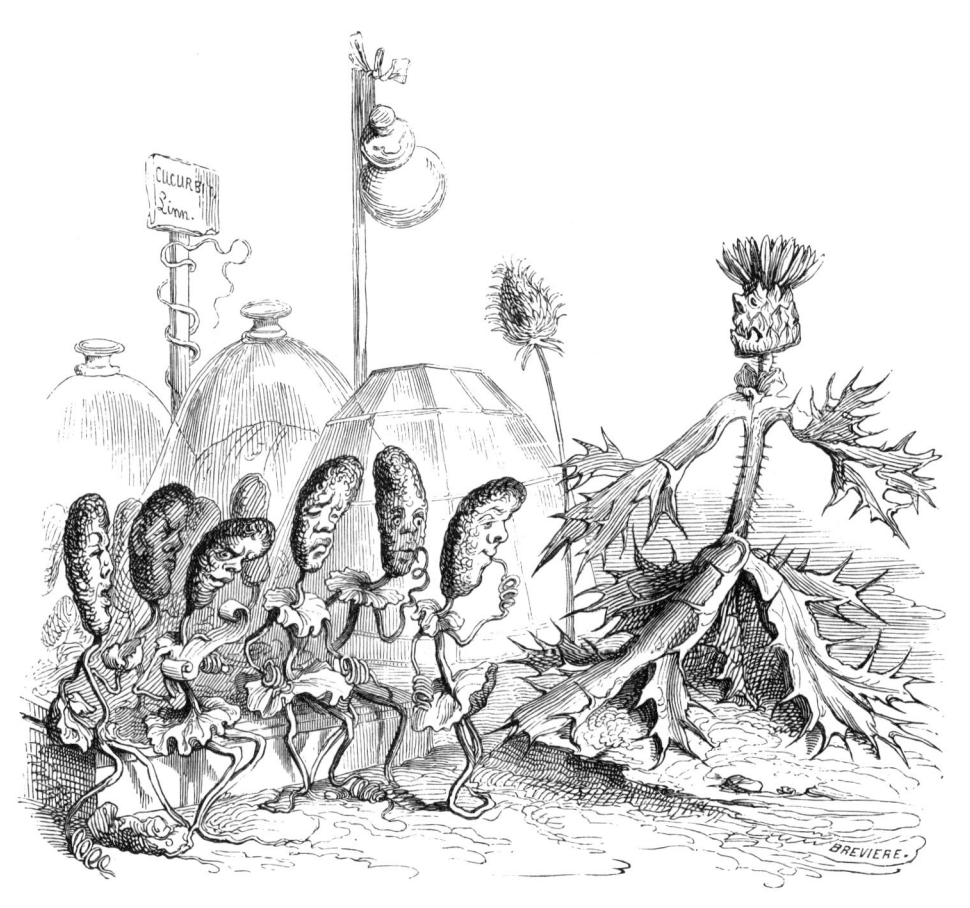

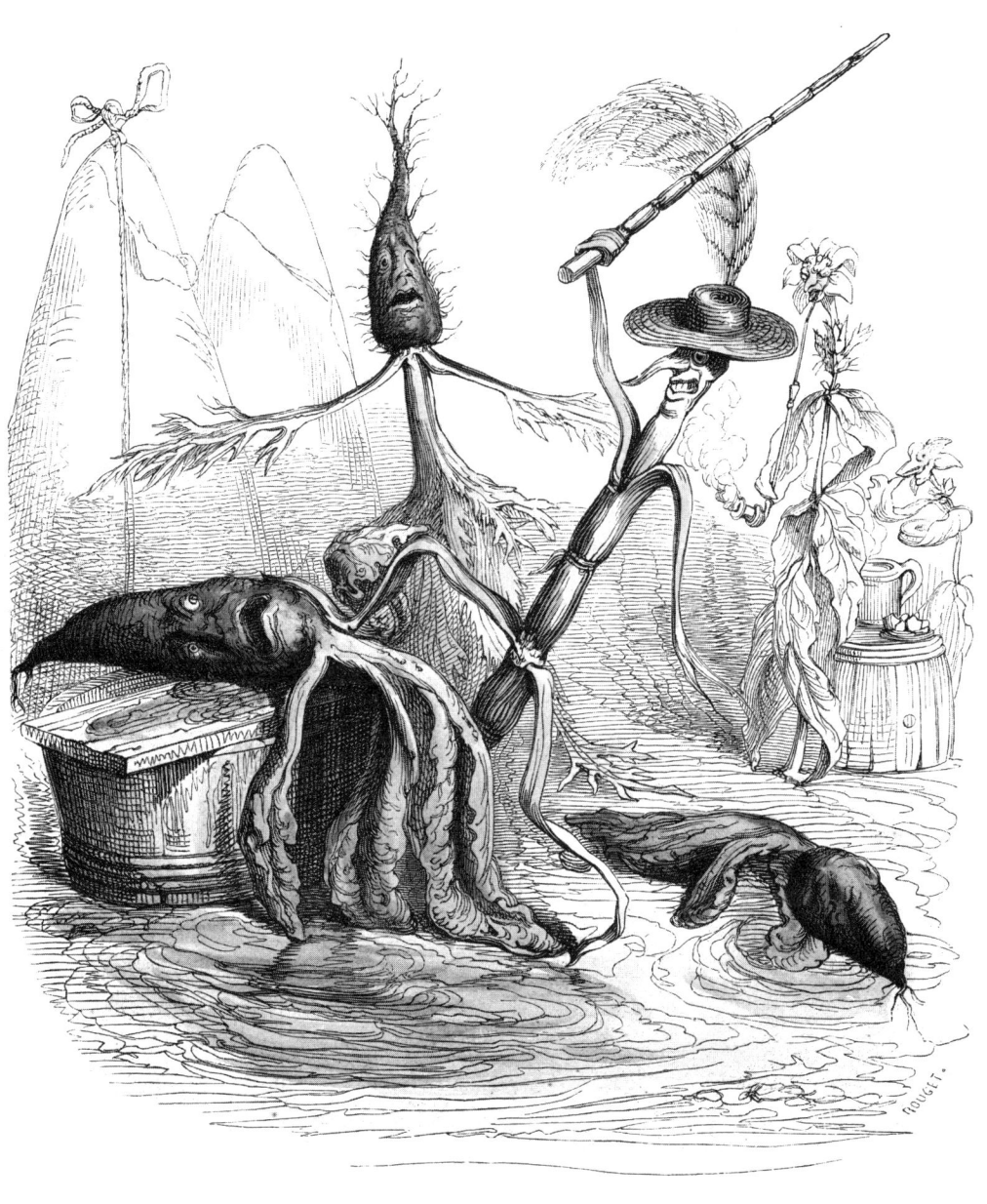

29. Artichokes, mushrooms and others vow to be food for man no longer. **30.** The proletarian thistle, fomenter of the revolt, harangues the gherkins. **31.** Fight between two "refined" gentlemen—the sugar cane and the sugar beet.

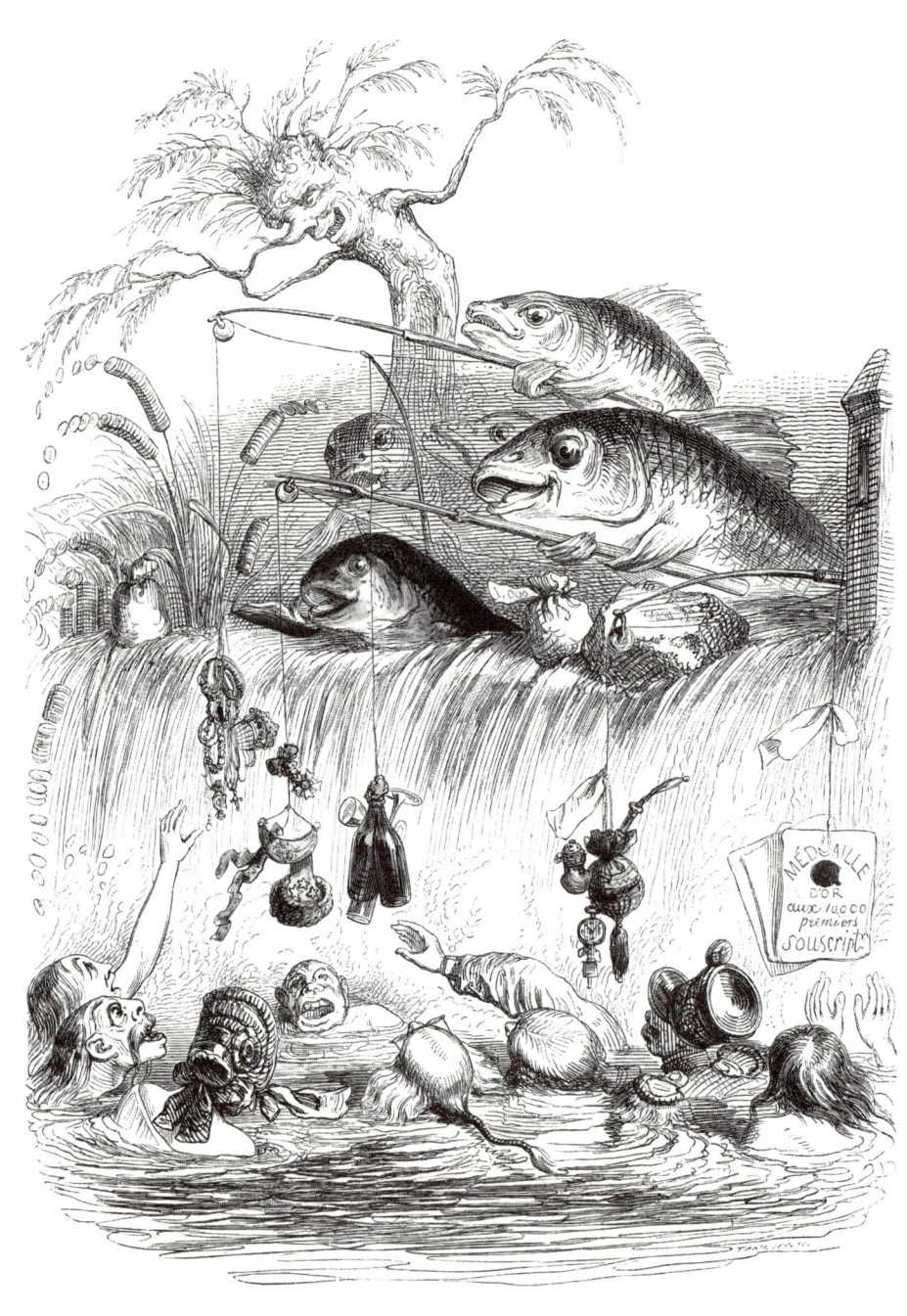

32. Fish fishing for people, using various desirable items as bait.   **33.** Satire on carriages: some as low-slung as armchairs, some as tall as steeples.   **34.** A dog walking his man.

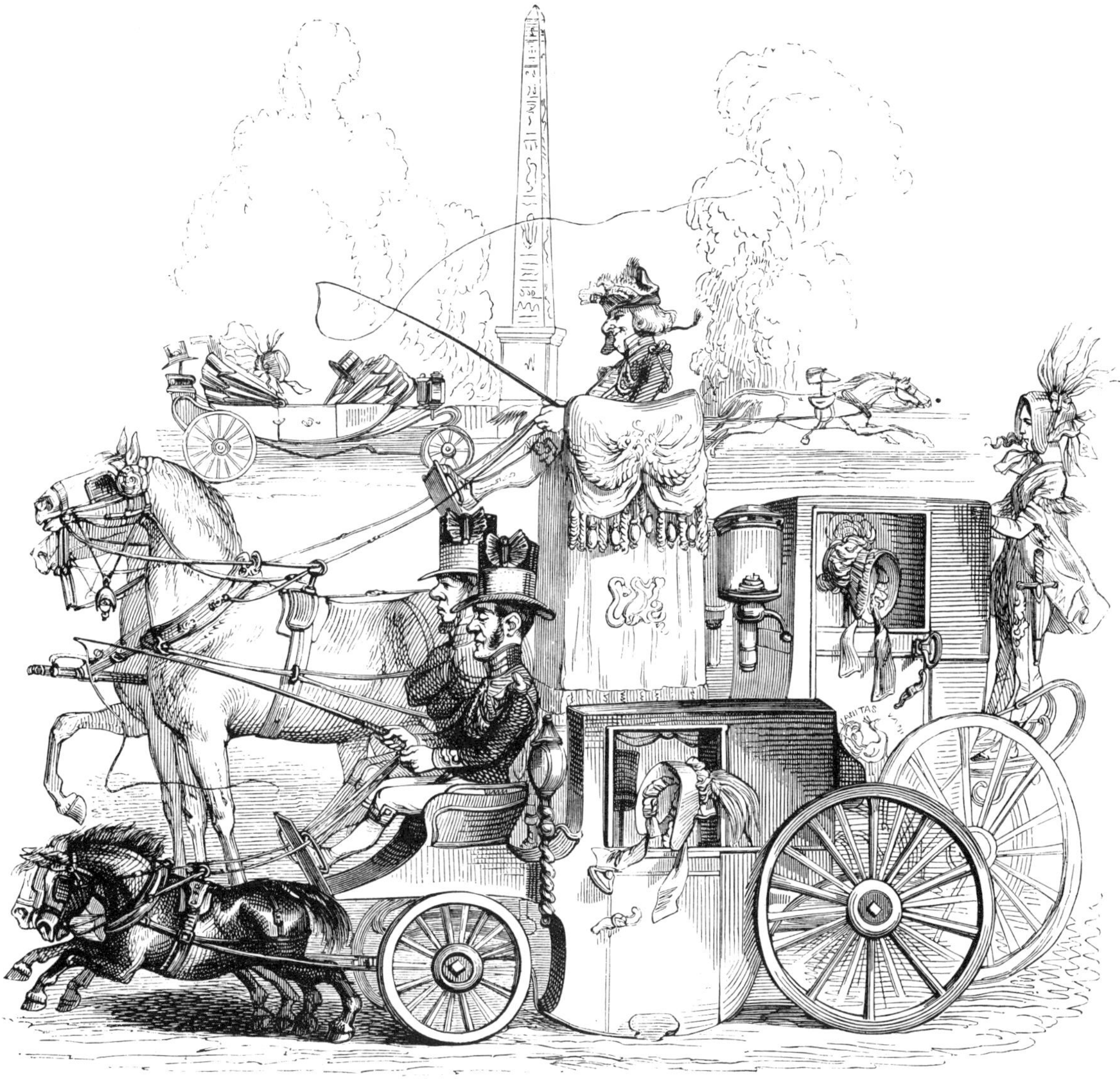

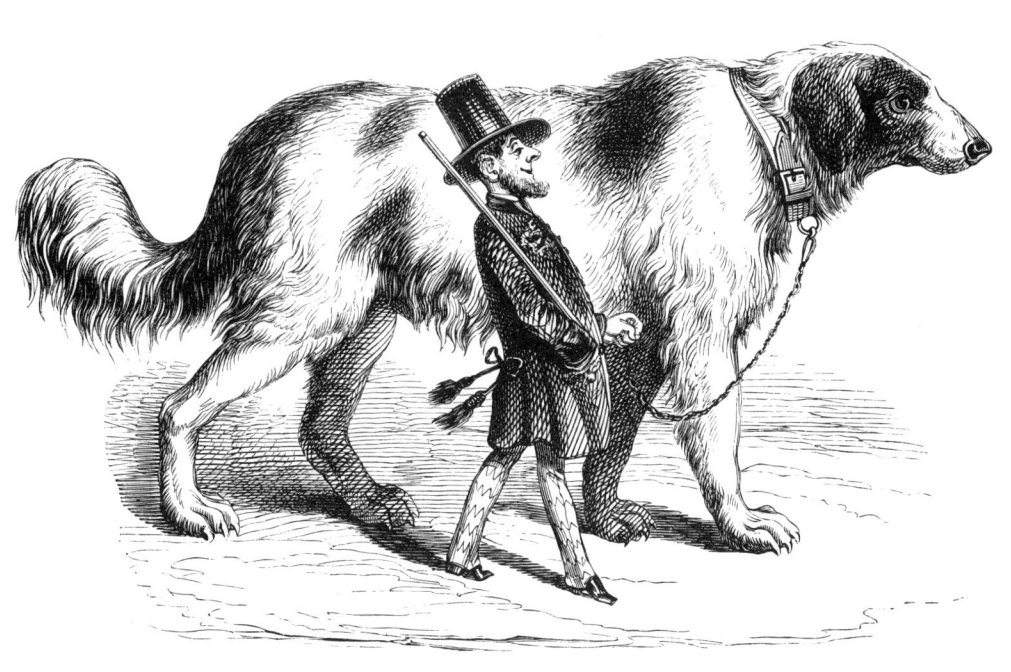

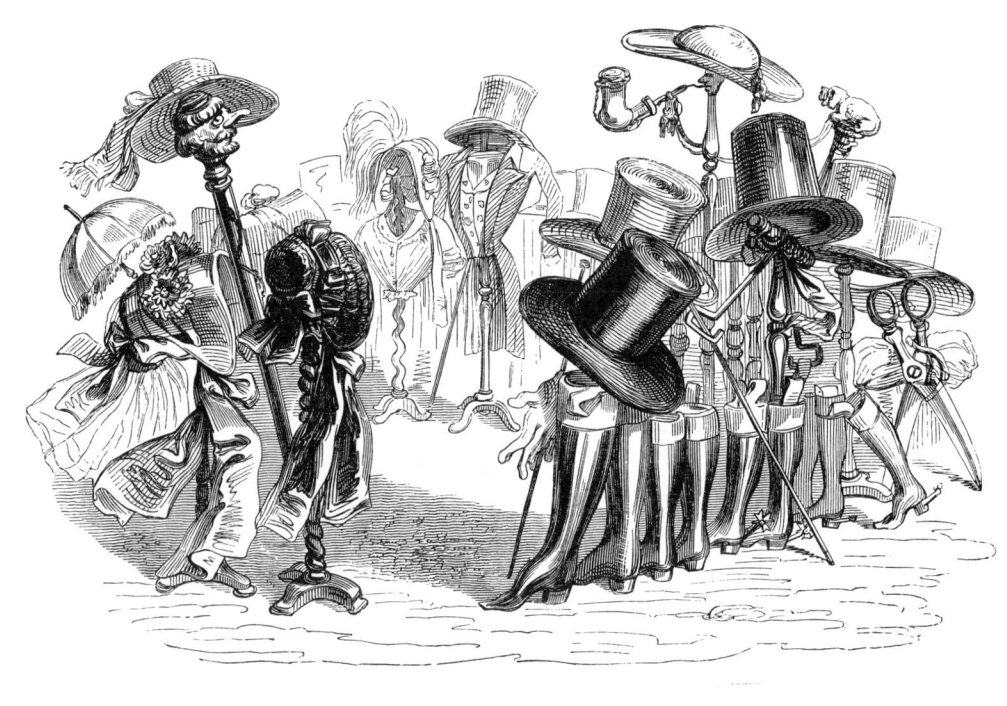

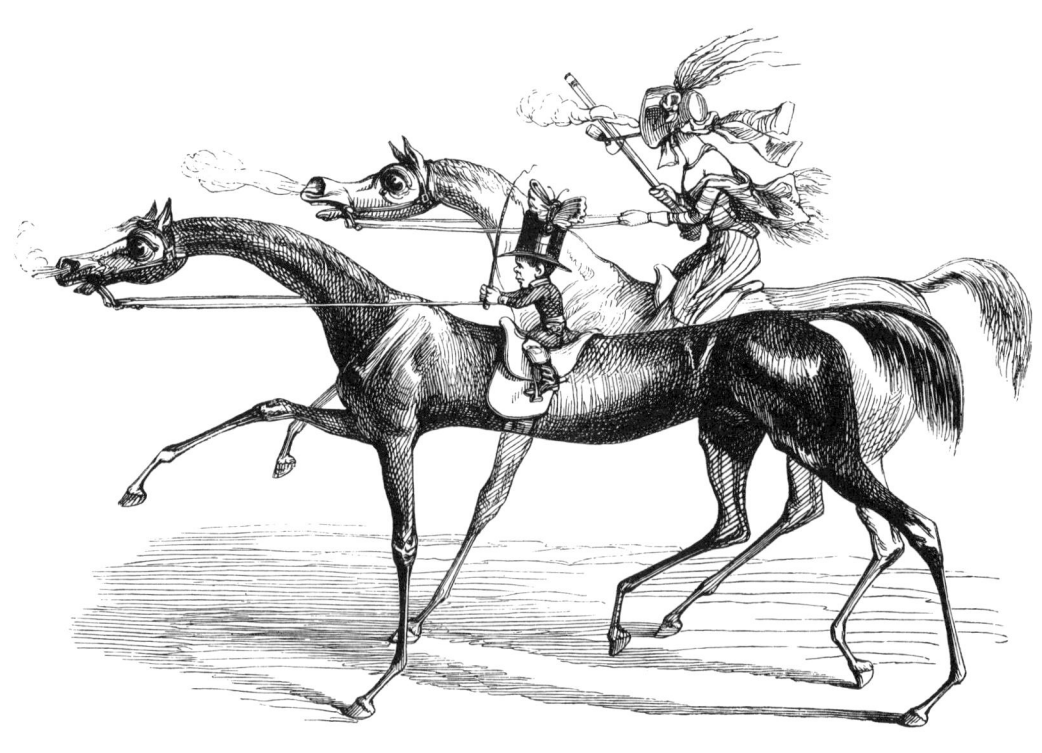

35. Fashionable people represented in public by their accoutrements. **36.** The Duchess of Sorrel with two of her English thoroughbreds, one mounted by her mechanically miniaturized groom.

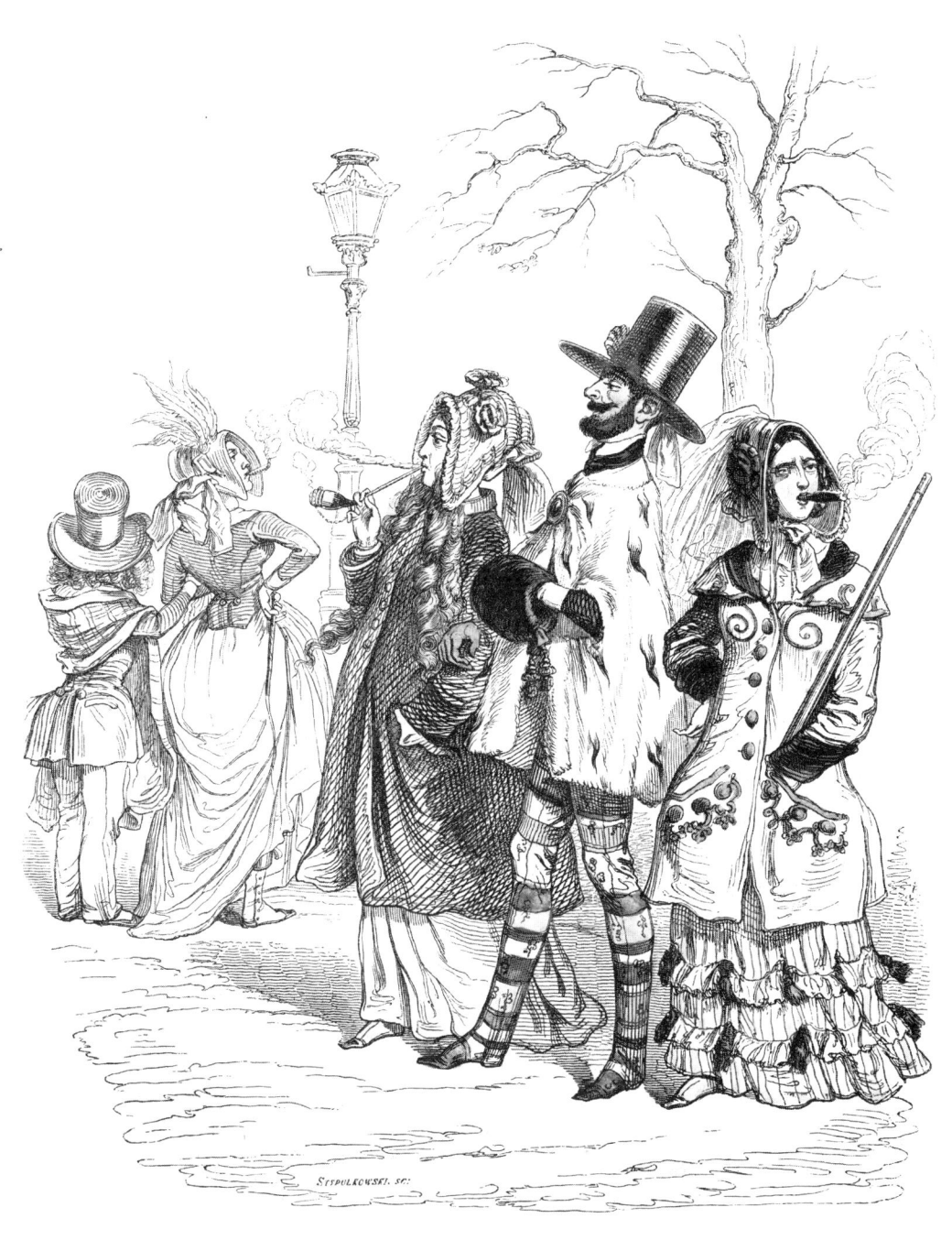

37. Dandyism and women's emancipation carried to the point of near-transvestism (satire on current trends).

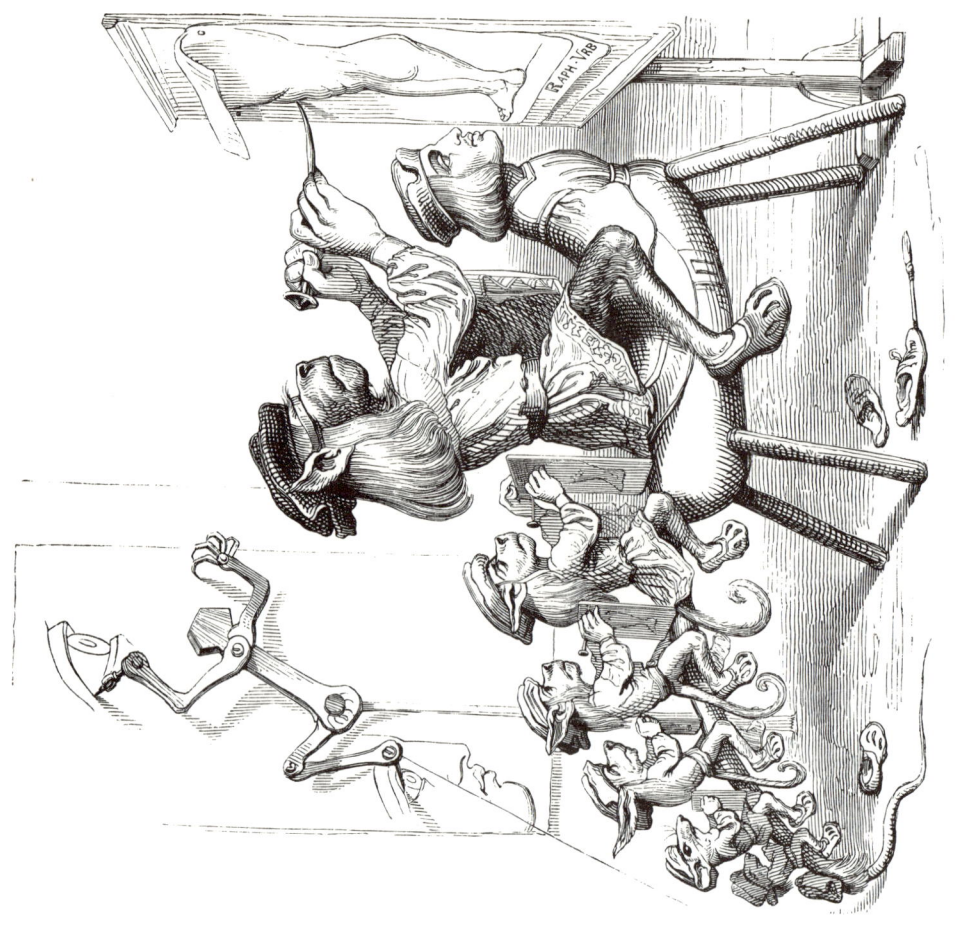

39. An academic teacher of painting and his pupils, mounted on a Raphael hobbyhorse, trace details from the old masters.

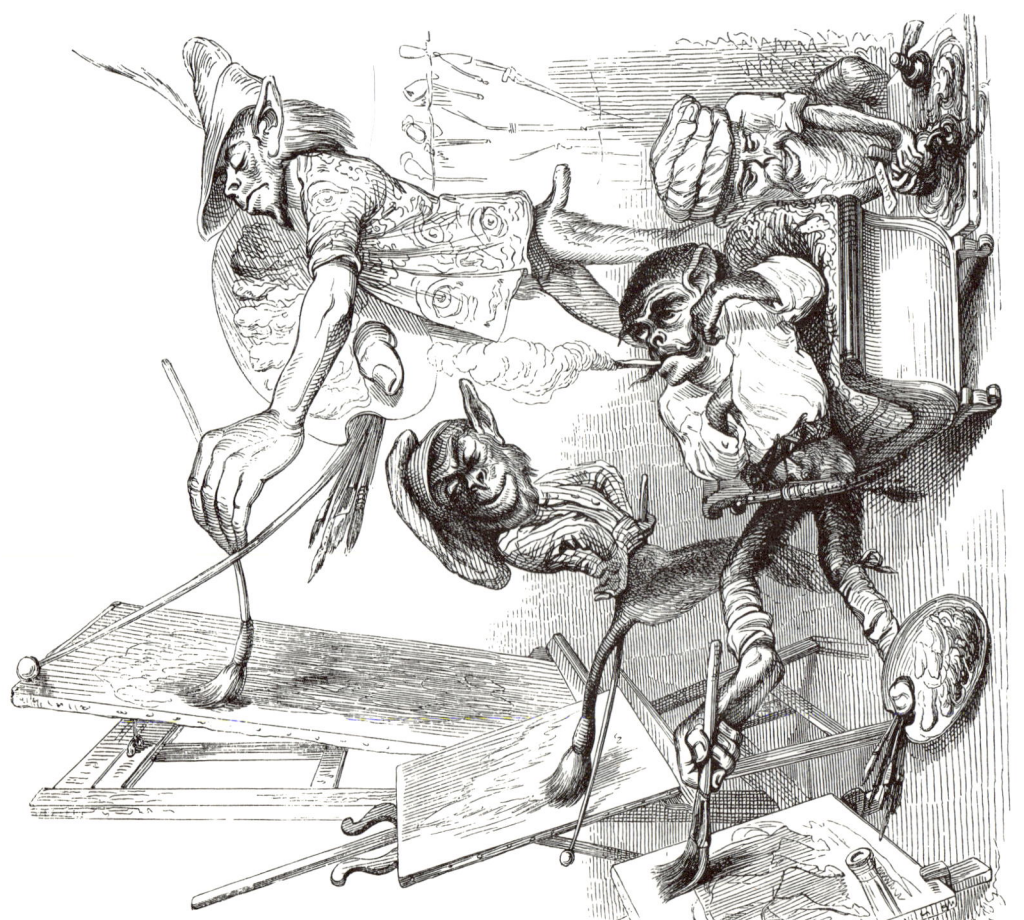

38. Painters who turn out many pictures in record time.

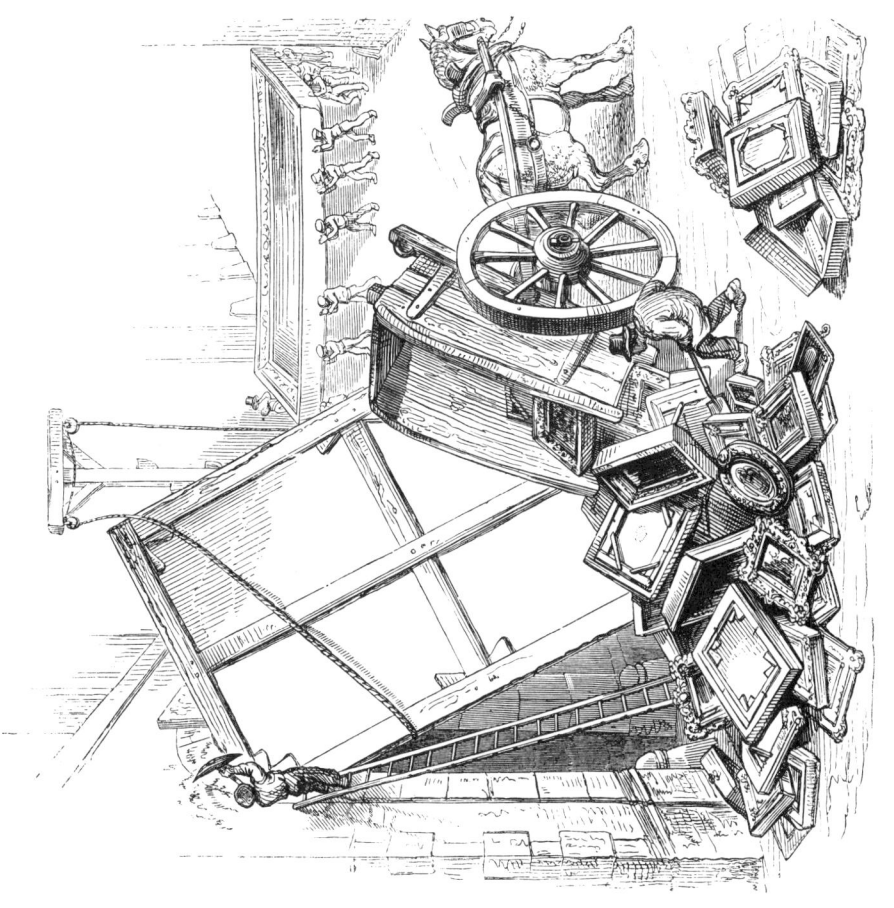

41. A portal of the Louvre is demolished to allow a vast academic canvas to be brought in.

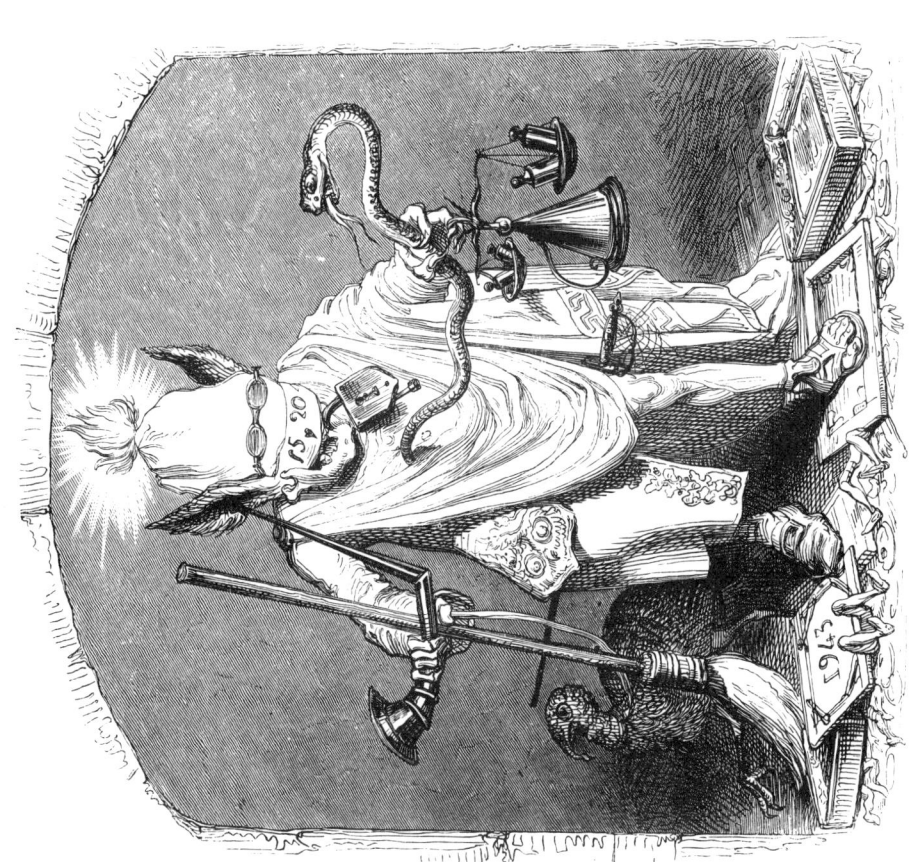

40. The expert who is to judge the pictures submitted by the artists.

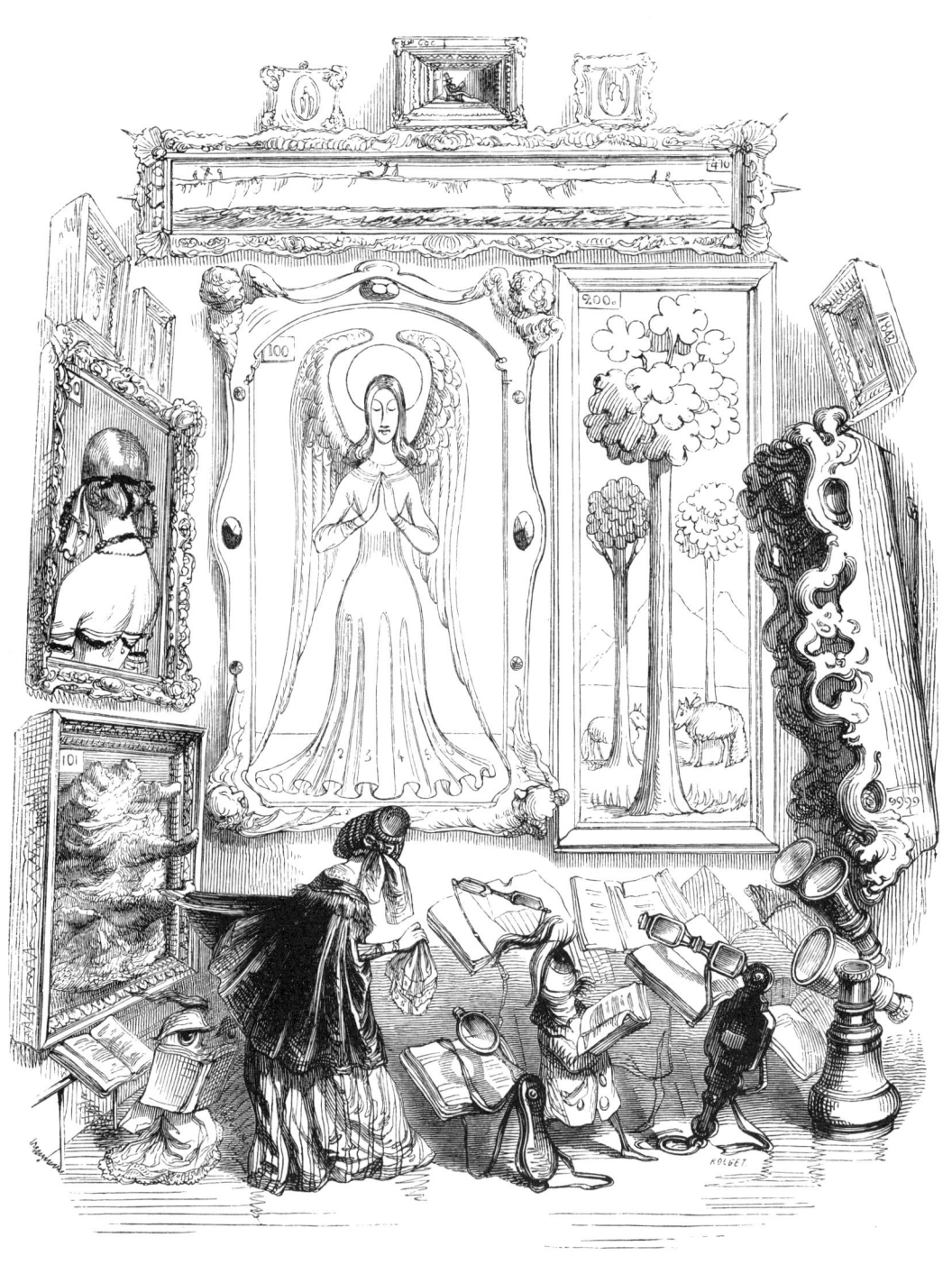

42. An exhibition room. **43.** An exhibition gallery. **44.** A great sculptor finishing his master-piece, "The Finger of God."

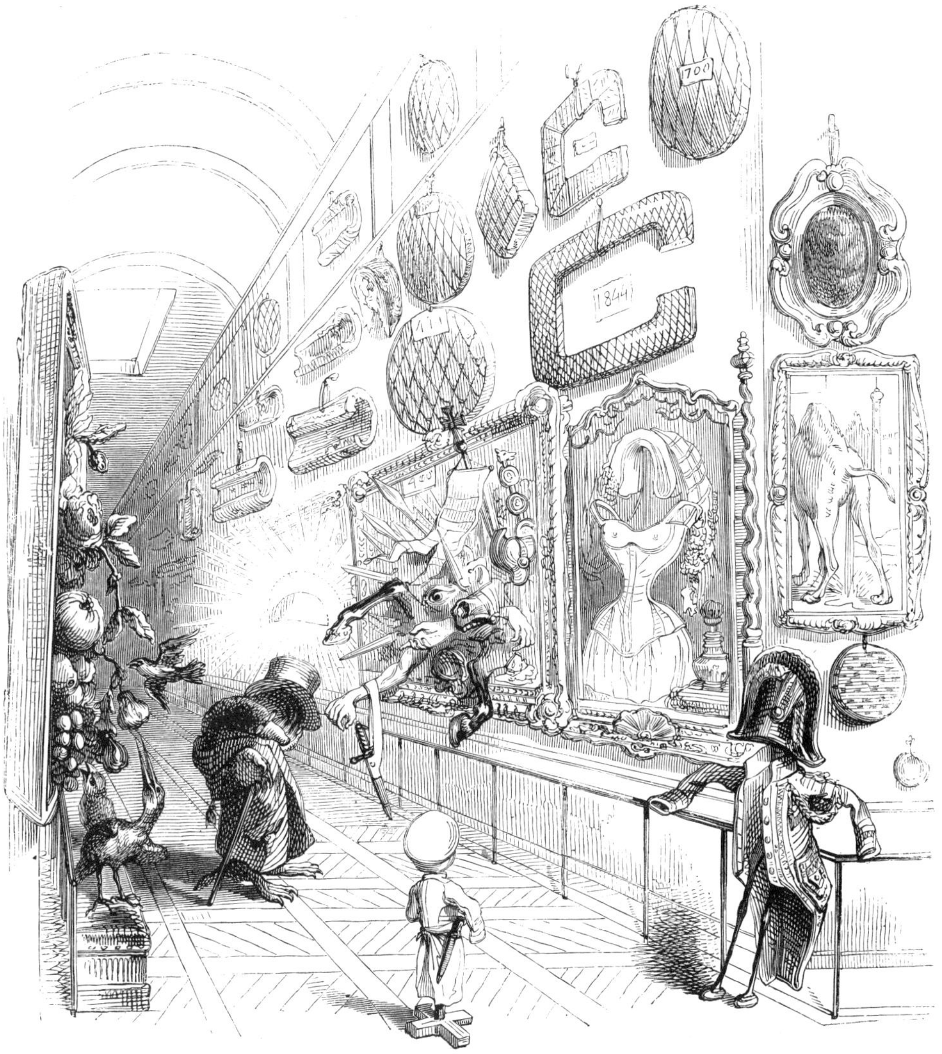

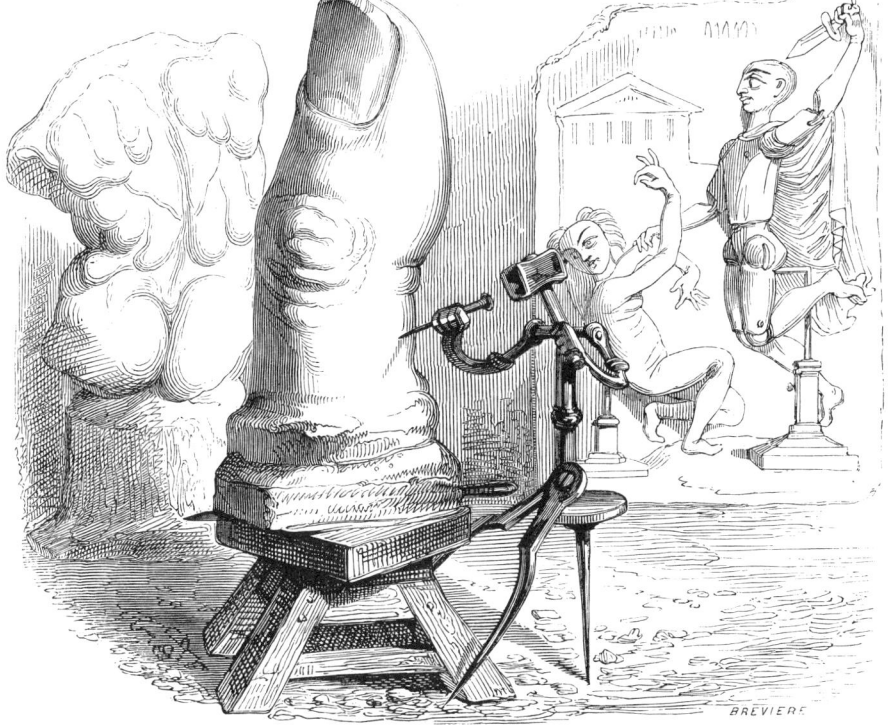

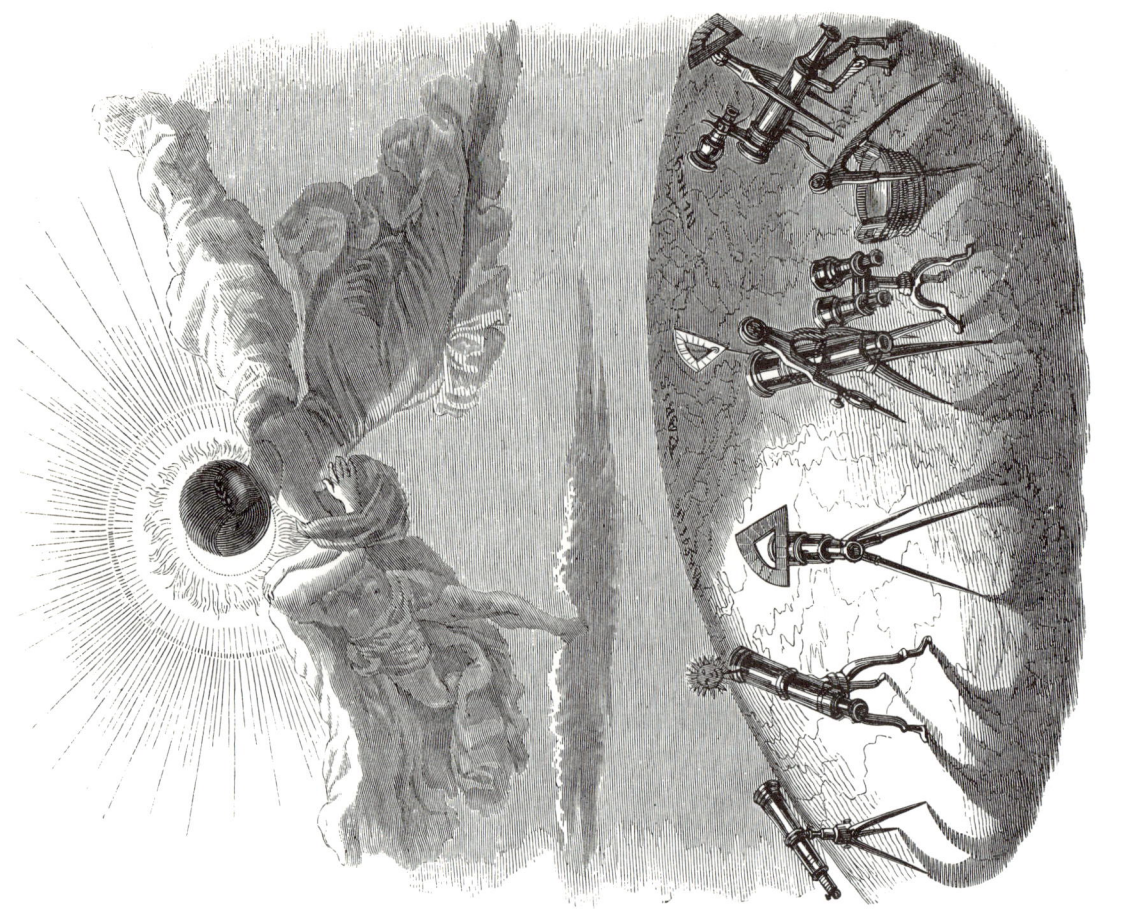

46. Astronomers on Earth, represented by their instruments, observe a solar eclipse—the Moon kissing the Sun.

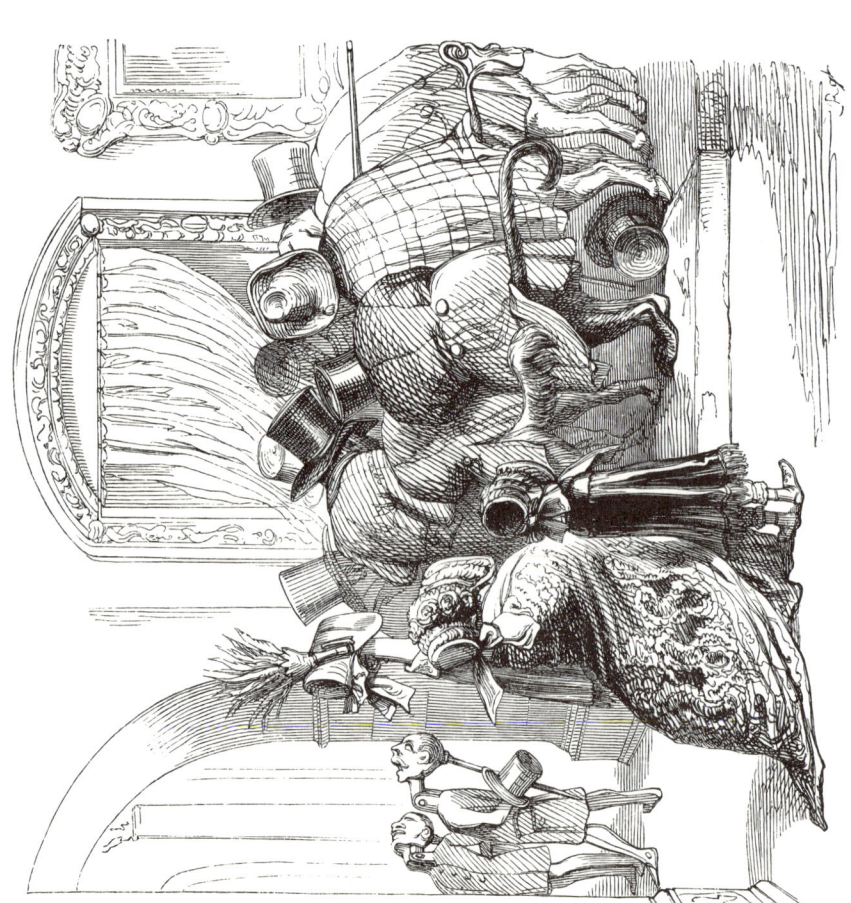

45. An exhibition room with licentious paintings.

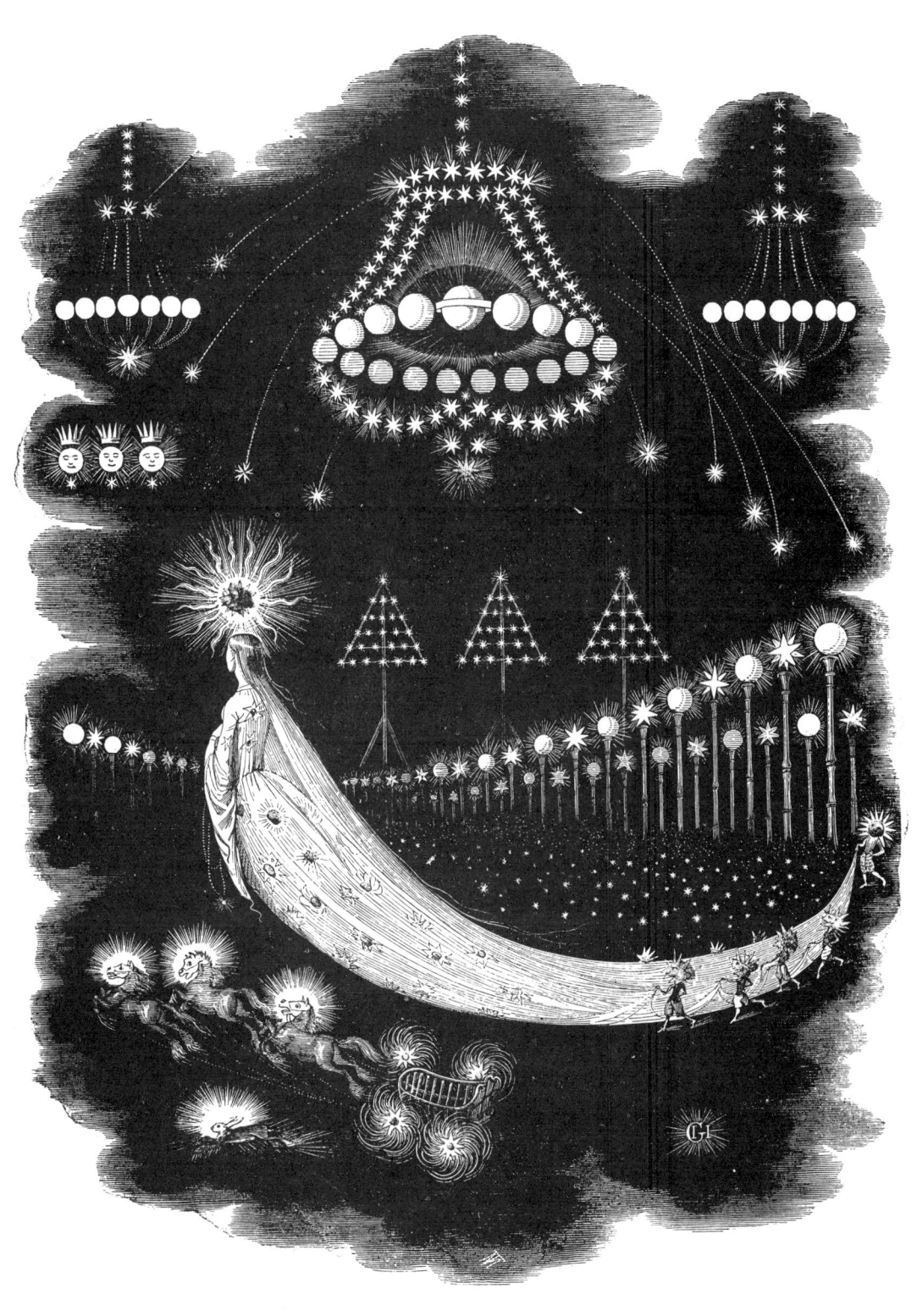

47. The passage of a comet across the sky.

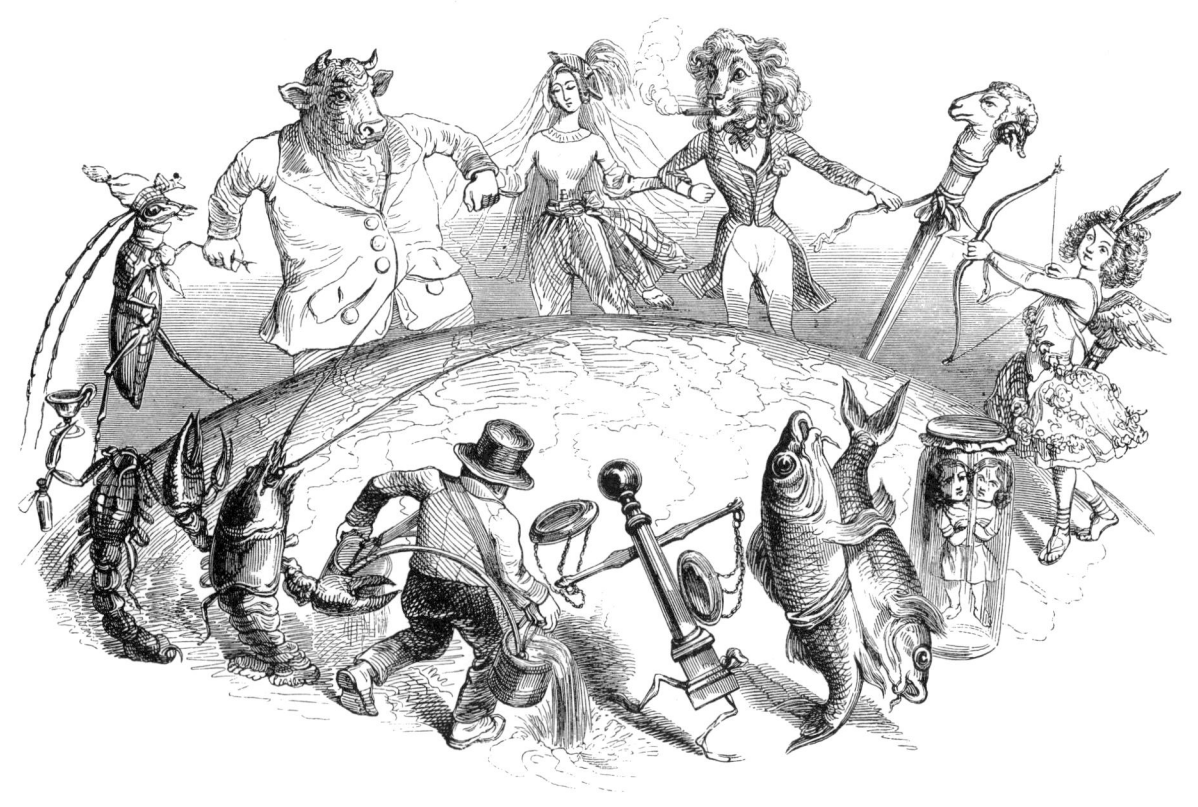

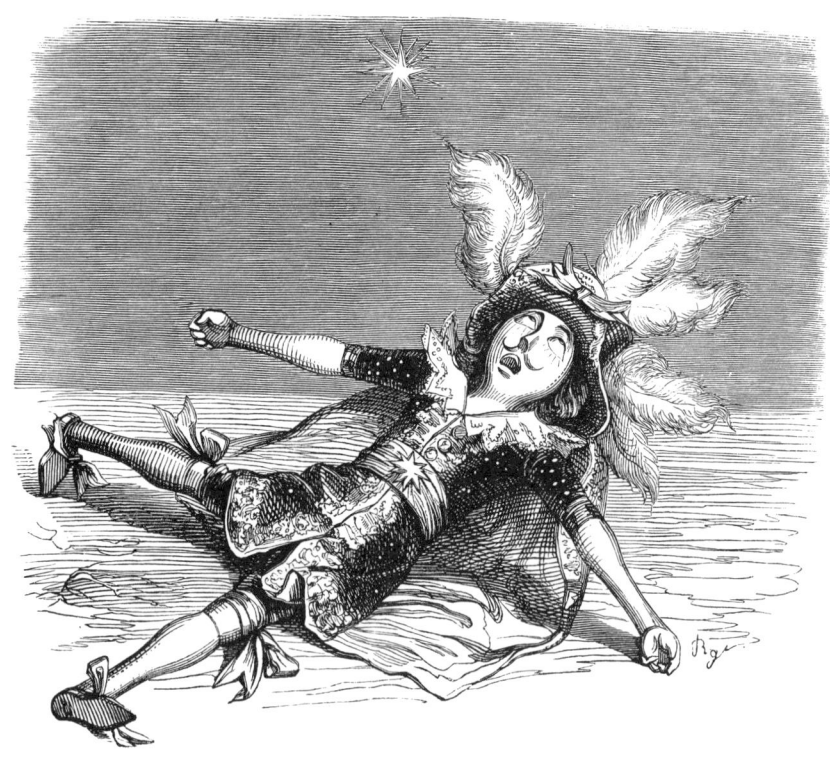

48. The constellations of the Zodiac, overjoyed at the eclipse, dance a saraband. **49.** The puppet faints when Venus appears. **50.** Venus in an opera box, with all eyes turned toward her. **51.** Venus as evening star.

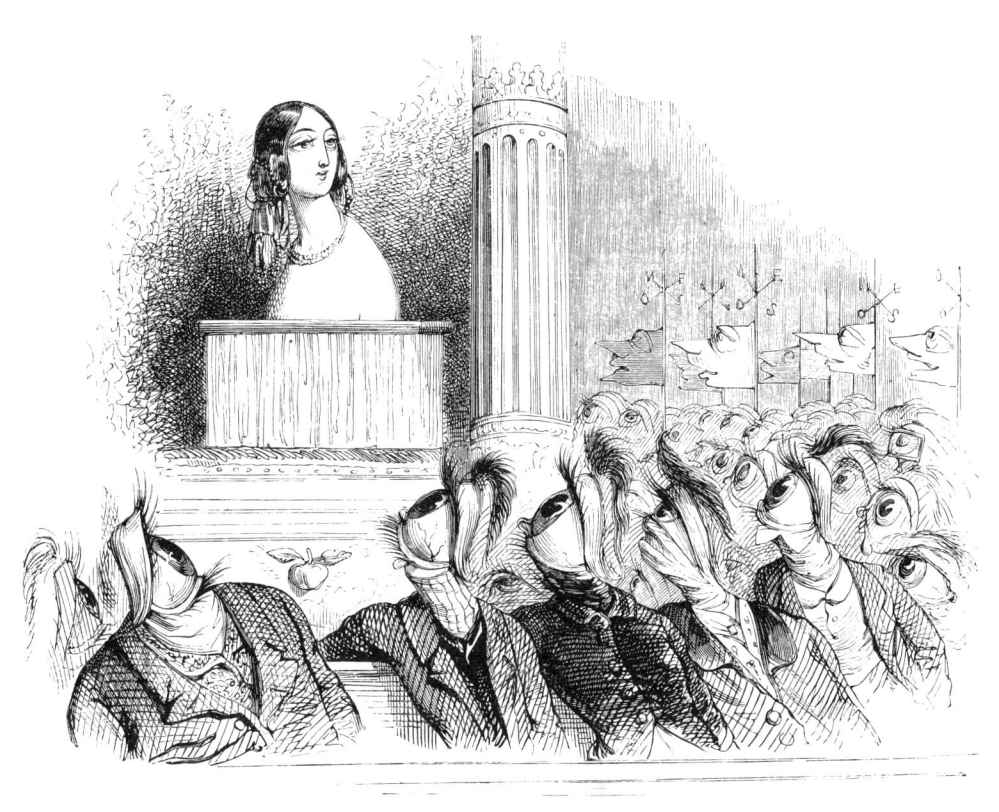

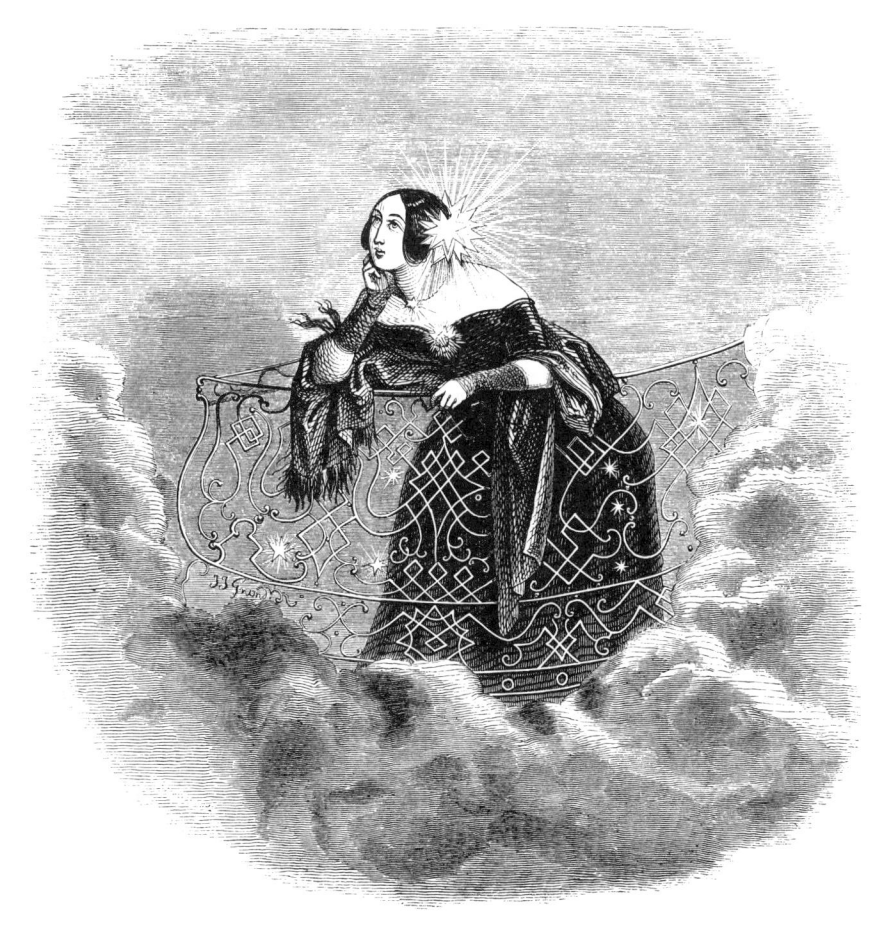

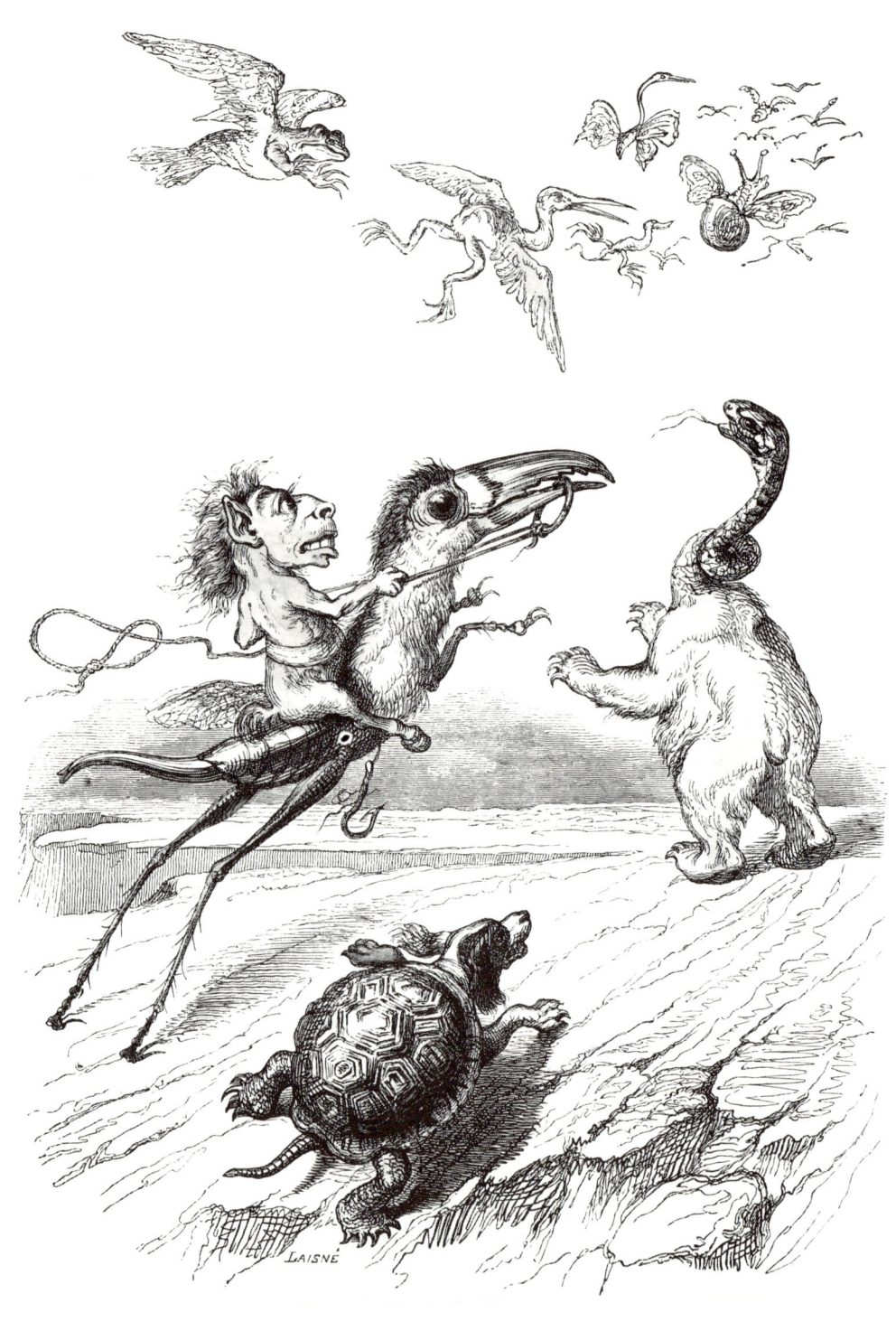

52. The centaur, with his turtle-hound, in pursuit of a boa-bear. **53.** Krackq visits the siren pool in the zoo. **54.** The cages of heraldic animals.

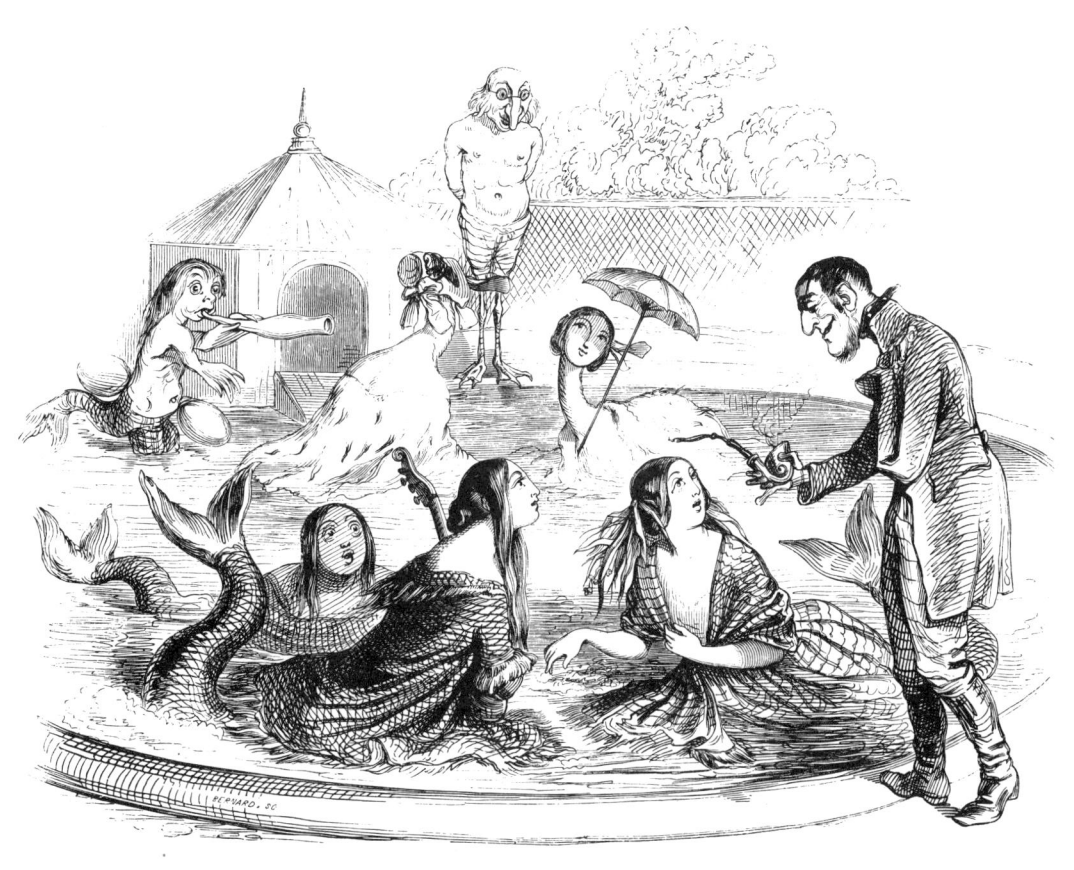

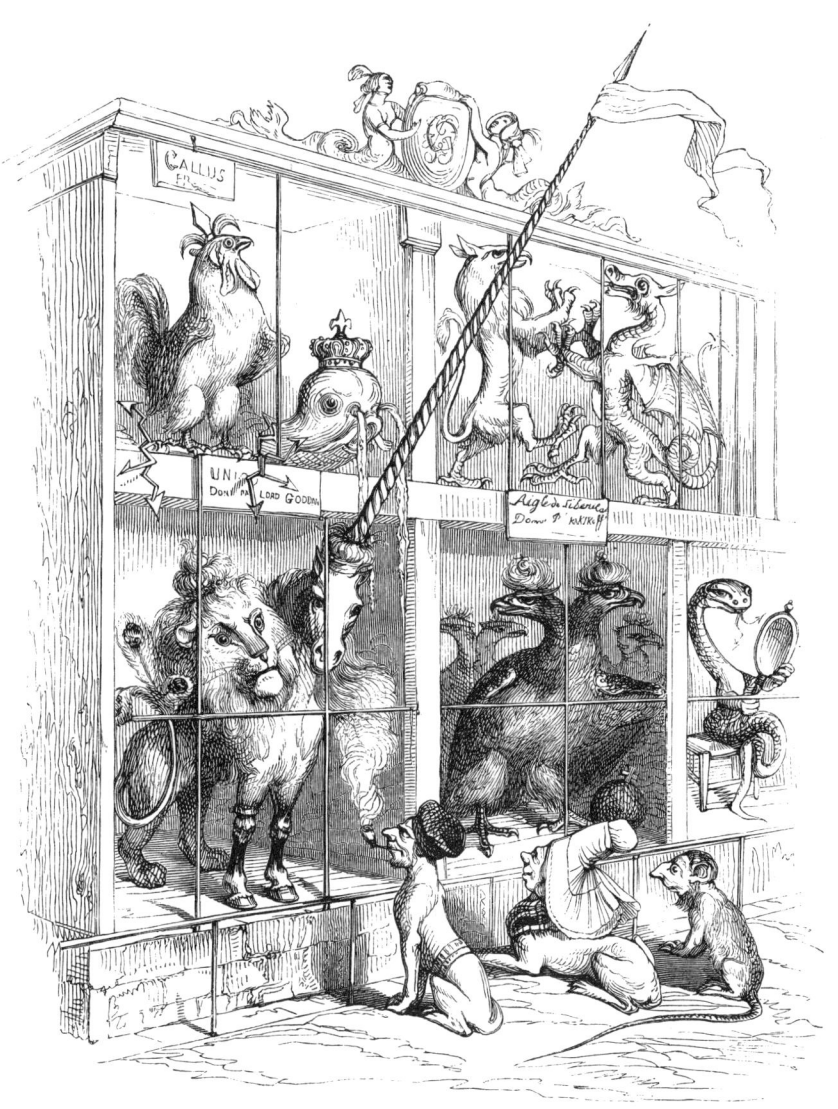

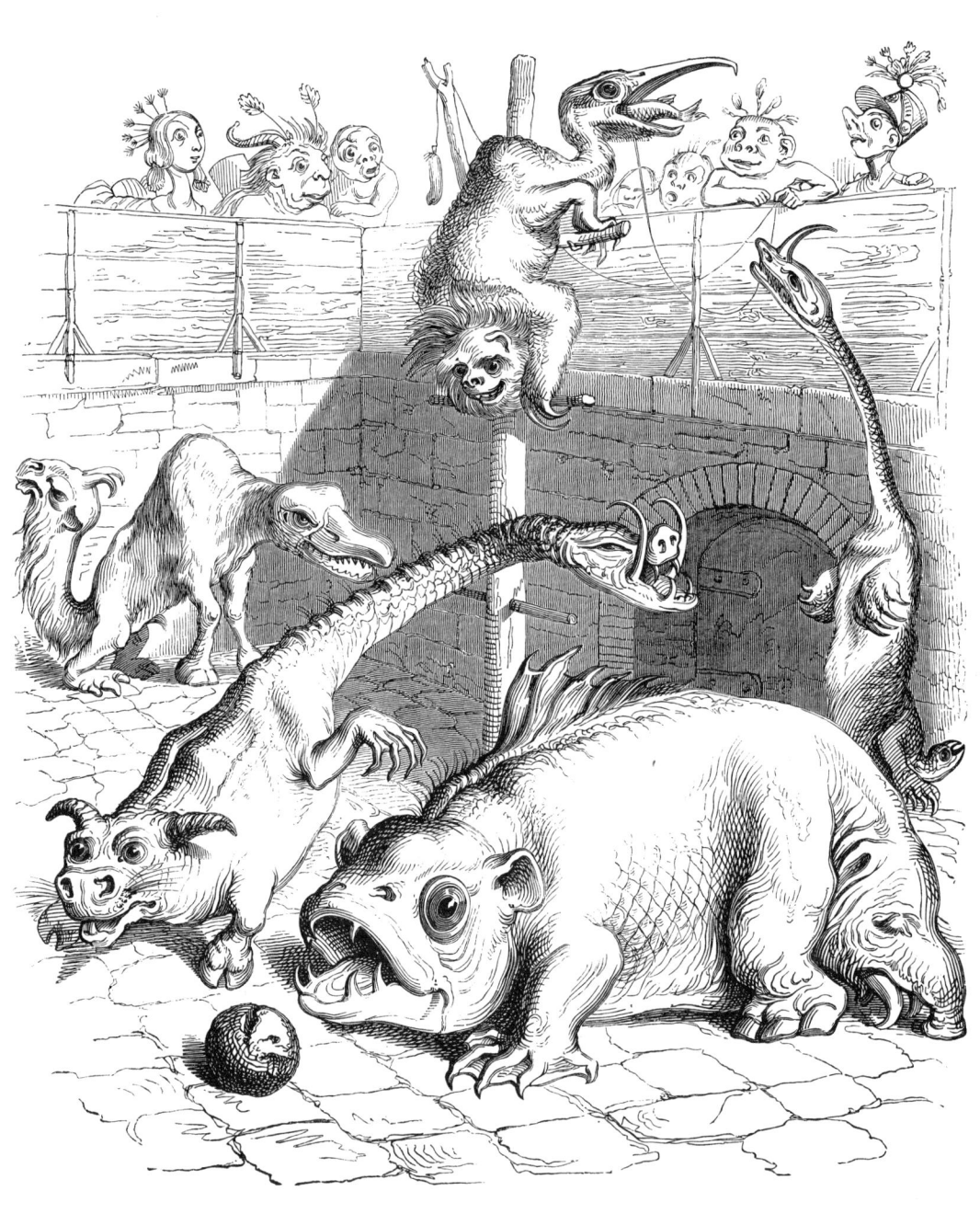

55. The pit of "doublivores" (animals that eat at both ends) at the zoo.

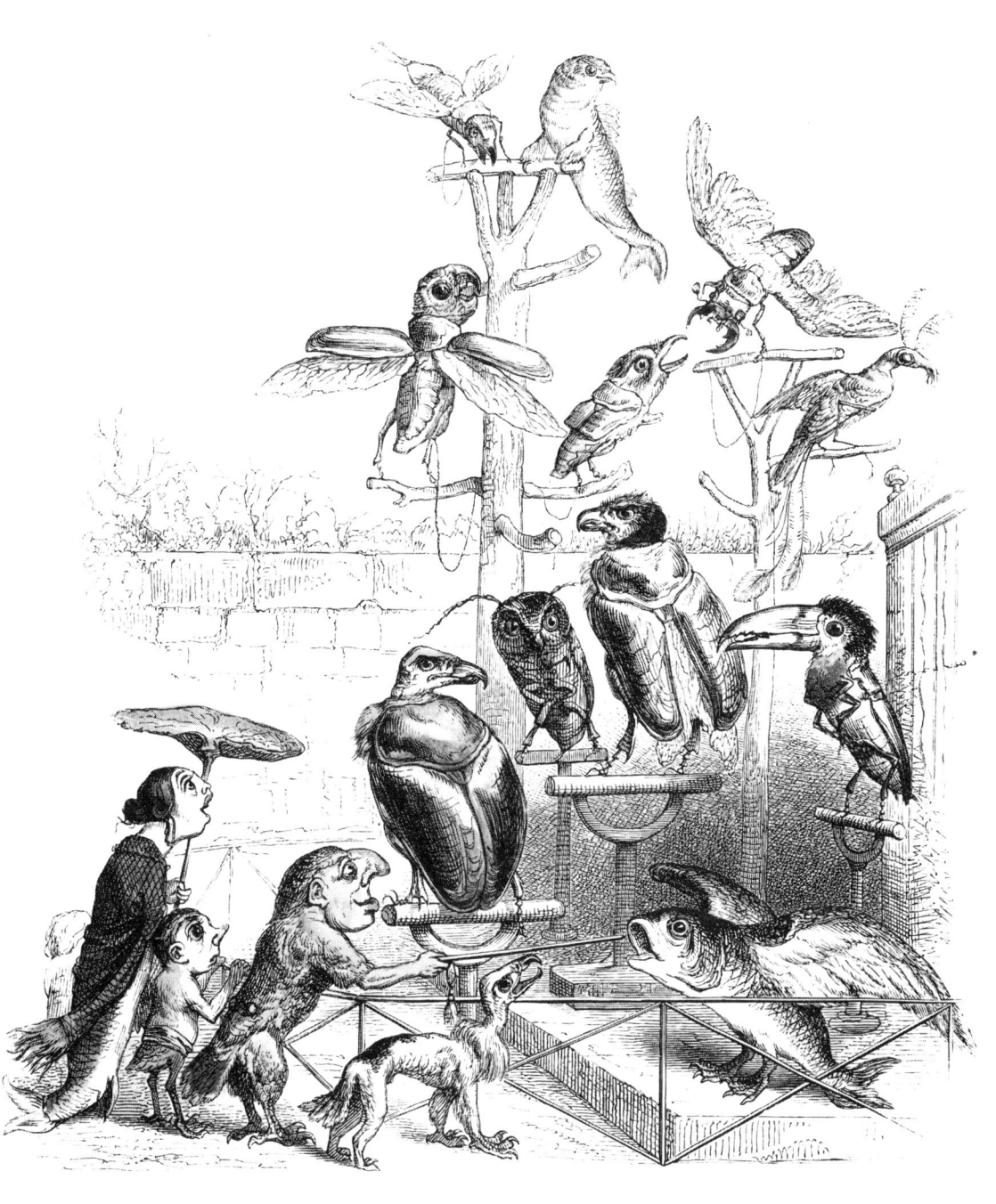

56. The bird collection at the zoo.

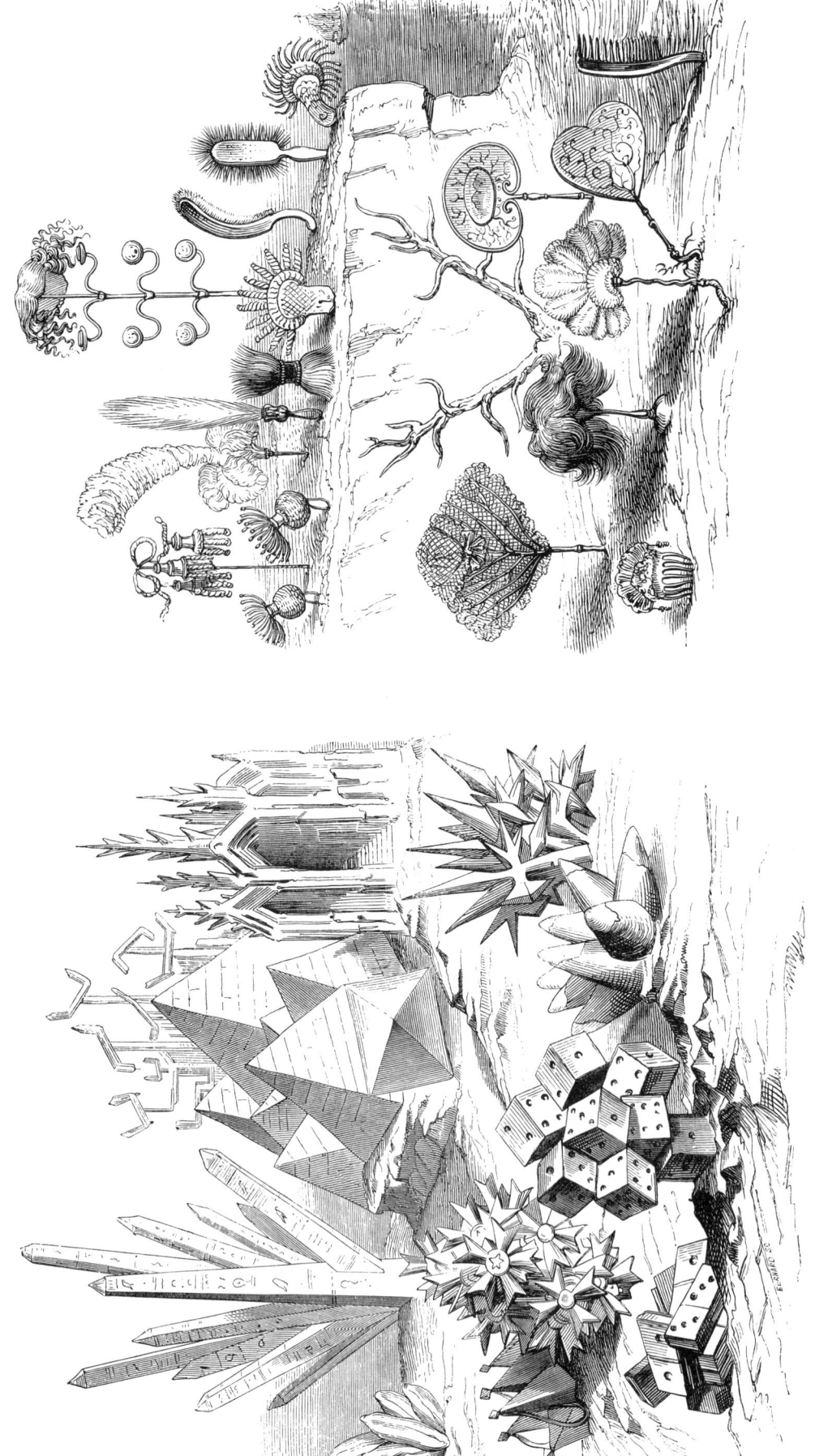

57. The mineralogical collection, showing that manmade buildings and objects are based on forms occurring in nature.

58. The marine life collection, showing that underwater plants and animals are based on forms invented by man—fans, wigs, combs, brushes, etc.

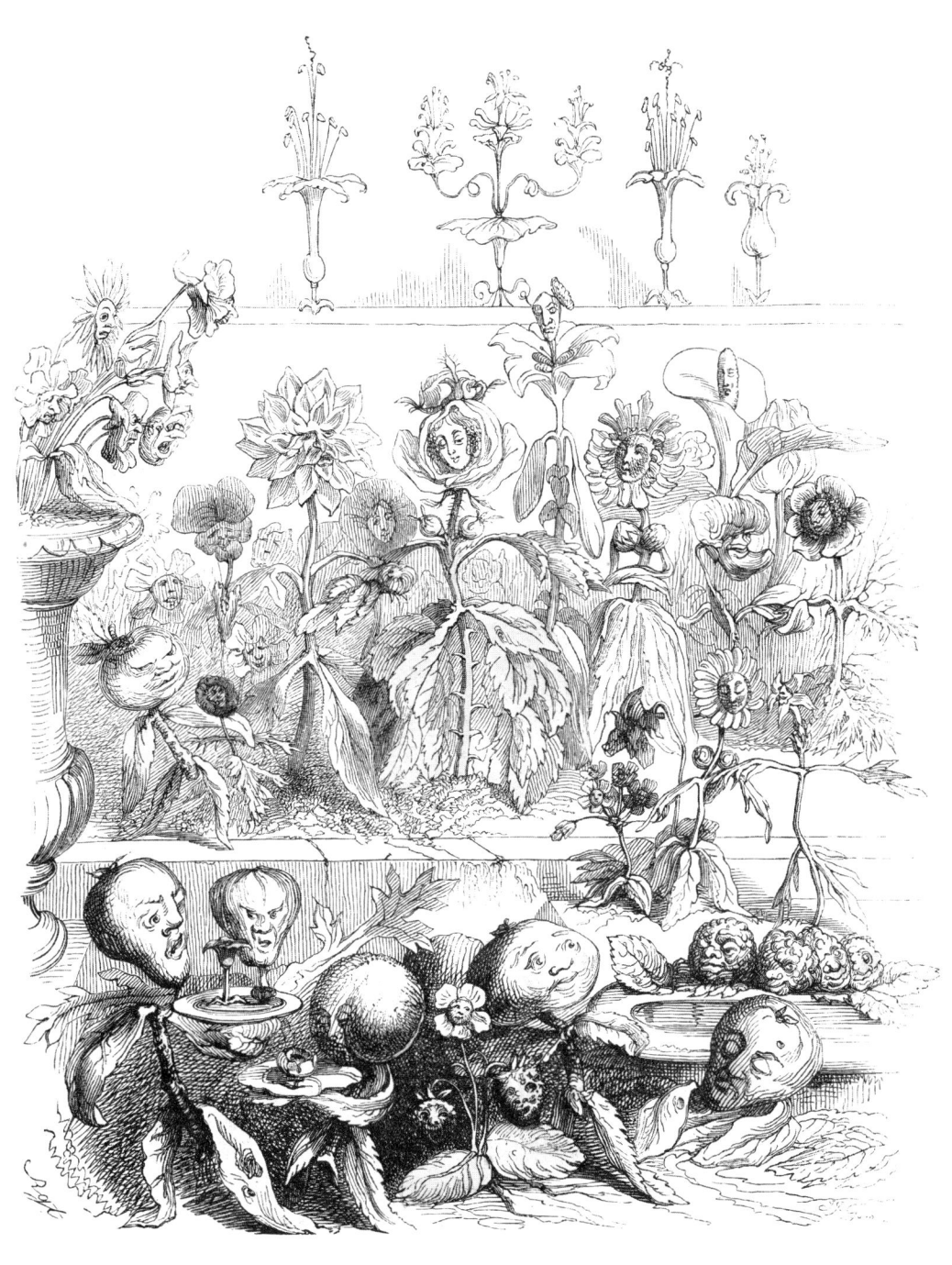

59. Flowers and fruits rejoice at the coming of spring.

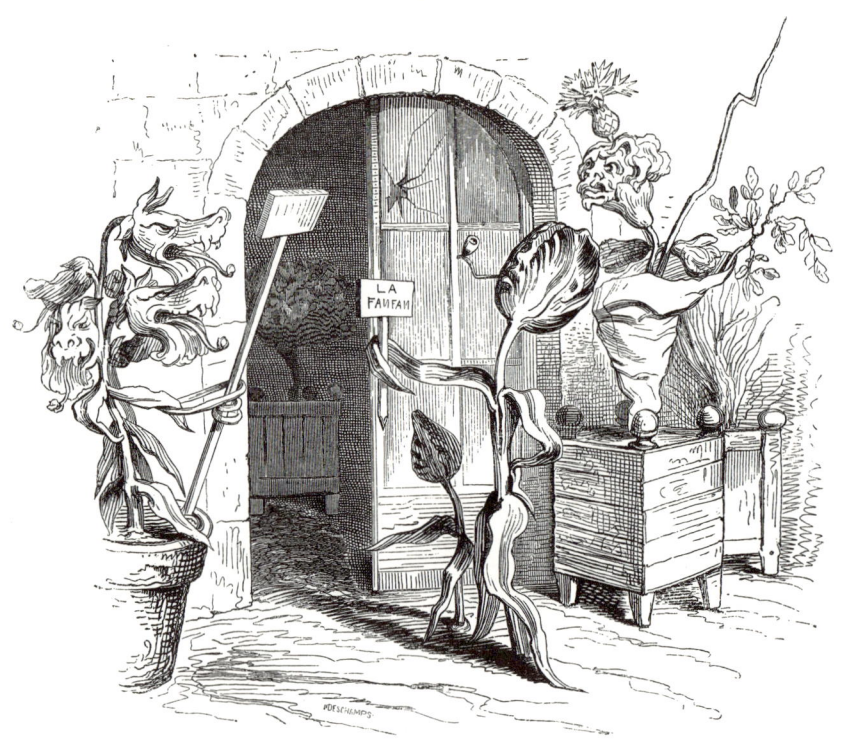

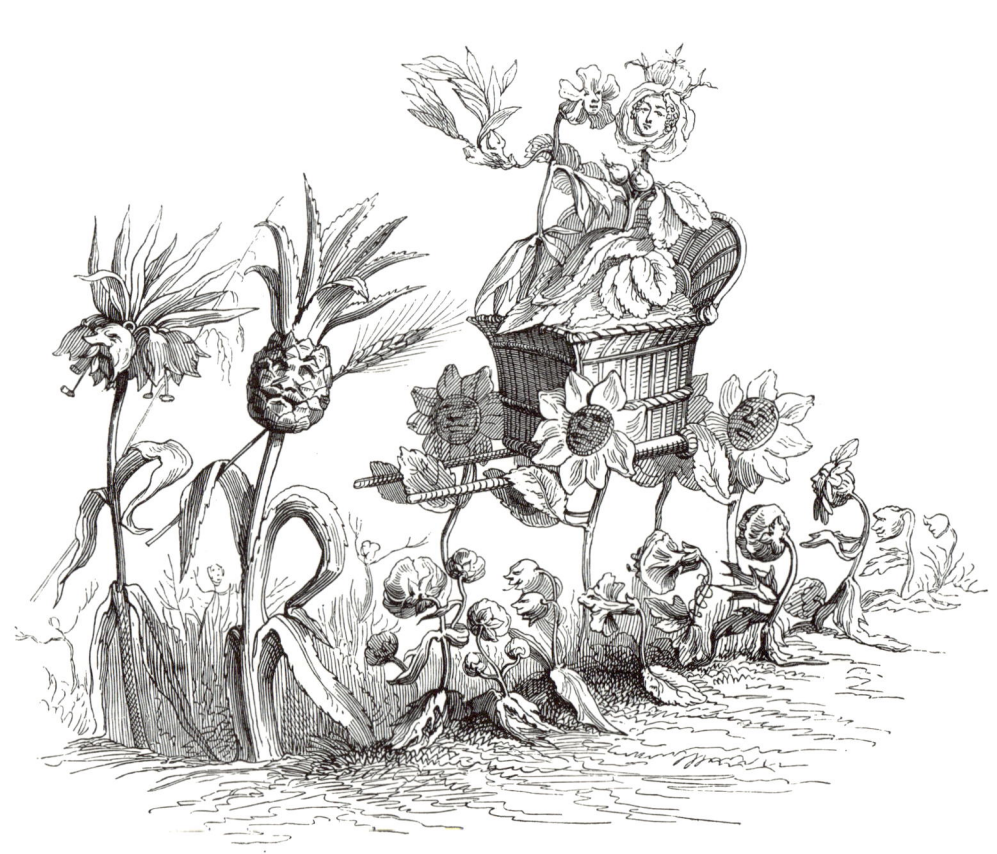

60. The entrance to a hothouse where a floral ball is being given. **61.** The rose, queen of the flowers, and her consort, the laurel, are borne in procession. **62.** Puff makes a "zigzag trip." **63.** Puff makes a trip by kite.

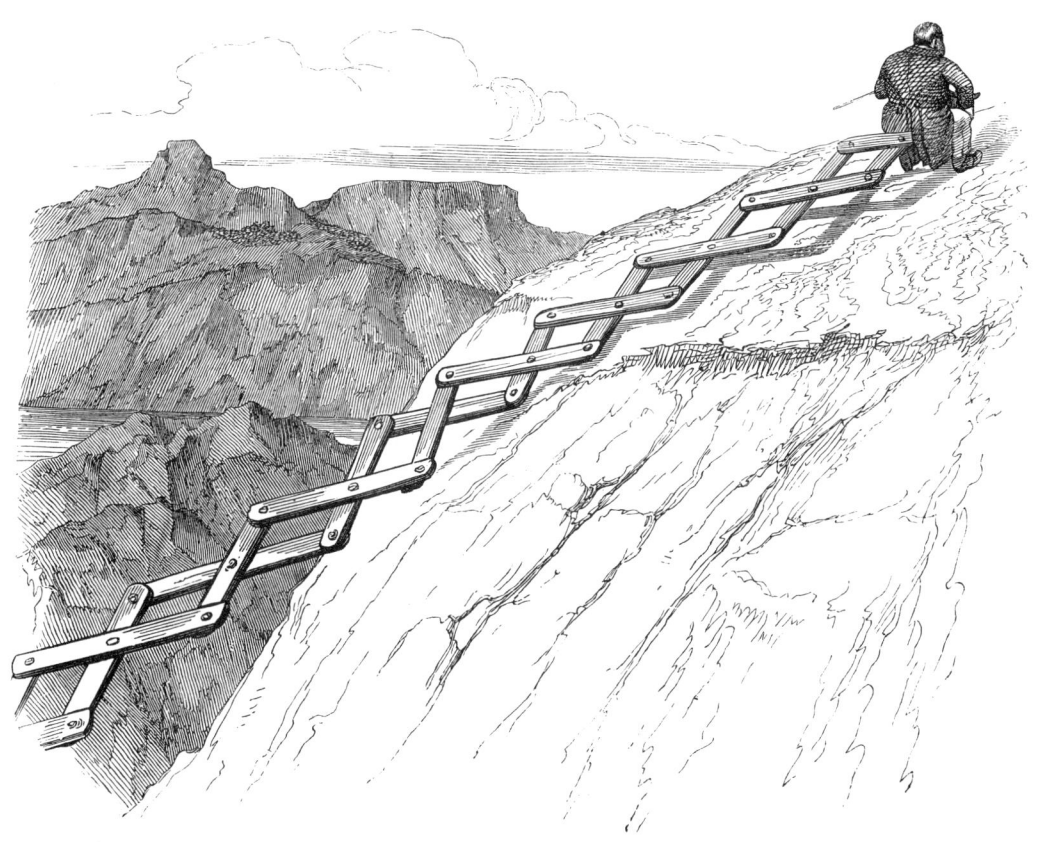

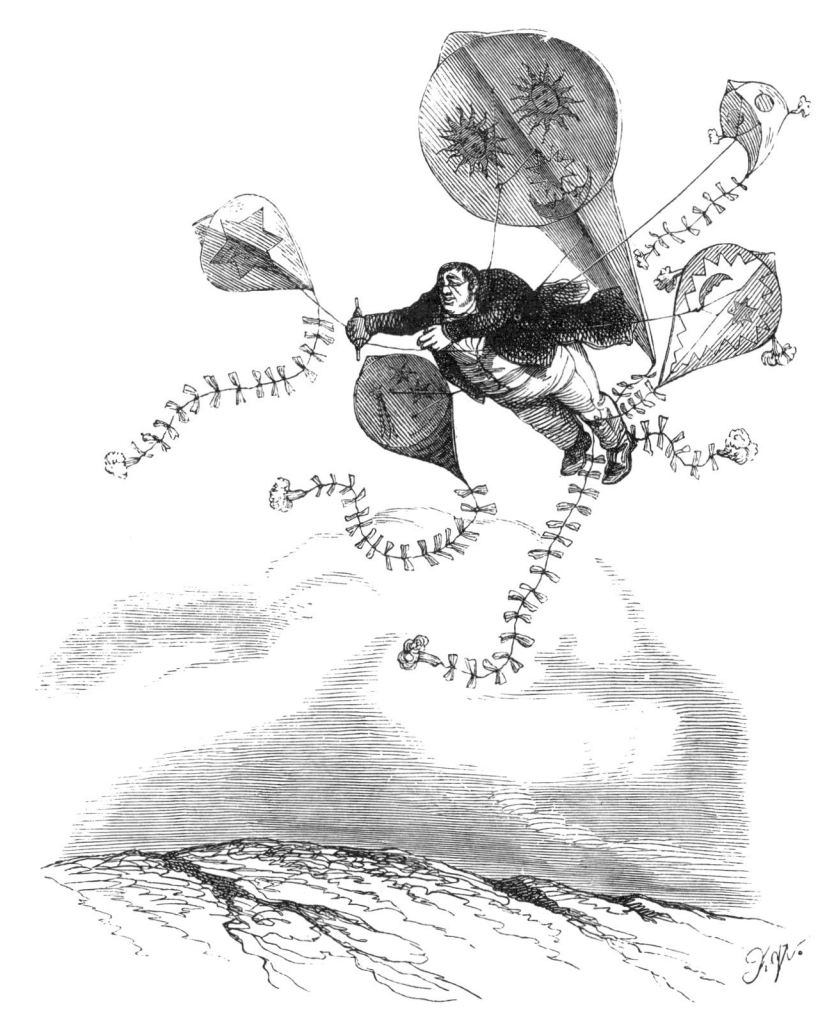

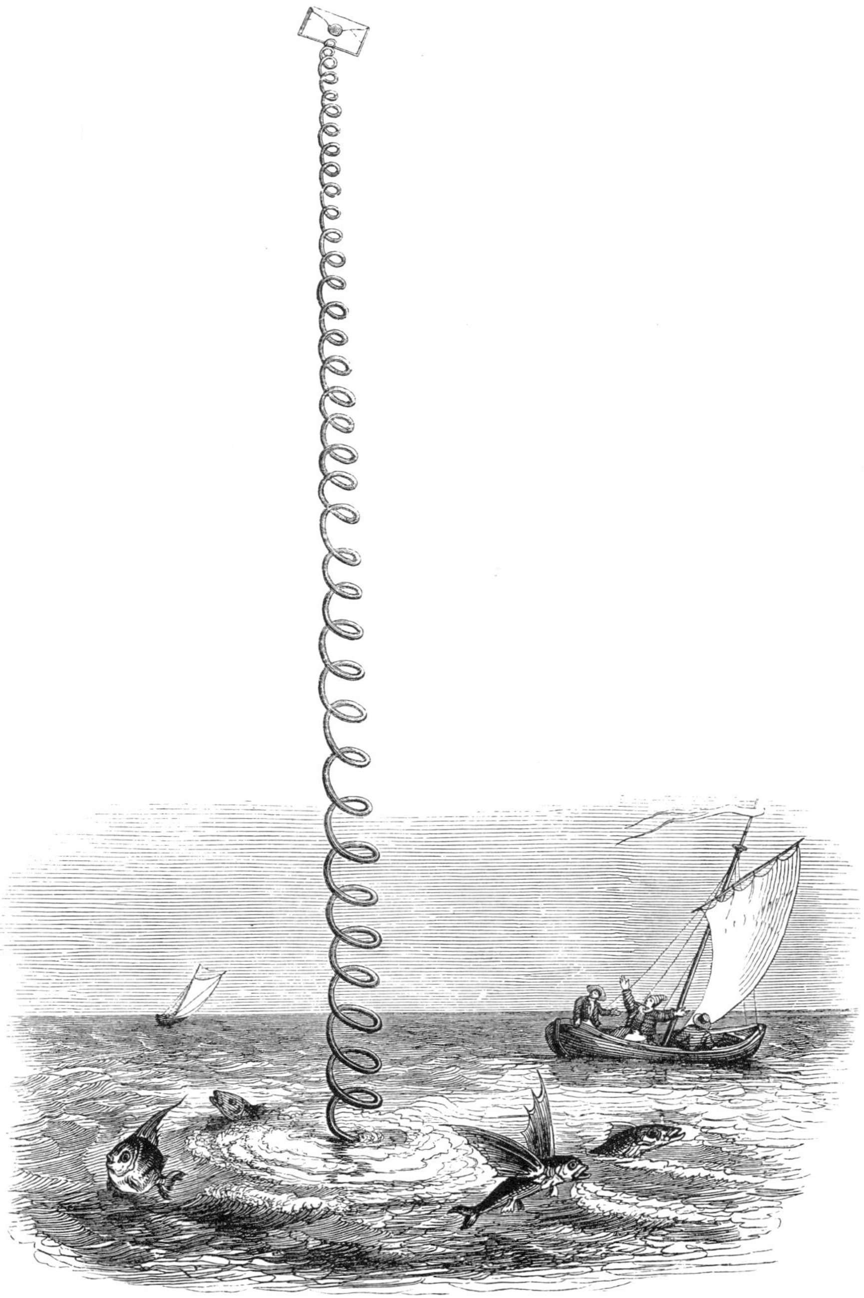

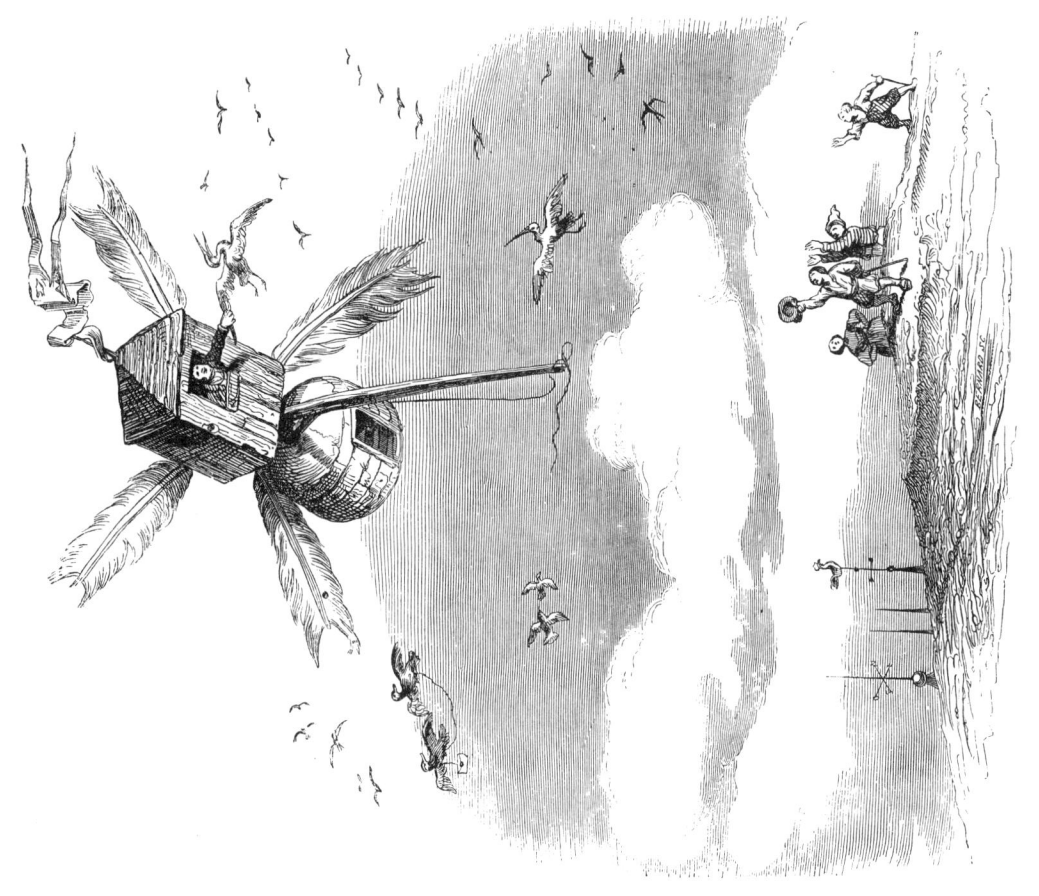

64. An undersea message from Krackq arrives by spring. **65.** Puff travels in a detached windmill.

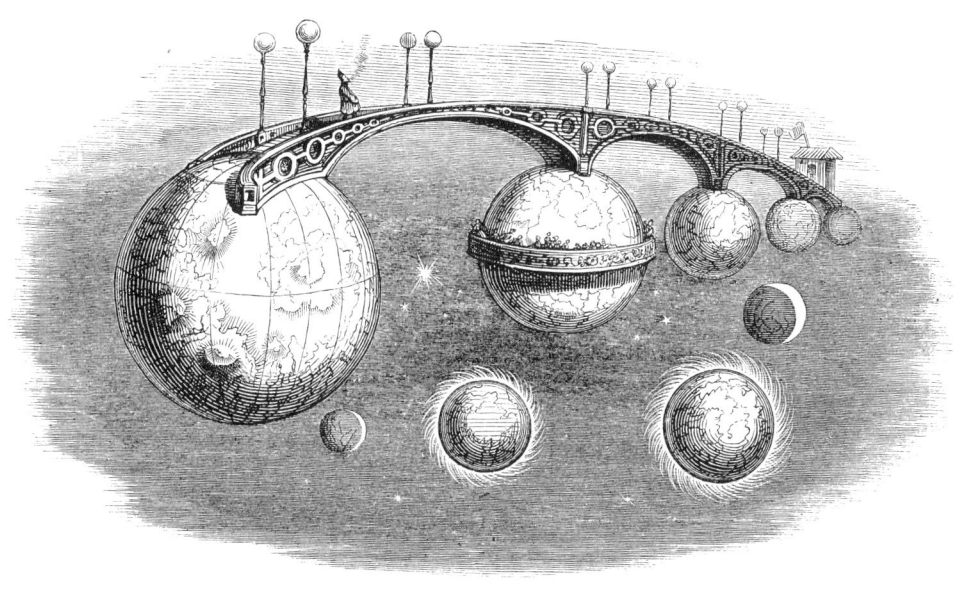

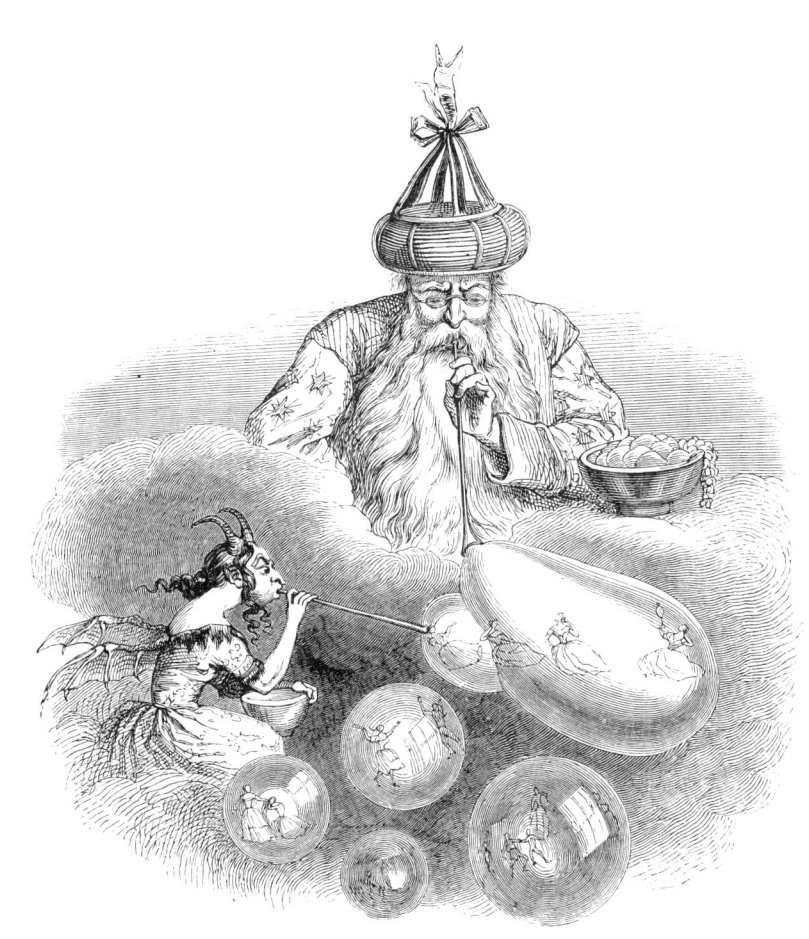

66. An interplanetary bridge. Saturn's ring is a balcony.   **67.** The secret of celestial mechanics: the worlds are soap bubbles blown by an old magician, who fails to notice that a female demon is insufflating love, jealousy and other woes into them.

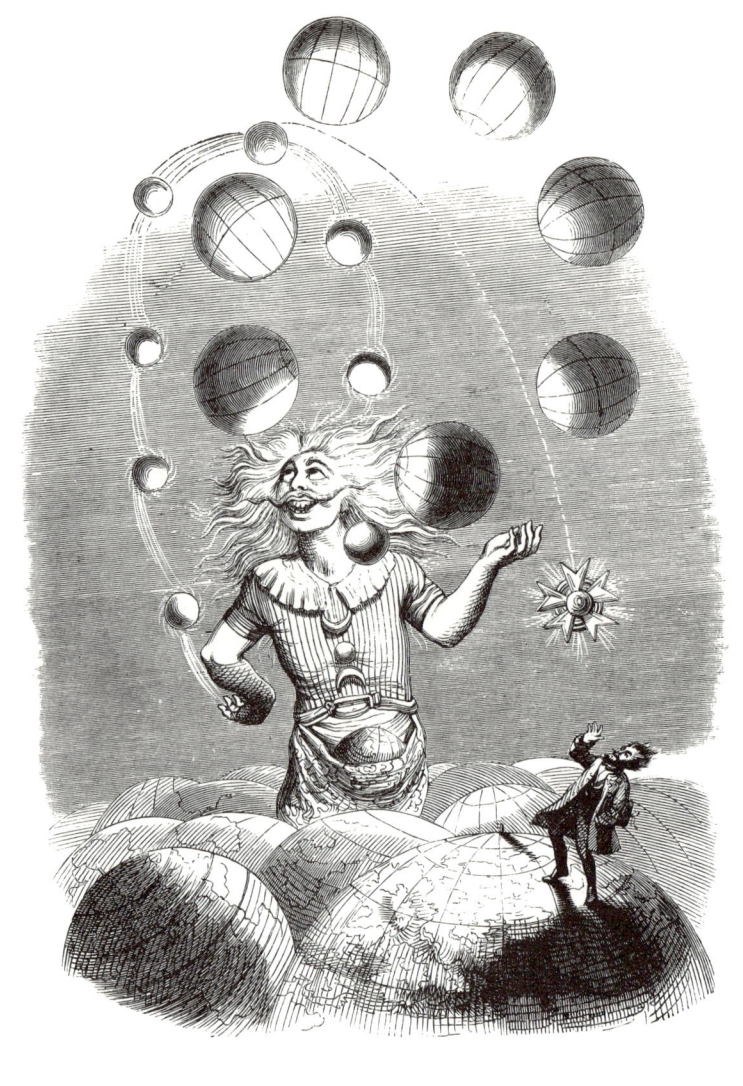

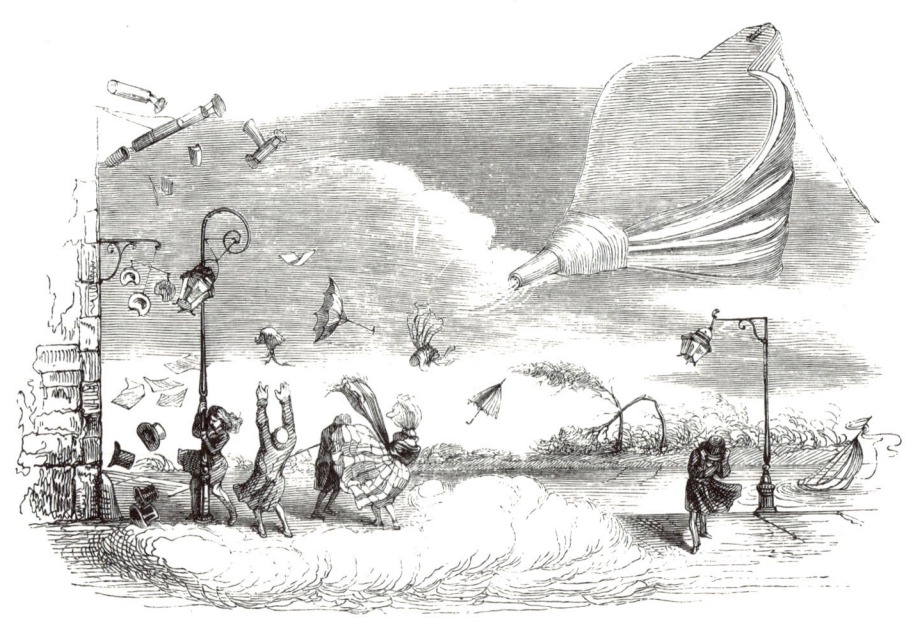

68. A juggler of universes, with a meteorite in the form of the Cross of the Legion of Honor.
69. The great bellows that causes hurricanes.

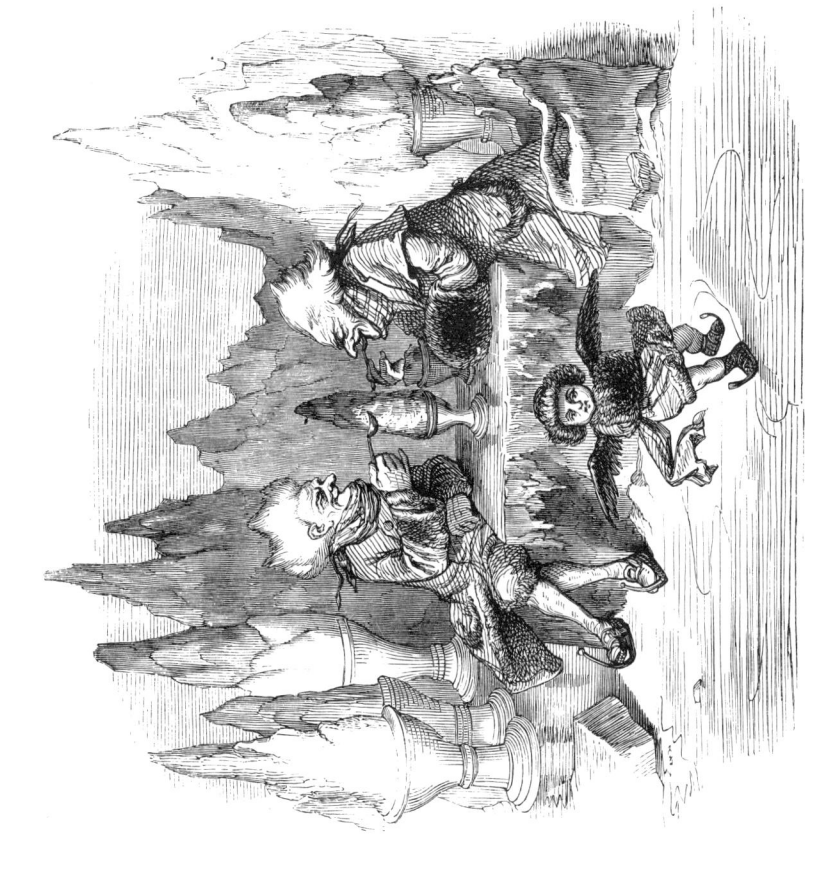

71. Hoarfrost and Rime, satellites of Winter, enjoying an ice at the North Pole.

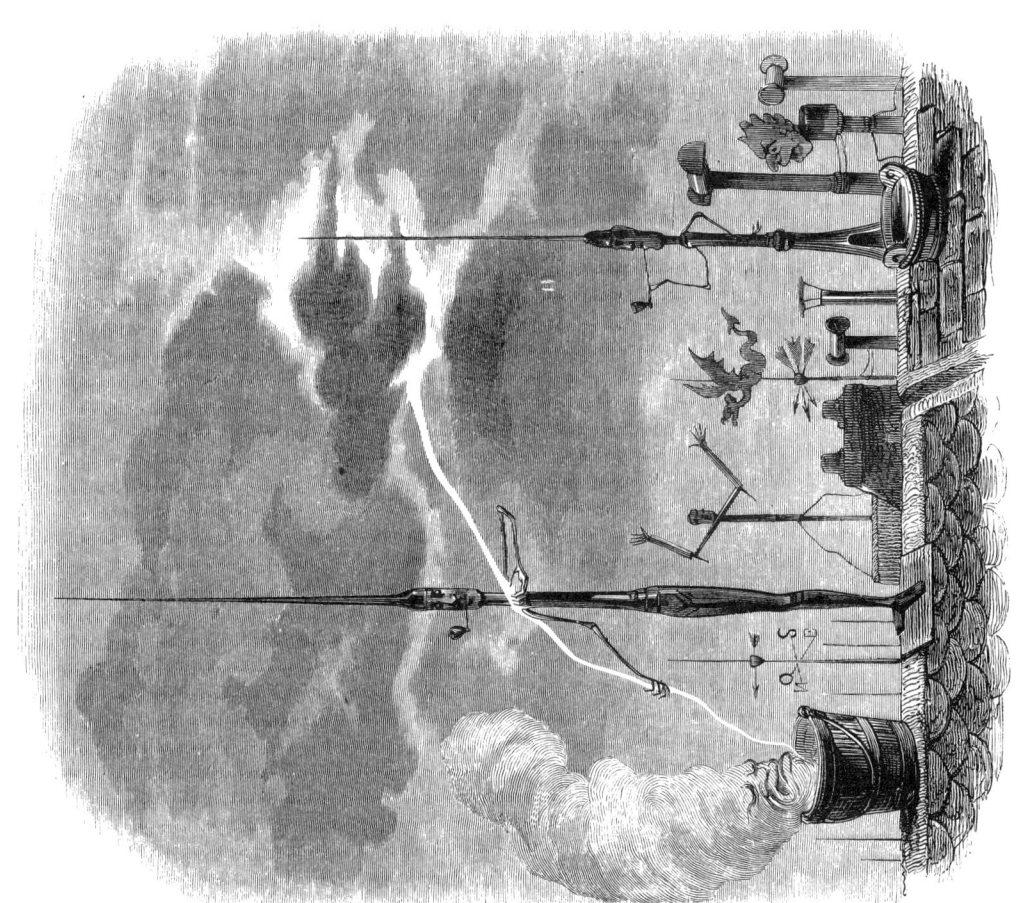

70. A lightning rod seizes a thunderbolt and extinguishes it in a bucket of water.

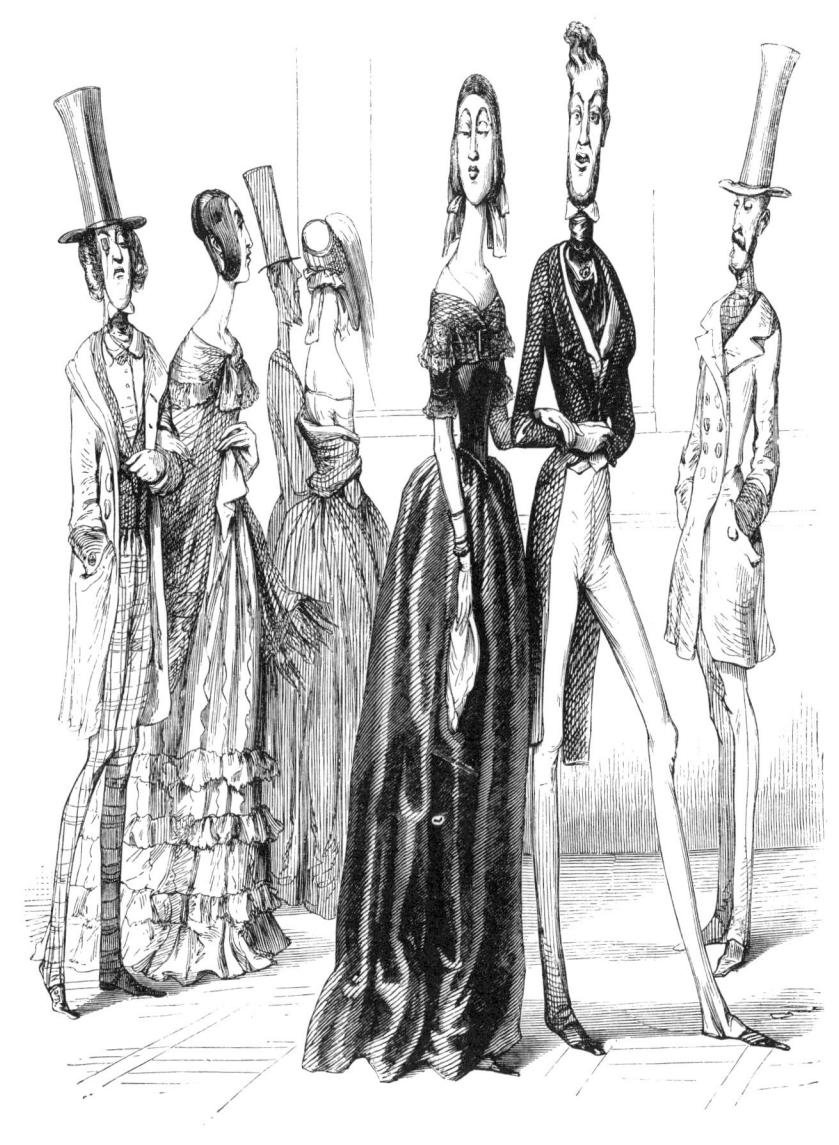

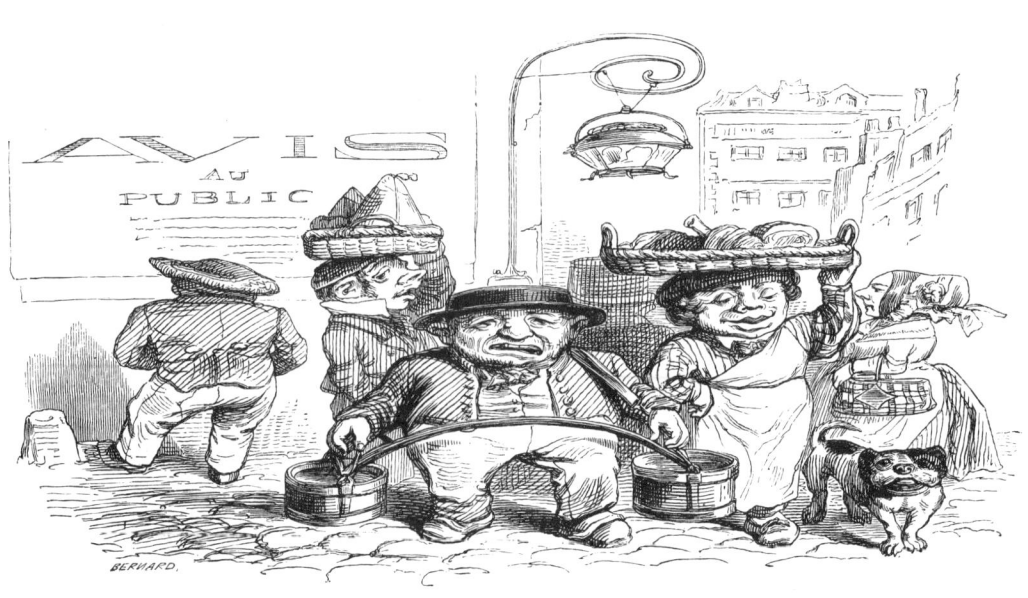

72–75. Scenes in the land where differences in rank are made visible by differences in size (No. 74 shows misalliances).

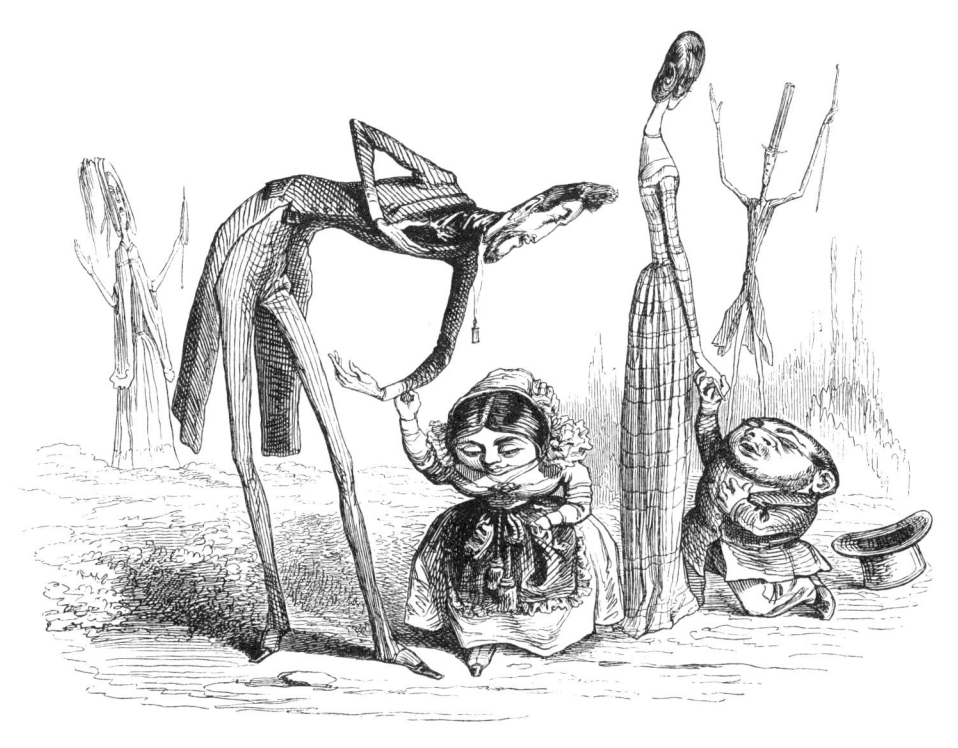

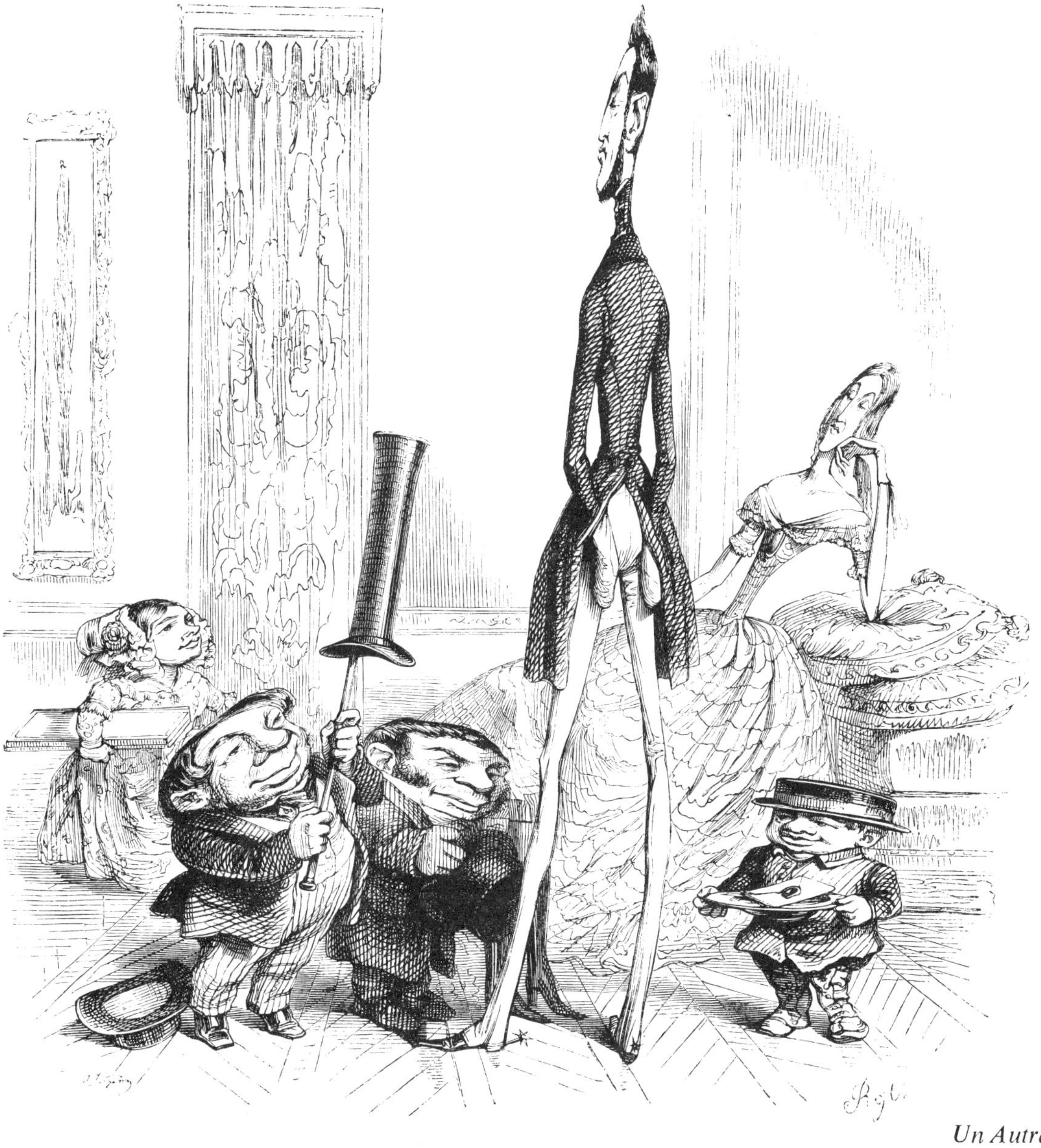

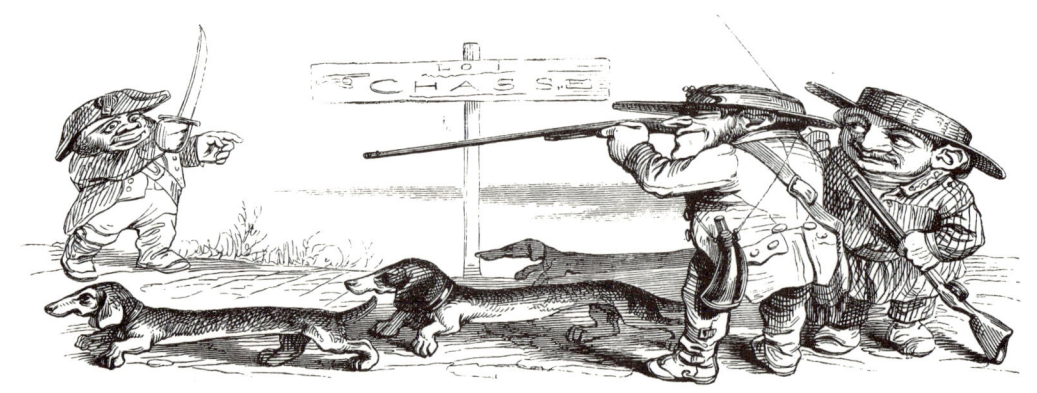

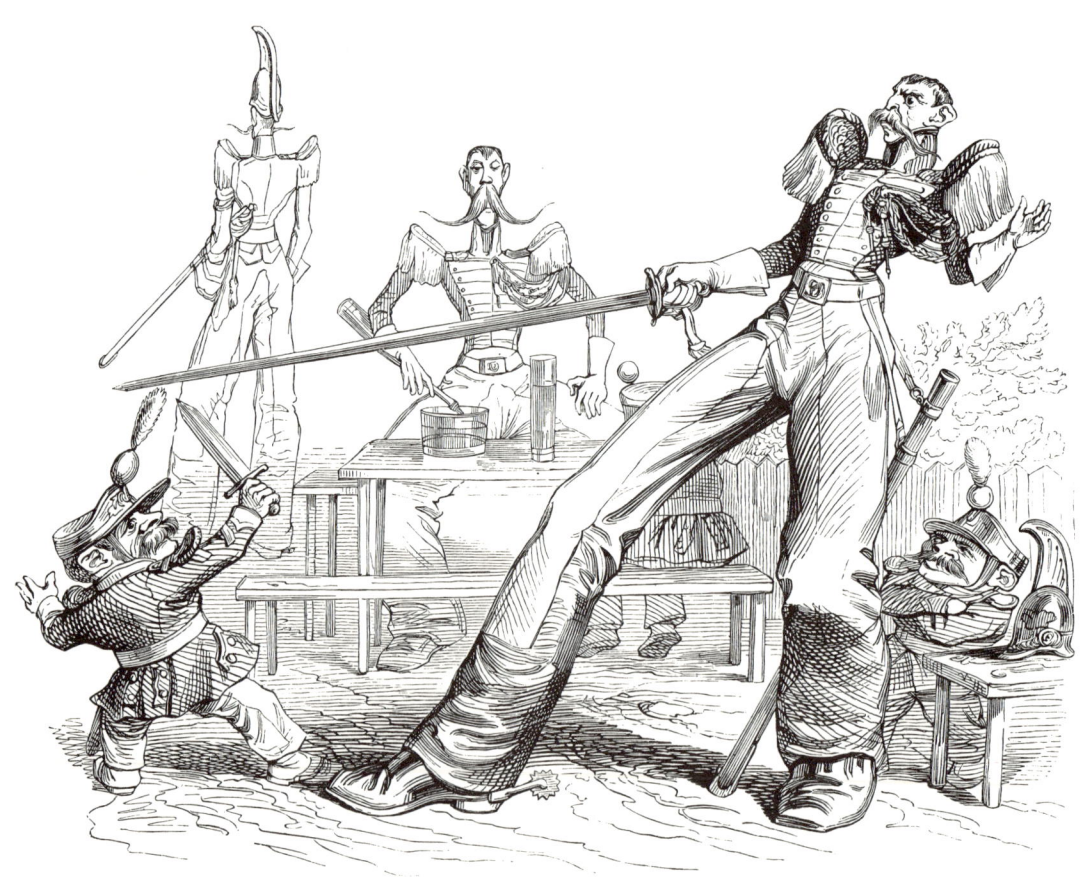

76. Poachers of small stature.   **77.** Duel between a high and a low soldier.

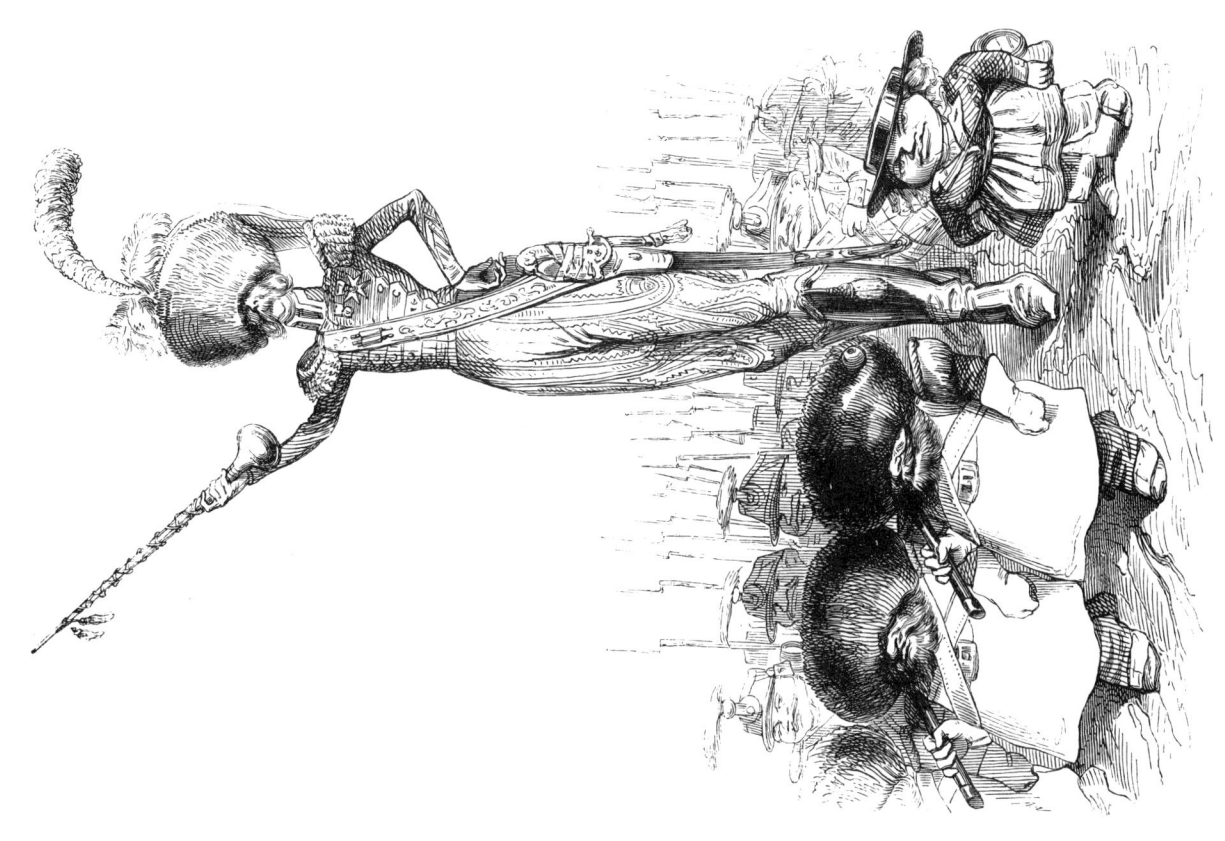

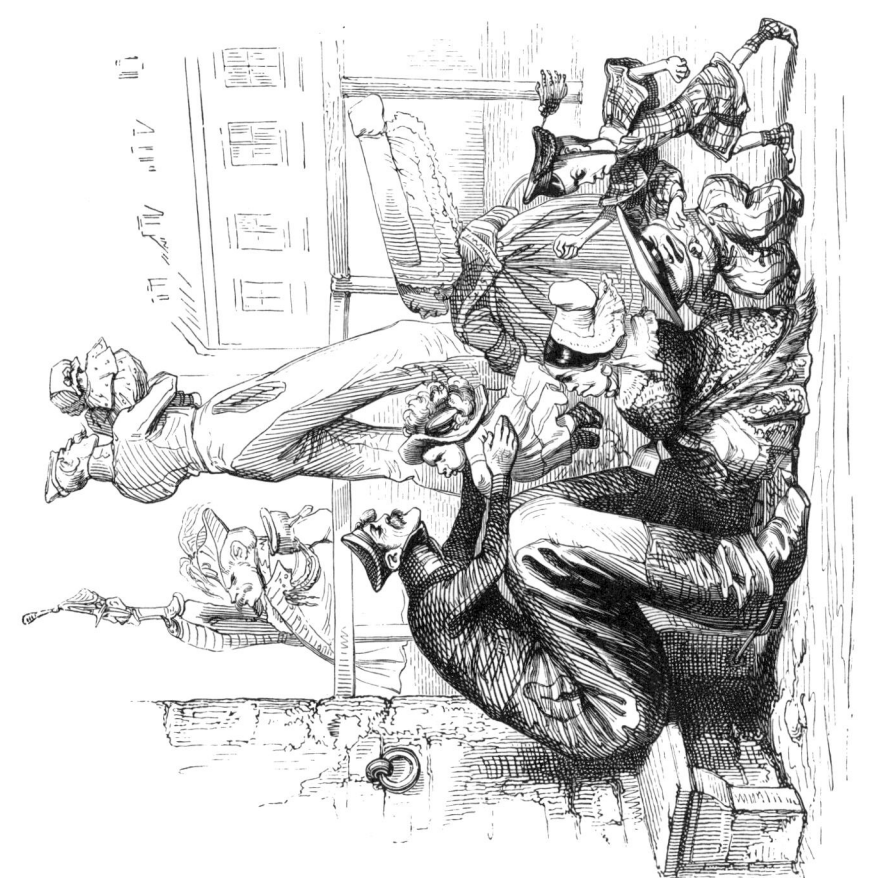

78. Local soldiers courting nursemaids. **79.** The tall inhabitants are natural-born drum majors.

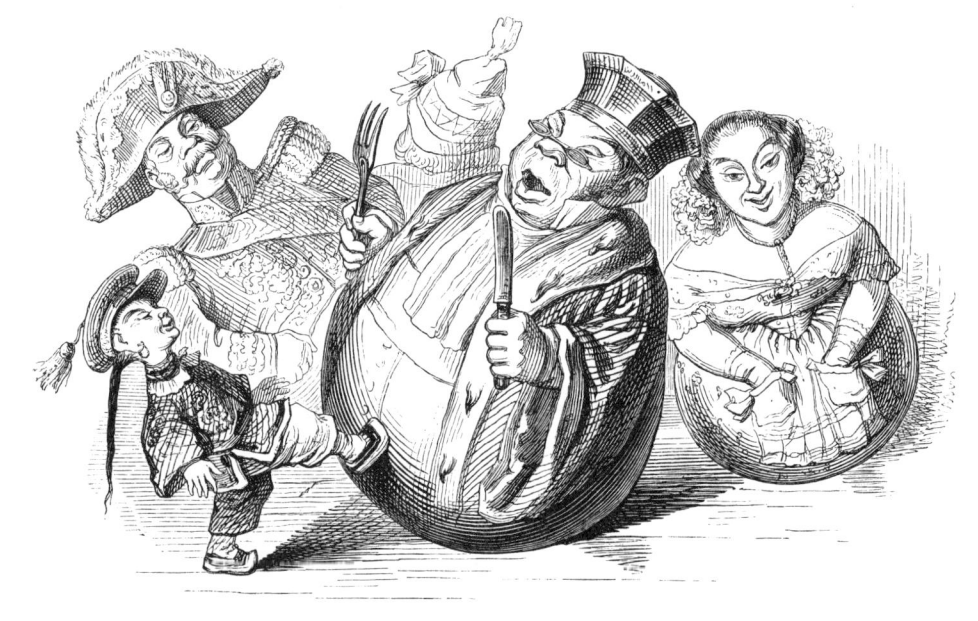

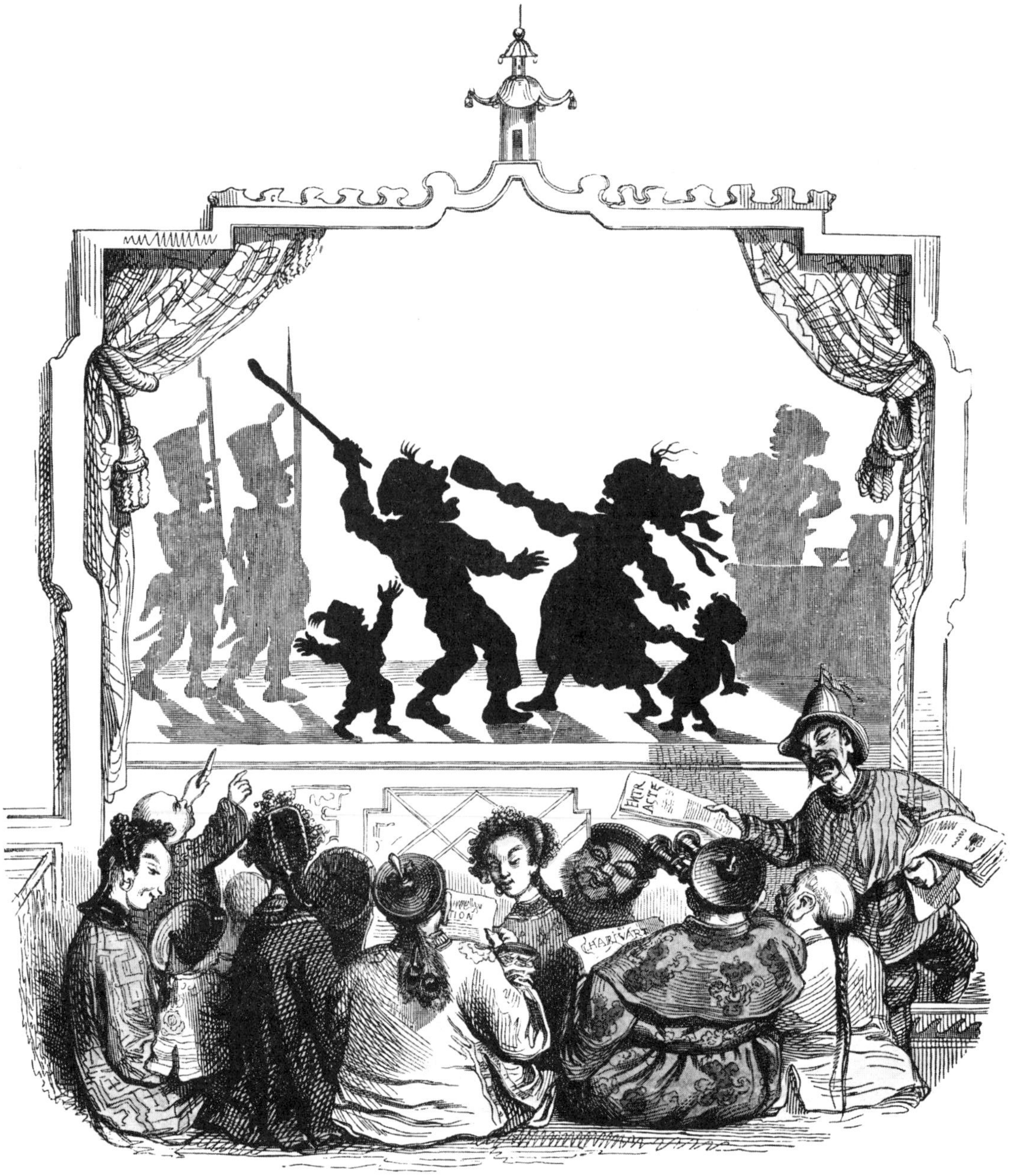

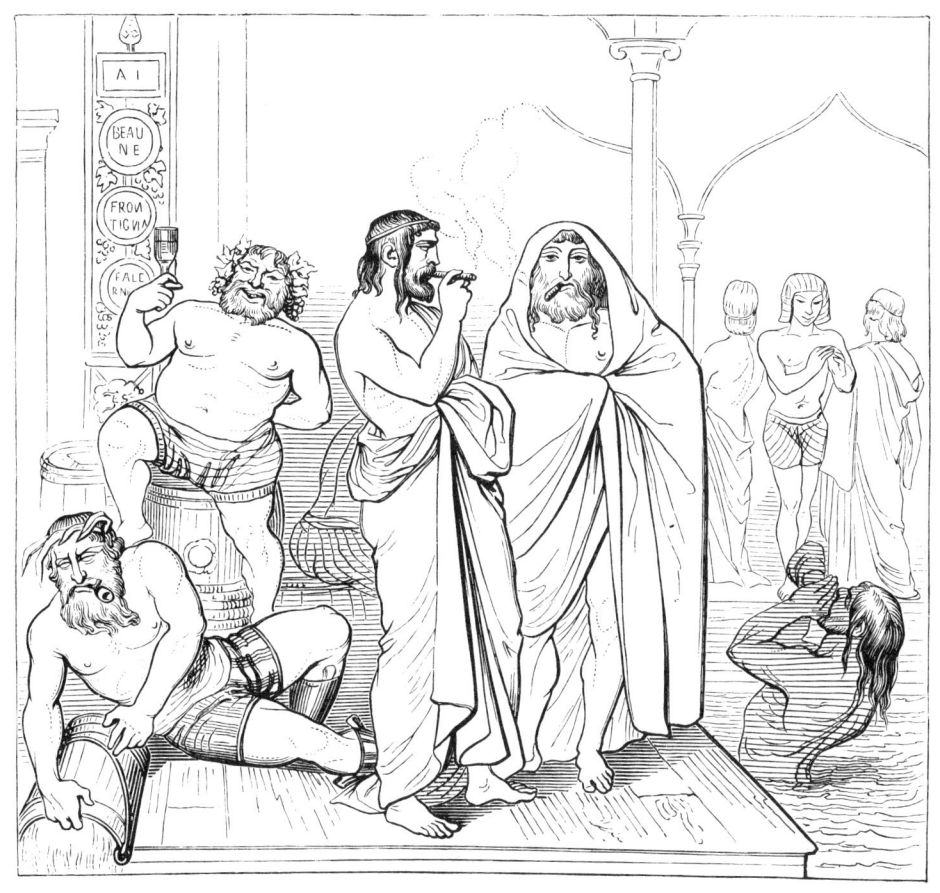

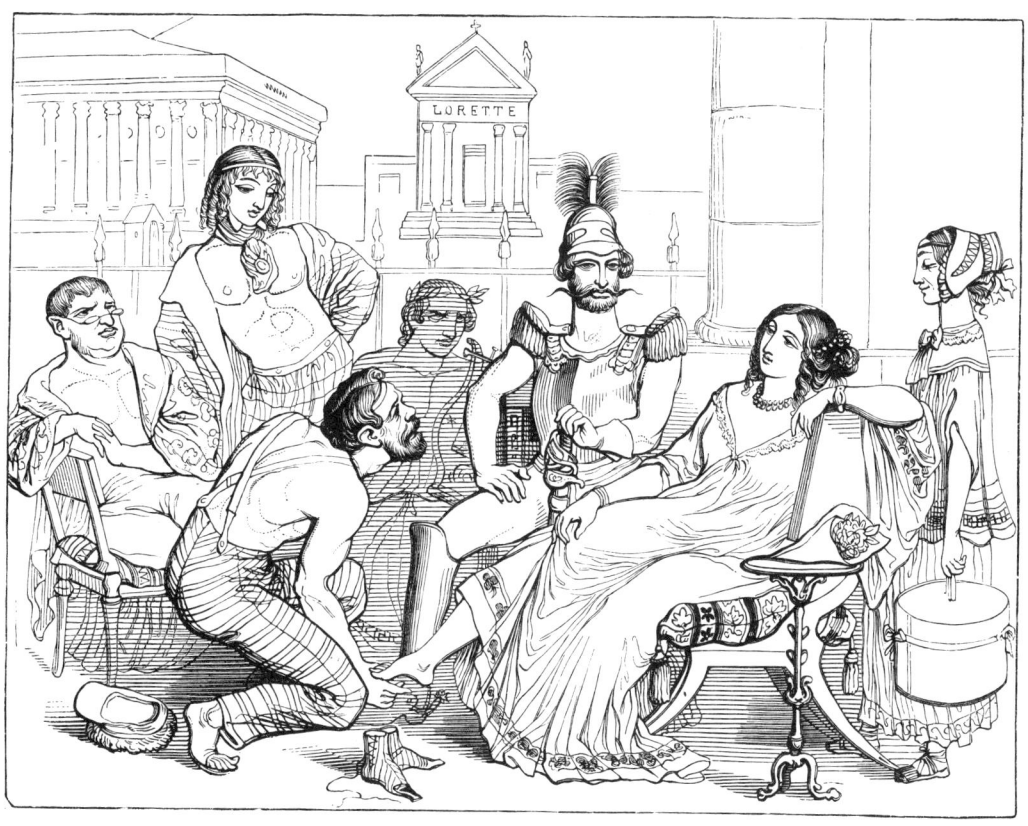

80. European figures as tumbler toys in China.
81. A group of Chinese at a "French-shadow"
play. **82.** The public baths of Rheculanum.
83. The salon of an "emancipated" lady of
Rheculanum.

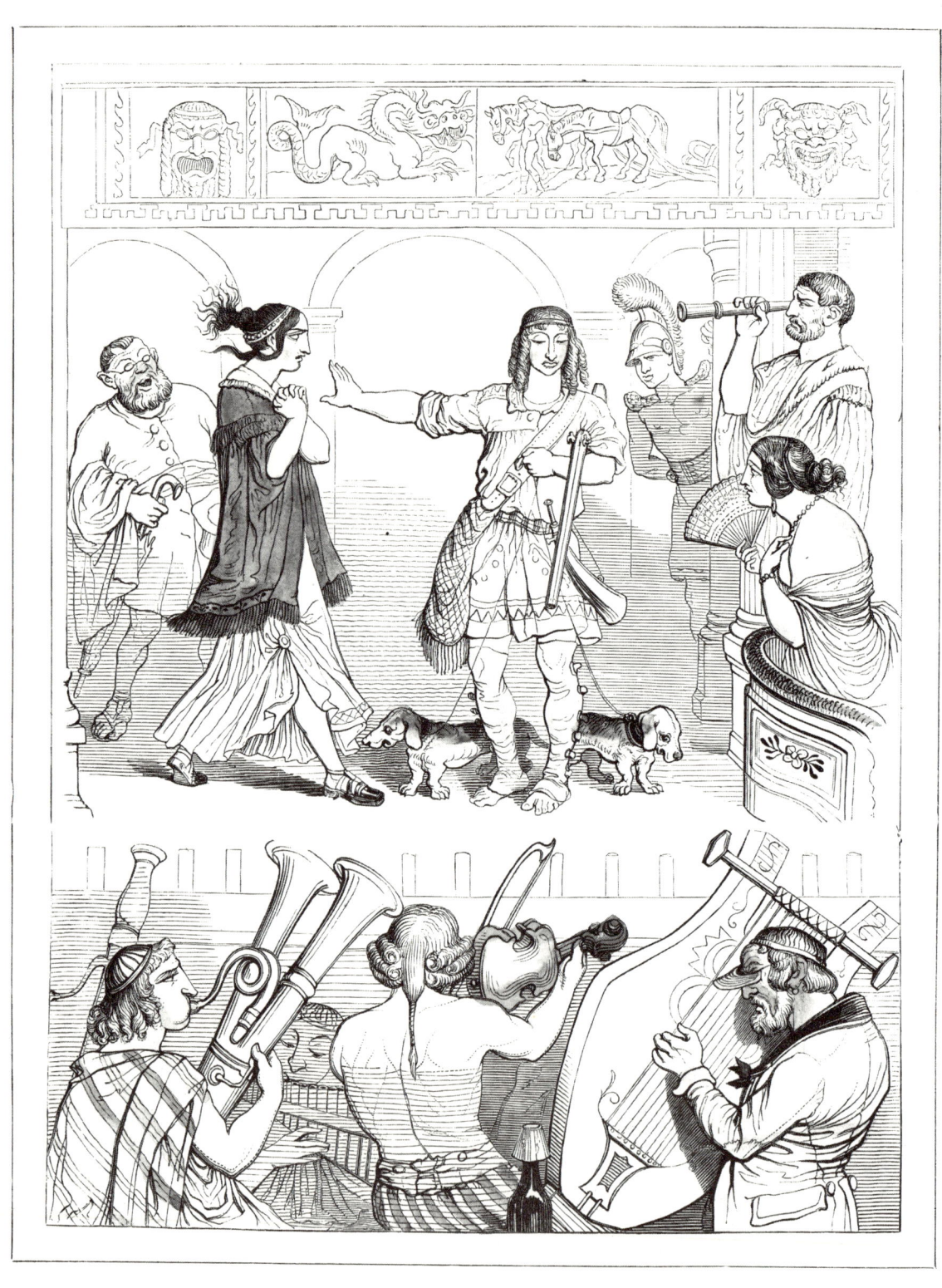

84. A performance of *Phèdre* in Rheculanum.

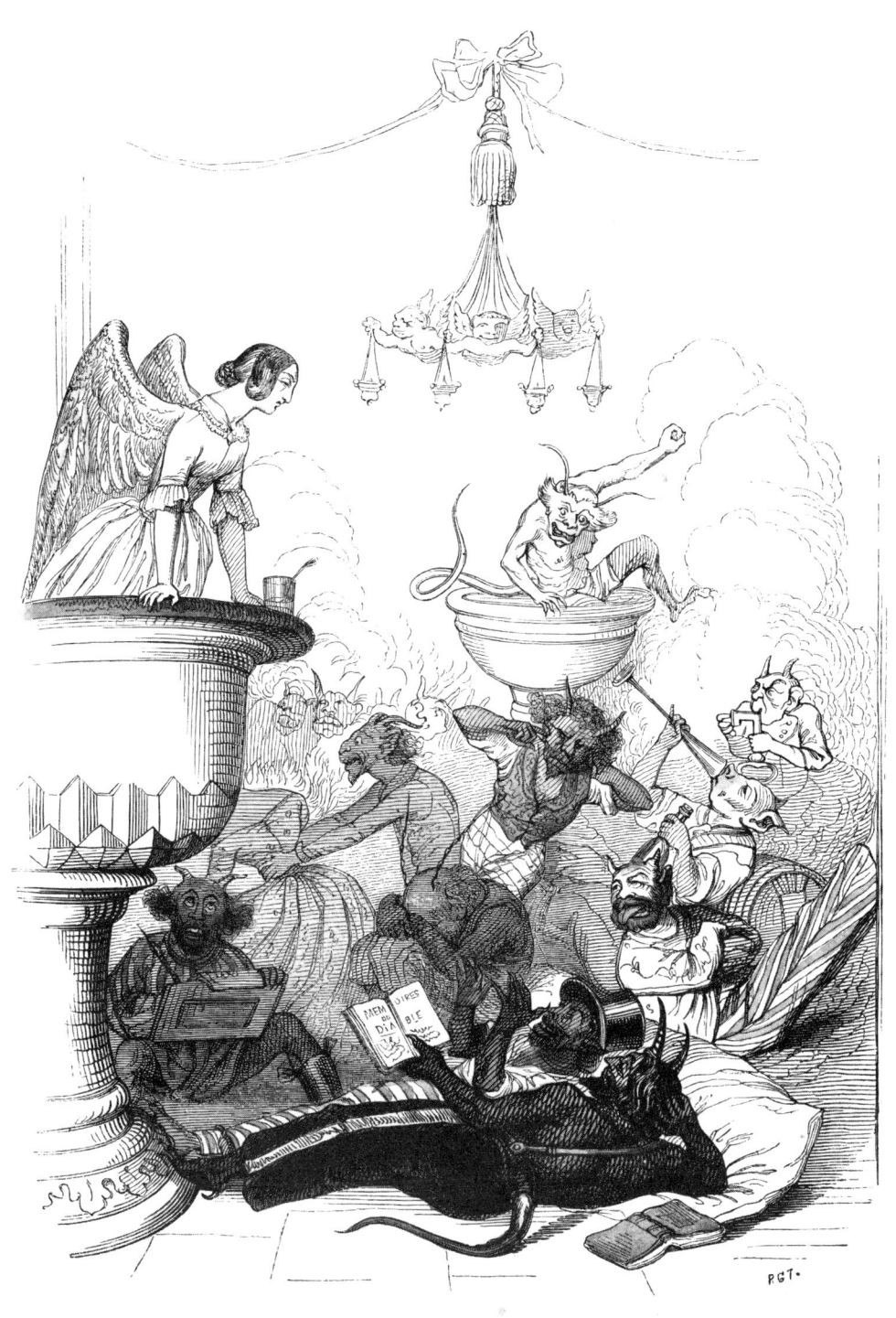

85. Demons tormenting angels.

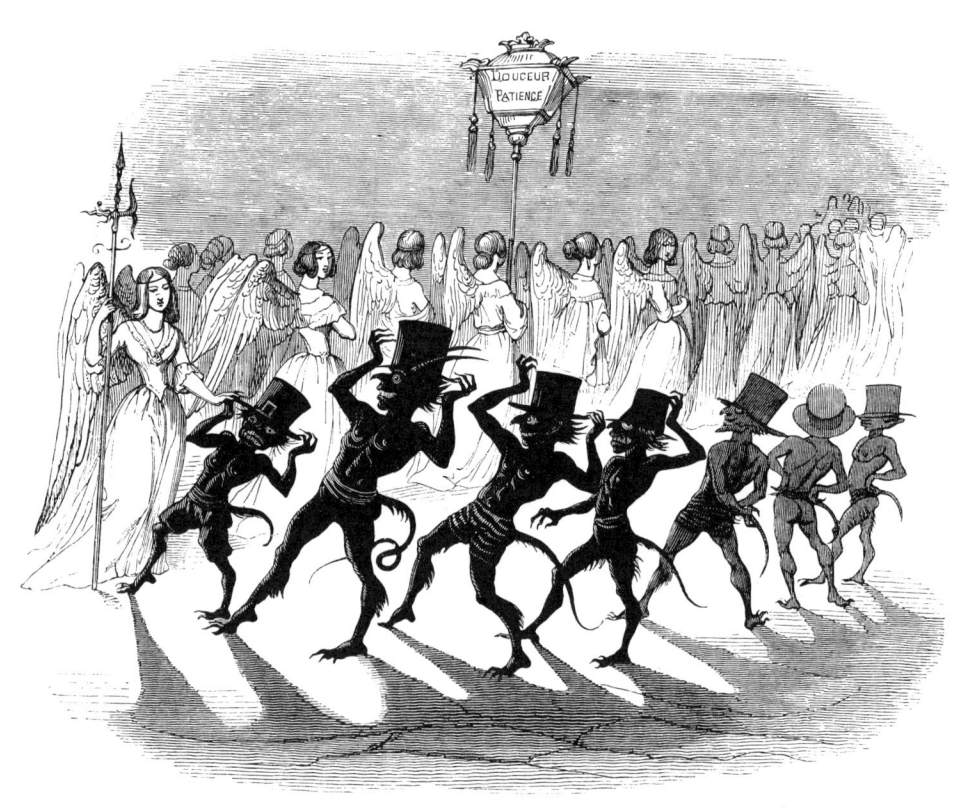

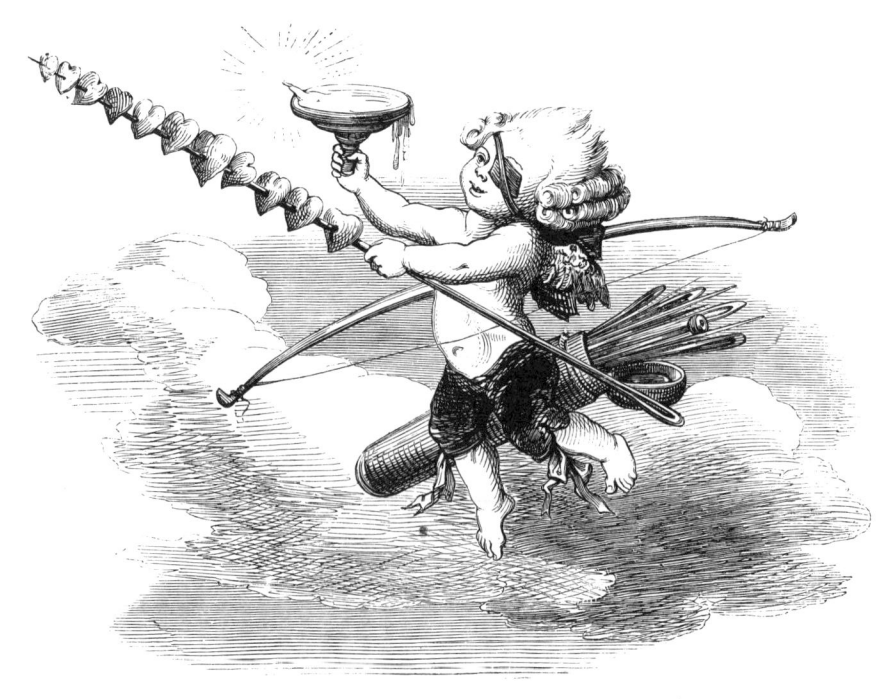

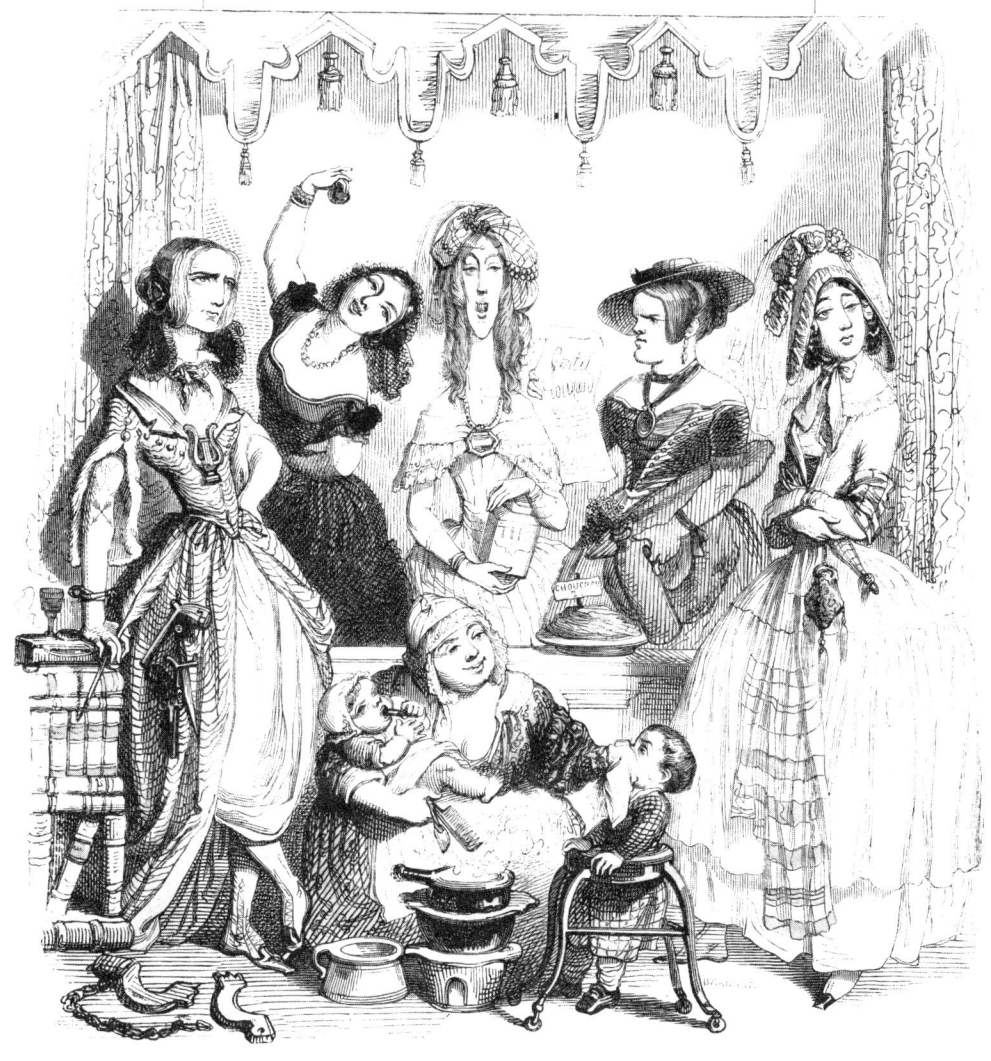

86. Demons mocking angels.   87. Cupid with his cup of tears and hearts on a spit.   88. An assortment of marriageable women.

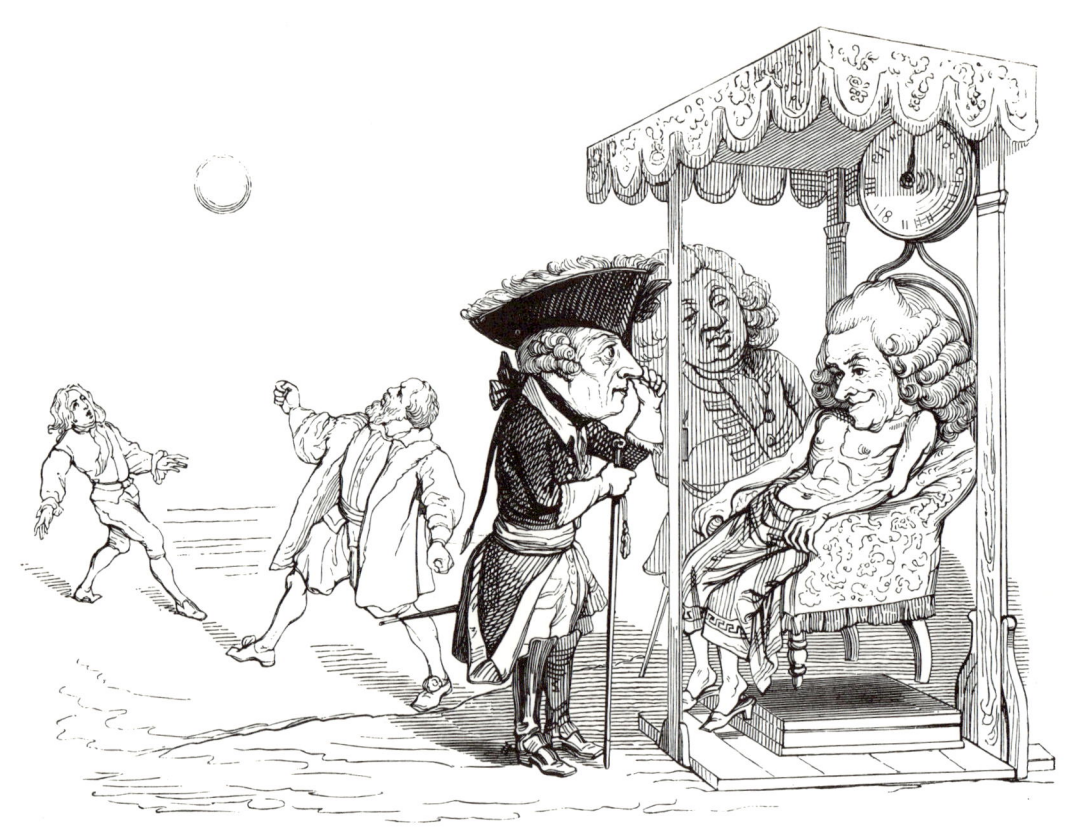

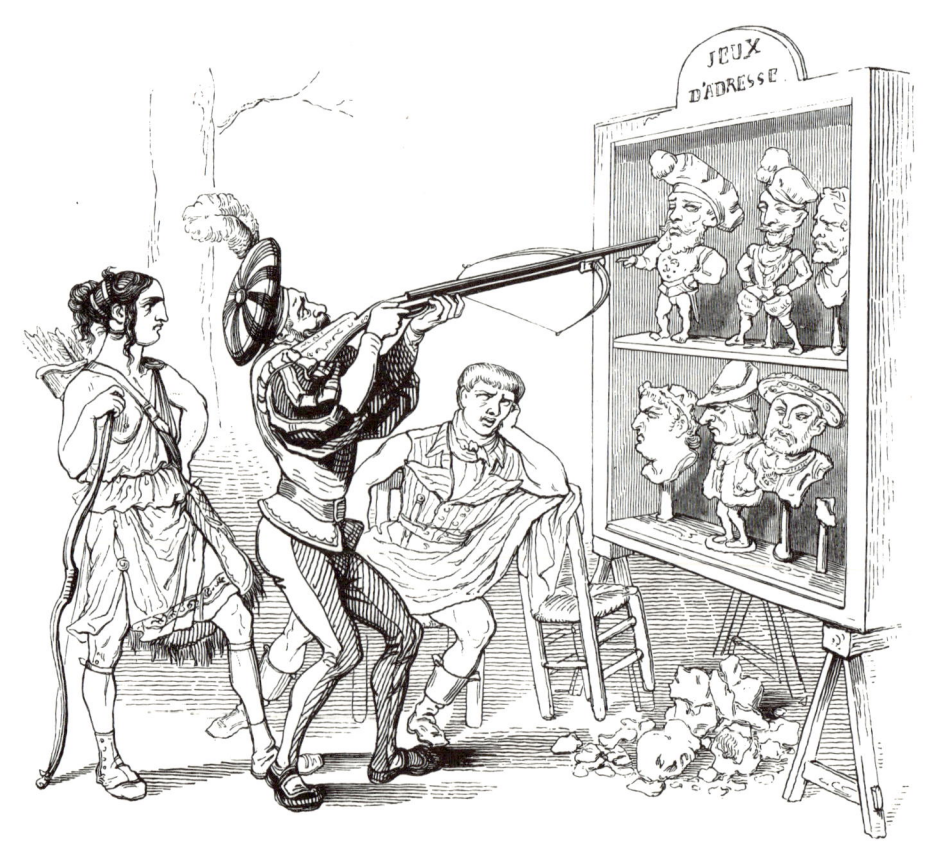

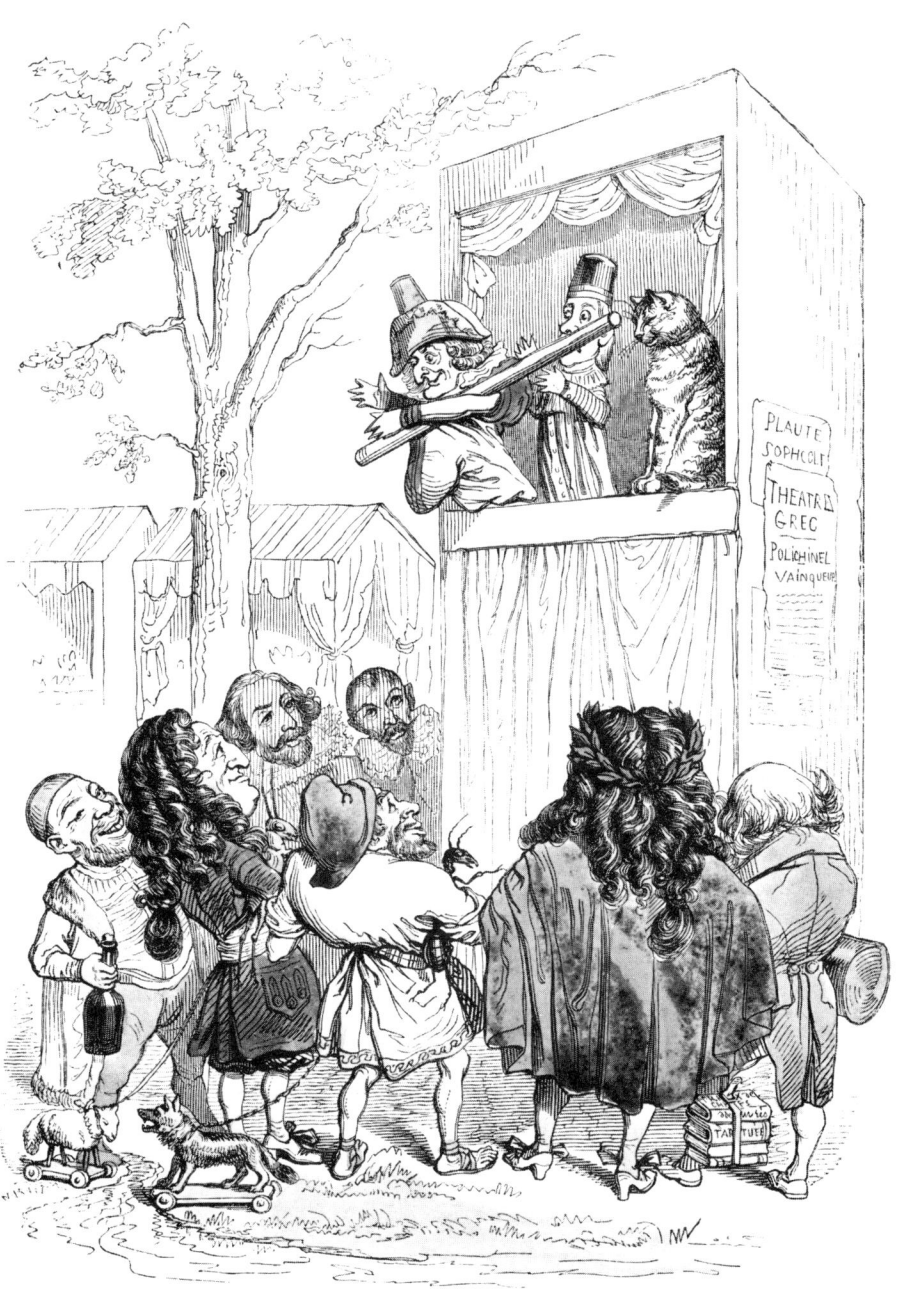

89. Voltaire and Frederick the Great weigh themselves, while Galileo and Newton play ball with a celestial sphere. **90.** Penthesilea and Brutus wait their turn while William Tell shoots at plaster tyrants. **91.** A puppet show attended by [going round the circle counterclockwise] Cervantes, Shakespeare, Rabelais, La Fontaine, Aesop, Molière and Picard.

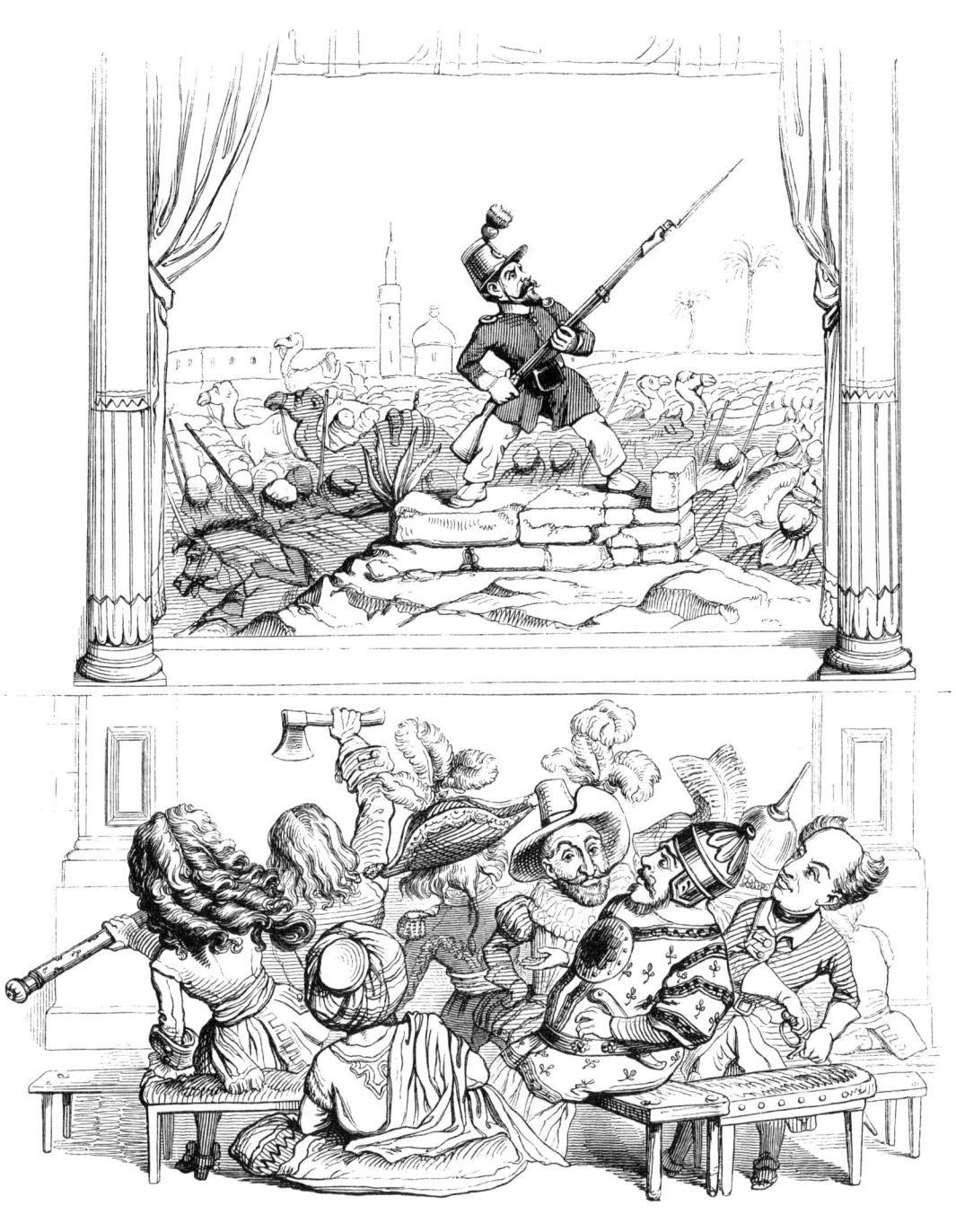

92. Great military figures of the past watch a play in which the exploits of French troops in Algeria are wildly exaggerated.

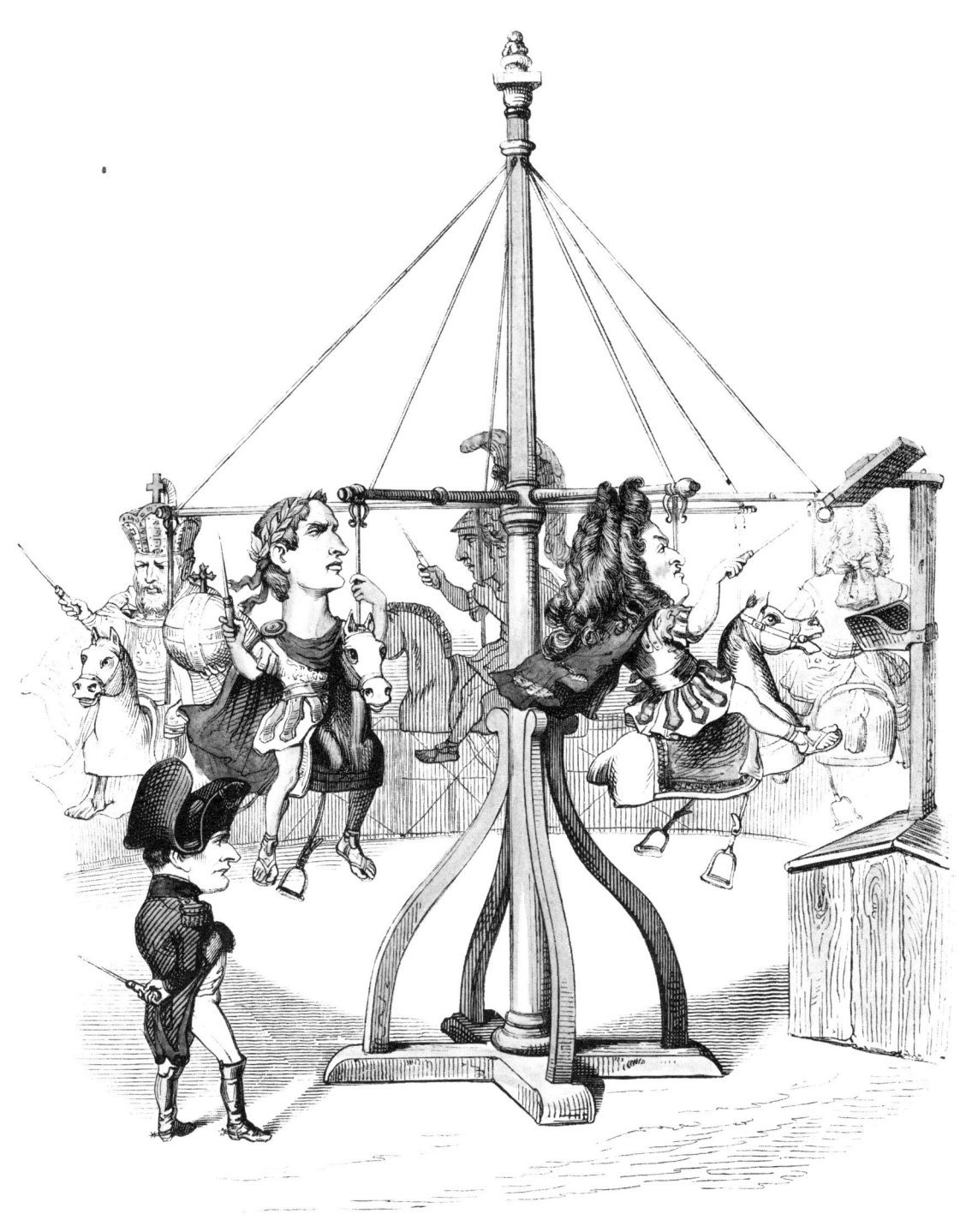

93. Great conquerors competing for the ring on a merry-go-round.

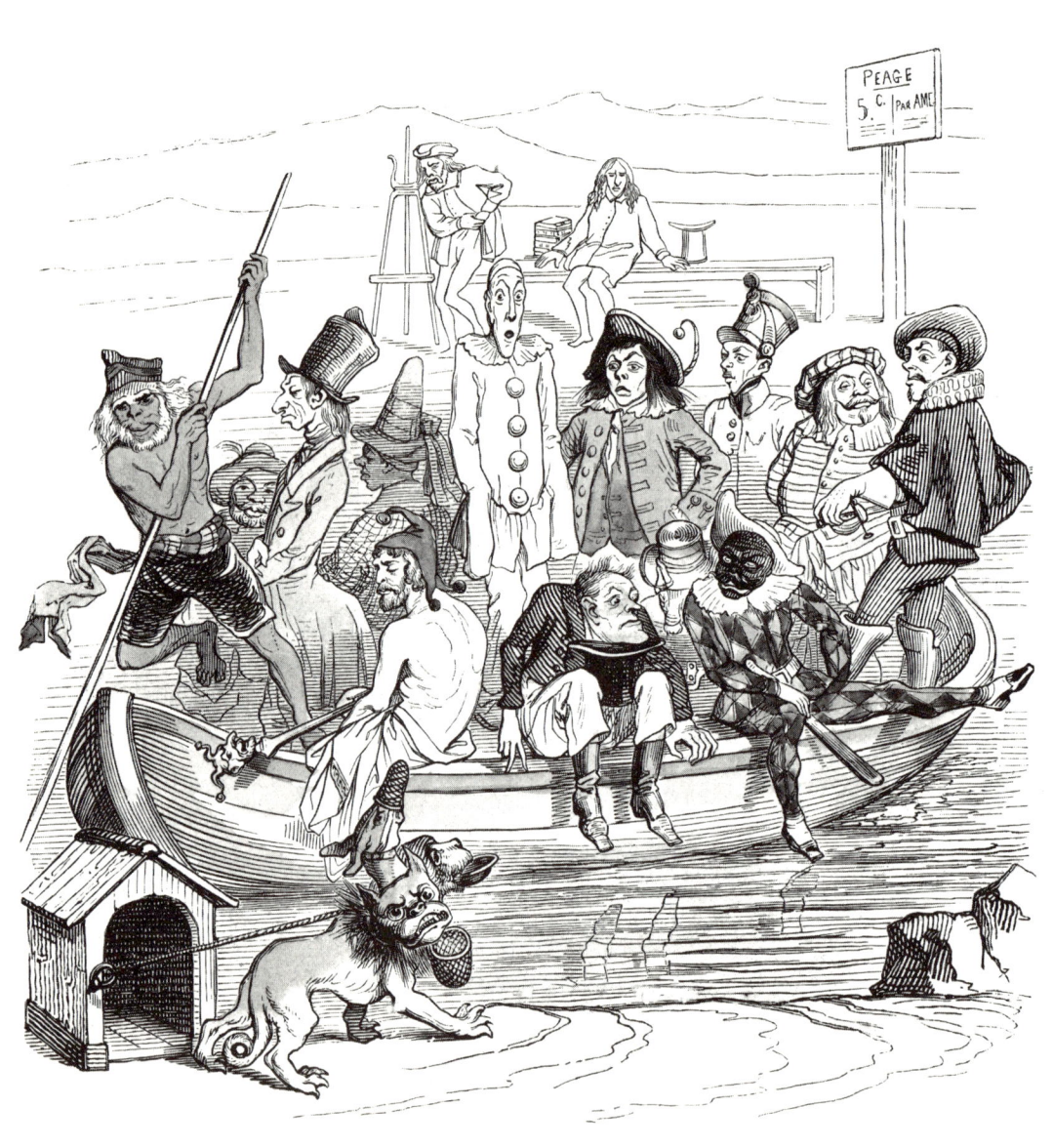

94. Charon's boat on the Styx filled with noted figures of fun.

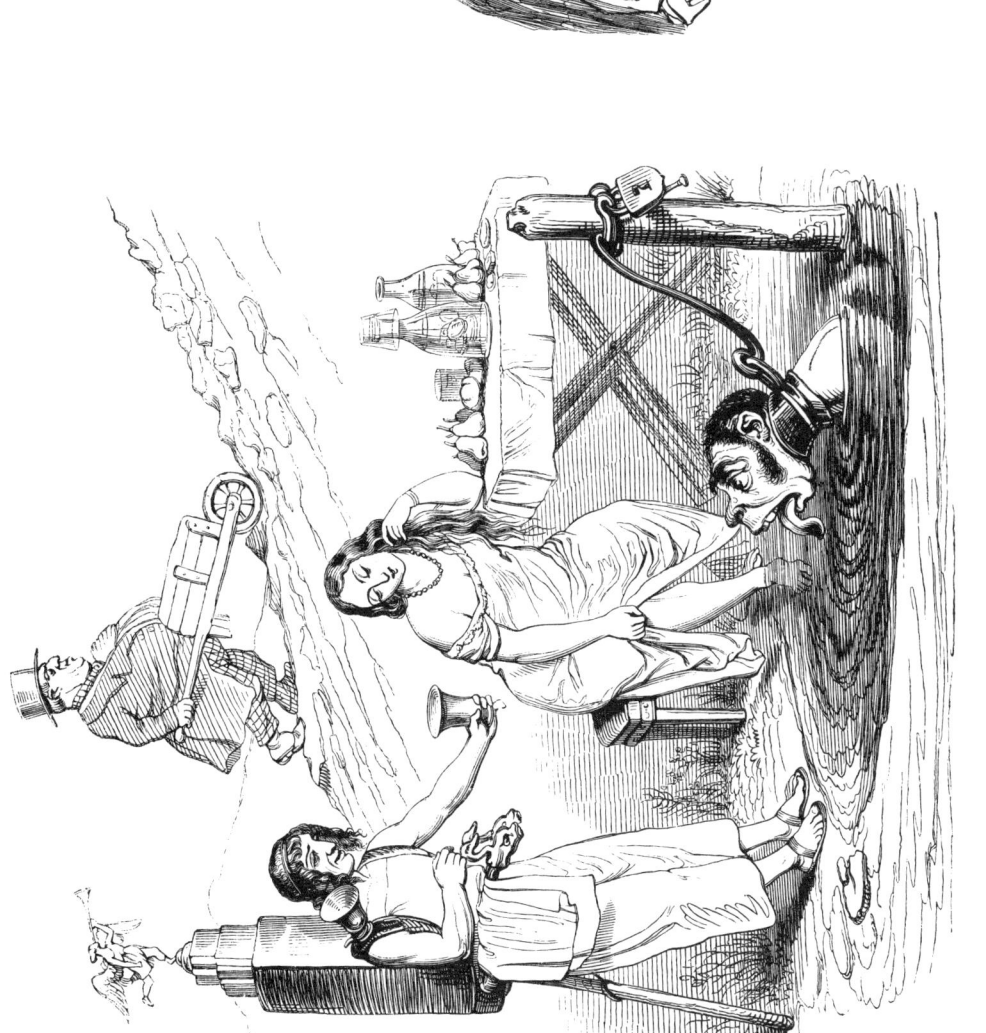

96. The three Fates.

95. The punishment of Tantalus interpreted as sexual longing; the myth of Sisyphus interpreted as gluttony.

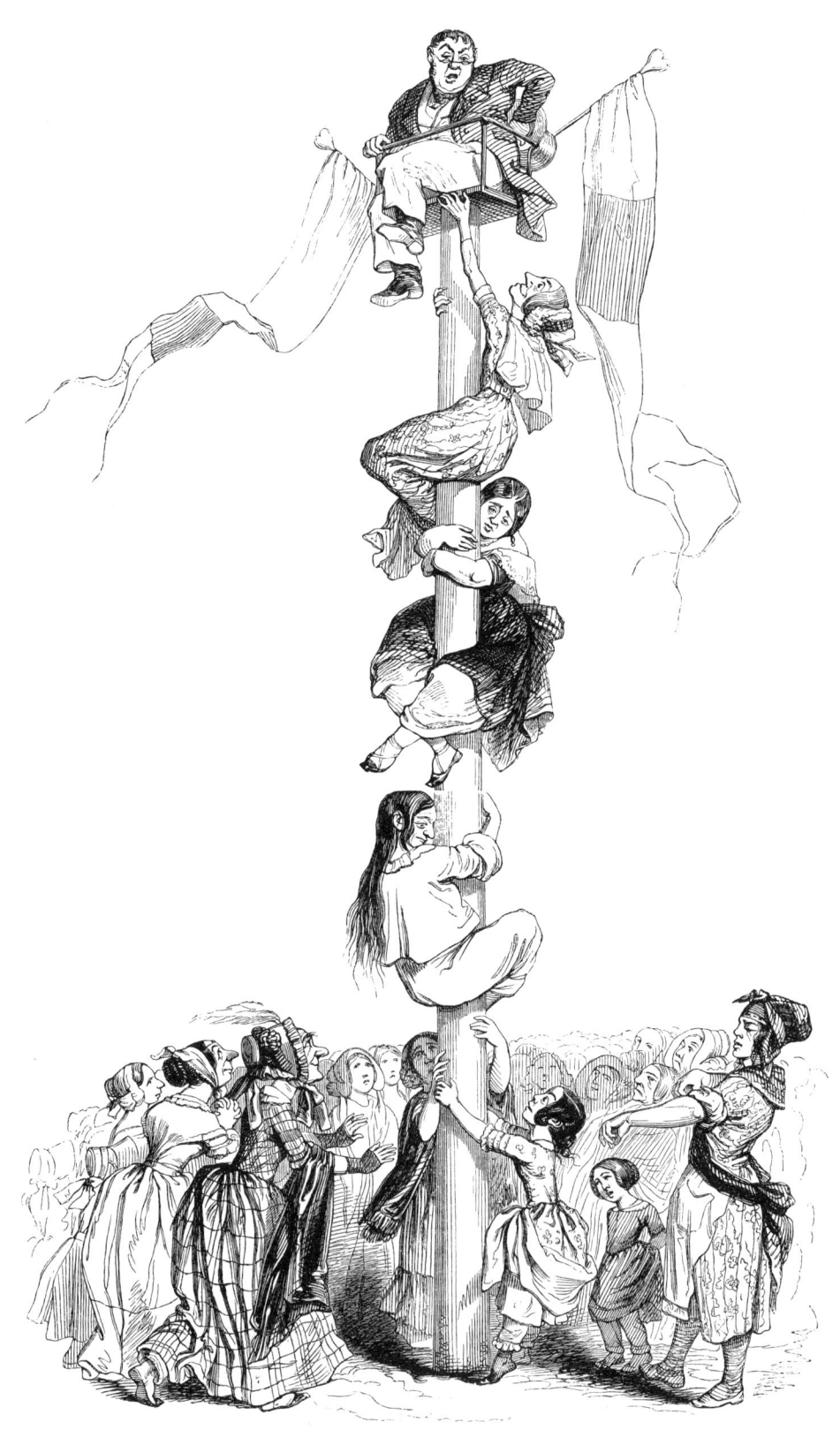

97. Old maids climbing a greased pole [carnival sport] to catch Puff for a husband.

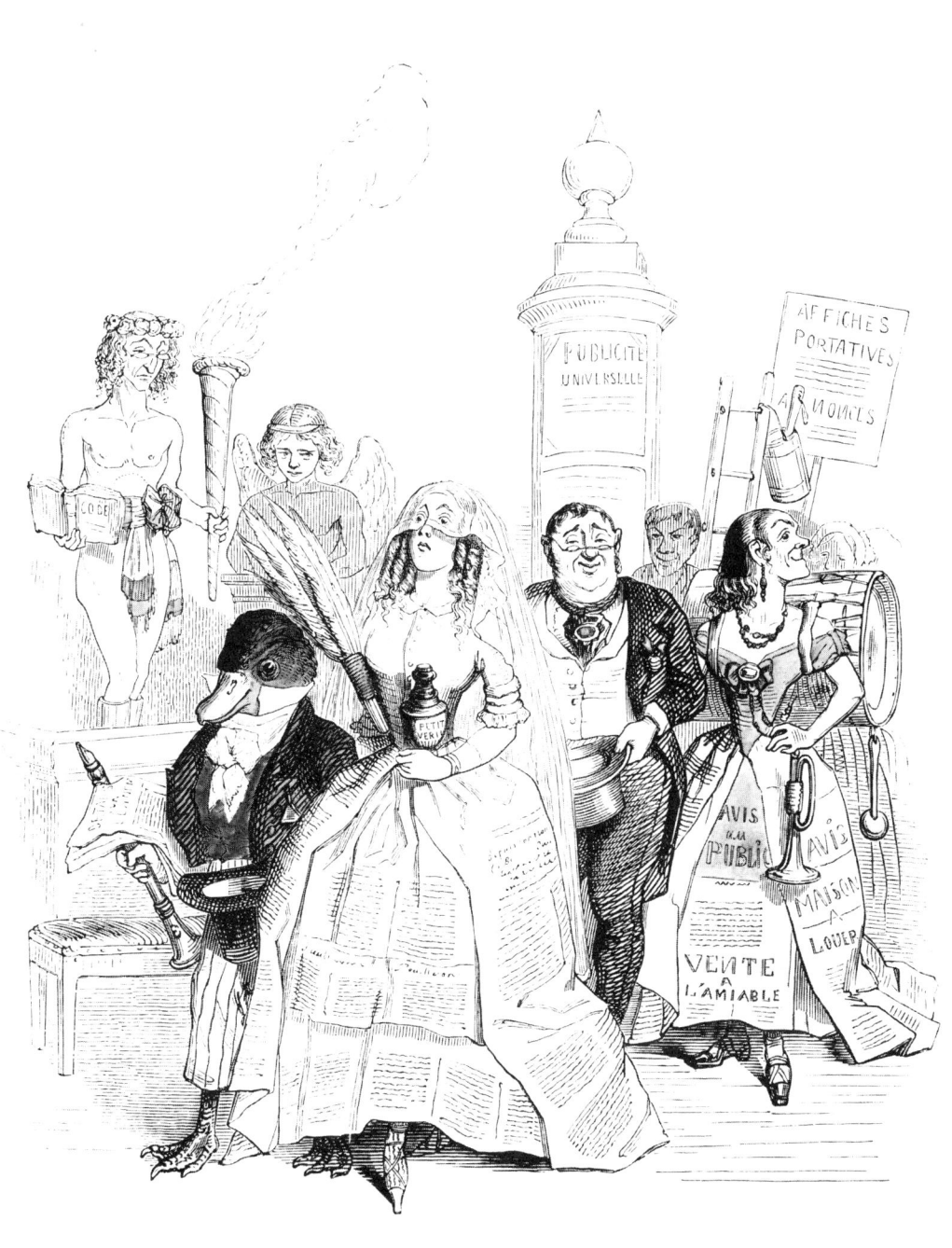

98. The wedding of Puff and Advertising.

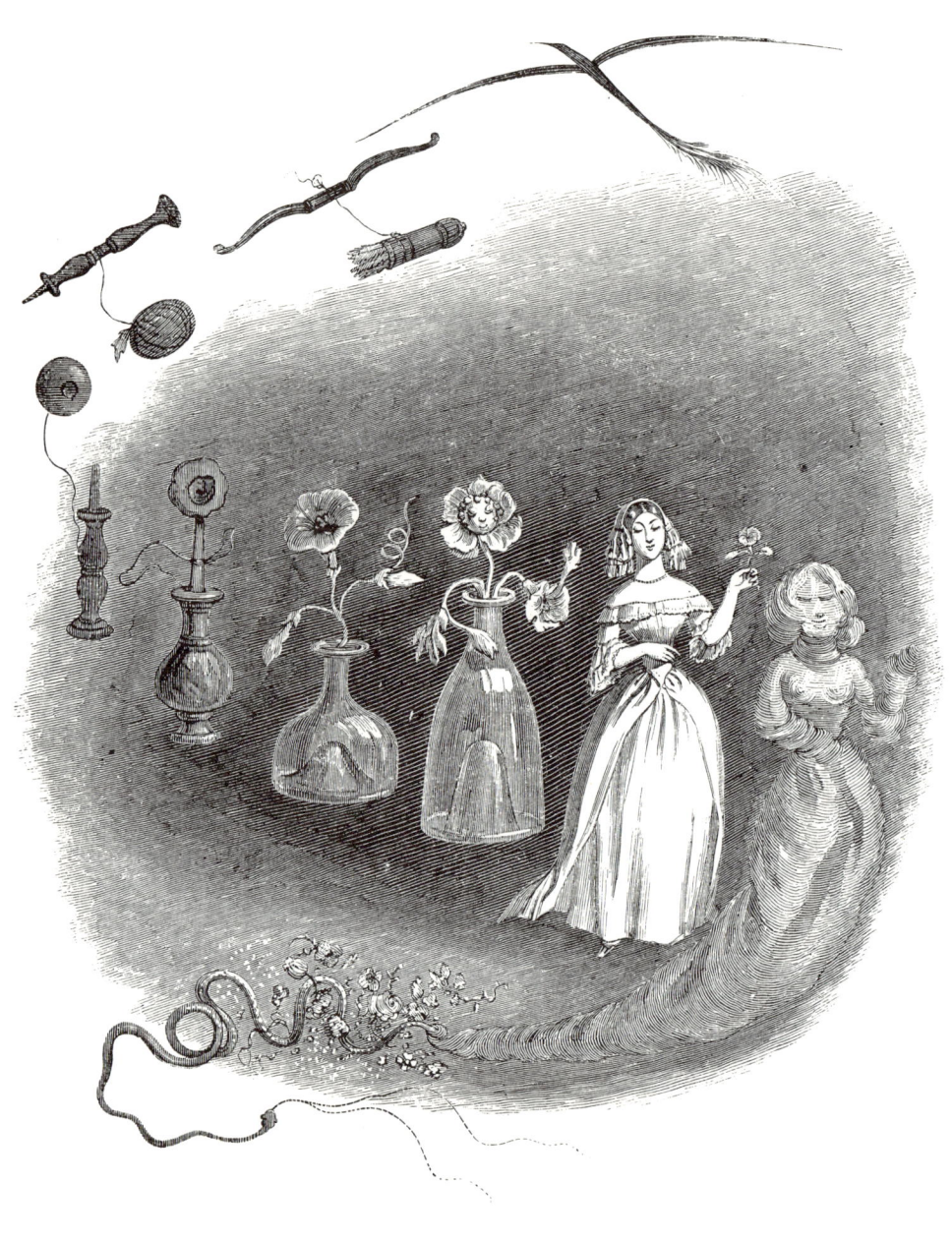

99. Hahblle's vision of his beloved Gertrude. **100.** A vision of the beloved tempted by riches.
101. A vision of the adoration of the Golden Calf (wealth).

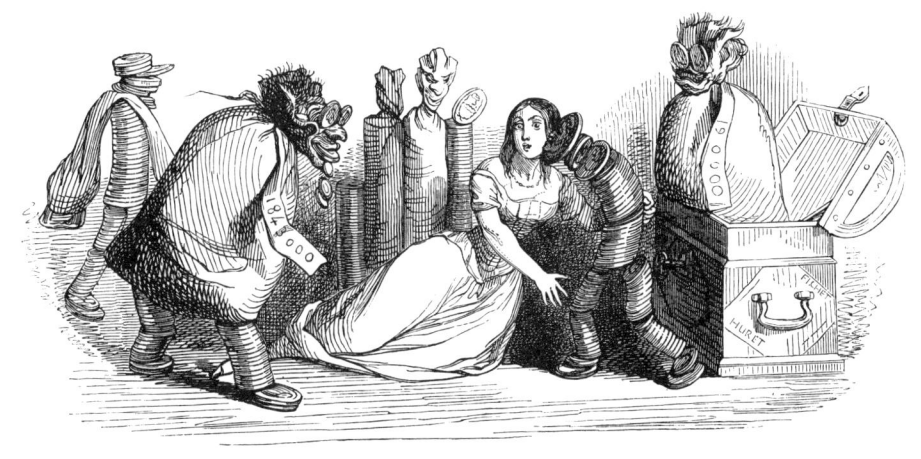

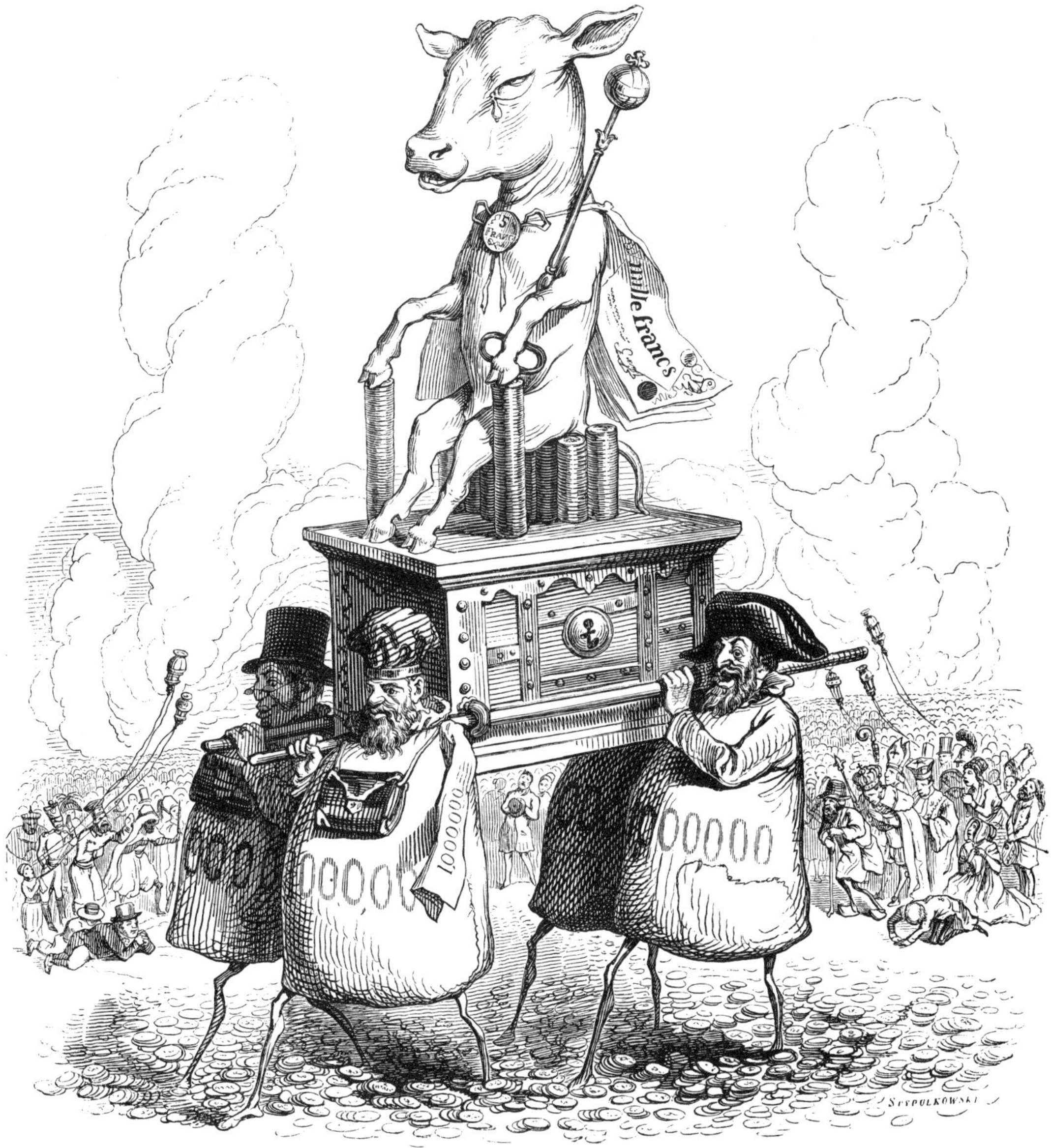

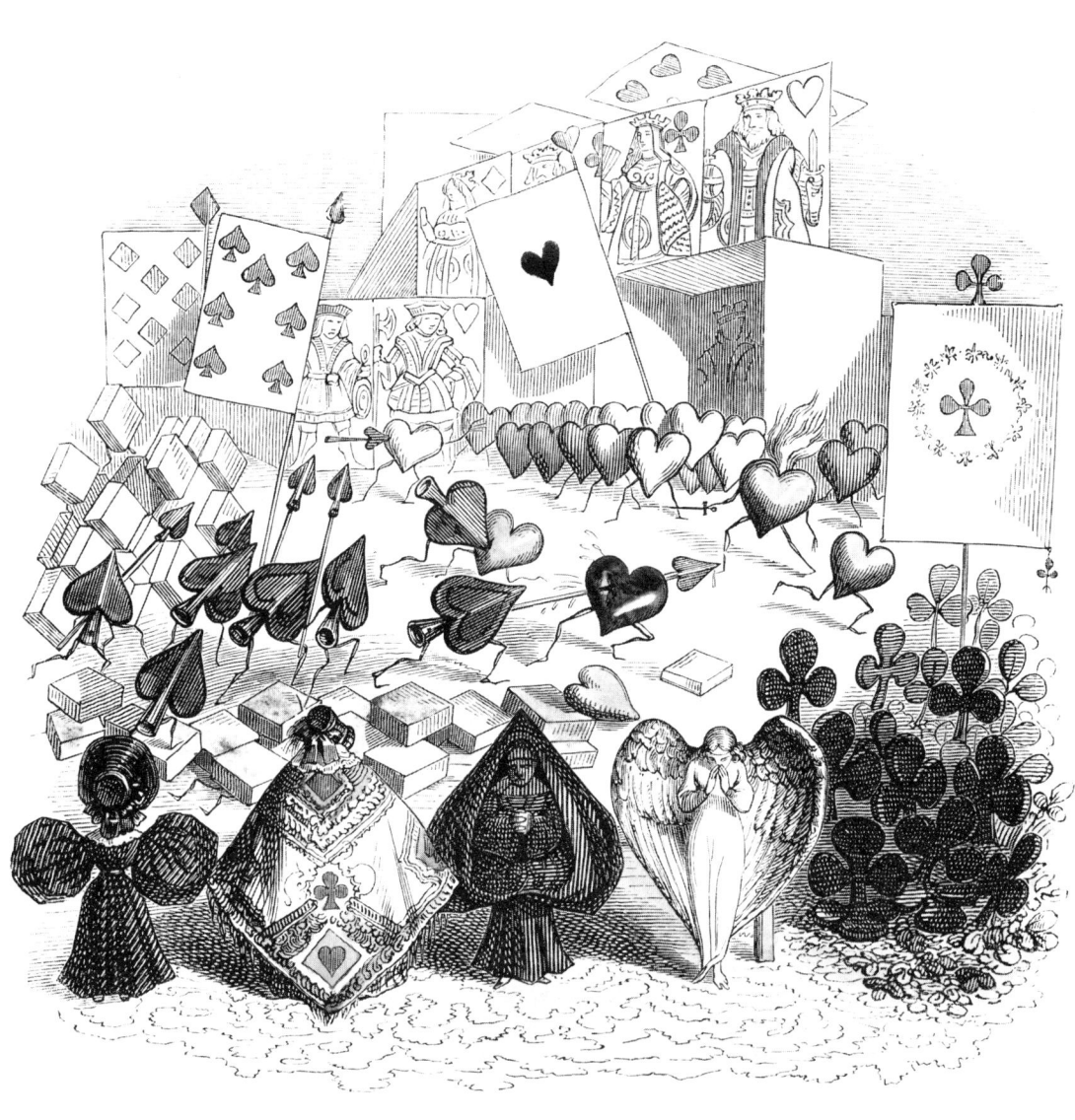

102. A vision of a battle of playing cards.   **103.** "Today social leveling is synonymous with compression."   **104.** Applying the discoveries of the phrenologists, society will eliminate crime and encourage virtue by physically altering the bumps on people's heads.

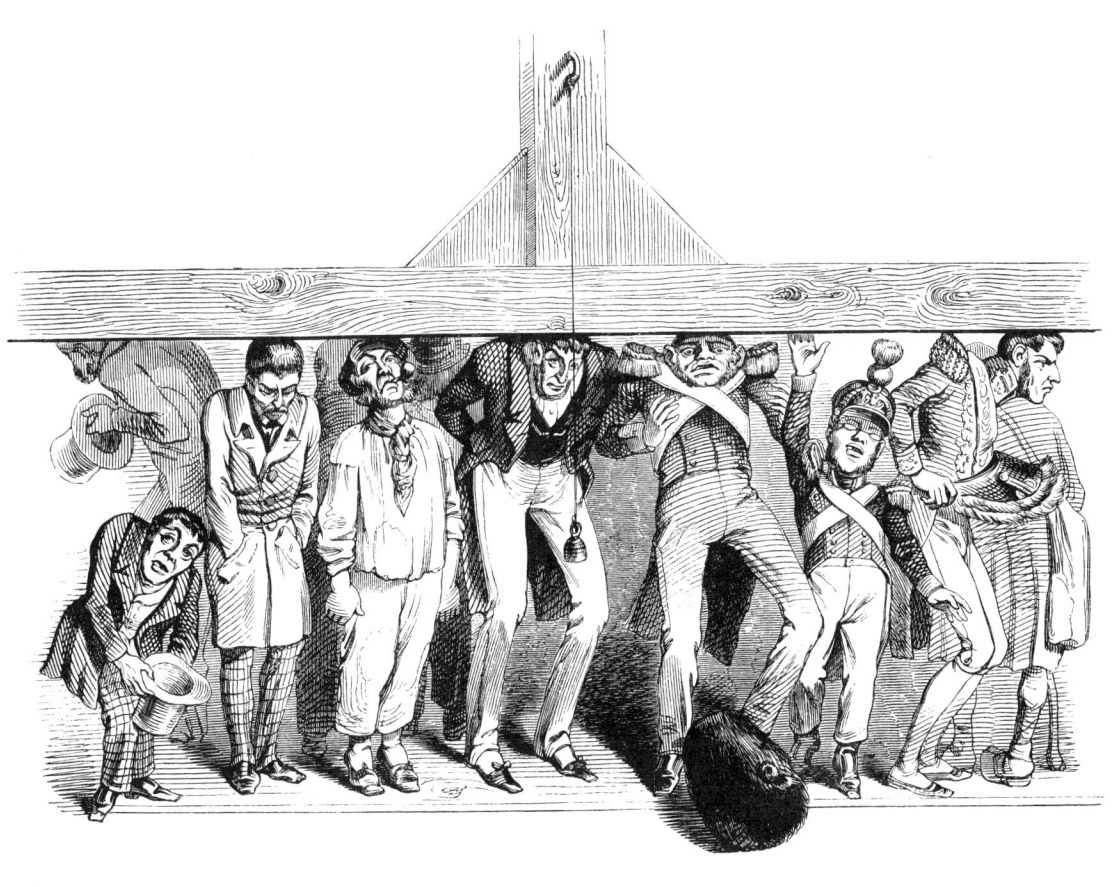

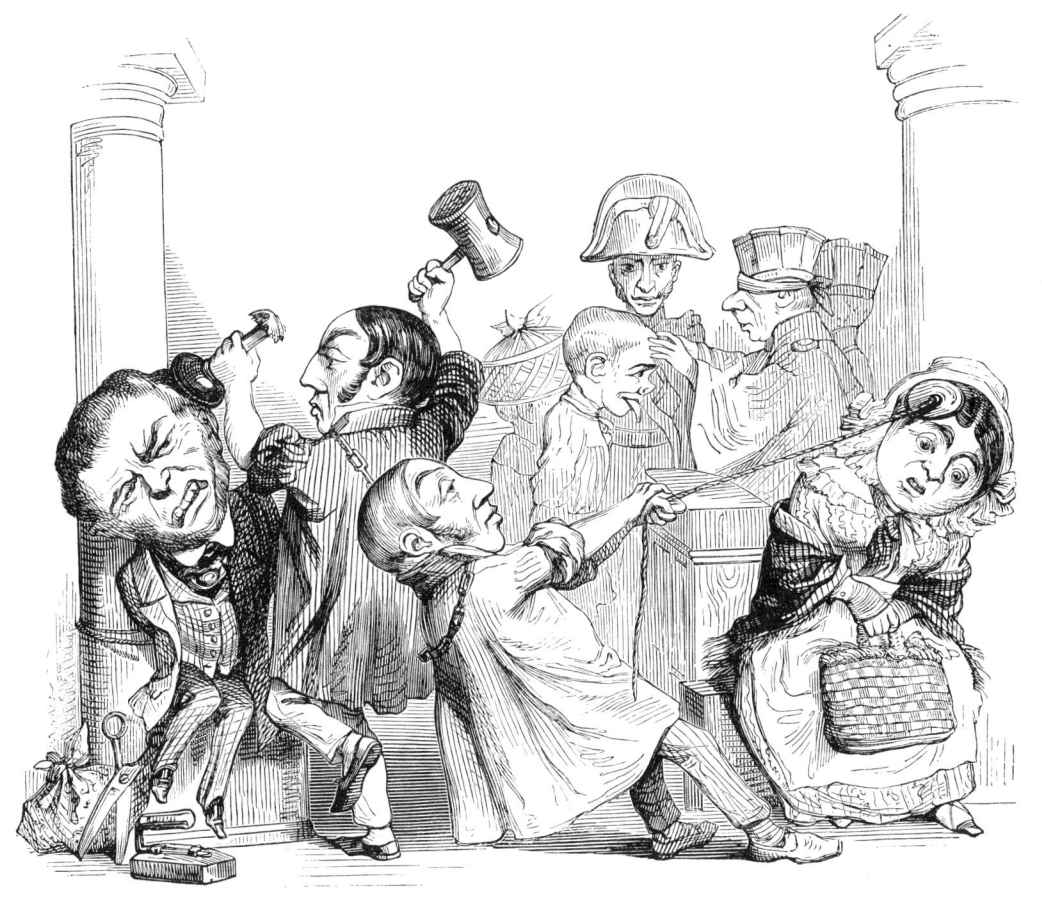

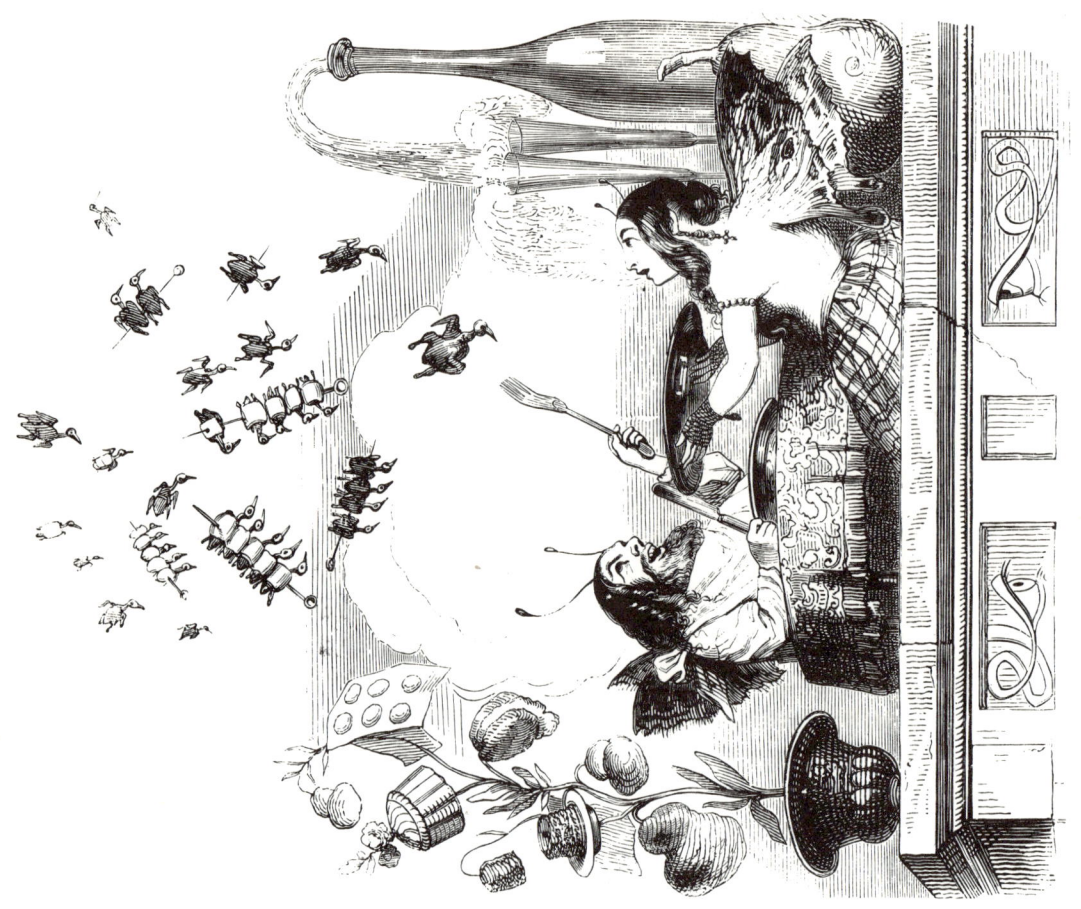

106. Human happiness—food for the asking—in the Fourierist utopia.

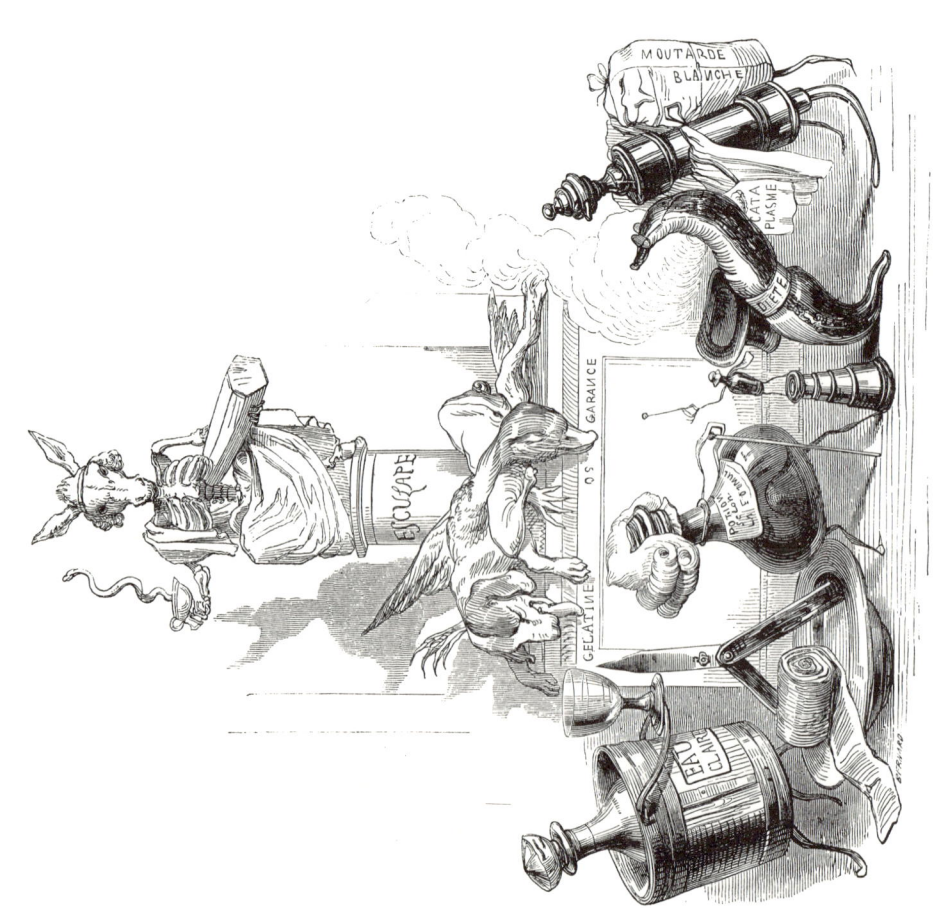

105. Allegory of Medicine.

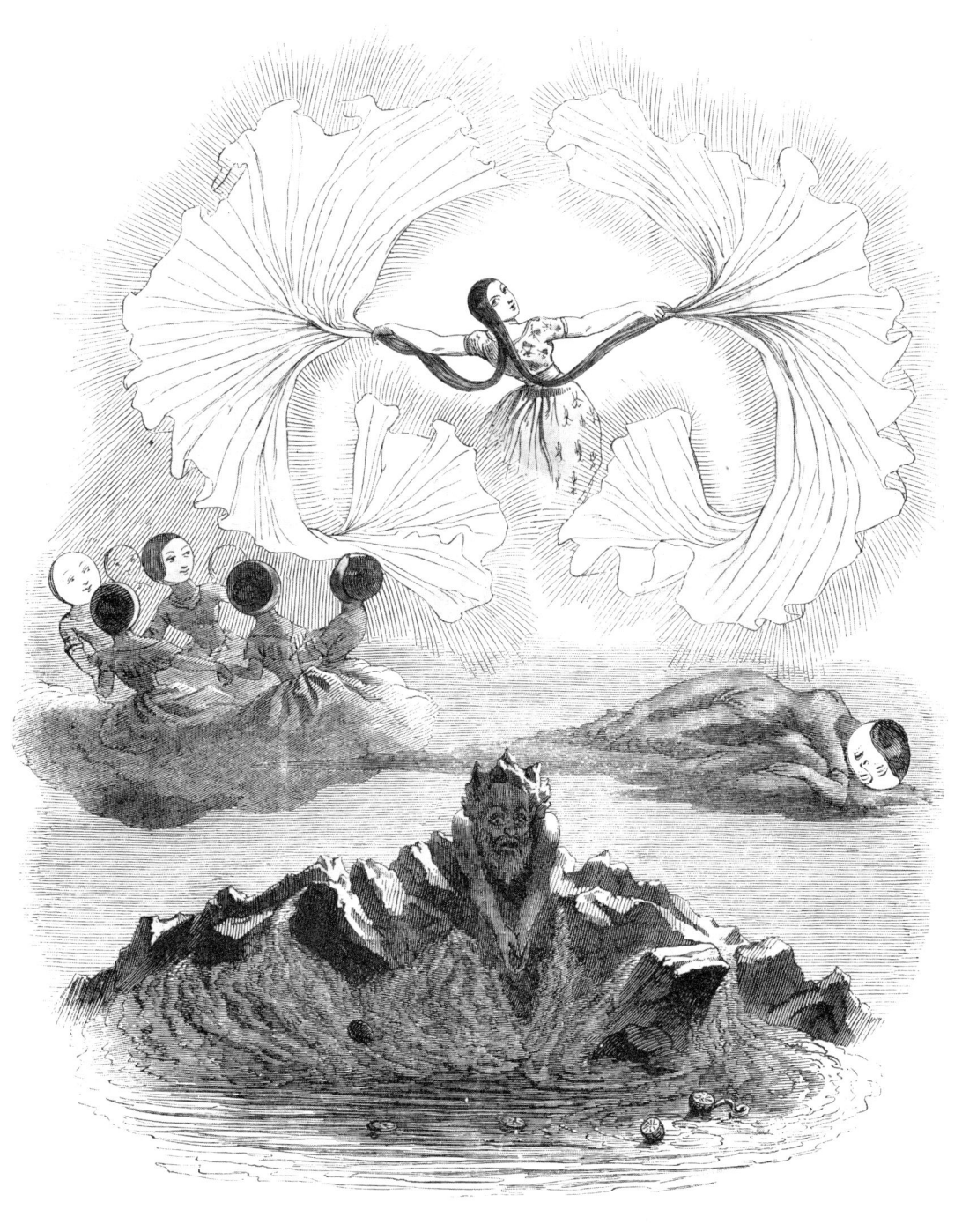

107. The new aspect of the heavens in the Fourierist utopia.

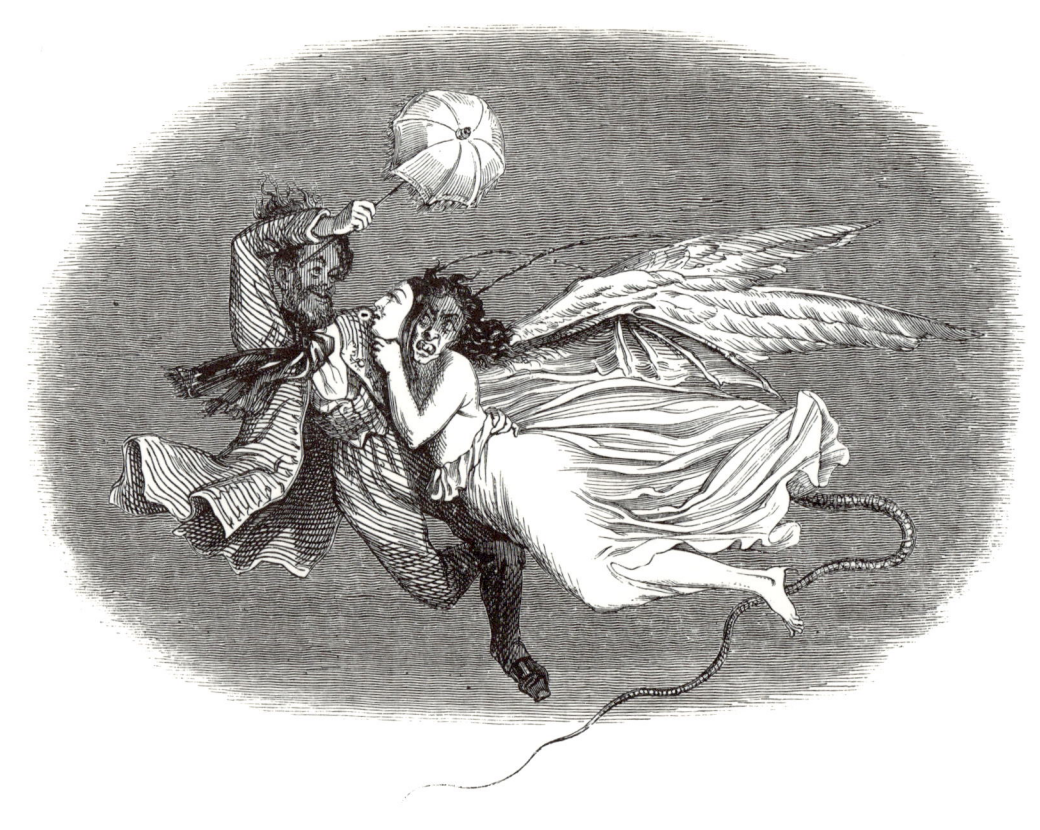

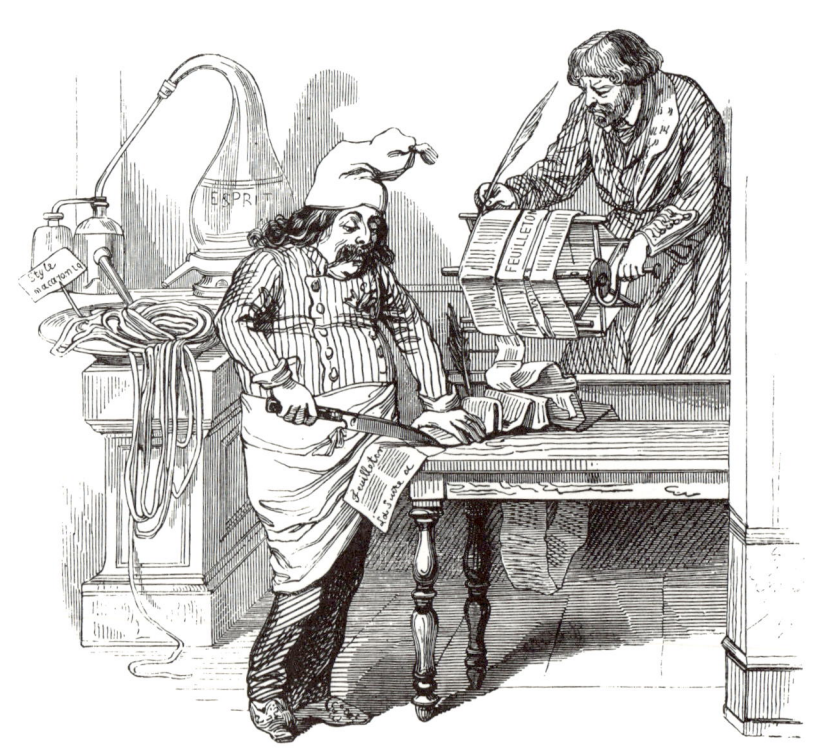

108. Hahblle's disappointment in love.   **109.** Literature being reeled off and sold in chunks.

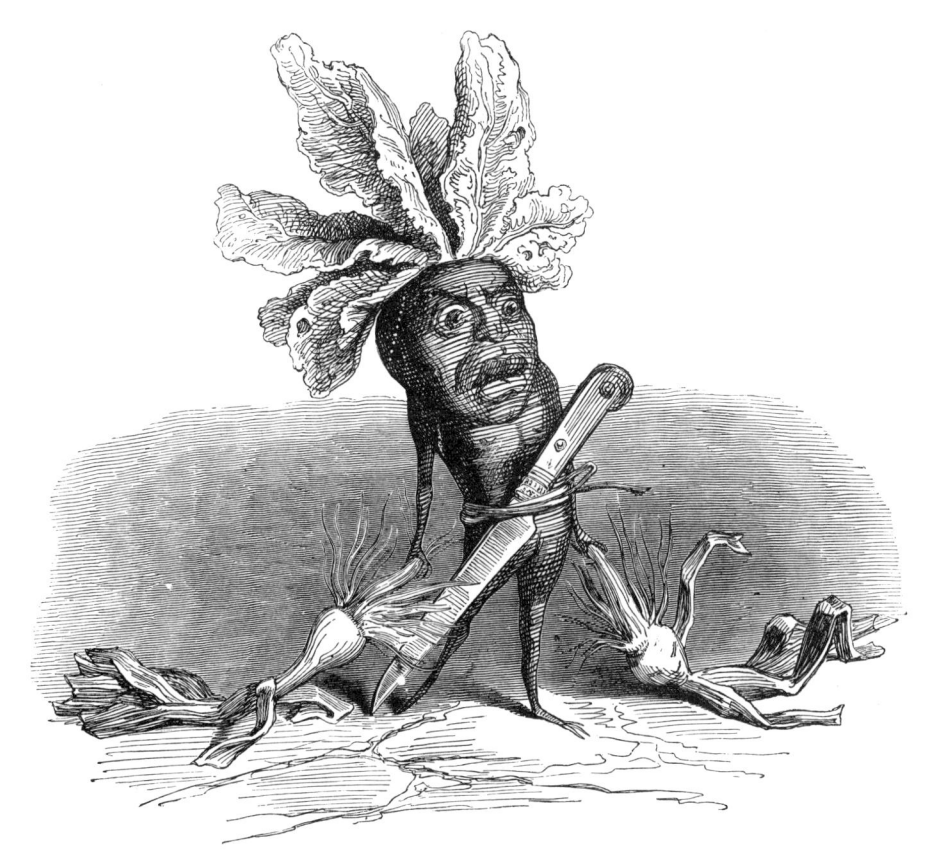

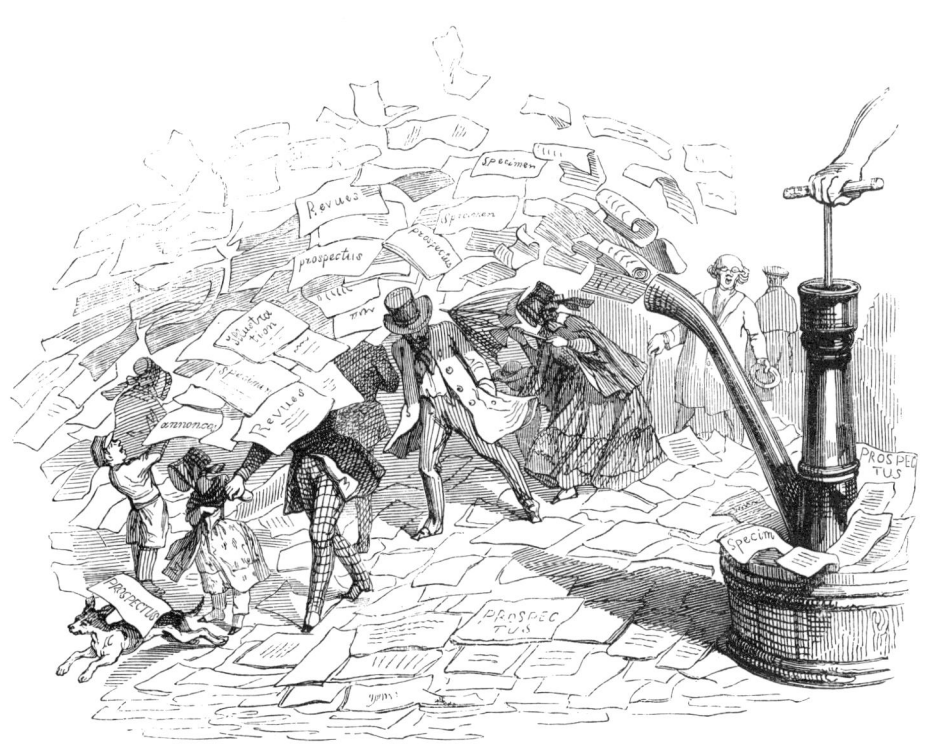

110. Allegory of the blood-and-thunder Romantic drama. **111.** A pump to flood a city with prospectuses and ads.

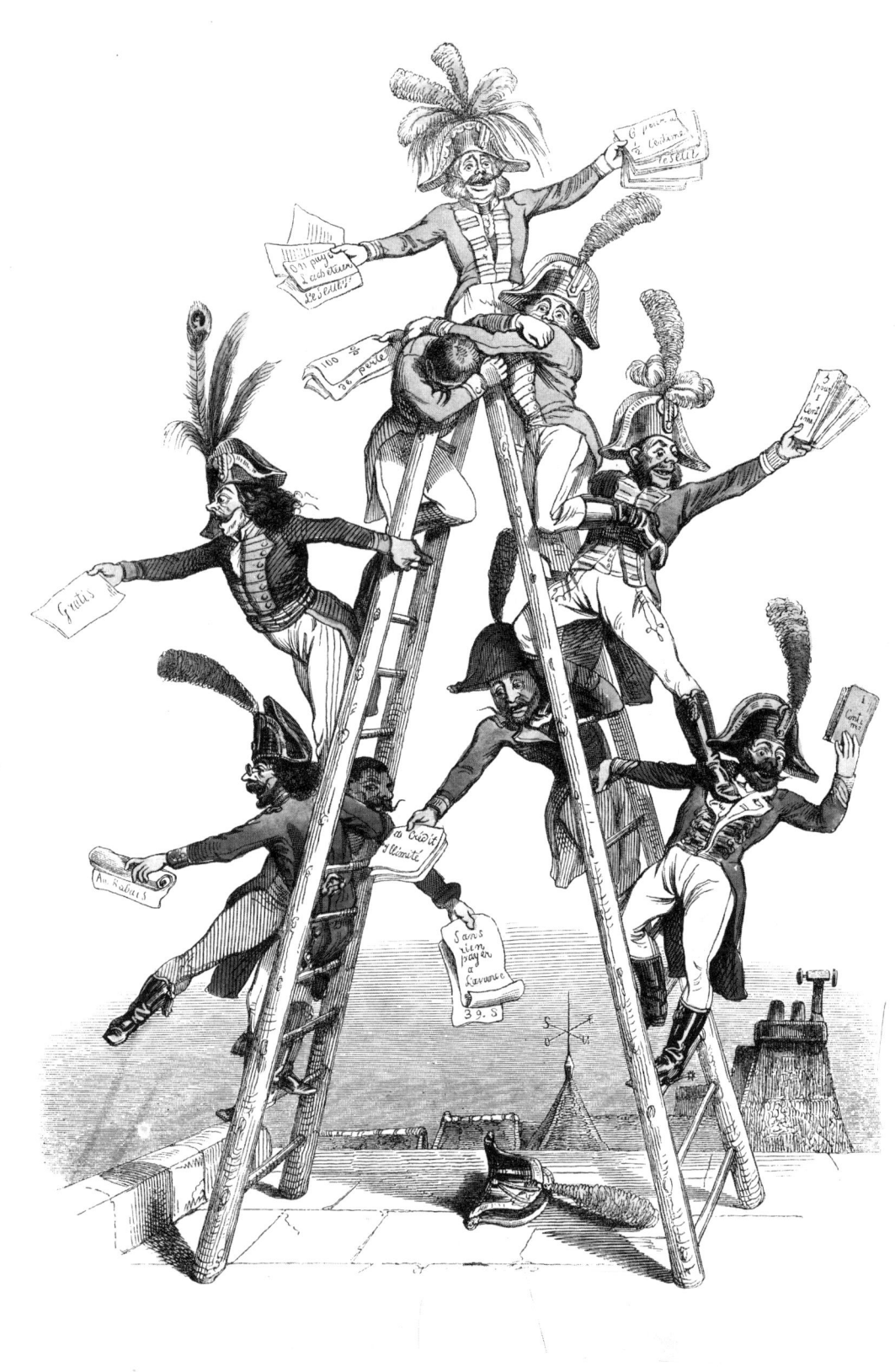

112. Criers advertising their bargains from the housetops.

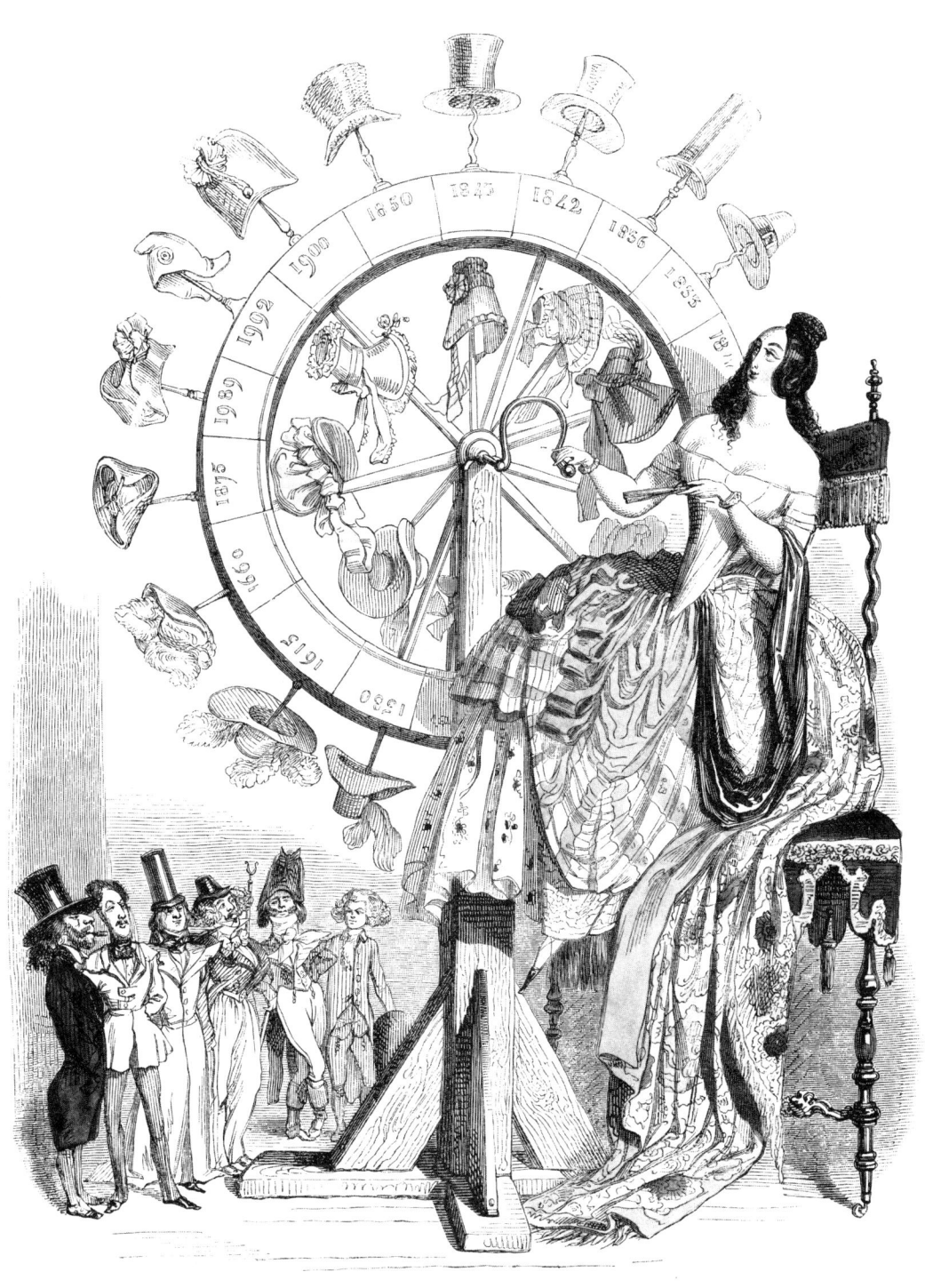

113. The wheel of Fashion.

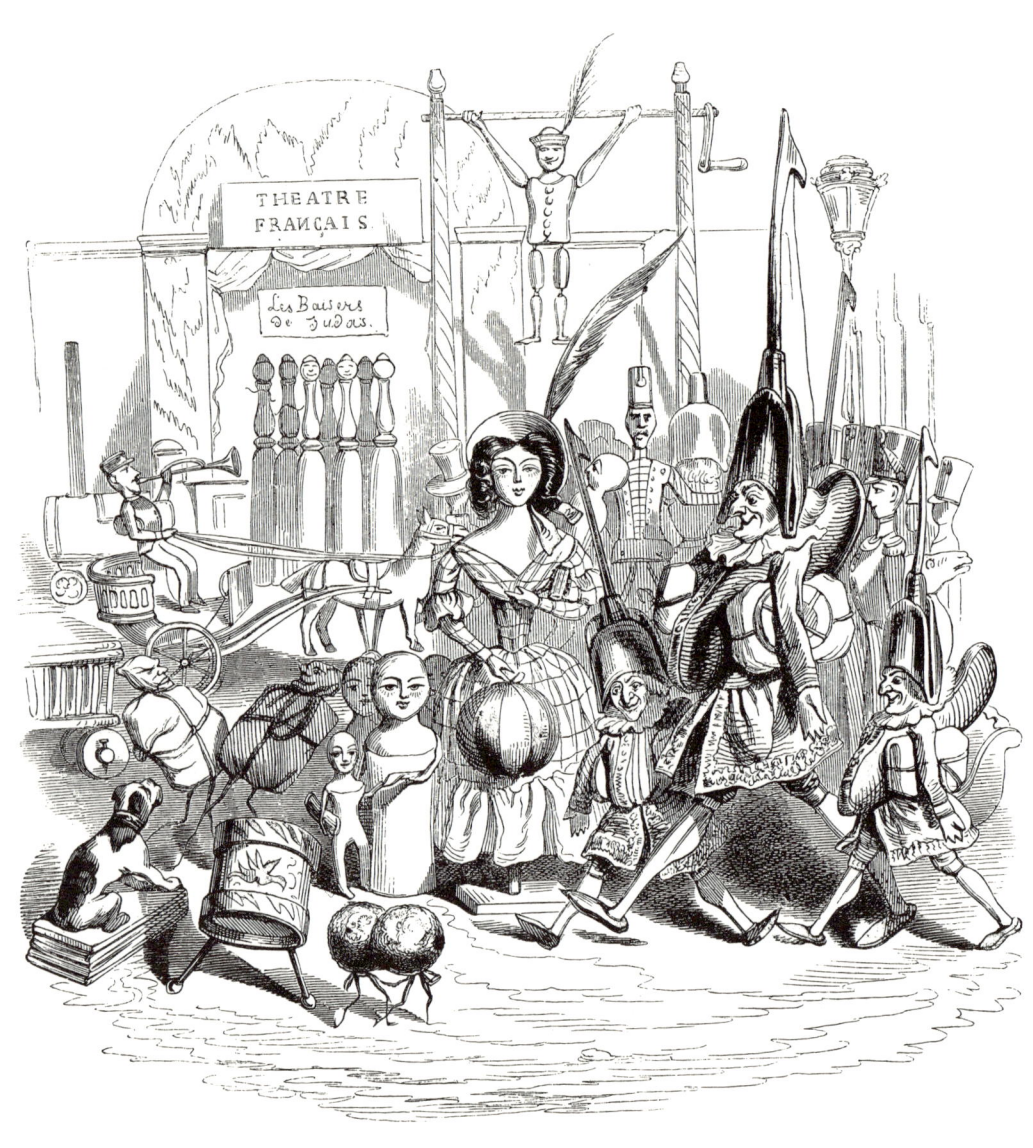

114. New Year's gifts that deliver themselves.

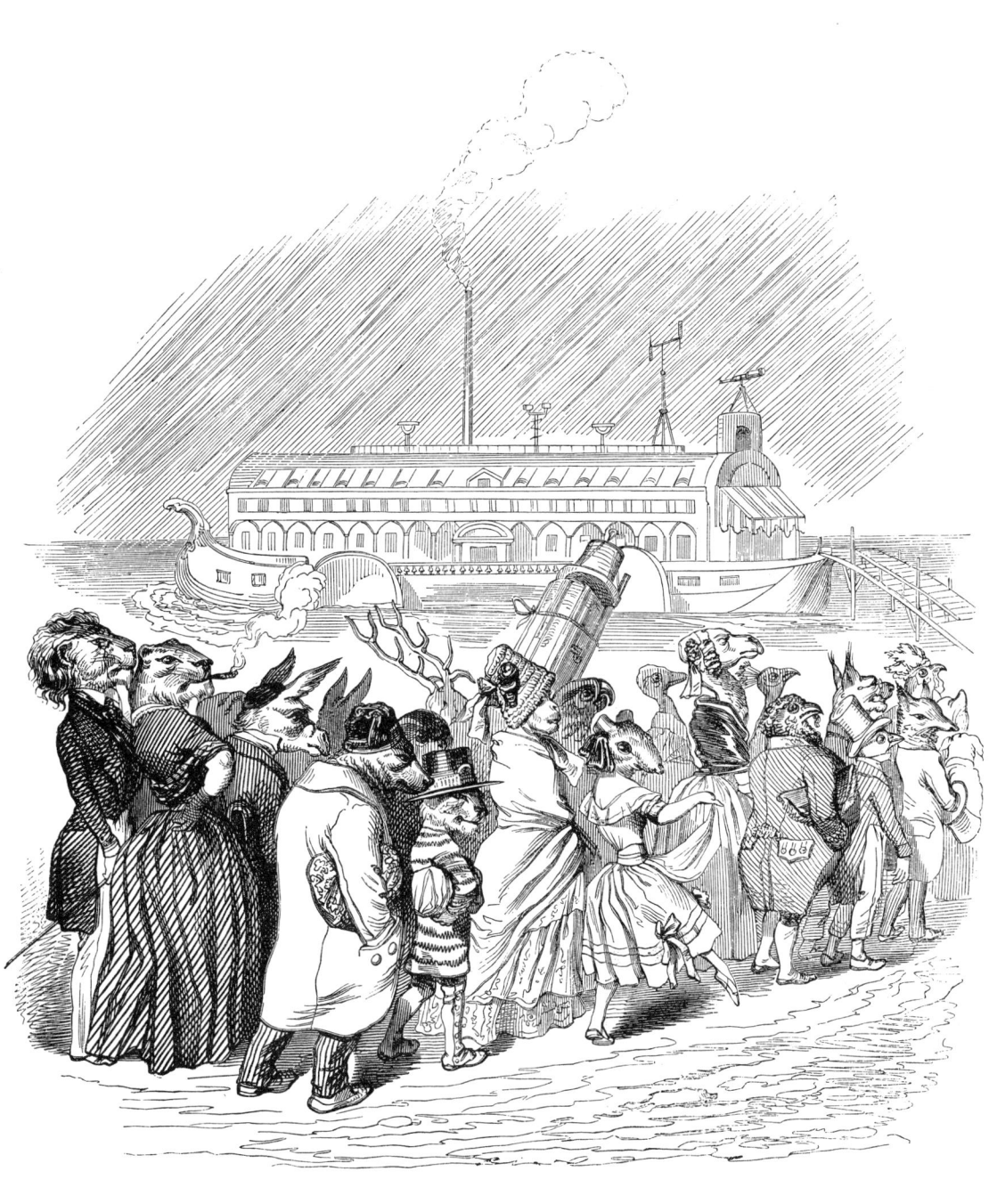

115. The animals entering the steam ark.

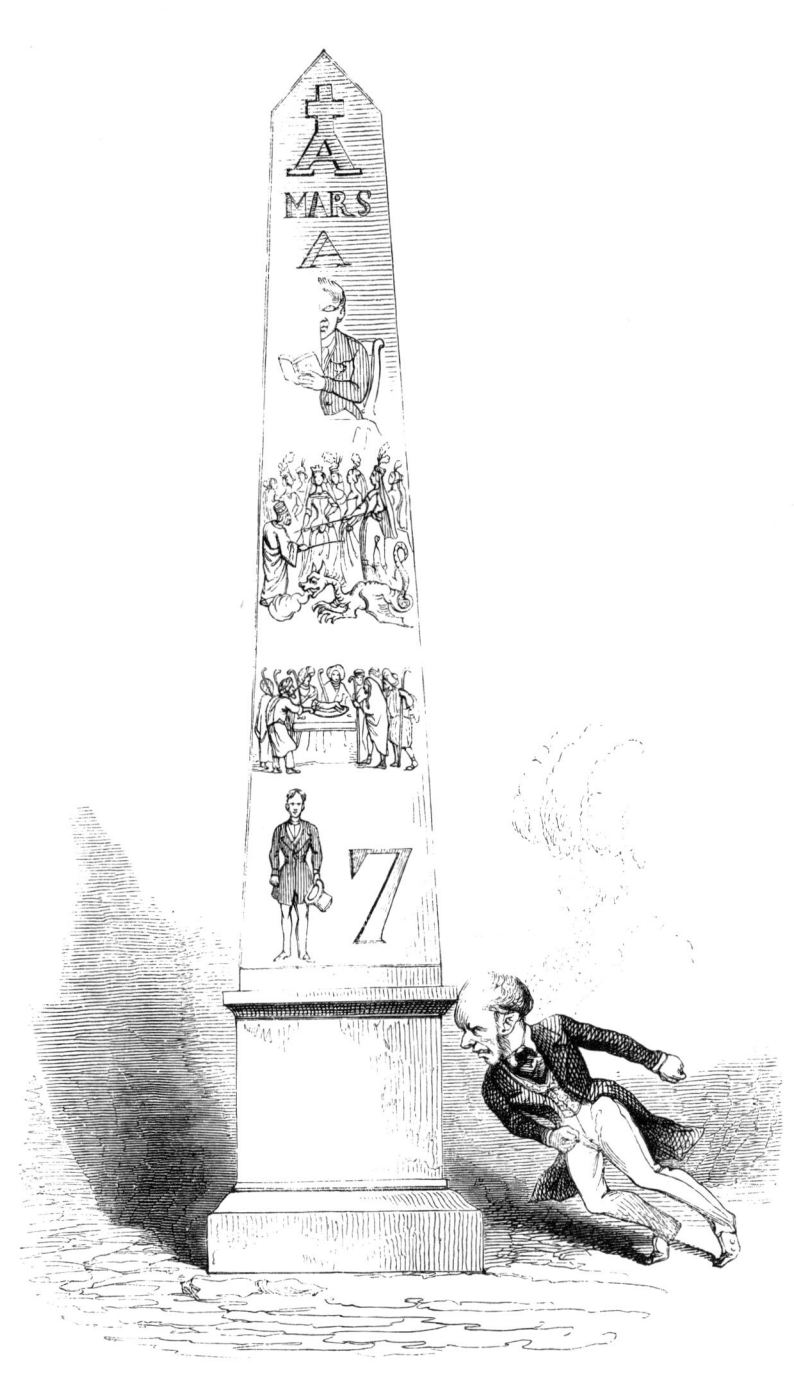

116. A punning rebus giving advice to the reader.   117. The pencil and the pen on Grandville's initials (J.-J. G.).   118. Headpiece of the table of contents (at the end of the book): the title.

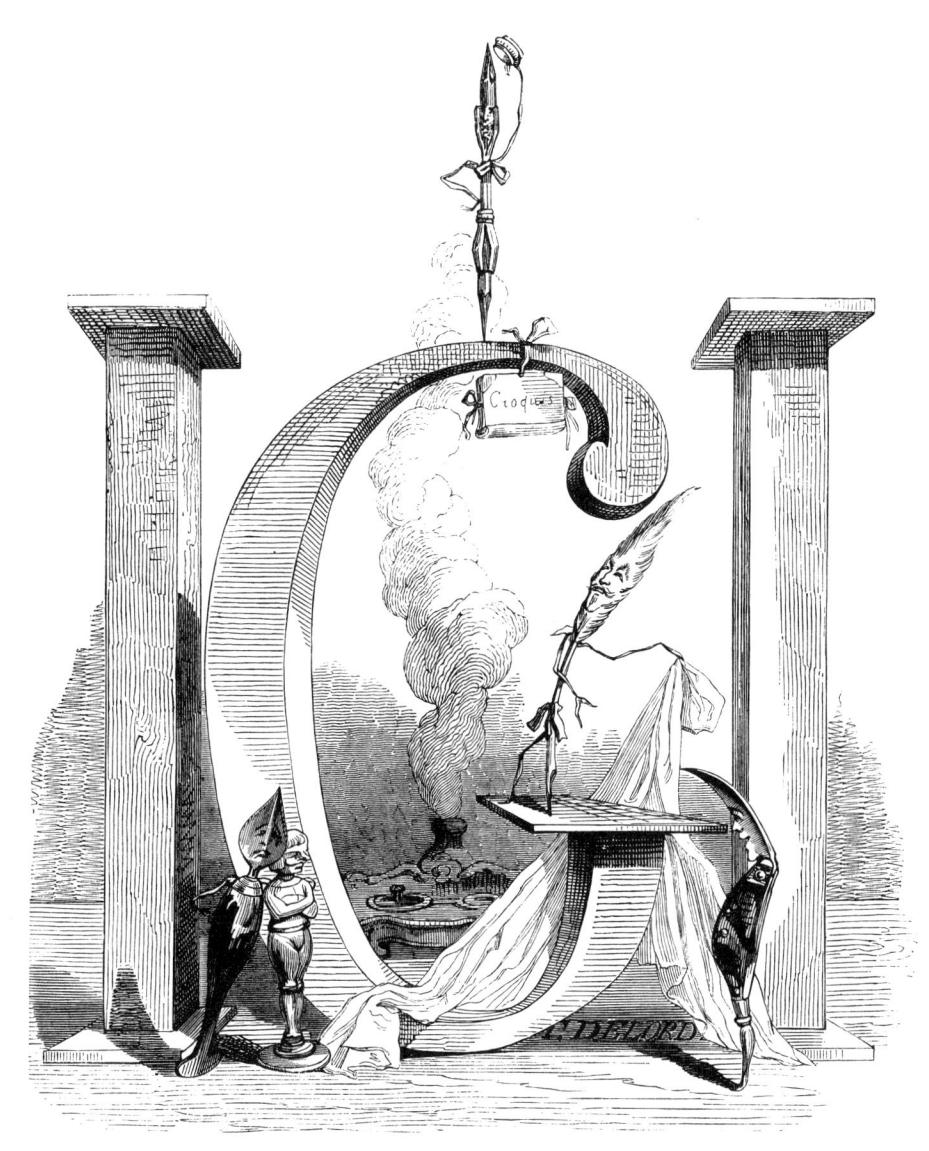

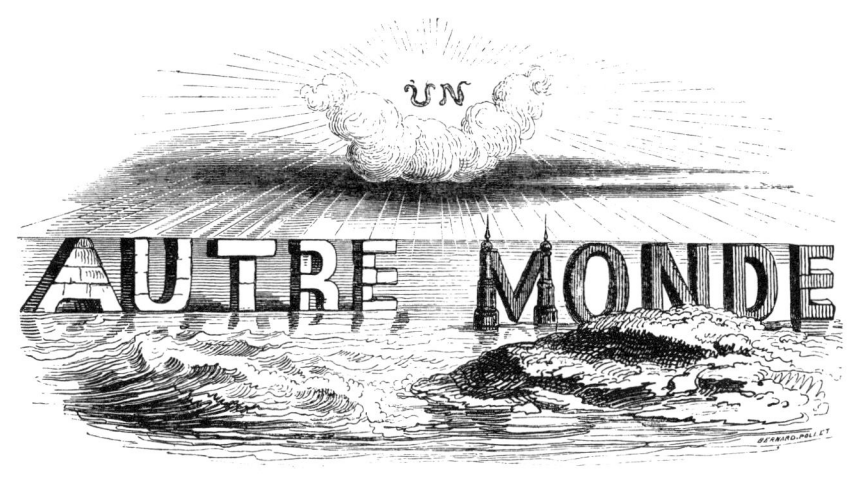

Les Animaux

THE ANIMALS

Synopsis of the Text
and Explanatory Notes on the Illustrations

119. Part title to Volume I (from the 1866 edition). The main inscription: "Public and Private Life of the Animals: Scenes of Manners." On the pot :"Triple fish paste" (for posting bills).

PROLOGUE
"General Assembly of the Animals"
and "Minutes of the Assembly"
by P.-J. Stahl (Pierre-Jules Hetzel)

The animals, considering themselves exploited and misrepresented by man, hold a secret nocturnal meeting in the Jardin des Plantes zoo in Paris. The fox convinces them that their best weapon is intelligence, and they desire to produce a book of, by and for animals, to be illustrated by Grandville (as an "honorary animal") and to be published by the sympathetic Hetzel and Paulin. The bulk of *Les Animaux* thus consists of the "animals' " literary contributions.

120. The parrot, who kept the minutes of the animals' assembly, proclaims his secrets from the housetops. **121.** A fly writes the "History of Animal Revolutions." **122.** Headpiece to the Prologue: the monkey, as editor-in-chief, receiving manuscripts from the animals. Sign on the wall: "Editorial office." The raven's manuscript is called "The Cadavers"; the owl's, "Midnight"; the swan's, "The Blue Lake." Sign on the inner room: "Composing room—no smoking." **123.** Frame illustration for the first page of the Prologue: the monkey-locksmith frees the animals from their cages for the secret meeting. **124.** At the assembly the chameleon assures the animals that he agrees with each one of them. **125.** The first installment of the animals' book is sold by street hawkers. The signs include Grandville's full name and his initials, the name and address of the publishers, and the date (1840) of the first installment of unbound pages (sold for 6 sous). On the sheet held by the young bulldog is an abbreviated form of an alternate title of the book: "The Animals Painted [by Themselves, and Drawn by Another]." Sign on house: "Subscriptions *not* taken here."

126. Second part title to Volume I. Animal signpainters and bill-posters. Note the spelling "Annimo." Down the sides of the sign are names of other books, some of which had already been illustrated by Grandville (La Bruyère, La Fontaine).

"Story of a Hare"
by P.-J. Stahl

An old hare tells his life story to a magpie. Born in 1830, he is orphaned during the last royal hunt of Charles X before the king's forced abdication in July of that year. After unhappy adventures with an ex-lackey of the king, the hare is sheltered by a kindly man as timorous as himself, a poor government clerk, who dies of chagrin when he loses his job. Back in the country, the hare is challenged to a duel, for no good reason, by a pugnacious rooster. The hare kills the rooster, to the great joy of the hare's second, the bulldog, whom the rooster used to awaken early every morning. In his native forest, the hare raises a family and grows old in relative tranquility.

127. The magpie, who wrote the hare's story from his dictation. **128.** An evil owl blocking the way of two young hares and their sister. This brief esipode does not form an integral part of the hare's story. **129.** The hare's new master, the timorous government clerk. **130.** The son of the new master, "like his father in every way." The text makes it clear that father and son are human beings, but Grandville portrays their hare-like nature. **131.** Mister Vulture, the hard-hearted landlord of the government clerk. The landlord, too, is supposed to be a man . . . but he *is* named Mister Vulture! The slip he is holding reads "Rent receipt." **132.** The pugnacious rooster who insists on fighting a duel with the hare. **133.** The rooster awakening the bulldog. **134.** "There are men who walk as beggars over the fertile earth." Though many characters in the *Animaux* stories are supposed to be men and women, this is the only full-fledged human being in Grandville's artwork for the book. And in this single instance, Grandville has not drawn one of the characters in the story but has illustrated a passing reflection on an aspect of life (the problem of the indigent).

"Memoirs of a Crocodile"
by Emile de la Bédollière

A selfish, voracious crocodile is transported to Paris after Napoleon's invasion of Egypt. There he becomes the property of an aristocratic bon vivant very similar to himself. When his owner prepares to eat him, he escapes. He swims all the way down the Seine, but is finally caught at Le Havre.

135. Convivial crocodiles at a banquet. The sign reads: "Pyramids Restaurant. For 18 sous you get 3 courses and a small carafe of wine." The obelisk from Luxor, which had been erected in the Place de la Concorde in 1836, apparently stimulated Grandville's imagination (see also No. 33). **136.** The crocodile's gluttonous owner. Again, the character is a human being in the text, but the illustration reveals his animal nature. In general, from this point on, the annotation for such instances will merely be "Human being in text." **137.** A patrol of the National Guard looking askance at revelers leaving a low-class drinking establishment. Such nocturnal roistering was also a vice of the crocodile's owner.

"Heartaches of an English Cat"
by Honoré de Balzac

Beauty, a female cat, is brought up by her old maid mistress in the stifling and hypocritical ways of English respectability. Taken to London, she is married to Puff, an aristocratic old cat who never consummates the marriage. Lovesick, Beauty takes up with Brisquet, a dashing young cat from the French embassy. When Puff learns of this, he divorces Beauty and has Brisquet killed by assassins.

138. Beauty's respectable mistress. She is meant to be a human being, and is *almost* one in the illustration. **139.** A young friend of the family asked to sing at an evening entertainment. Human being in text. **140.** Beauty meets Puff, her aristocratic future husband. The portrait on the wall is signed by Grandville. **141.** When Beauty becomes lovesick, the first doctor called in proposes curing her with an enema. **142.** Beauty with her gallant French lover, Brisquet. The paper that has fallen from his pocket reads: "State secrets."

"The Adventures of a Butterfly"
by P.-J. Stahl

A fickle butterfly decides to marry a damsel-fly [a type of dragonfly] but she is unfaithful almost immediately. Flying off into a big city, he is burned up in a gas jet.

143. The marriage of the butterfly and the damsel-fly. The sign reads: "Registry office. Hall of marriages." **144.** Acrobats entertain the guests at the wedding party. **145.** A concert at the wedding party. **146.** An old butterfly. This drawing is inspired by a reflection in the text that it was just as well that the butterfly died young since it is unbecoming to be old and frivolous.

"Animals As Doctors"
by Pierre Bernard

Tired of being treated by veterinarians, the animals learn medicine themselves and almost succeed in killing a dog with a broken paw.

147. The sick dog, attended by a sow, has his case discussed by the diagnosticians: a sloth, a leech, a dugong, a crane, a Spanish fly and others. **148.** In the hospital, the surgeons are a shark and a saw-fish, and the medical students are rats, ravens and vultures. For an earlier portrayal of medical students as ravens, see Fig. B of the Introduction. **149.** A medical student. **150.** A disabled ex-soldier. This is one of Grandville's odd liberties with the text. The story speaks of the sick dog as an "invalid," and the artist has drawn another type of *invalide,* an army pensioner. The building complex in the background is—naturally!—the Hôtel des Invalides in Paris.

"The Animals' Criminal Court"
by Emile de la Bédollière

An open-and-shut case of a wolf killing an ewe and a lamb is handled with near-human inefficiency and slowness.

151. In prison, the wolf reads the *Idylls* of Mme. Deshoulières—which concern sheep! In the most famous of her *Idylls,* the seventeenth-century poetess compared her fatherless children to poor lost sheep. **152.** When the wolf is convicted, broadsheets appear recounting his crime in moralistic platitudes. The bird at the lower right represents the popular versifier inspired by the sensational crime.

"The Bear"
by L. Baude (Louis Baudet)

An intellectual bear seeks solitude in the mountains. He is captured by men and sold to an innkeeper, who then sells him to the British poet Lord B[yron], who happens to pass by during his travels. The bear lives two years in Scotland with Lord B——. When Lord B——, on his way to fight for the freedom of Greece, comes to France with the bear, the latter escapes. Tired of solitude and poetry, the bear becomes a very domestic husband and father.

153. The bear living alone in the mountains. The book says: "The sweetness of solitude." **154.** The bear in the bosom of his family. The fez was part of men's indoor informal dress. **155.** The bear is a good father.

"Handbook for Animals Desirous of Honors"
by Honoré de Balzac

[The word used for "handbook" is *guide-âne,* literally "guide the donkey."] Out for fame and fortune, a country schoolteacher brings his donkey to Paris and camouflages it as a rare zebra. He uses it to uphold a theory of "animal unity" opposed to the teachings of the great taxonomists. As wealth and titles rain down upon him, he compromises with the other side, but the hoax is never revealed. The false zebra is sold to the London zoo, where he lives happily, awaiting immortality as a stuffed specimen in a museum.

156. In the country, the donkey emulates his schoolteacher owner, and teaches classes himself. The dunce cap has human ears. **157.** In Paris, an academician comes to examine the rare animal. Human being in text. In the background is the Institut de France, seat of the Académie Française and the Académie des Sciences. **158.** A disciple of the schoolteacher gives popular lectures on the new theory. This drawing is strongly reminiscent of the print "What a Golden Beak!" in Goya's *Caprichos* (see Fig. G of the Introduction). **159.** The ex-schoolteacher, now an illustrious man of learning and a political power. **160.** "The Museum of Natural History is the Pantheon of animals." The Panthéon in Paris was used as a burial place for great men, like Westminster Abbey in London. The initials of the "sculptor" are Grandville's.

"The Philosophical Rat"
by Edouard Lemoine

A philosophic old rat consoles his gloomy, world-weary young ward. He also brings a pair of human lovers together by eating a document that stood in the way of their marriage.

161. The wise rat thumbs his nose at the world's alarms. Grandville's initials and the date. **162.** The misfortunes of rats: indigent, they are refused aid by the greedy rich. **163.** The resourcefulness of rats: with courage and brains they can escape from traps and cats.

"Journeys of a Parisian Sparrow to Find the Best Form of Government"
by George Sand [actually by Balzac]

[The sparrow represents the lively and saucy working-class Parisian.] The sparrow visits the island of the ants [England], an imperialistic oligarchy; the land of the bees, a divine-right monarchy; and, in the Russian steppes, the egalitarian republic of the wolves, who subsist on rapine.

164. The island of the ants [satire on England]. Details: St. Paul's Cathedral, a judge in robes and wig, a crate of opium, a sack with Grandville's initials. **165.** Fraternity among the wolves. The costumes allude to the Revolution of 1789 and, indeed, the drawing is strongly reminiscent of actual Revolution-period prints with wolves and sheep as characters (see Fig. H of the Introduction). The banner reads: "The rights of wolf. Section of rabid enthusiasts."

"A Trapped Fox"
by Charles Nodier

A fox tells the writer of the story that he is deeply in love with a hen, although she prefers her barnyard rooster. The fox, when young, had received lessons in morality from a kindly old dog who forgave him for stealing grapes on his property. Later, as a member of a raiding party of foxes, the fox fell in love with, and saved the life of, the hen—but she continues to disdain him. Finally the hen is slaughtered by a human being for food, and the loyal fox, trying to save her, is trapped and killed. The writer suspects, however, the the fox really wanted all along to make a meal of her himself.

166 & 167. Fisher folk. **168.** A butterfly hunter. These are not characters in the story; the pastimes of fishing and butterfly hunting are merely mentioned in passing. **169.** The young fox hauled before the dog-landowner for stealing grapes. **170.** The foxes of the raiding party eat soft-boiled eggs while the mother hen weeps. **171.** The fox fruitlessly seeks the hen's affections.

"Pistol's First Drama Review"
by Jules Janin

Pistol, the dog of a drama critic [Janin], reviews a performance of trained animals [satire on a "modern" Romantic play]. Relinquishing his active life for that of a reviewer, he dies of boredom.

172. The third-rate musicians who perform the incidental music for straight plays. On the sheet music: "Score." The ducks emerging from the bell of one instrument stand for sour notes (*canards* in French). **173.** A group of actors in repose. **174.** The hero of the play in his brief moment of grandeur. **175.** Birds and snakes in the audience hissing and whistling at the villain. In France, whistling is a sign of audience disapproval. The parrot and snake in the front row are using the hollow stems of their keys as whistles. **176.** The climax of the play: the noble heroine still loves the hero even when he is disheveled and grimy. The music on the stand consists of "animated notation" of the type Grandville had drawn for the periodical *Le Magasin pittoresque*.

"Memories of an Old Crow"
by P.-J. Stahl

A widowed crow decides to spend her life traveling and writing accounts of her travels. She visits an old château that has been partially altered by a parvenu banker. Haughty arriviste owls live on the terraces of the new wing; a poor but noble old falcon, together with some lizards and other animals, lives in the crumbling old section. The female owl runs off with a lover, and her husband dies soon after. Later the banker has the old wing destroyed and the residents perish. But the crow has already moved on to Paris, where she finds repose and happiness with an old male crow, an admirer of hers from the days of their youth.

177. The crow's husband dies at the cathedral of Strasbourg. **178.** The crow sets down her travel experiences. **179.** The falcon who lives in the unrepaired part of the château. His costume is *ancien régime*, indicating both loyalty to pre-Revolution mores and inability to buy newer clothes. **180.** A neighbor and protégé of the falcon—a field mouse occupied with burrowing. **181.** Petty modern hunters (in contrast with the falcon's memories of grand hunts). **182.** A banker. The drawing probably refers to the human banker who bought the château. **183.** The lizards who lived in the old wing of the château. **184.** The ridiculous female owl who lived in the altered wing of the château. **185.** After his wife has run off, the male owl consults a fortune-telling carp for advice and witnesses this scene of divination.

"Journey of an African Lion to Paris"
by Honoré de Balzac

An African lion is curious to see what Parisian lions are like [the term *lion* (feminine, *lionne*), borrowed from English, was the one then used in French to indicate wealthy dandies]. He is able to roam about Paris quite freely (guided by an officious dog) since it is Carnival time and he is thought to be in costume.

186. The dog who shows the lion around Paris. **187.** A café scene. The café depicted is like the famous Tortoni's that stood on the Boulevard des Italiens. The sign reads: "Ices and sherbets." **188.** A lion (dandy) of Paris with his young page. These young servants were then known as tigers, an appellation not lost on Grandville, who added stripes to the boy's coat for good measure. The sign on the advertising pillar reads "Lion's Pommade." **189.** A *lionne* of Paris. **190.** A scene at a Carnival ball. **191.** "Animal passions break out in man." In the text, this phrase refers to Carnival time, but the artist gives it a different slant by depicting a monkey dressed as a sans-culotte of the Revolutionary period.

"To the Reader"
by P.-J. Stahl (closing of Volume I)

More fine stories and drawings are promised to the animal readers by the animal editors of the book.

192. "Goodnight, then, dear reader. Go home, lock your cage well, sleep tight and have pleasant dreams. Until tomorrow."

193. Part title to Volume II. **194.** Second part title. See the text synopsis immediately following for the events depicted. Sign on the gallows: "A quarter hour of public exposure." On the lamppost: "Animal justice." On the billboard: "Notice," "Petition of the flies," "Proclamation: Animals!" On the paste-pot: "Stronger and stronger paste."

"Another Revolution"
by P.-J. Stahl

Dissatisfaction leads to a revolt of the animals against the monkey, parrot and rooster who edited the first volume. The fox takes advantage of the general turmoil to make himself the powerful sole editor. The former editors are condemned to be hanged (though the parrot and the monkey contrive to find substitute victims for themselves). A new billposter promises to use better paste.

195. Frame illustration for the first page of text: the fox becomes sole editor. **196–200.** Assorted activities during the animal revolution. 196: Animals faithful to the old editors on the lookout for trouble. 197: A beetle reading the paper issued by the old editors during the troubles. 198: The seditious gnats having indulged in oratory about sacrificing their heads, the vulture examines the value of such heads. 199: The Hercules beetle, leader of the rebellious insect forces. 200: Law-abiding people who stay home and mind their business. Combinations of bats and owls were frequently used in allegorical art to represent ignorance, obscurantism and reaction; compare Goya's *Caprichos*. **201.** The bison speaks out at a meeting of the rebels.

202. Another fiery orator demanding speedy action. The text states that a hyena is making this speech, but the animal portrayed is a caracal (a type of lynx); the head here is very similar to that in the scientific rendering of this animal (not drawn by Grandville) in Boitard's *Jardin des Plantes* (see comment to No. 55, in *Un Autre Monde*). Elsewhere Grandville has drawn a hyena very accurately, so this instance of animal substitution cannot be taken as an error on his part. **203.** During the revolt, walls are covered with political manifestos. The dog is dressed like a laborer. **204.** A loyal guardian of the old regime on sentry duty. **205.** The heavy infantry of the rebellious insects. **206.** Animals bringing complaints to the old editors. Sign on the wall: "Bureau of complaints, demands, petitions, etc." The donkey's paper: "Complaints. We, the undersigned subscribers, ..." The parrot's paper: "The editors' replies. Gentlemen . . . ." Papers on the floor at the lower right: "Threats," "Complaints" and the signature of the wood engraver, Tamisier. **207.** At the rebels' victory banquet, the showy hoopoe acts as steward. **208.** A gallant gentleman toasts the fair sex. **209.** After the fox is in power, the animals continue to draw up many petitions, which are systematically ignored.

"Memorable Journeyings of Old Man Toad"
by Louis François L'Héritier de l'Ain

While lying in wait outside a beehive, the toad hears the queen tell the story of a marmot of Savoy [these rodents were trained and exhibited on the street by little Savoyard ragamuffins in French cities]. The marmot is captured and forced to join a traveling troupe. Her sad adventures in Paris include incarceration in both the zoo and a dog pound. When she manages to arrive home, the old rural ways no longer suit her and she dies of chagrin.

210. The hedgehog, a disagreeable neighbor of the toad. **211.** The marmot family preparing to hibernate. **212.** A performing tortoise in the marmot's troupe. **213.** The brutal director of the troupe. Human being in text. **214.** A mother kangaroo in the zoo. **215.** The marmot dreams that she is an independent exhibitor, owner of performing junebugs. **216.** The dog pound. The violin on the wall is a verbal-visual pun on *violon*, used as a slang word for "jail." **217.** A female greyhound who got lost and was impounded. **218.** A bee-nursemaid in the hive giving her charges bread and honey. **219.** The kingfisher, a rival of the toad as a consumer of bees.

"Sufferings of a Click-Beetle"
by Paul de Musset

A young click-beetle is told by a capricorn-beetle sorcerer that he will suffer all his life from seeing through social façades too clearly. A man-about-town junebug introduces him to the life of salons, to musicians, painters and females of doubtful virtue, but the click-beetle prefers the down-to-earth company of ladybugs.

220. The capricorn beetle casting the click-beetle's horoscope. **221.** The elegantly narrow-waisted wasps one meets in society. **222.** A grand concert, with a virtuoso pianist. On the piano score: "Eternal variations on the air . . . ." **223.** A painting of the animalcules that live in a drop of water. Reminiscent of William Heath's print (c. 1828), "Monster Soup Commonly Called Thames Water." **224.** A painted-lady butterfly, a potential danger to young insects.

"Topaz the Portrait Painter"
by Louis Viardot
A Brazilian monkey, pet of a Parisian painter, is convinced of his own great talent and goes to art school, but to no avail. When the daguerreotype is invented, he learns to take pictures and sets up shop in his native jungle. There he is partially successful until a dissatisfied elephant smashes his equipment.

> **225.** Topaz on his way to an art lesson. **226.** Topaz retouches a daguerreotype in his studio, to a chorus of comments by gawkers. **227.** Topaz taking a picture. His assistant, Sapajou, is preparing a plate. The subject of the portrait is fastened to keep him still during the rather long exposure time required. The sign reads: "2 seconds of public exposure" (joking allusion to the exposure of criminals; see No. 194). Topaz's abandoned palette, brushes and maulstick are tied to a bough. **228.** Pictures of Topaz's customers. The labels read: "1 second in the shade," "⅓ second," "¼ second," "In dusk, 1/11 minute," "In moonlight, 1/12 minute," "Topaz and Sapajou, Monkerreotypists. Licensed, pensioned, patented. Tricksters Square, Dusky Avenue (New France)." *Nouvelle-France* was actually the name for France's former North American colonies; perhaps the reference is to French Guiana, once called *France équinoxiale.*

"Heartaches of a French Cat"
by P.-J. Stahl
One of two poor sister cats leaves home to better her condition and becomes a worldling, addicted to vanity. But her husband—none other than the scalaway Brisquet, whose death in England (see "Heartaches of an English Cat") was merely a rumor originated by him to regain his amorous liberty—deserts her for an exotic Chinese cat. She returns to live with her sister, now happily married. Never again does she pay heed to suitors.

> **229.** The poor mistress of the two sister cats, who lives by sewing. Human being in text. **230.** The heroine pays more attention to her evil genius, who promises wealth, than to her guardian angel. **231.** After her adventures, she turns a deaf ear to toms who come courting. **232.** The Chinese beauty.

"Letters from a Swallow"
by Marie Mennessier-Nodier
A swallow with literary aspirations sets out to see the world and, after many unsatisfactory relationships with various birds, returns to Paris sadder and wiser.

> **233.** The swallow meets a nightingale tenor who advises her to live for pleasure. The song is called "By a brilliant chirping." **234.** The problems of an authoress mother. On the box: "Kitchen salt." **235.** Tragedy in a robin family: a fledgling falls from the nest while a bird of prey is near. **236.** A shrike, stepmother of two warblers, makes their life miserable. The open book contains the notes of the scale. On the eggshell: "Vinegar."

"The Seventh Heaven"
by P.-J. Stahl
A German turtledove, orphaned at an early age, goes mad from disappointed love; his sweetheart dove, tired of waiting for his return from a journey, has married another. He spends his days in reverie and writes poetry, finally dying in an asylum. Then his sweetheart, whose existence is no longer necessary to her grown children, follows him in death. In his last literary work, the turtledove had recounted a dream in which he died and found his loved one in the seventh heaven.

> **237.** The moment of the turtledove's passing, as recounted in his poem. A bird of prey represents Death. This drawing and No. 240, two of Grandville's best (and most mystical), have given rise to extensive psychoanalytical interpretations. **238.** The turtledove loses his parents while still very young. **239.** His sweetheart, now mother of a numerous brood. **240.** The turtledove becomes a solitary dreamer. **241.** Vision of the lovers' souls reunited in the seventh heaven.

"The Love of Two Creatures"
by Honoré de Balzac
[This story is a conscious imitation of the numerous tales by E. T. A. Hoffmann in which everyday events are echoed by events on another plane of existence.] A professor of the Jardin des Plantes is striving to mate a male scale insect imported from Mexico; if the experiment is successful, cochineal (red dyestuff made from the insects) could be produced in French Algeria. While the insect refuses all mates, so does the professor's ambitious young assistant remain cool to the love of the professor's daughter. Finally the insect finds an ideal mate—but the now-famous young scientist marries an ugly heiress!

> **242.** The professor with a paper container of scale insects which he will place on a cactus (they will colonize it as parasites). **243.** The male cochineal insect rejecting the advances of imperfect mates. **244.** A volvox epidemic strikes the near-microscopic world of the scale insects. Volvox is a sort of plant-animal link, a protozoon that contains chlorophyll. **245.** Guards encircle the ideal mate, who is still in the larval stage. **246.** A strange insect called the "misocamp," fond of eating scale insects. Grandville liked this insect character of his, which reappears in several of the drawings in this book. **247.** The courtship of the scale insects. **248.** The ugly and silly heiress whom the young man marries. Human being in text.

"Life and Philosophic Opinions of an Auk"
by P.-J. Stahl

An auk travels to many lands in quest of happiness, but never finds it. One of the places he visits is called Happy Island, but the inhabitants are selfish and lazy, not really happy [satire on a Fourierist phalanstery—see note to No. 106].

249. On Happy Island, all children are reared communally—by serpents and other dangerous animals. On the bucket: "Watered-down milk." **250.** A study hall on Happy Island. Sign: "French divans."

"A Letter from the Giraffe of the Jardin des Plantes"
by Charles Nodier

The giraffe gives its (satirical) impressions of human beings. [The giraffe of the Jardin des Plantes came as a gift from Mohammed Ali, ruler of Egypt, in 1827, and was still alive when *Les Animaux* appeared. The animal created a tremendous sensation when it first arrived, and remained one of the sights of Paris.]

251. The giraffe of the Jardin des Plantes. The cow in the background probably represents the two cows that originally came to Paris with the giraffe and nursed it. **252.** In her letter, the giraffe mistakes the monkey house in the zoo for the Chamber of Deputies in session. On the urn: "Secret ballot." **253.** Two modern lovers in the zoo. Human beings in text—a young man with a bison's beard and a girl with gazelle's eyes. They express their love in fashionable metaphysical terminology.

"Story of a White Blackbird"
by Alfred de Musset

[In French, "a white blackbird" (*un merle blanc*) is an expression denoting a great rarity.] A young blackbird is driven from the nest by his father for being white and whistling incorrectly. The young bird wonders what species he really belongs to. He flies with a messenger pigeon for a while, but faints from exhaustion. A socialite magpie, accompanied by a tempting dove, tells him he is an all-white Russian magpie, but when he whistles, the other two birds fly away. Then he meets a cockatoo-poet, who is too egoistic to pay him any mind. Next he spends a night in the woods with an assortment of birds, none of whom claim kinship with him. Hearing a human being use the expression *merle blanc*, he realizes his worth and becomes insufferably proud. He composes a vast autobiographical epic that makes him famous, and receives a marriage proposal from an English blackbird who claims to be white also. After their marriage he learns that she has been whitening herself artificially, and he leaves her. In the solitude of the forest, he expresses his jealousy of the seemingly happy nightingale, who confides in him that he himself is hopelessly in love with the rose, and the rose dallies only with insects.

254. As his mother weeps, the young white blackbird is disowned by his father. **255.** The magpie and the dove come to the aid of the exhausted white blackbird. **256.** The cockatoo-poet. His costume is that of a member of the Académie Française. On his papers: "The King of the Cockatoos, disorderly drama," "Melodrama, archidrama," "Crested [i.e., dandified] odes," "Poems without rhymes," "The Shadows, fugitive poems." **257.** An unfriendly old dove, one of the birds encountered in the woods by the white blackbird. **258.** The blackbird discovers his wife's cosmetic secrets. **259.** The nightingale and the rose.

"Funeral Oration for a Silkworm"
by P.-J. Stahl

The funeral of a silkworm is recounted.

260. The death's-head moth gives the signal for the procession to begin. **261.** The silkworm's funeral procession. **262.** A silk mill. **263.** The praying mantis tells the insects: "To die is to be reborn into a better life."

Last Chapter
by P.-J. Stahl

Learning of the animals' various rebellions, the zookeepers manage to lock them all up again. The human beings responsible for the book are also placed in the zoo by the police—except for Grandville and Stahl. The latter cannot be found [because he is merely an alias of the publisher, Hetzel].

264. Animals from distant countries arriving too late to join in the rebellion. **265.** Another latecomer. **266.** [Drawing by Français.] Grandville sketching Hetzel, Balzac and Janin, who are locked up in the zoo, along with other contributing writers. Above the heads of the trio: "It is forbidden to throw anything into the cages." On the fence: "No smoking" and "Donated by the Prince de Joinville [a son of King Louis-Philippe]." François-Louis Français (1814–1897), who did illustrations for several books around this time, became an important landscape painter.

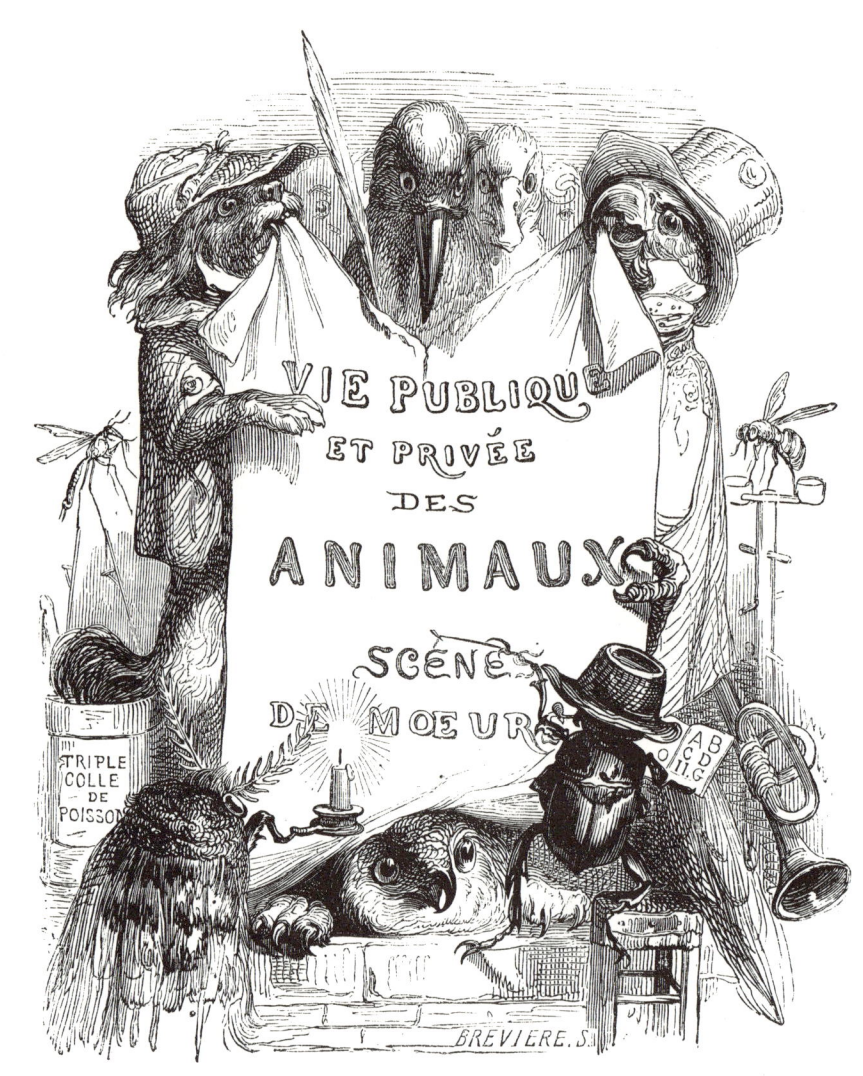

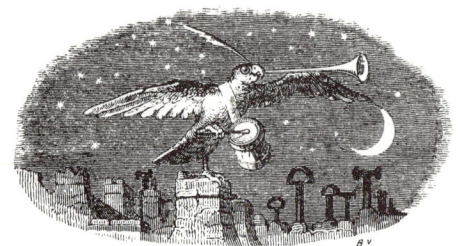

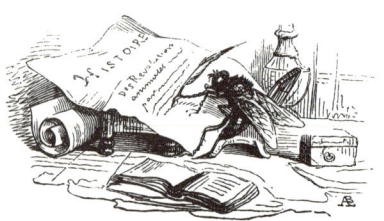

119. Part title to Volume I (from the 1866 edition). **120.** The parrot, who kept the minutes of the animals' assembly, proclaims his secrets from the housetops. **121.** A fly writes the "History of Animal Revolutions."

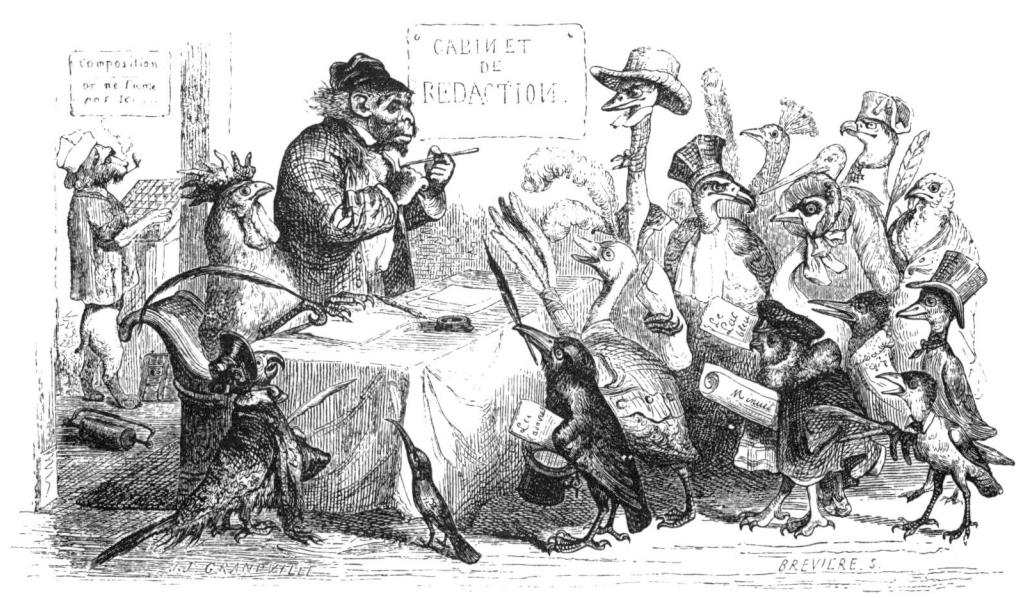

PROLOGUE.

ASSEMBLÉE GÉNÉRALE DES ANIMAUX.

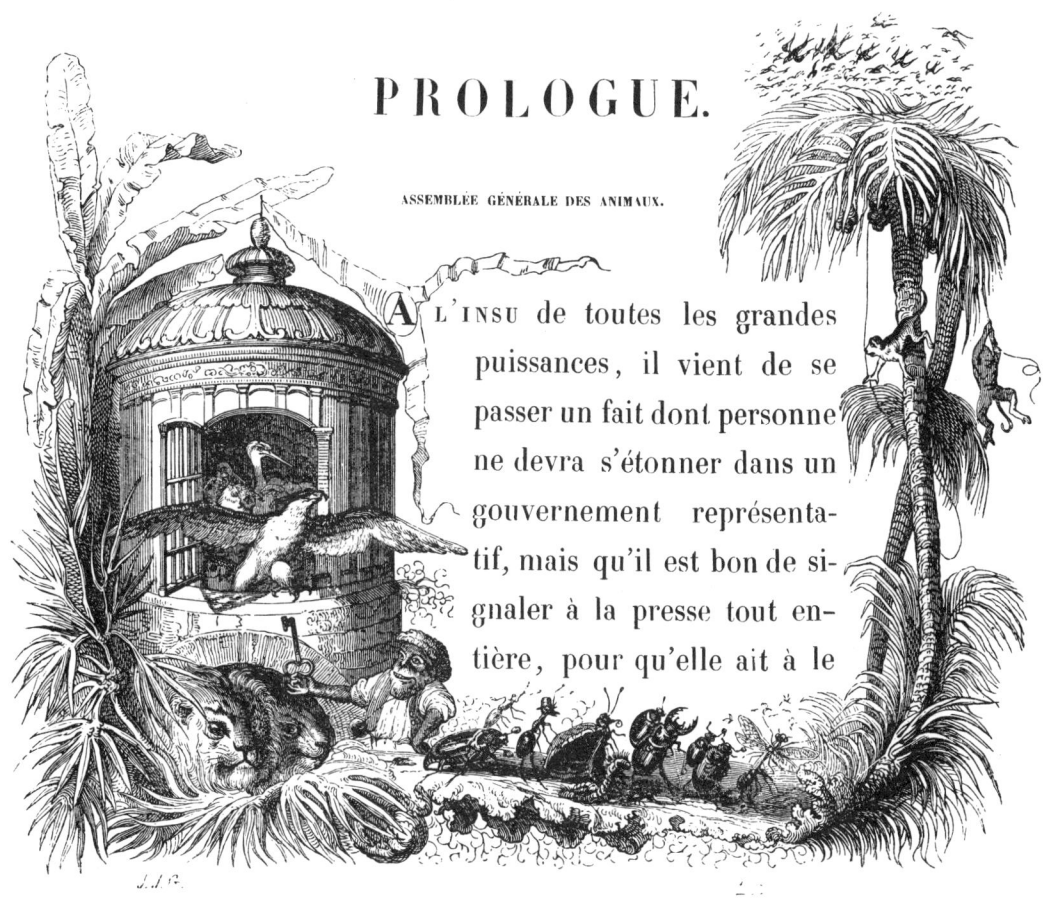

A L'INSU de toutes les grandes puissances, il vient de se passer un fait dont personne ne devra s'étonner dans un gouvernement représentatif, mais qu'il est bon de signaler à la presse tout entière, pour qu'elle ait à le

122. Headpiece to the Prologue: the monkey, as editor-in-chief, receiving manuscripts from the animals. **123.** Frame illustration for the first page of the Prologue: the monkey-locksmith frees the animals from their cages for the secret meeting.

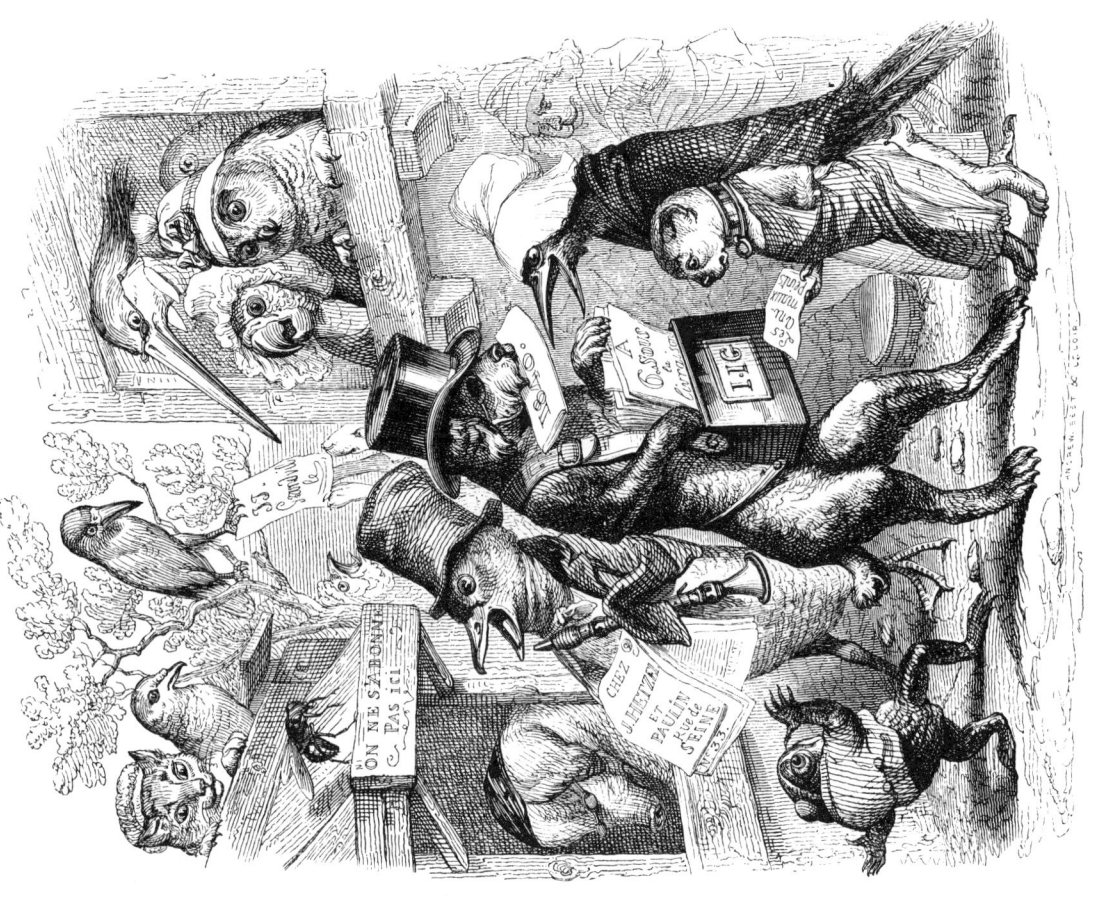

125. The first installment of the animals' book is sold by street hawkers.

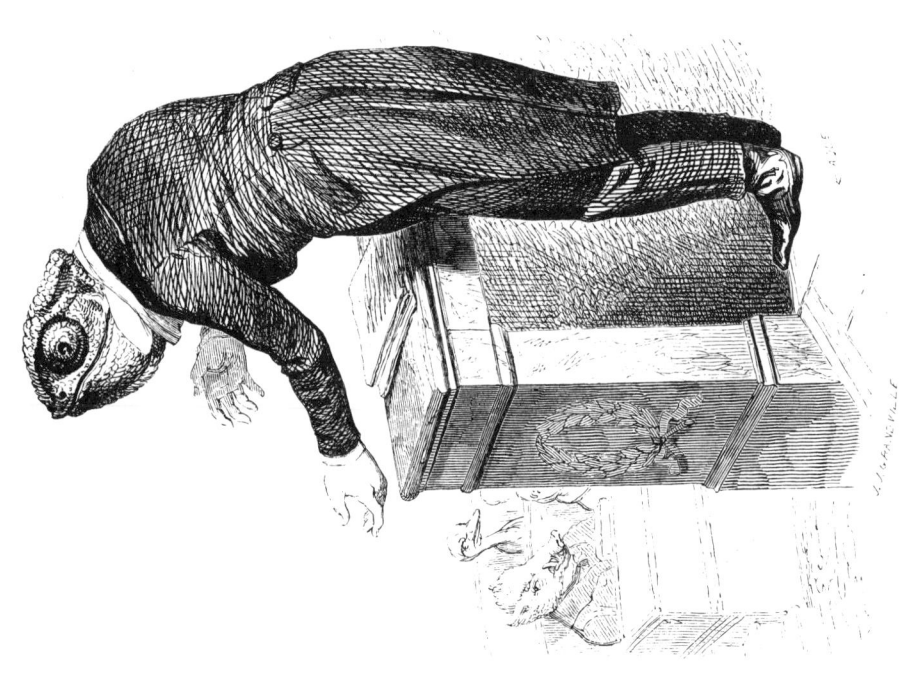

124. At the assembly the chameleon assures the animals that he agrees with each one of them.

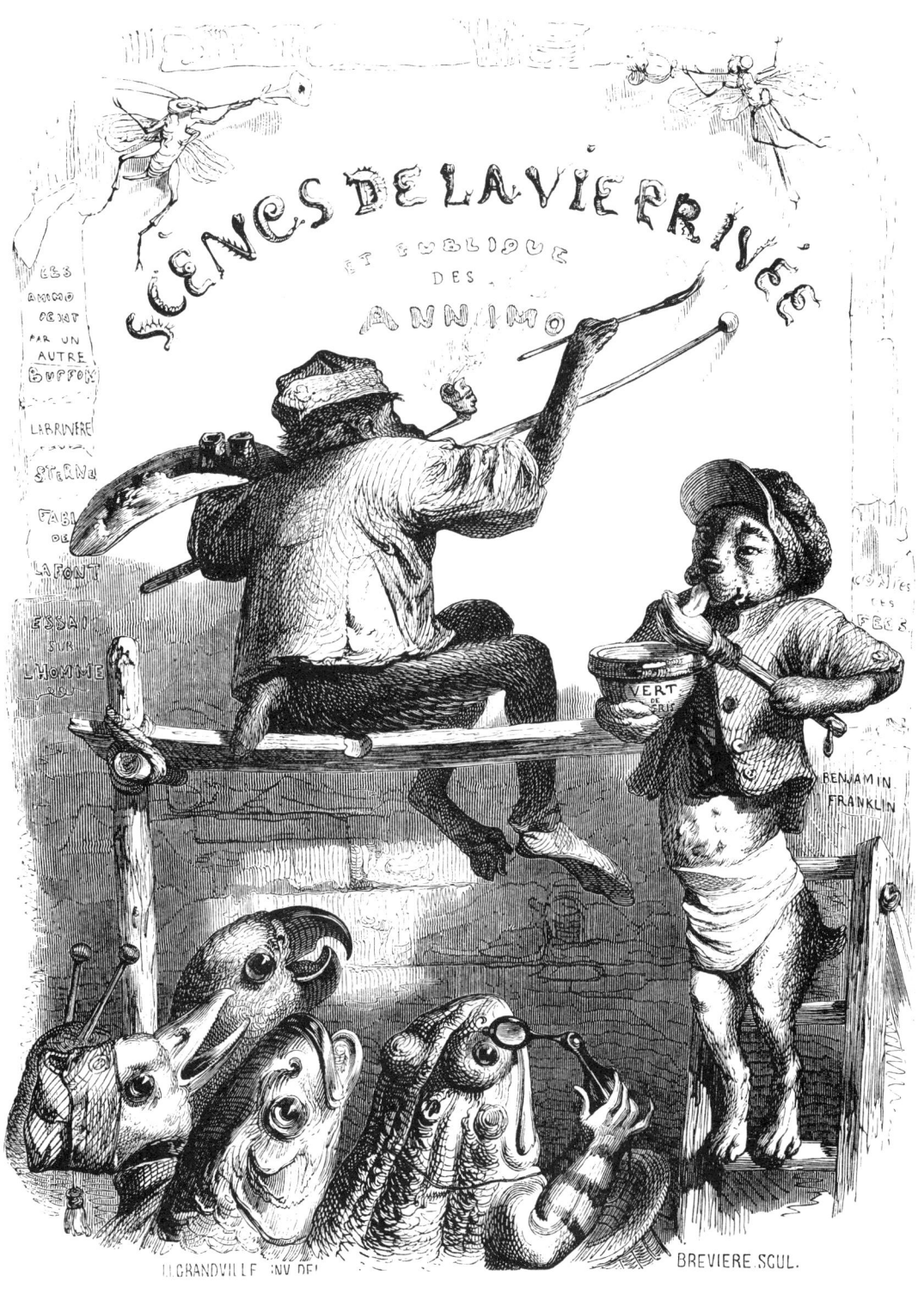

126. Second part title to Volume I. Animal sign-painters and bill-posters. Note the spelling "Annimo." Down the sides of the sign are names of other books, some of which had already been illustrated by Grandville (La Bruyère, La Fontaine).

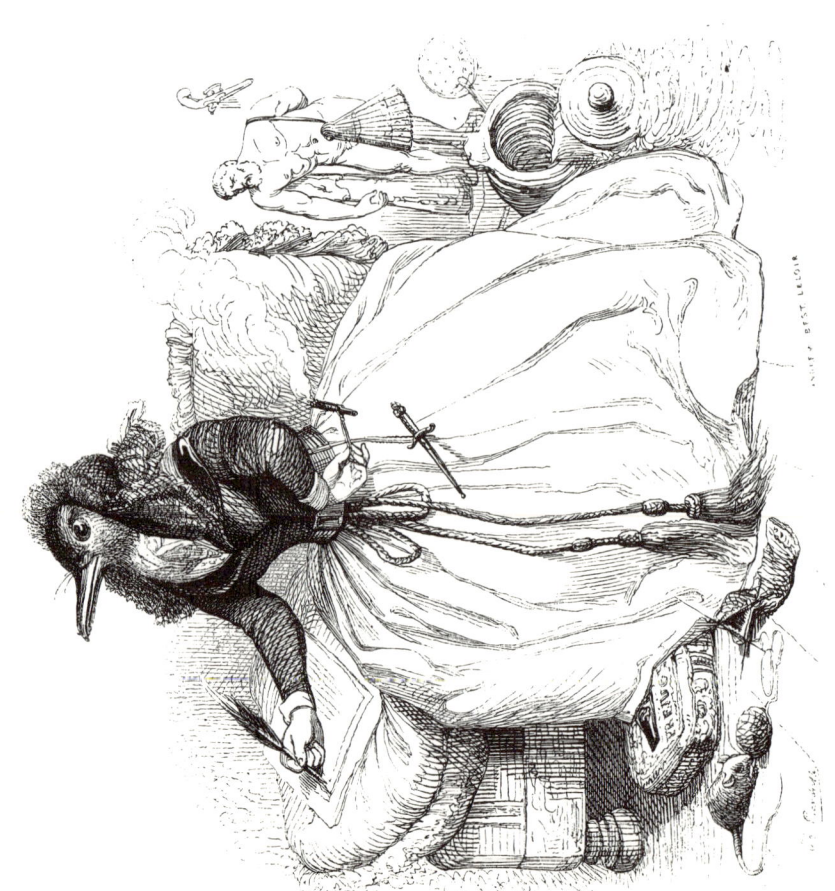

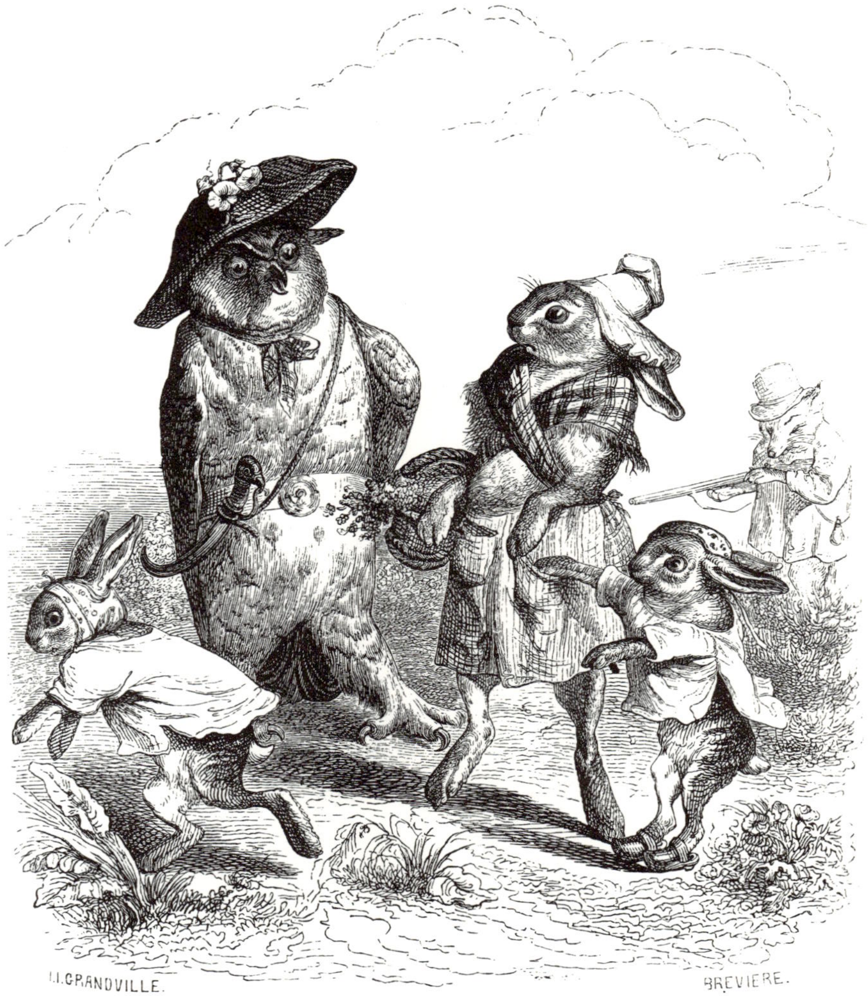

128. An evil owl blocking the way of two young hares and their sister.

127. The magpie, who wrote the hare's story from his dictation.

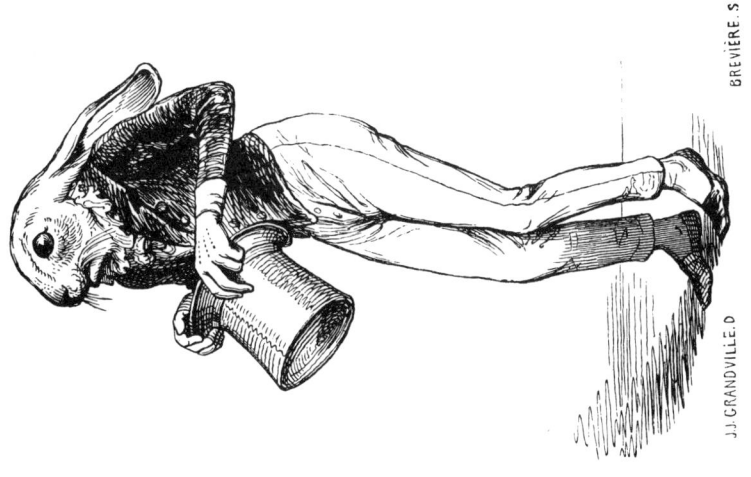

130. The son of the new master, "like his father in every way."

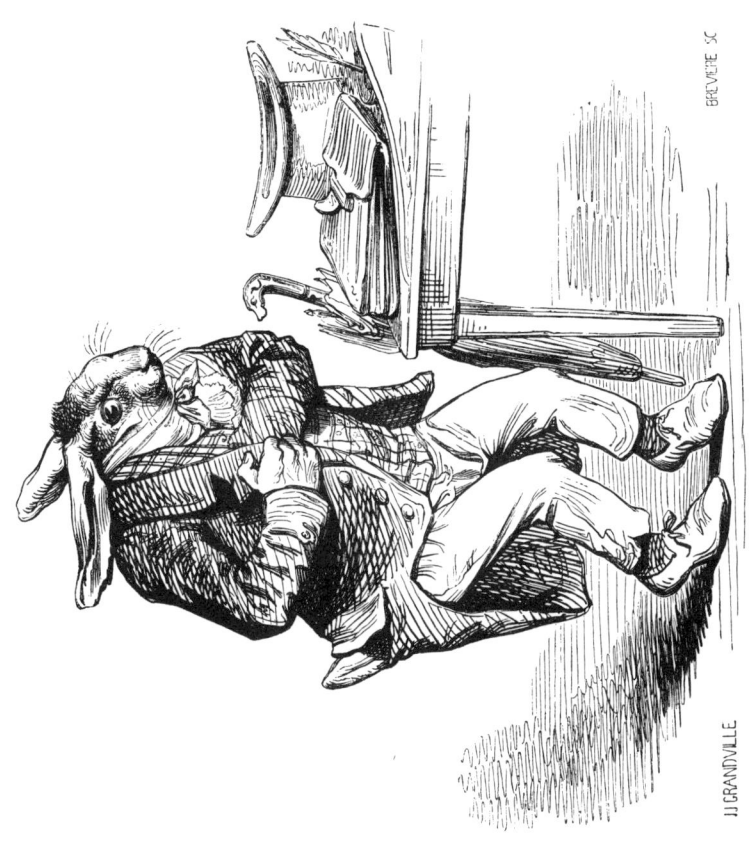

129. The hare's new master, the timorous government clerk.

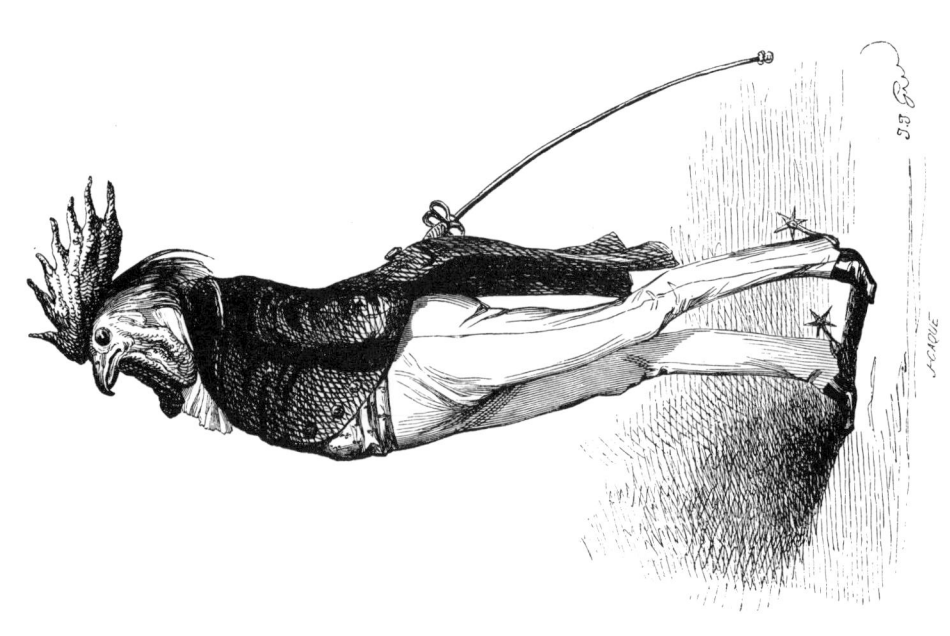

132. The pugnacious rooster who insists on fighting a duel with the hare.

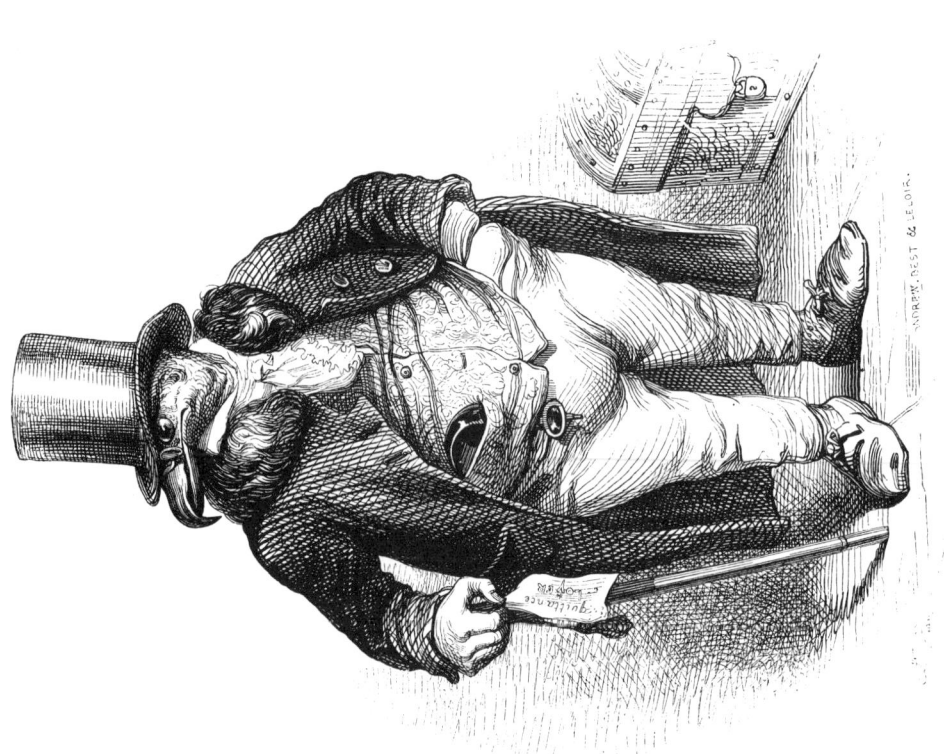

131. Mister Vulture, the hard-hearted landlord of the government clerk.

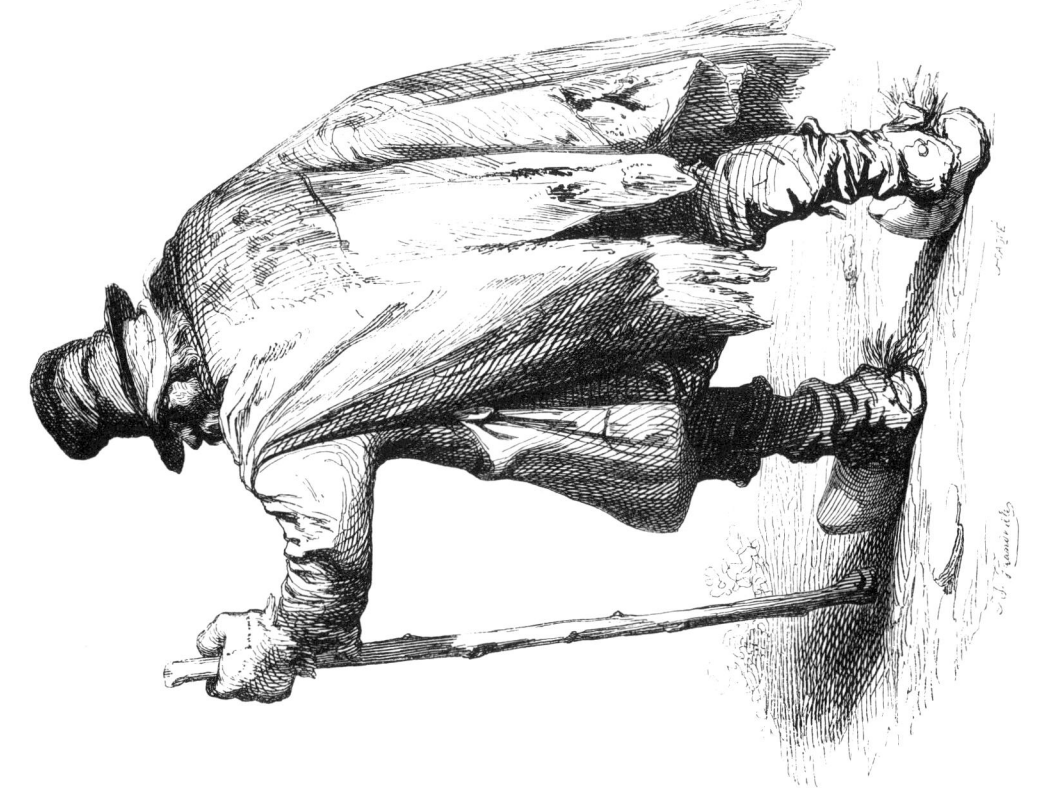

134. "There are men who walk as beggars over the fertile earth."

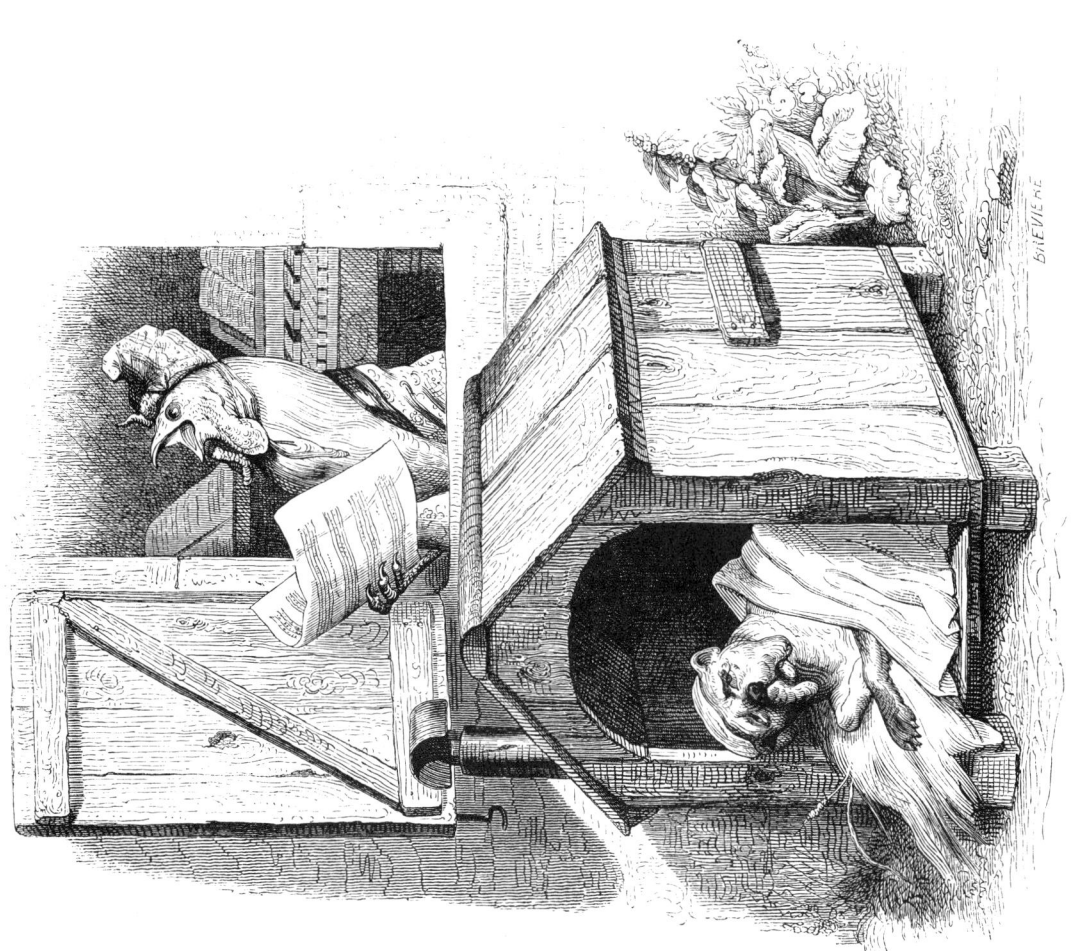

133. The rooster awakening the bulldog.

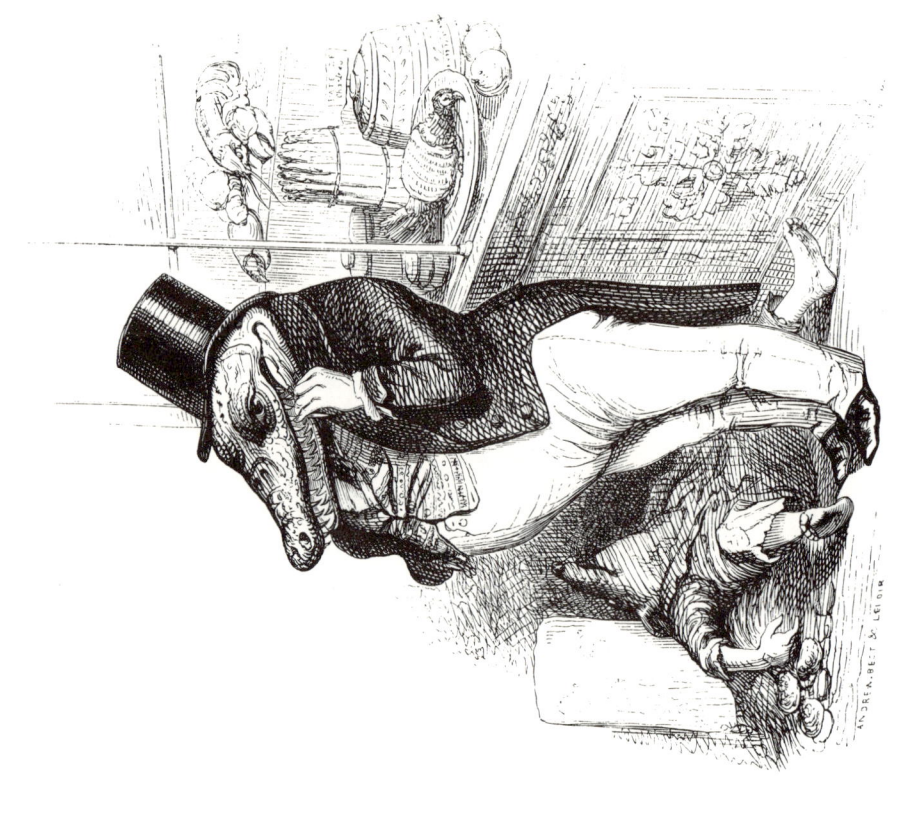

136. The crocodile's gluttonous owner.

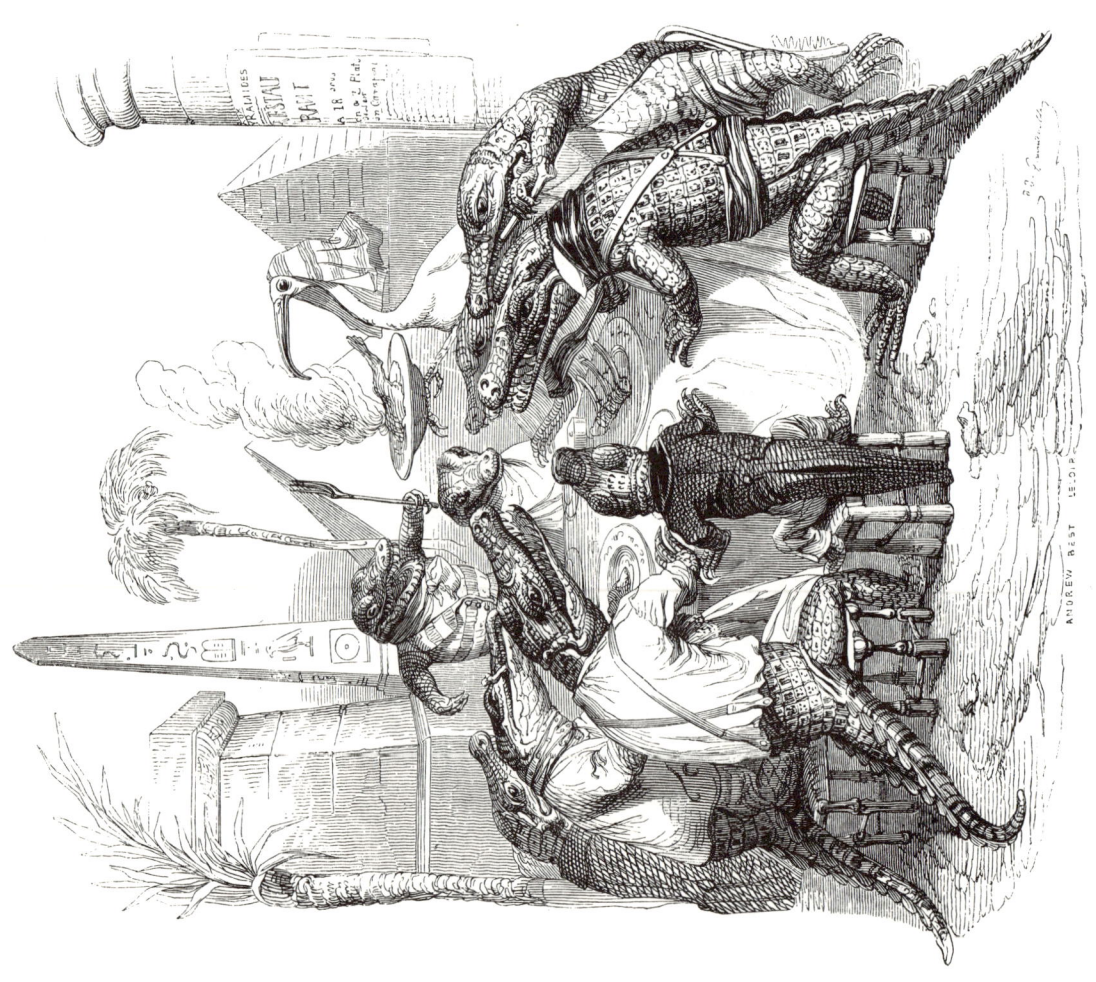

135. Convivial crocodiles at a banquet.

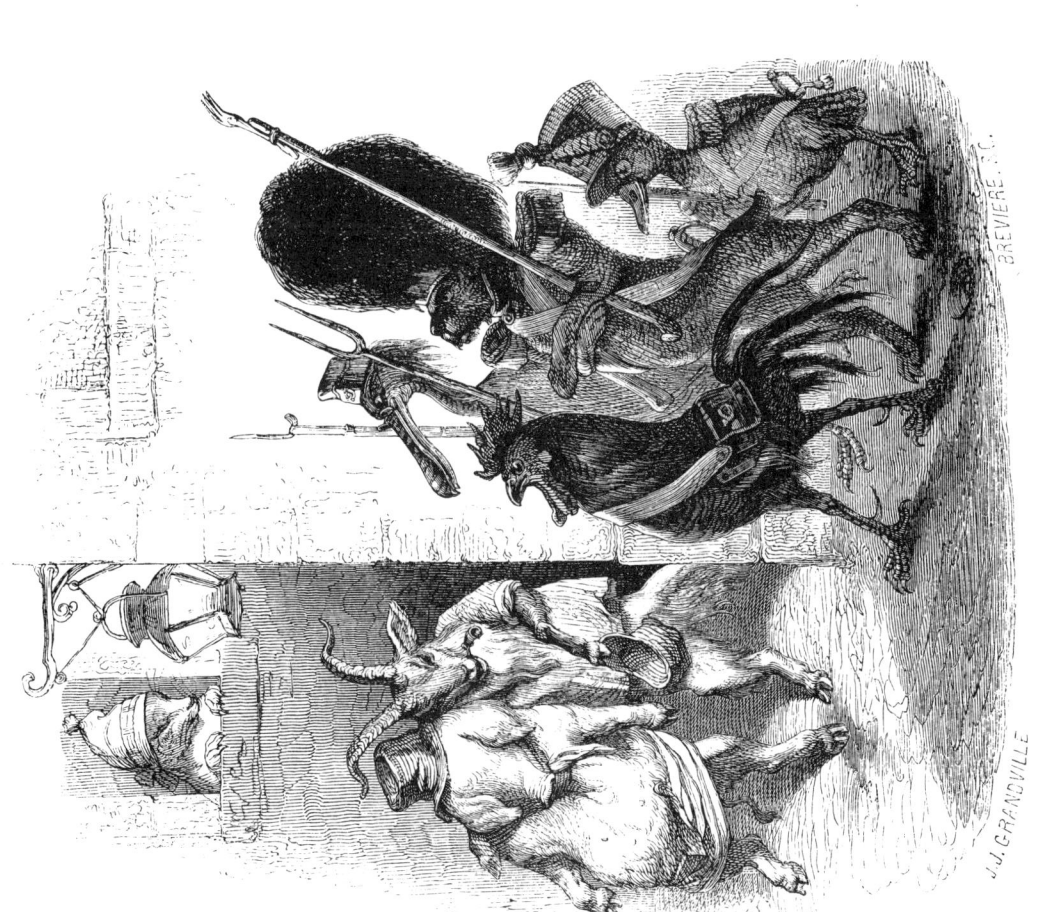

138. Beauty's respectable mistress.

137. A patrol of the National Guard looking askance at revelers leaving a low-class drinking establishment.

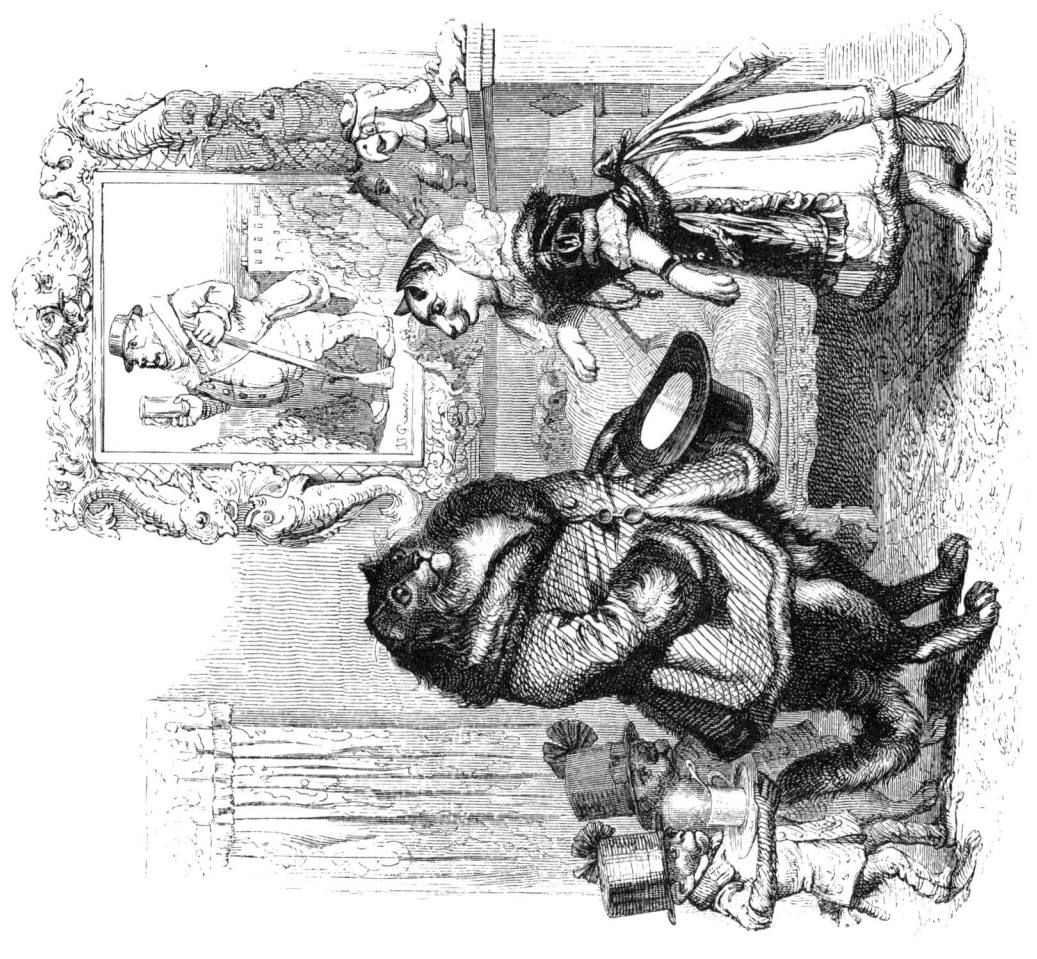

140. Beauty meets Puff, her aristocratic future husband.

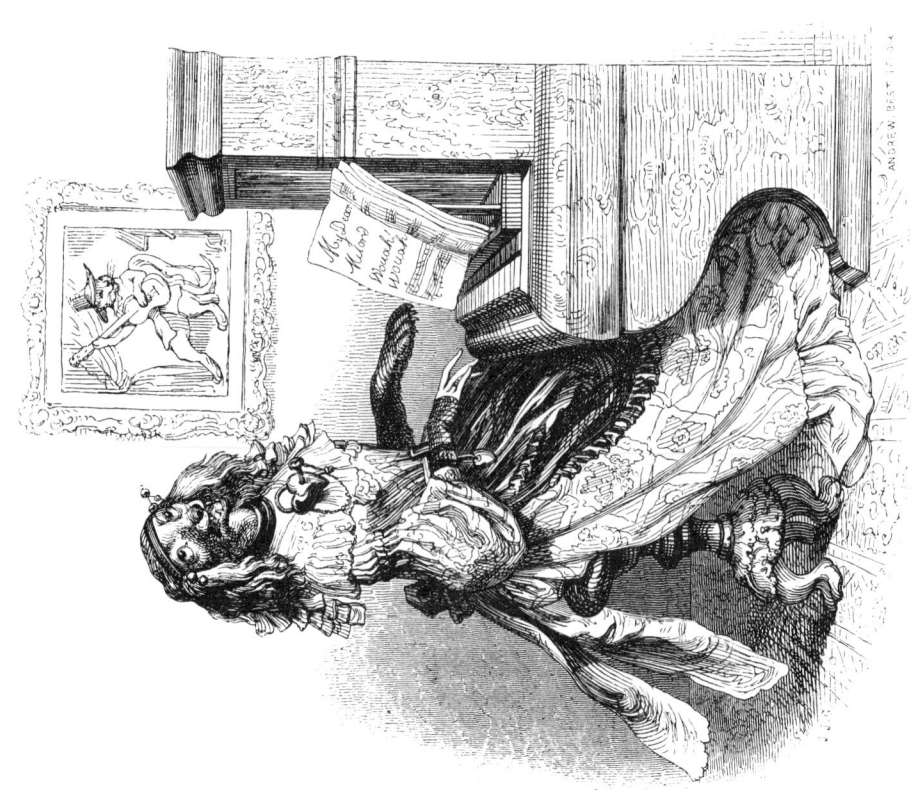

139. A young friend of the family asked to sing at an evening entertainment.

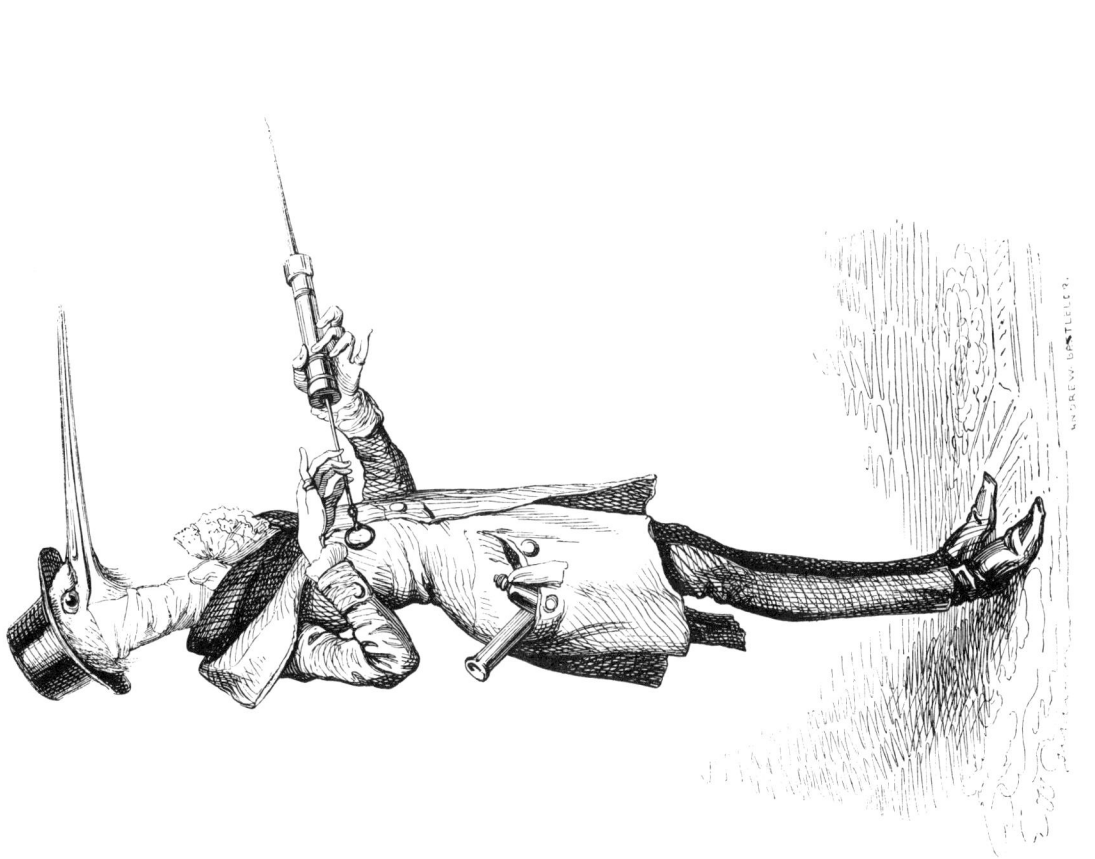

141. When Beauty becomes lovesick, the first doctor called in proposes curing her with an enema.

142. Beauty with her gallant French lover, Brisquet.

Les Animaux 103

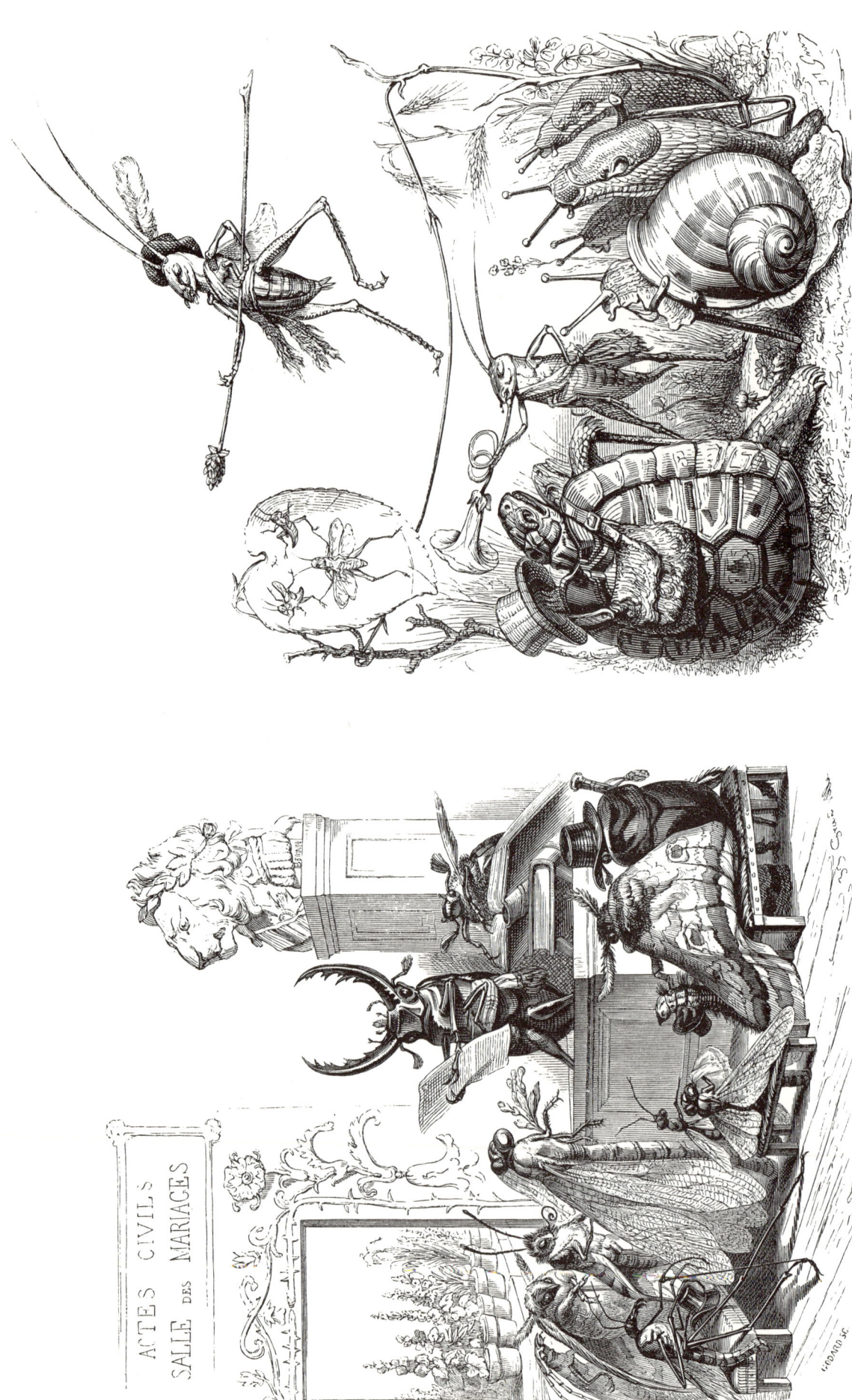

144. Acrobats entertain the guests at the wedding party.

143. The marriage of the butterfly and the damsel-fly.

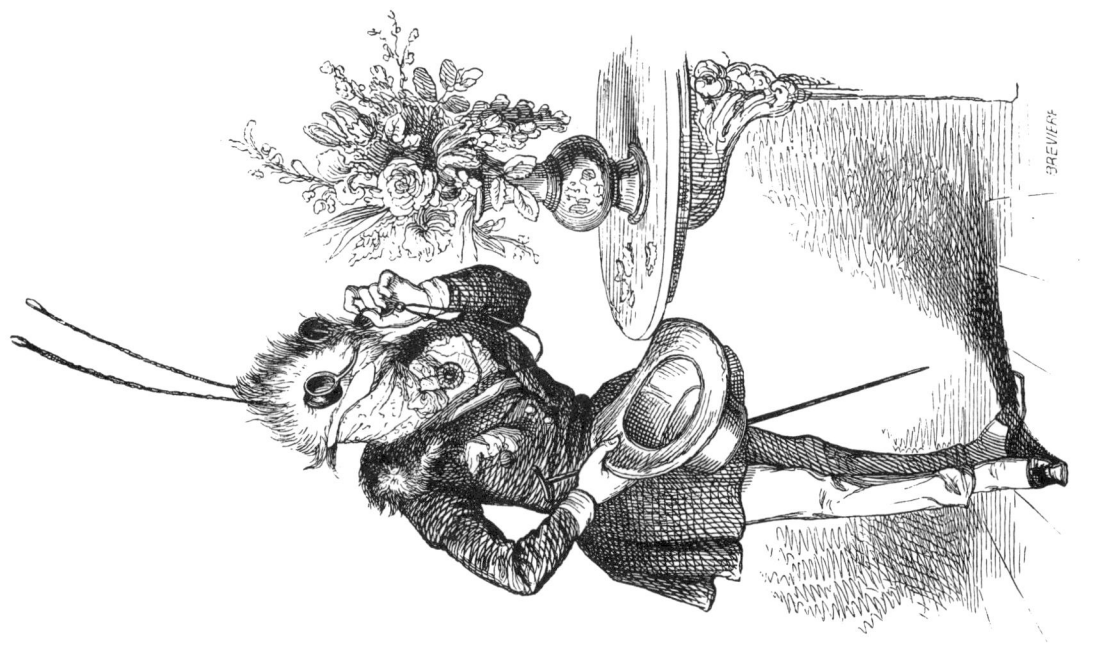

146. An old butterfly.

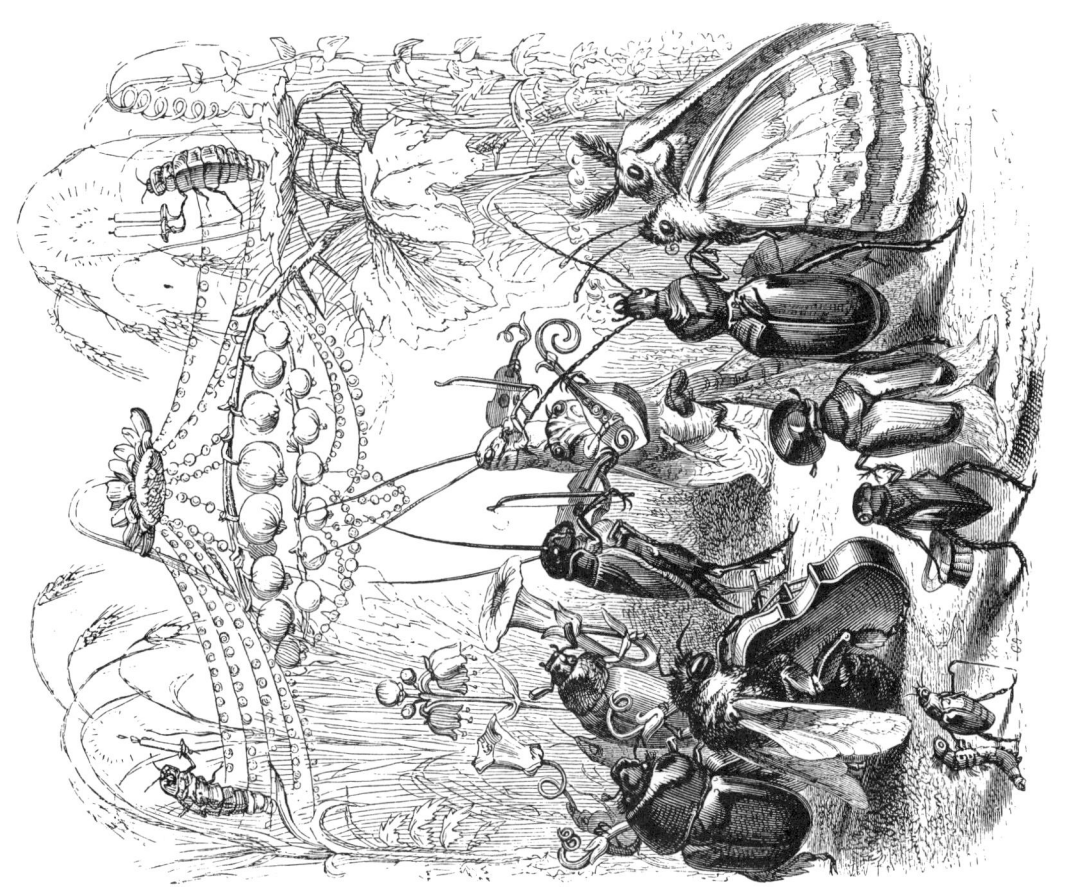

145. A concert at the wedding party.

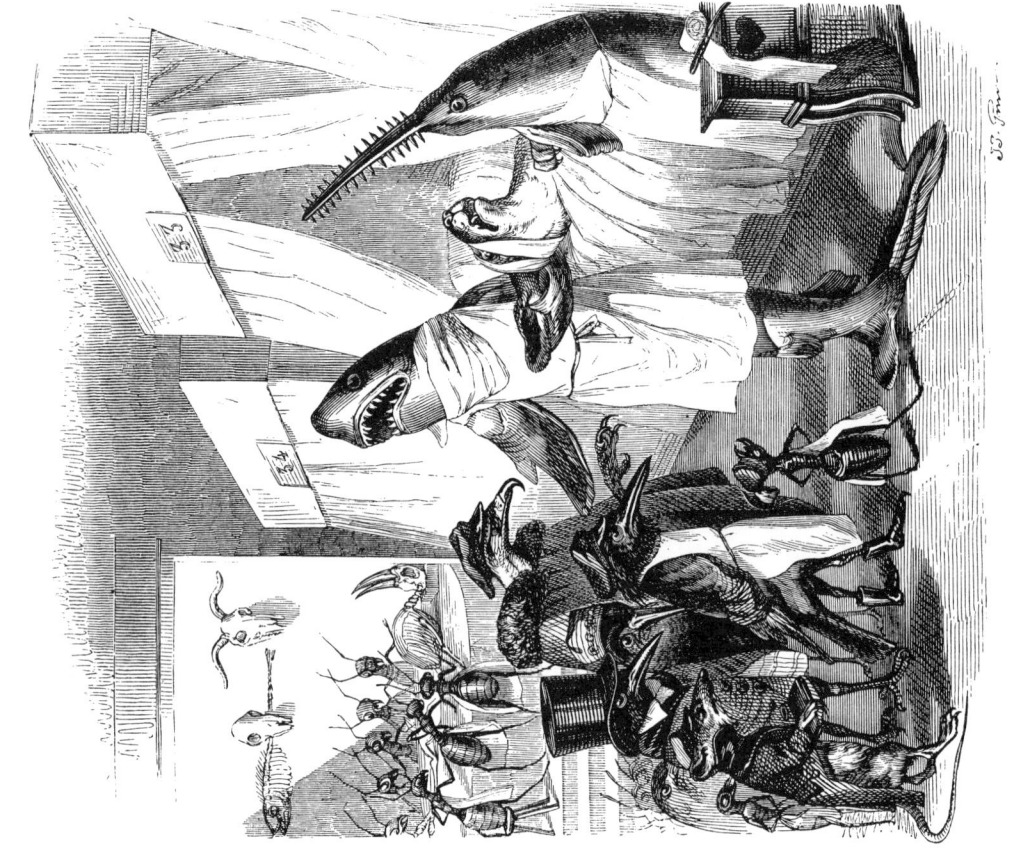

148. In the hospital, the surgeons are a shark and a sawfish, and the medical students are rats, ravens and vultures.

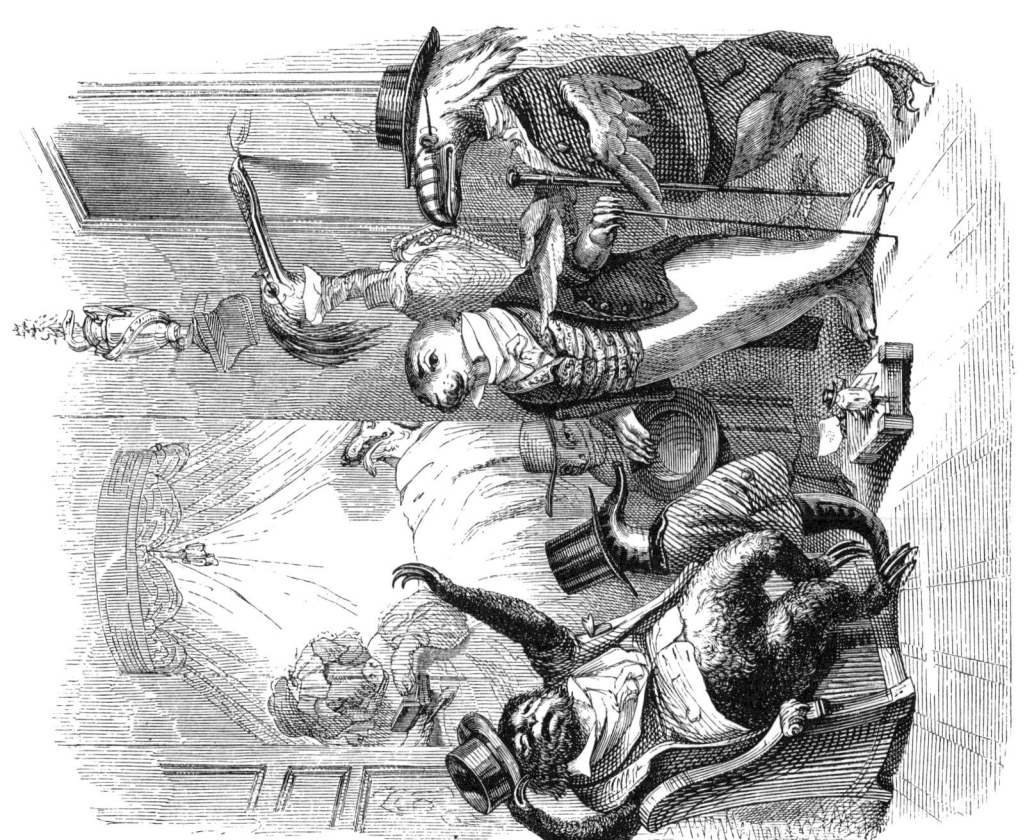

147. The sick dog, attended by a sow, has his case discussed by the diagnosticians: a sloth, a leech, a dugong, a crane, a Spanish fly and others.

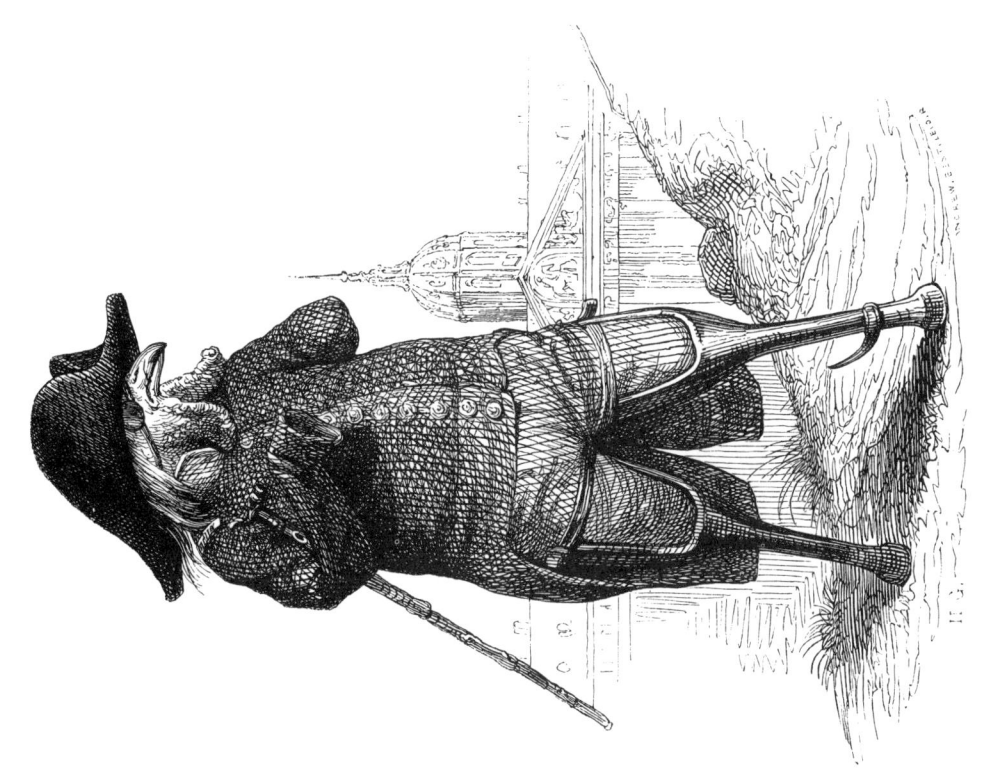

150. A disabled ex-soldier.

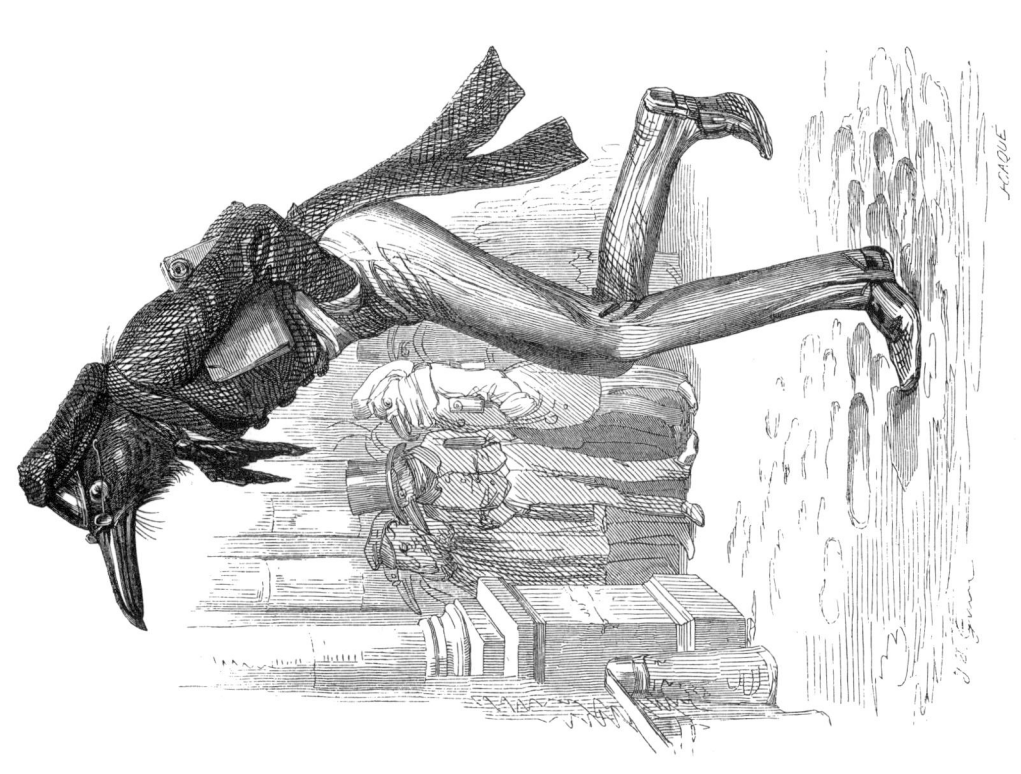

149. A medical student.

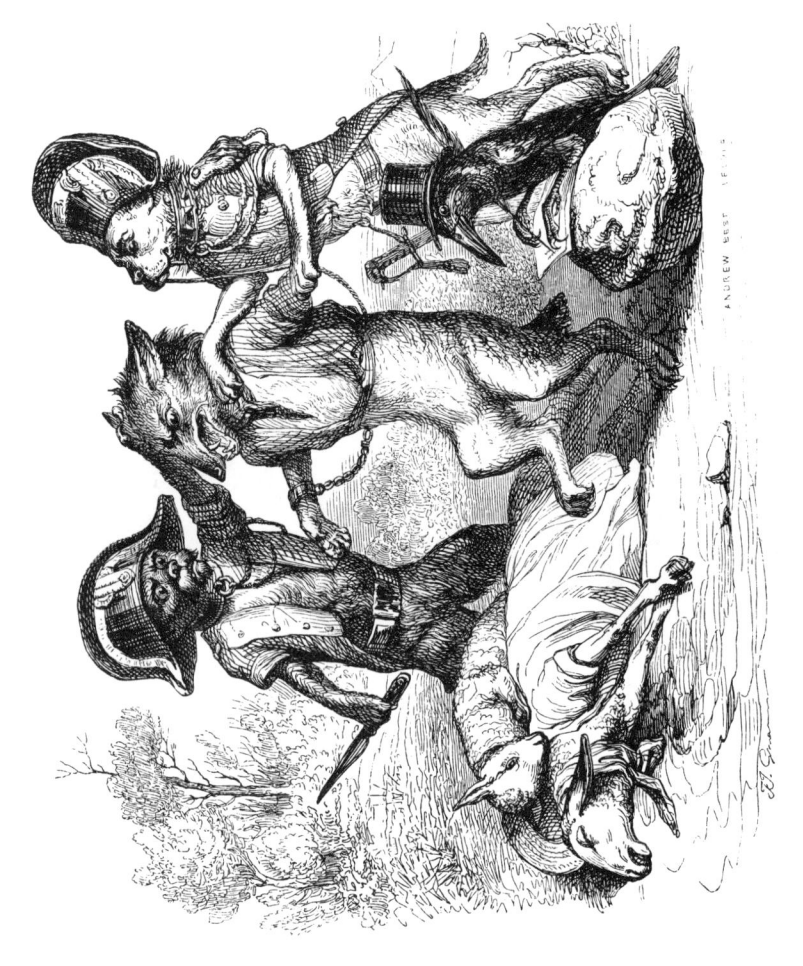

152. When the wolf is convicted, broadsheets appear recounting his crime in moralistic platitudes.

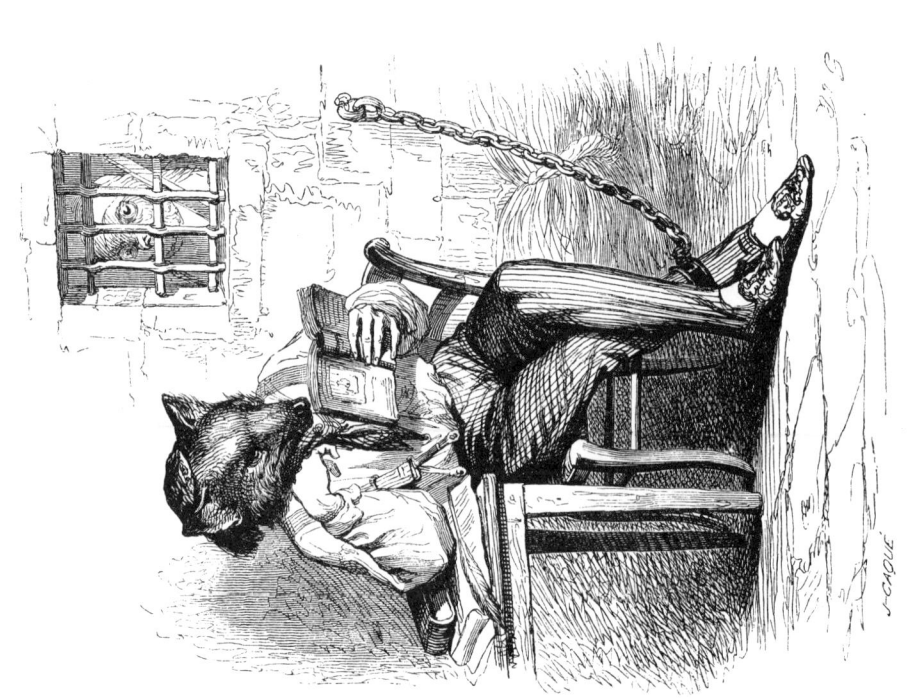

151. In prison, the wolf reads the *Idylls* of Mme. Deshoulières—which concern sheep!

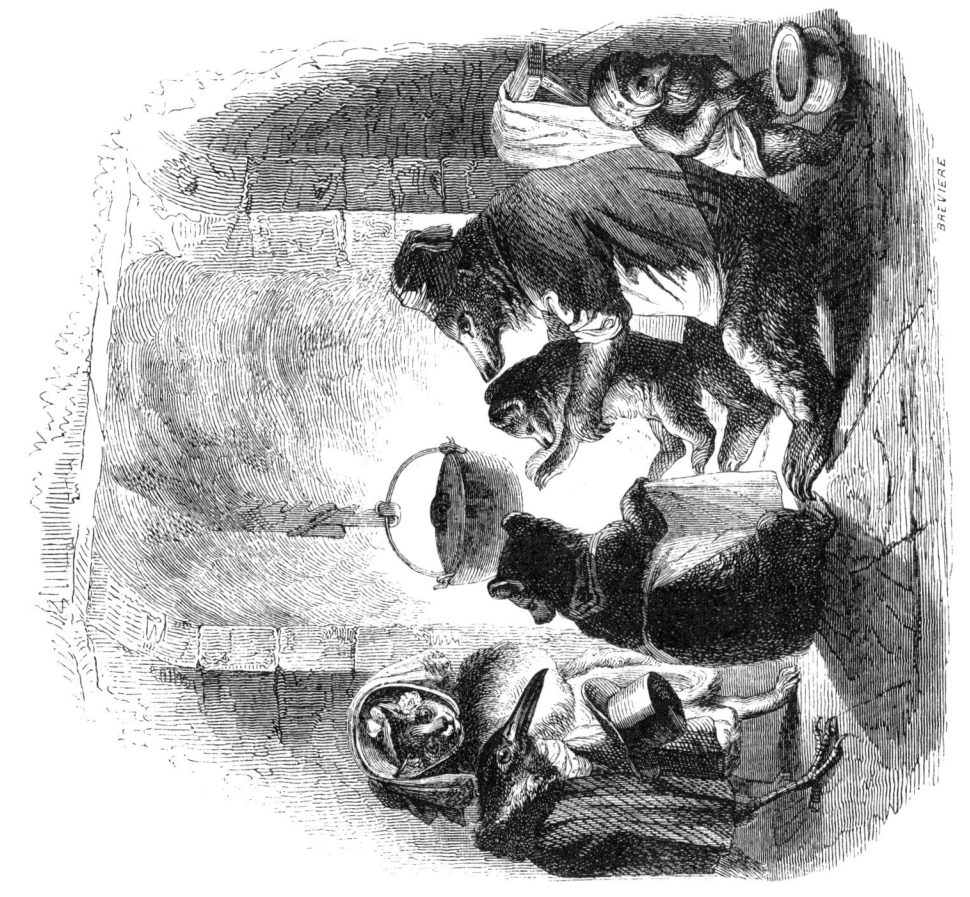

154. The bear in the bosom of his family.

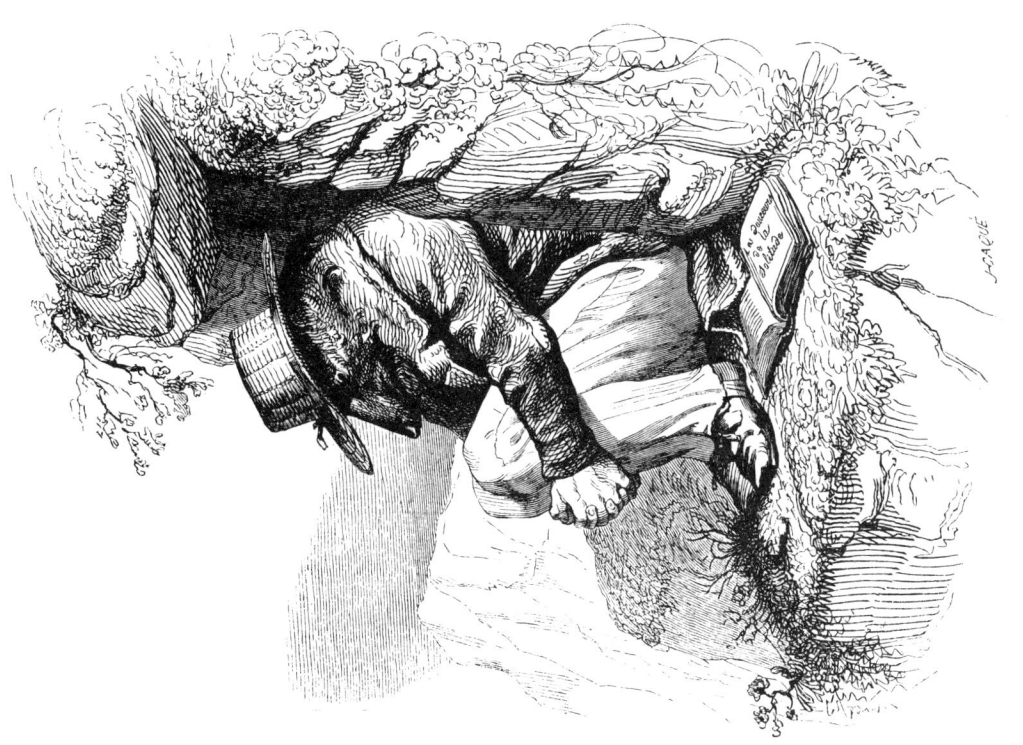

153. The bear living alone in the mountains.

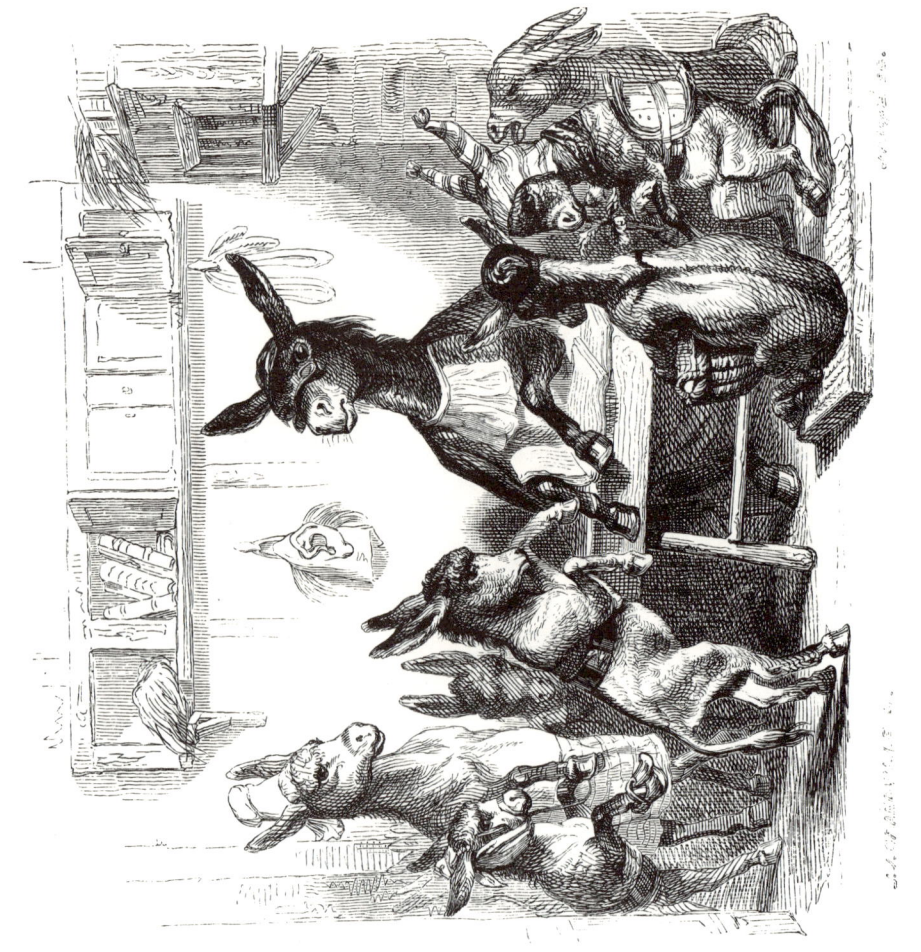

156. In the country, the donkey emulates his schoolteacher owner, and teaches classes himself.

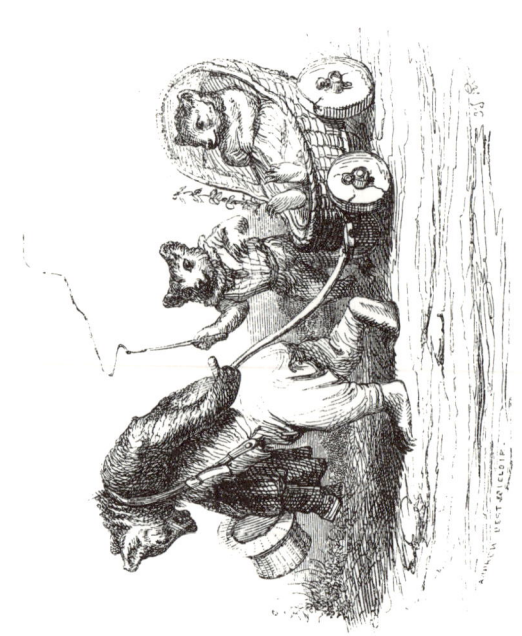

155. The bear is a good father.

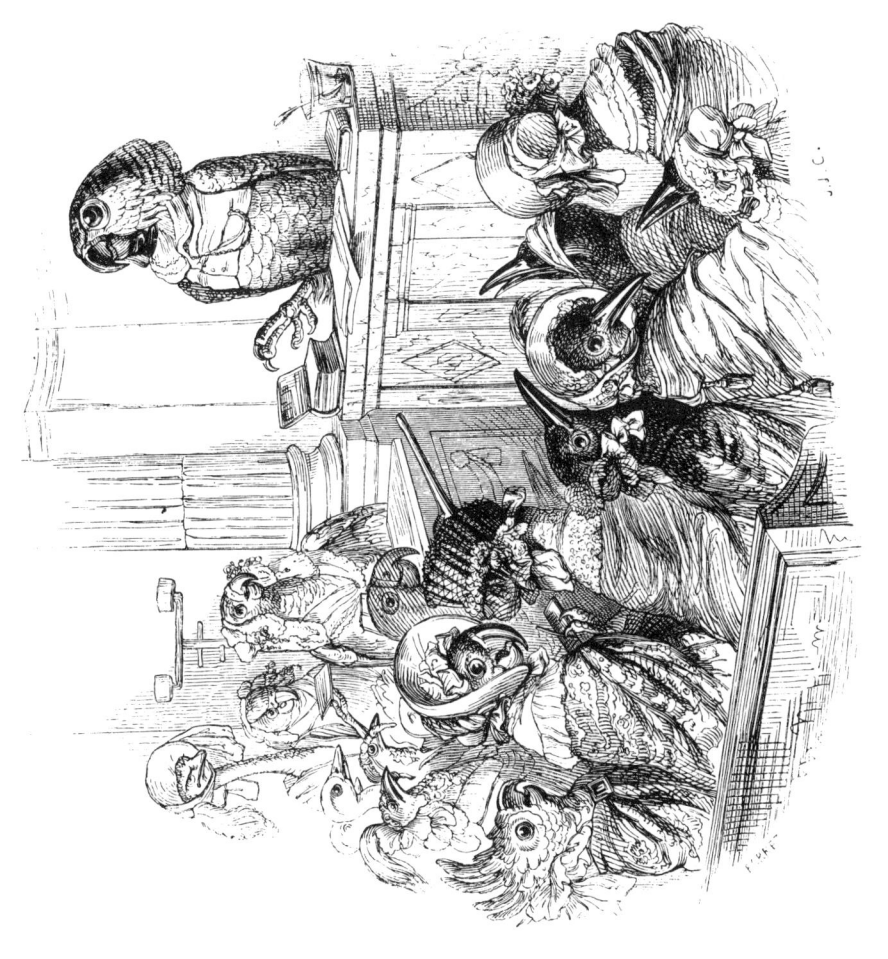

158. A disciple of the schoolteacher gives popular lectures on the new theory.

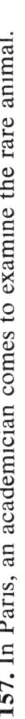

157. In Paris, an academician comes to examine the rare animal.

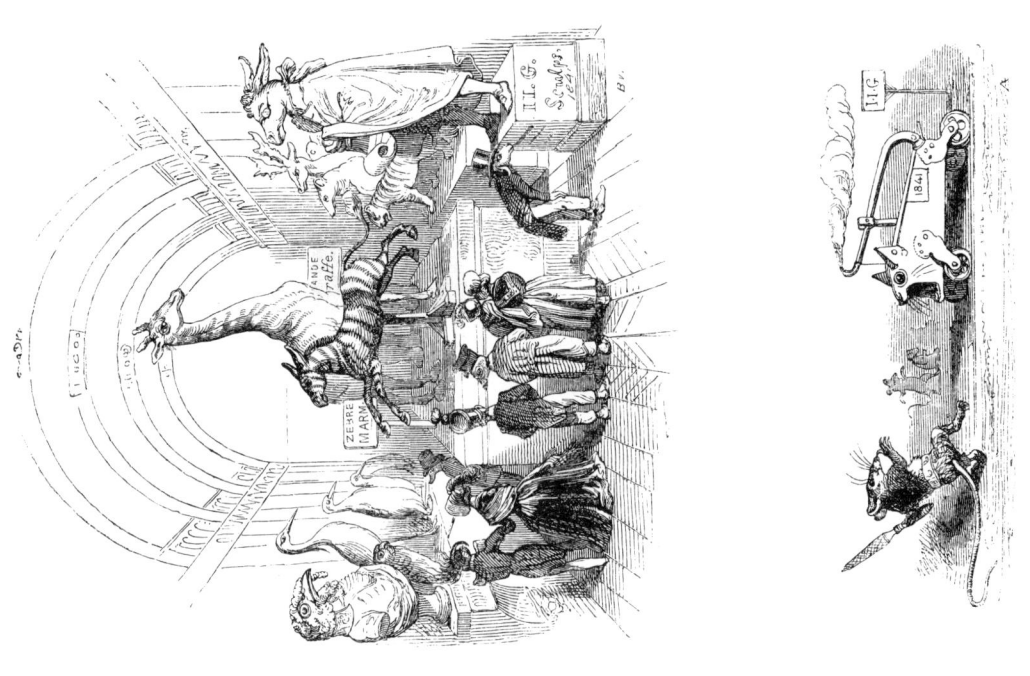

160. "The Museum of Natural History is the Pantheon of animals." **161.** The wise rat thumbs his nose at the world's alarms.

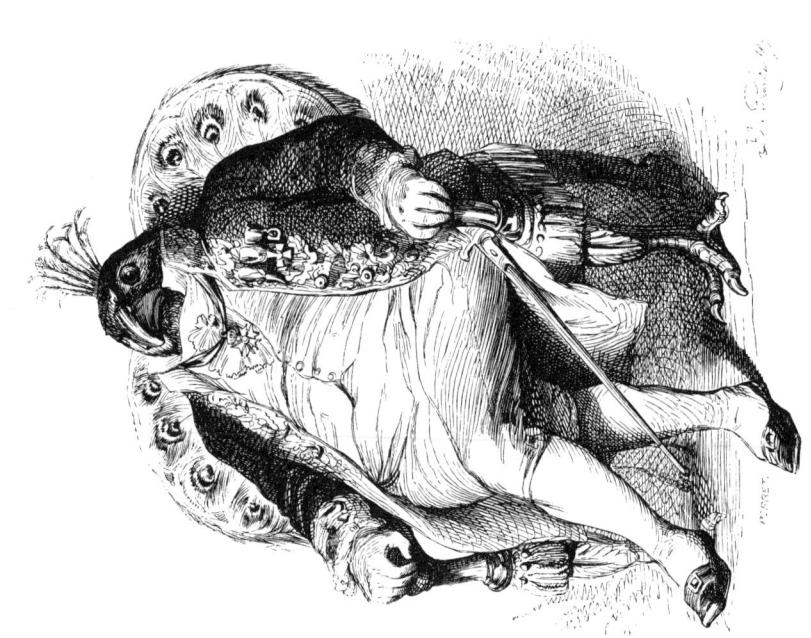

159. The ex-schoolteacher, now an illustrious man of learning and a political power.

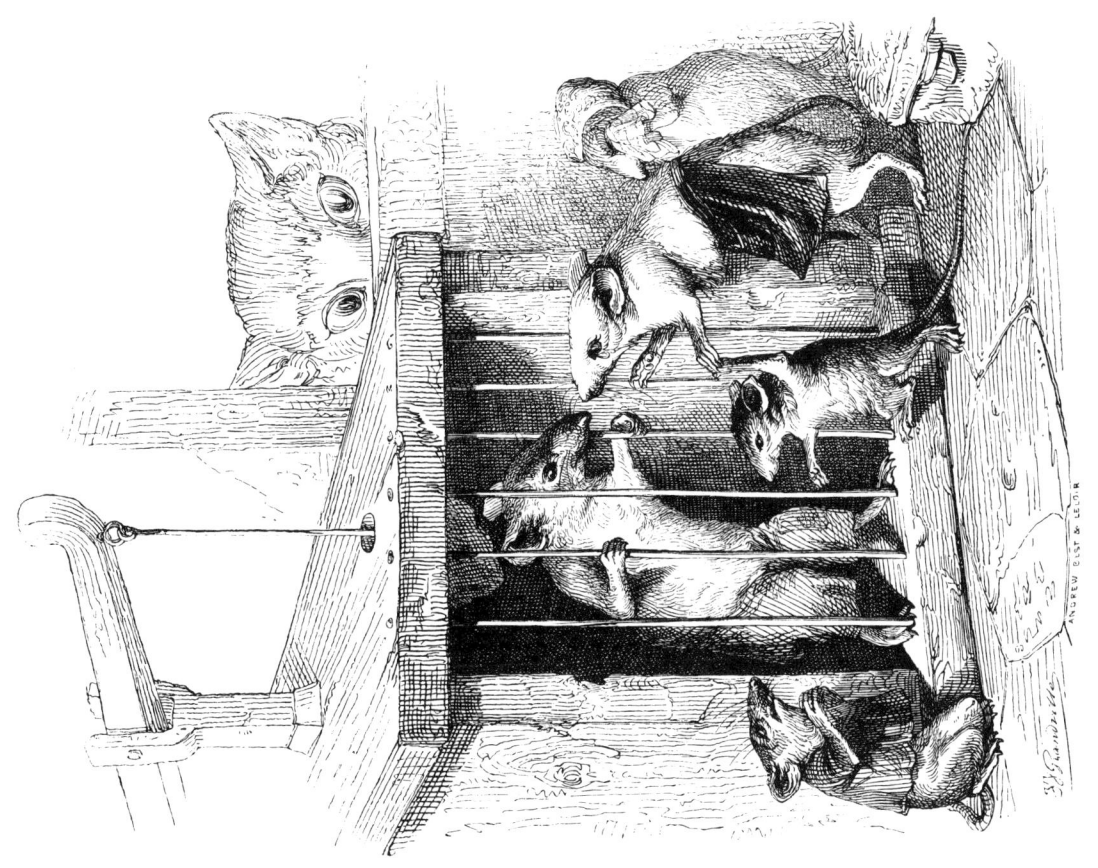

163. The resourcefulness of rats: with courage and brains they can escape from traps and cats.

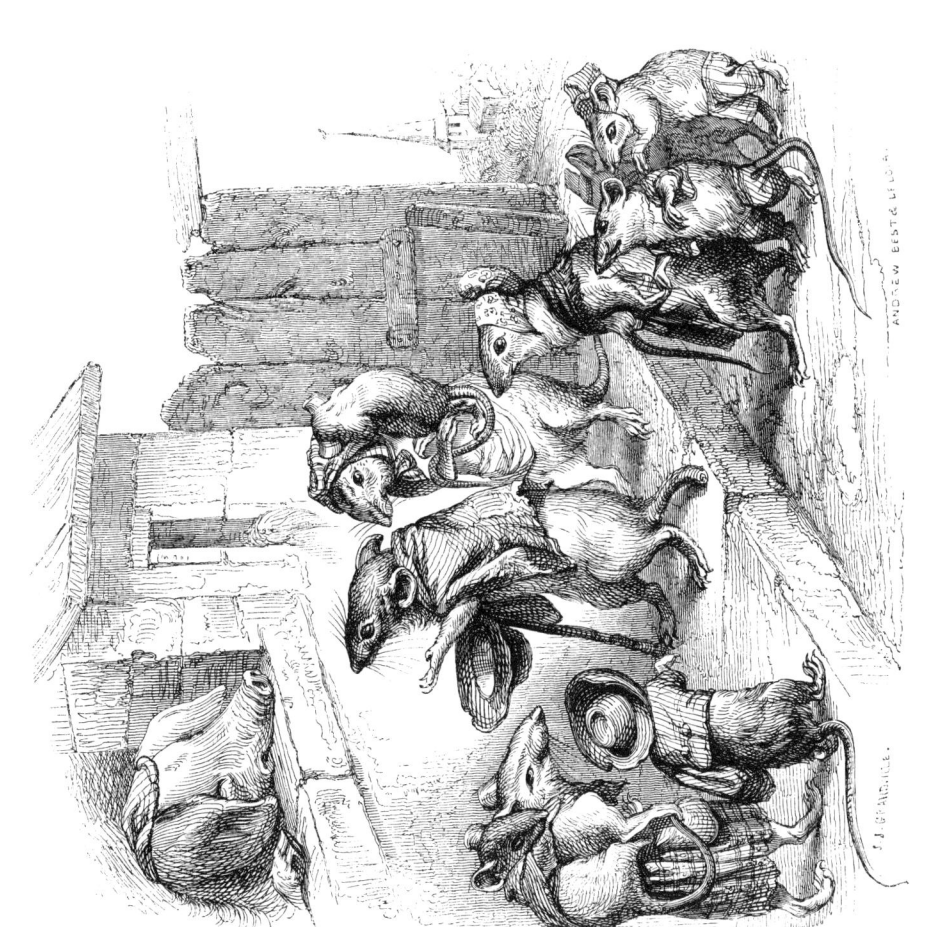

162. The misfortunes of rats; indigent, they are refused aid by the greedy rich.

Les Animaux 113

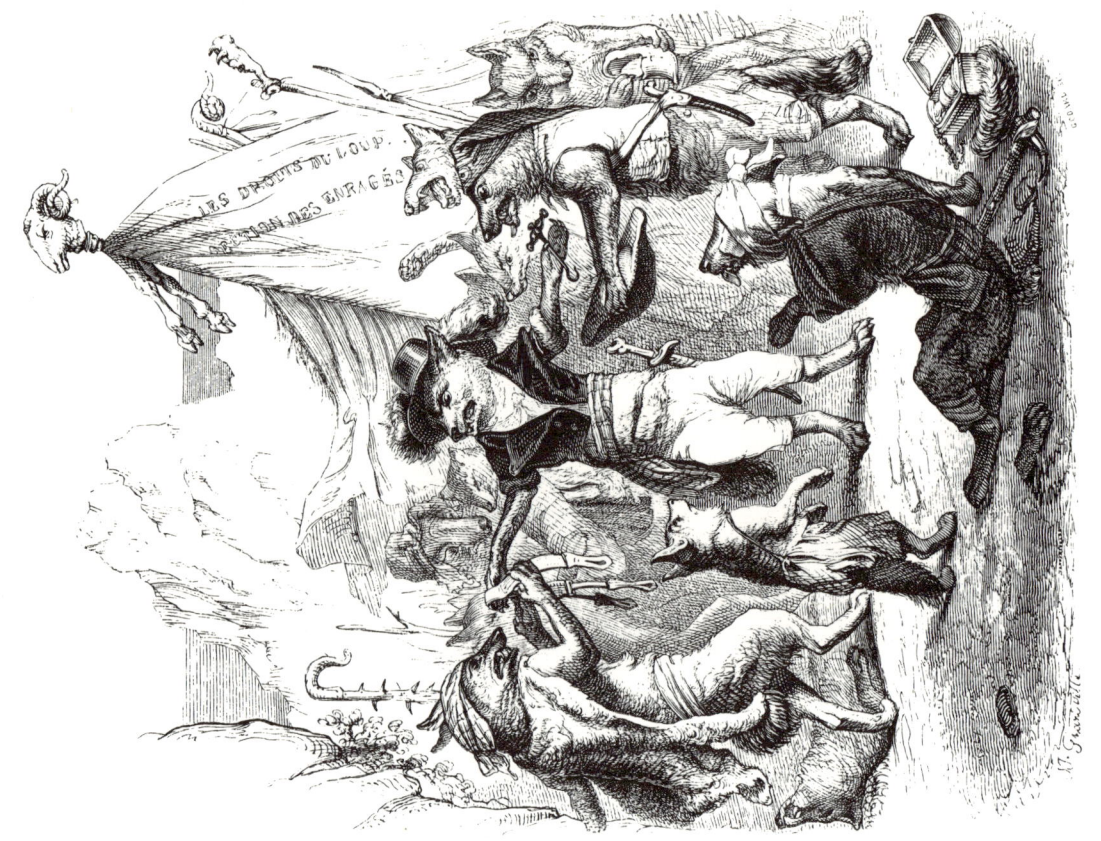

165. Fraternity among the wolves.

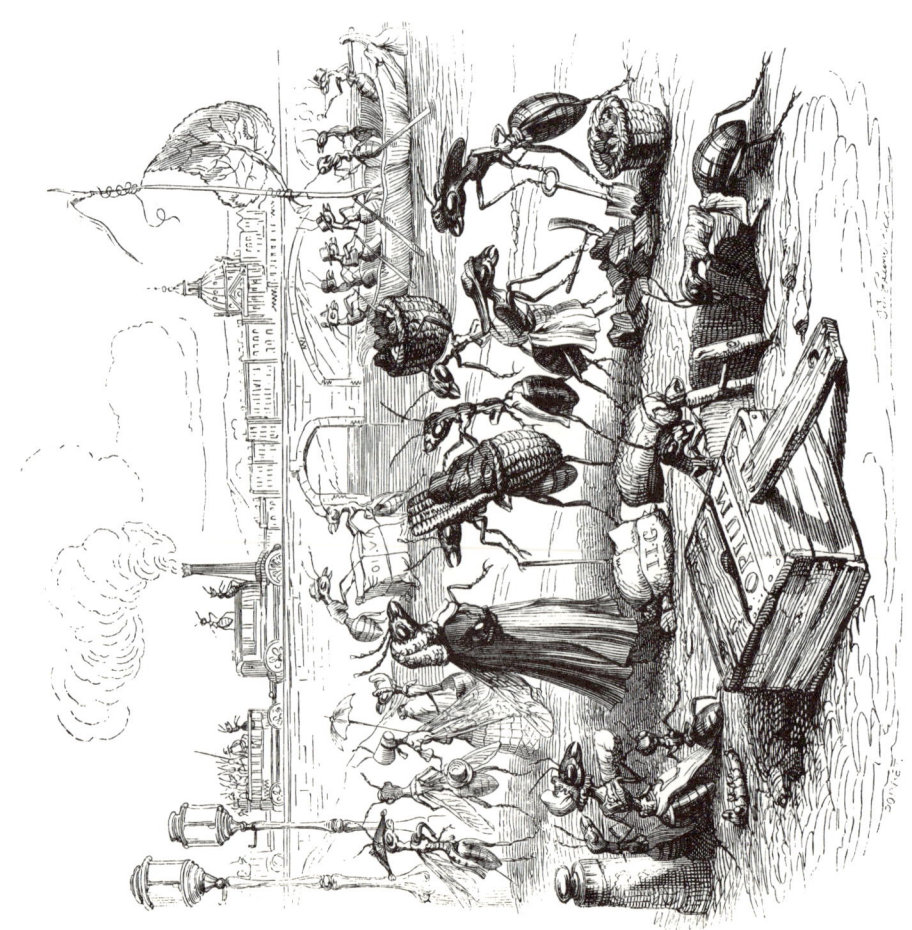

164. The island of the ants [satire on England].

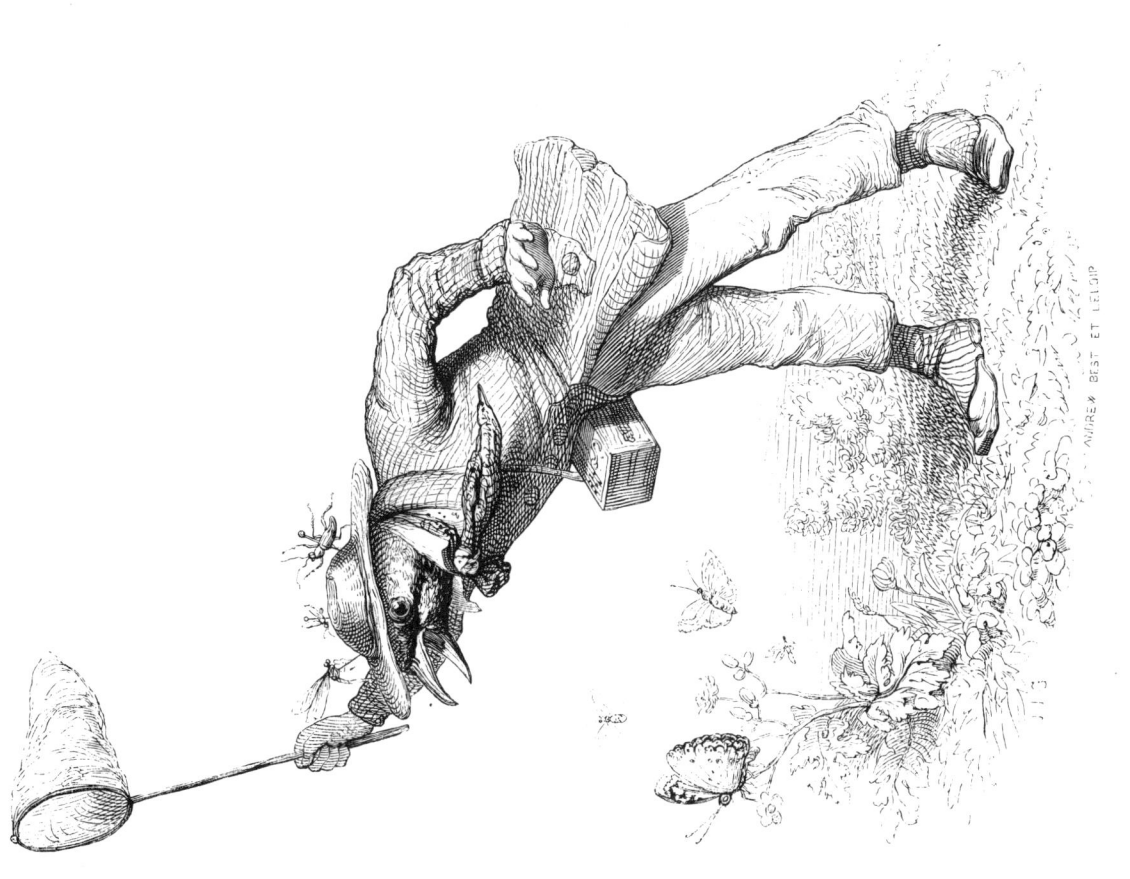

166 & 167. Fisher folk. **168.** A butterfly hunter.

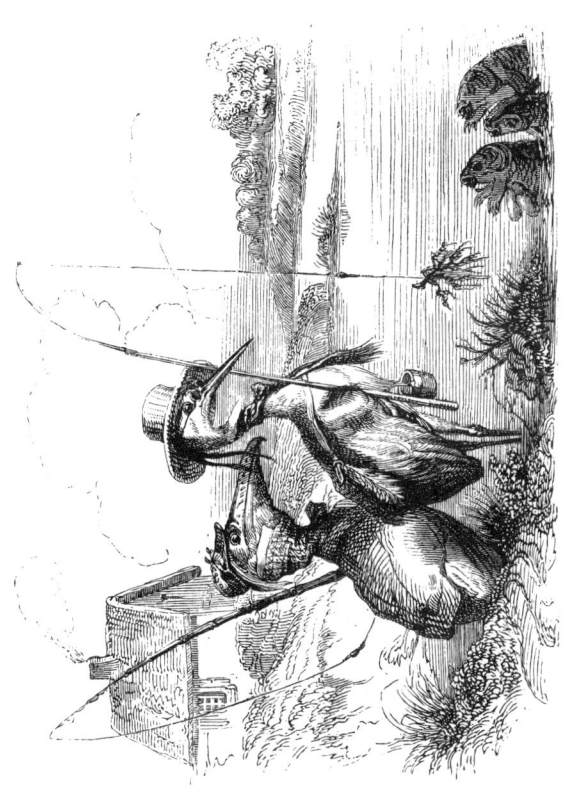

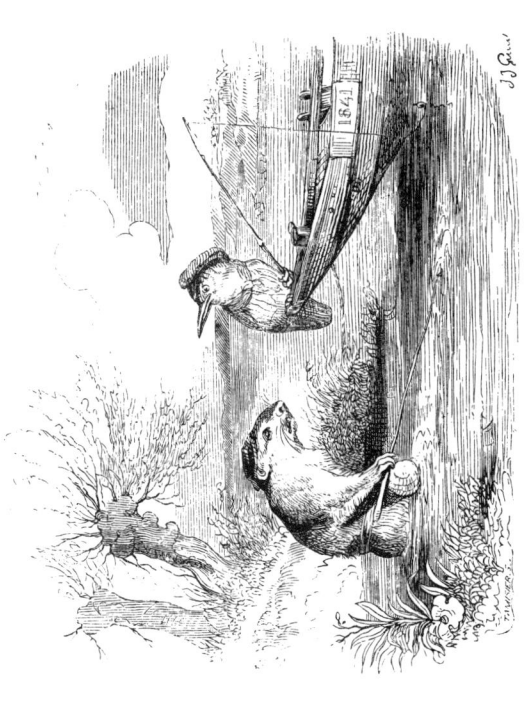

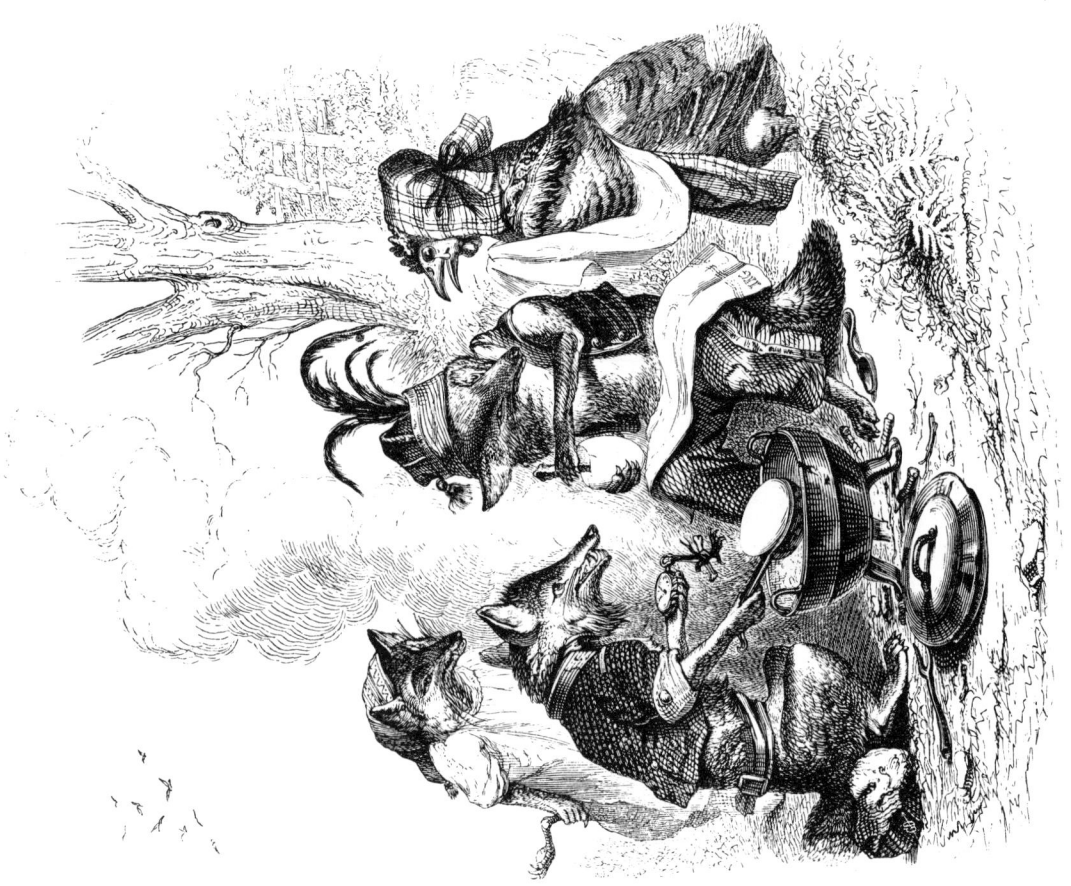

170. The foxes of the raiding party eat soft-boiled eggs while the mother hen weeps.

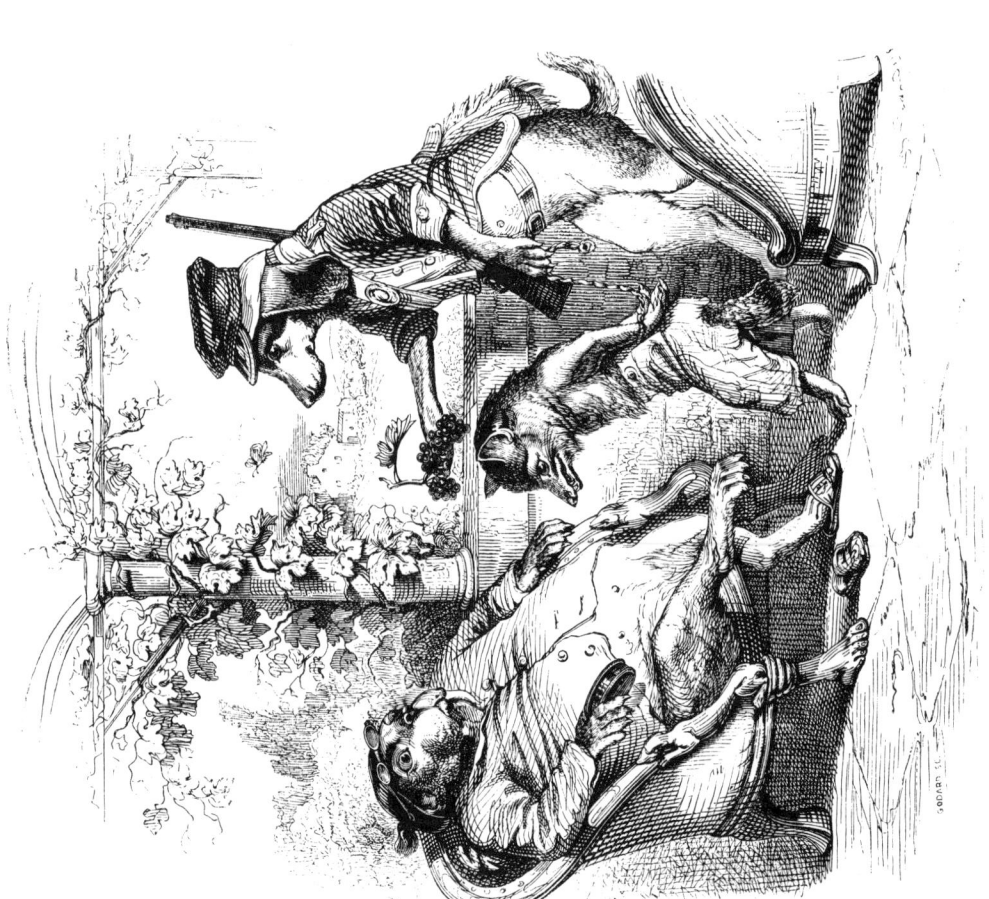

169. The young fox hauled before the dog-landowner for stealing grapes.

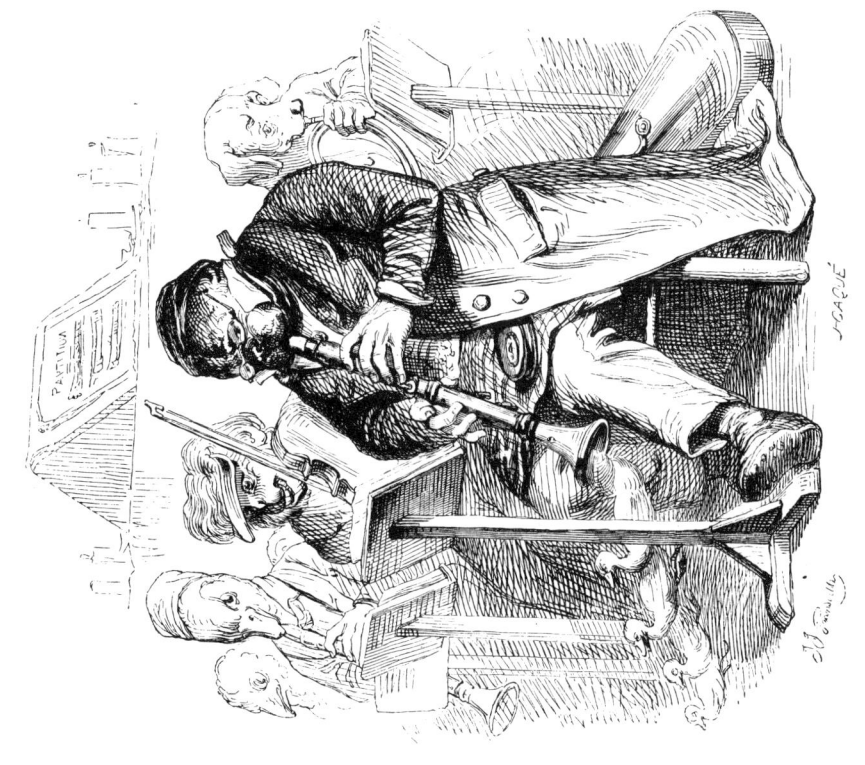

172. The third-rate musicians who perform the incidental music for straight plays.

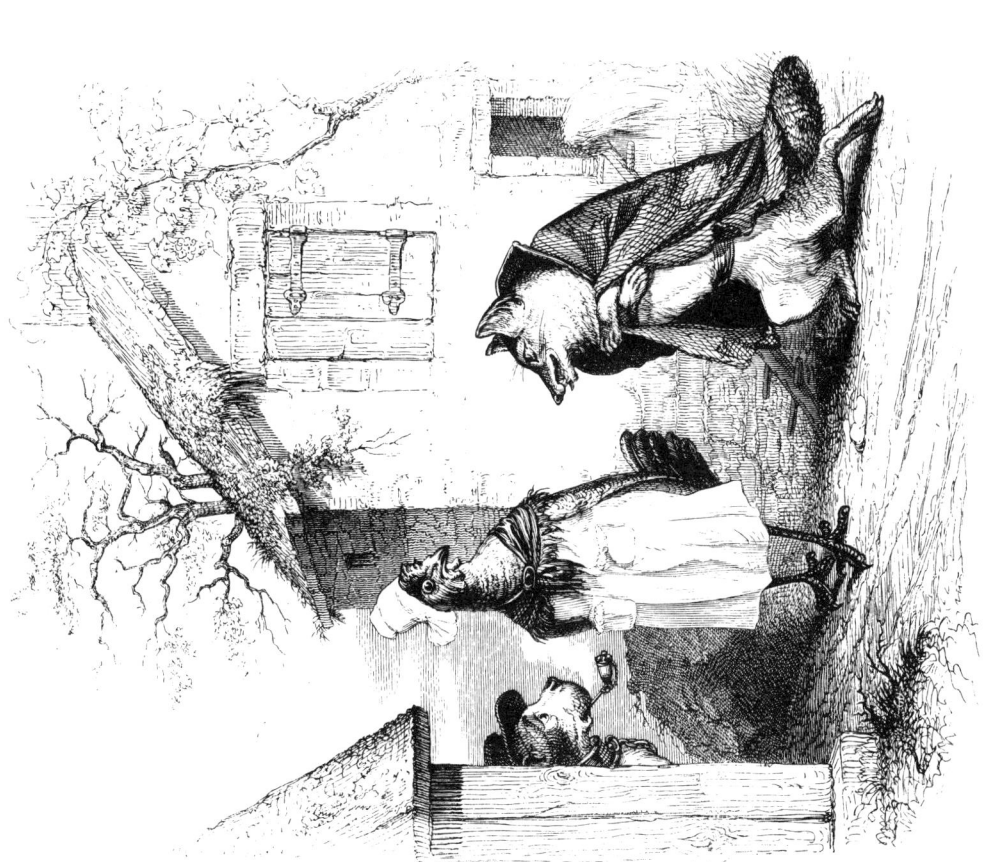

171. The fox fruitlessly seeks the hen's affections.

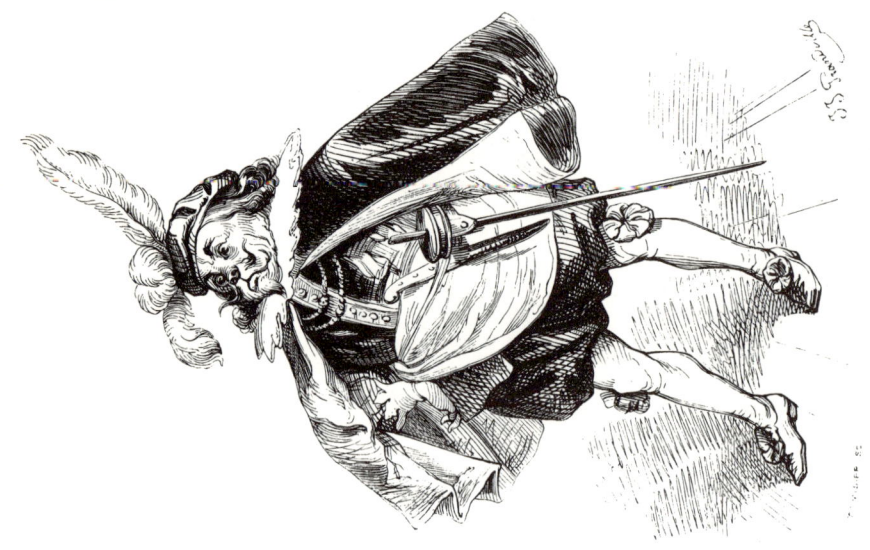

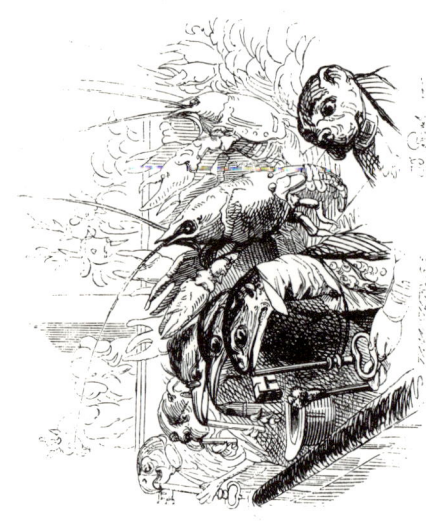

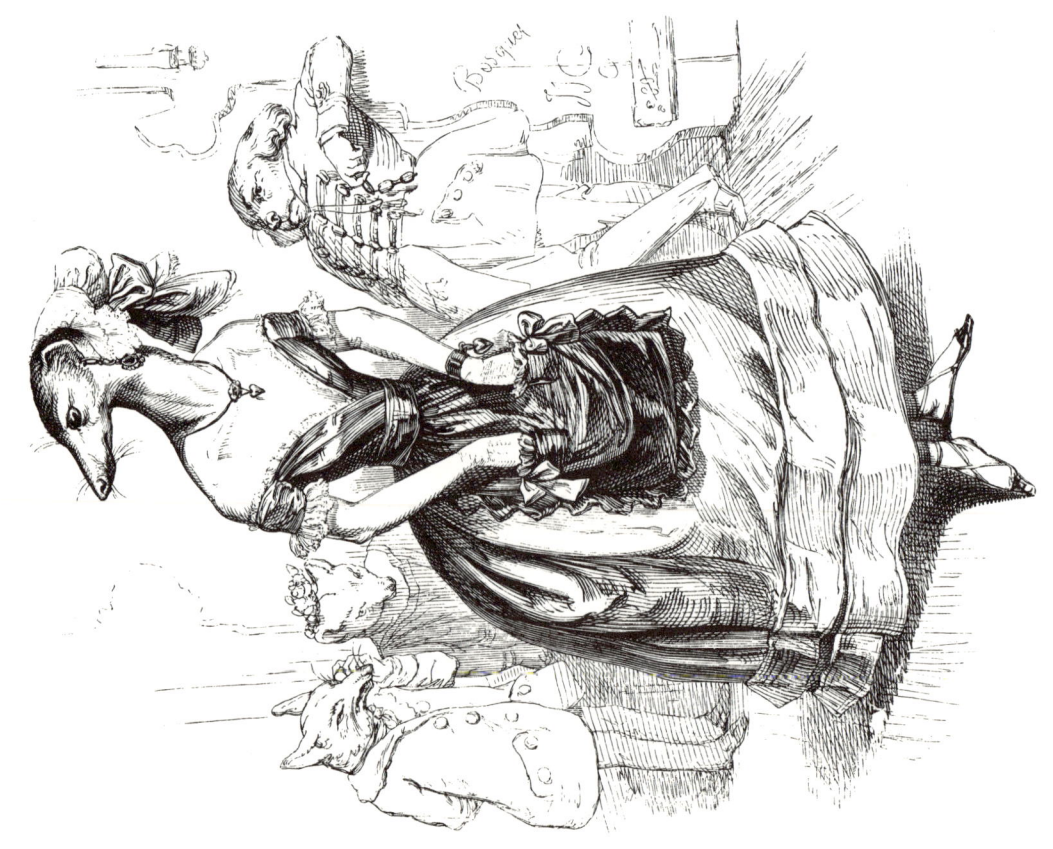

173. A group of actors in repose. **174.** The hero of the play in his brief moment of grandeur. **175.** Birds and snakes in the audience hissing and whistling at the villain.

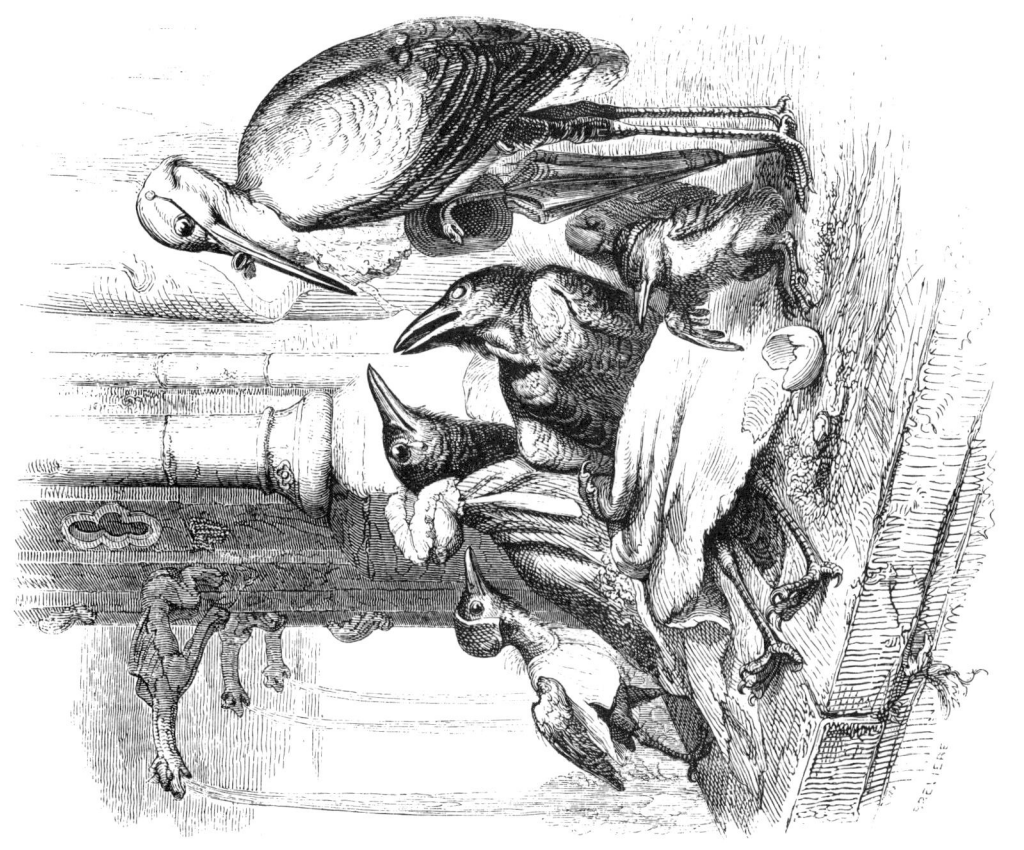

177. The crow's husband dies at the cathedral of Strasbourg.

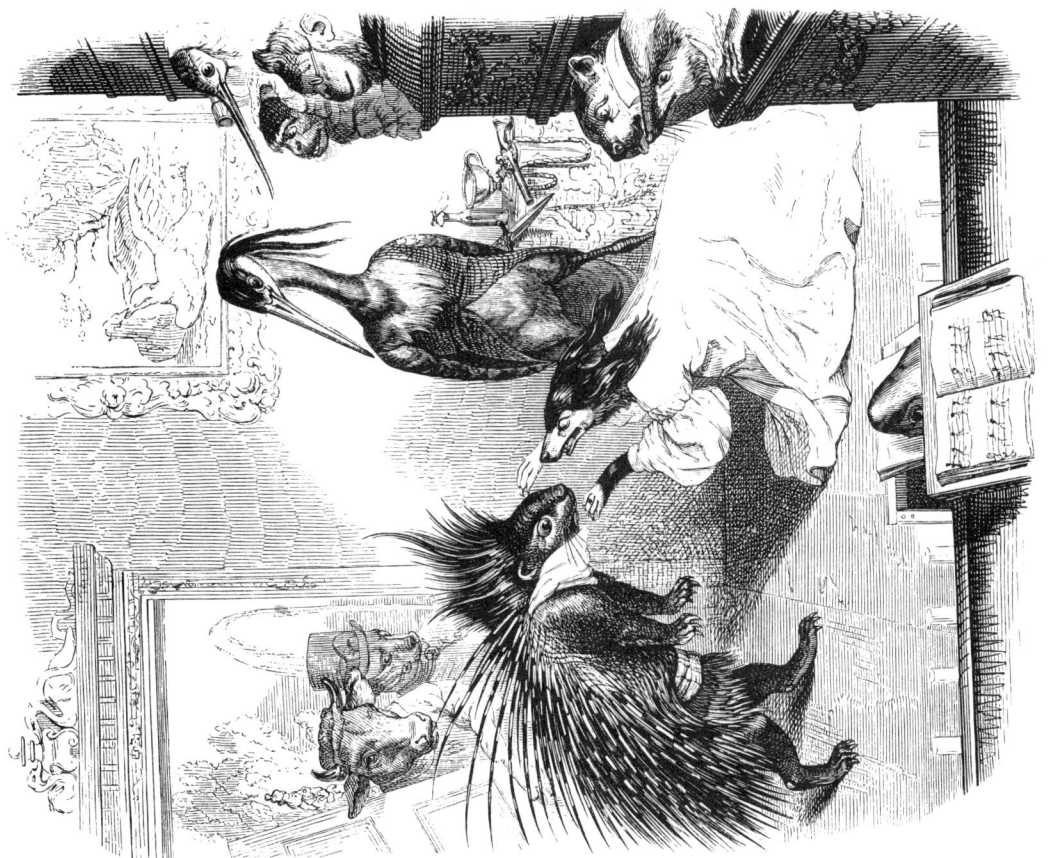

176. The climax of the play: the noble heroine still loves the hero even when he is disheveled and grimy.

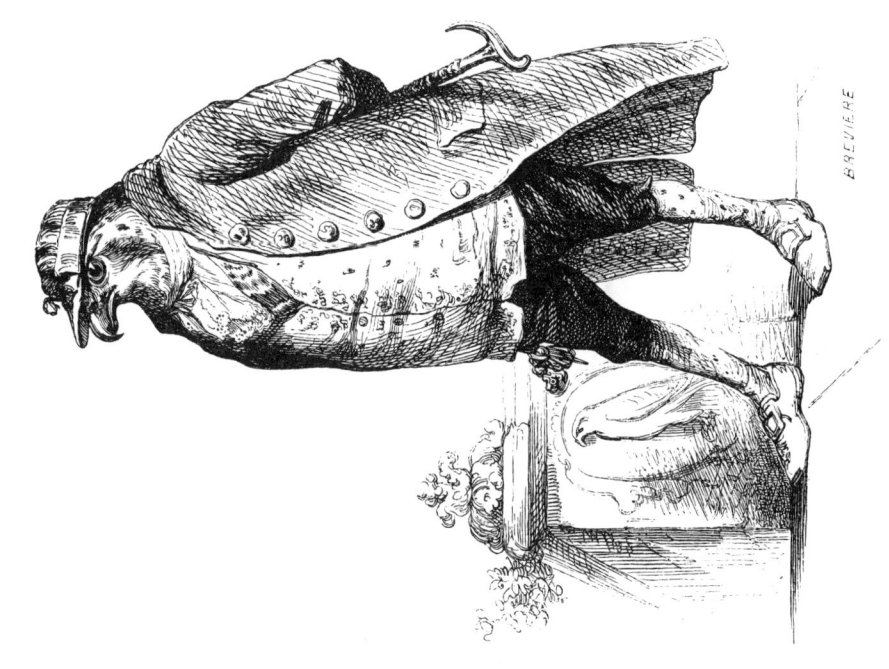

179. The falcon who lives in the unrepaired part of the château.

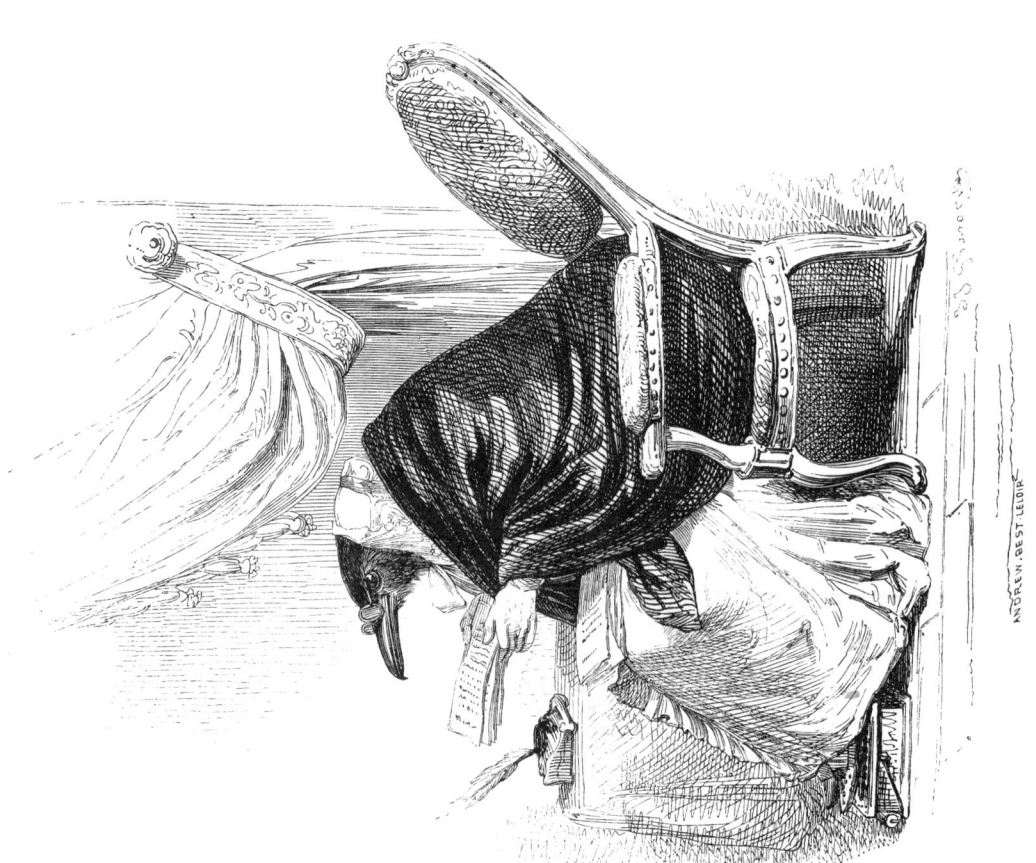

178. The crow sets down her travel experiences.

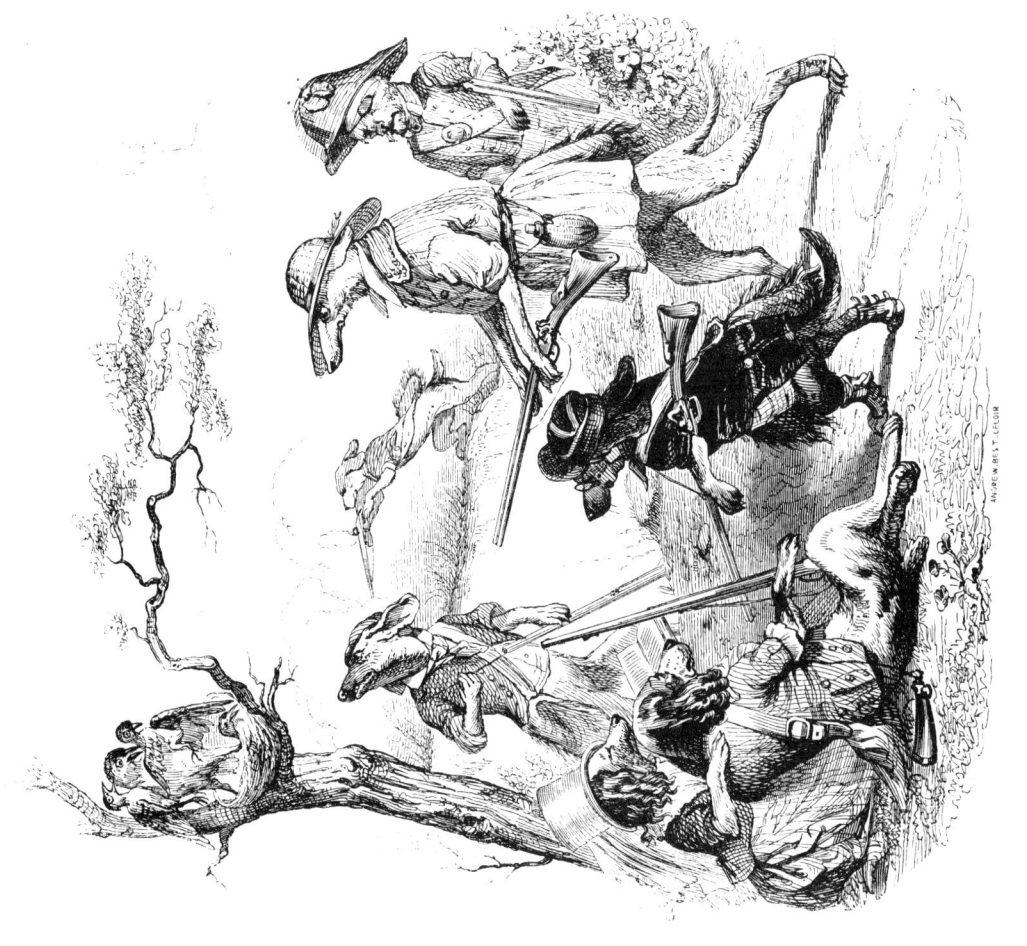

181. Petty modern hunters (in contrast with the falcon's memories of grand hunts).

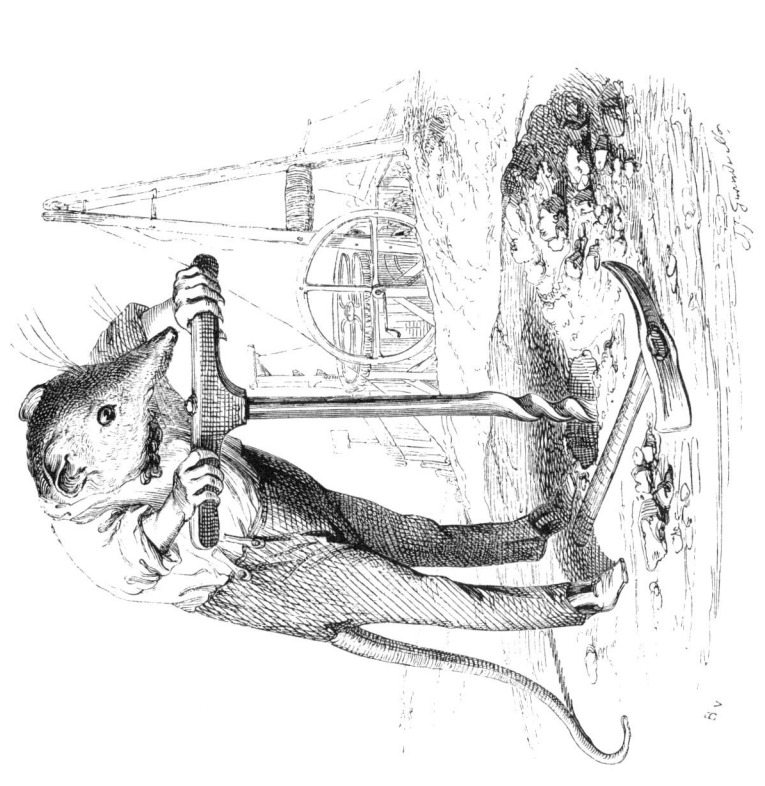

180. A neighbor and protégé of the falcon—a field mouse occupied with burrowing.

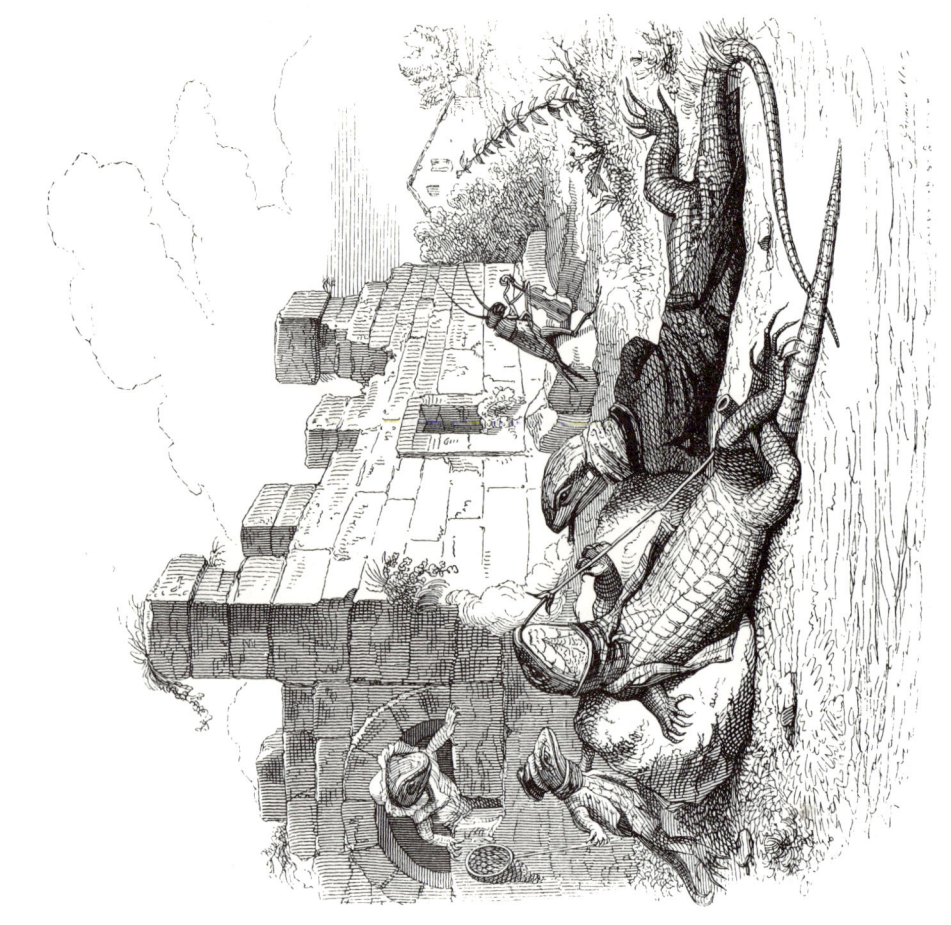

183. The lizards who lived in the old wing of the château.

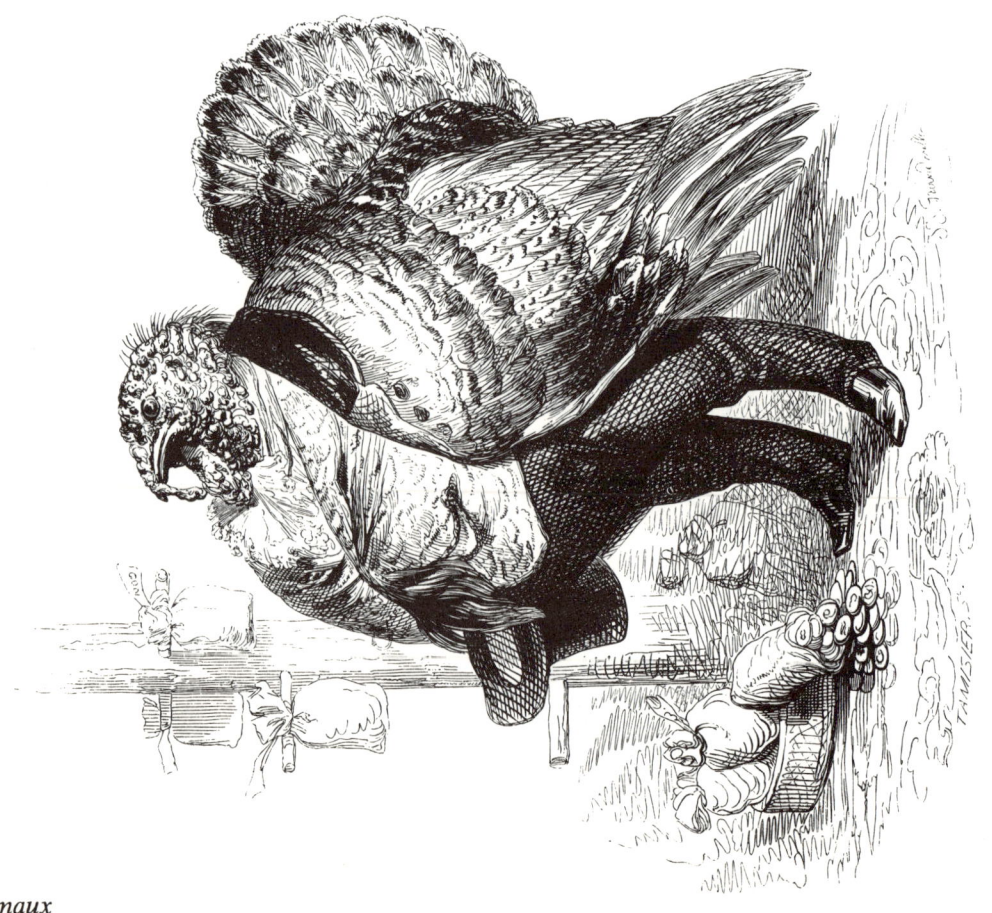

182. A banker.

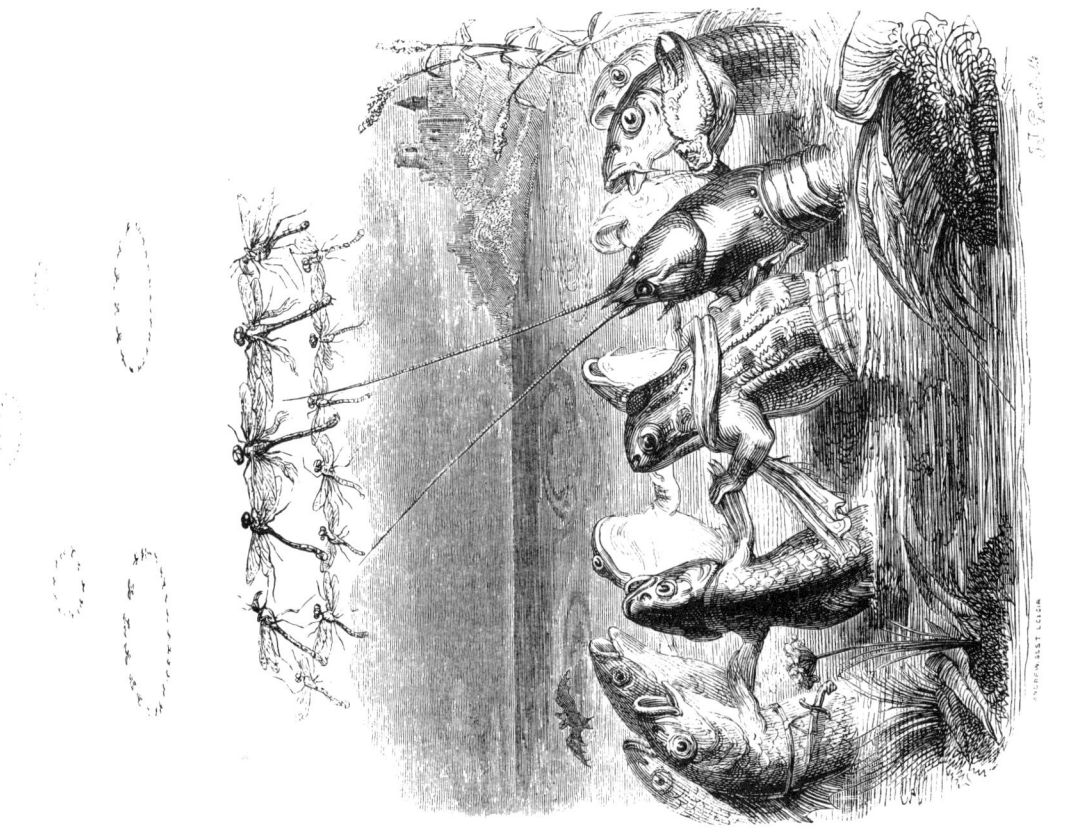

185. After his wife has run off, the male owl consults a fortune-telling carp for advice and witnesses this scene of divination.

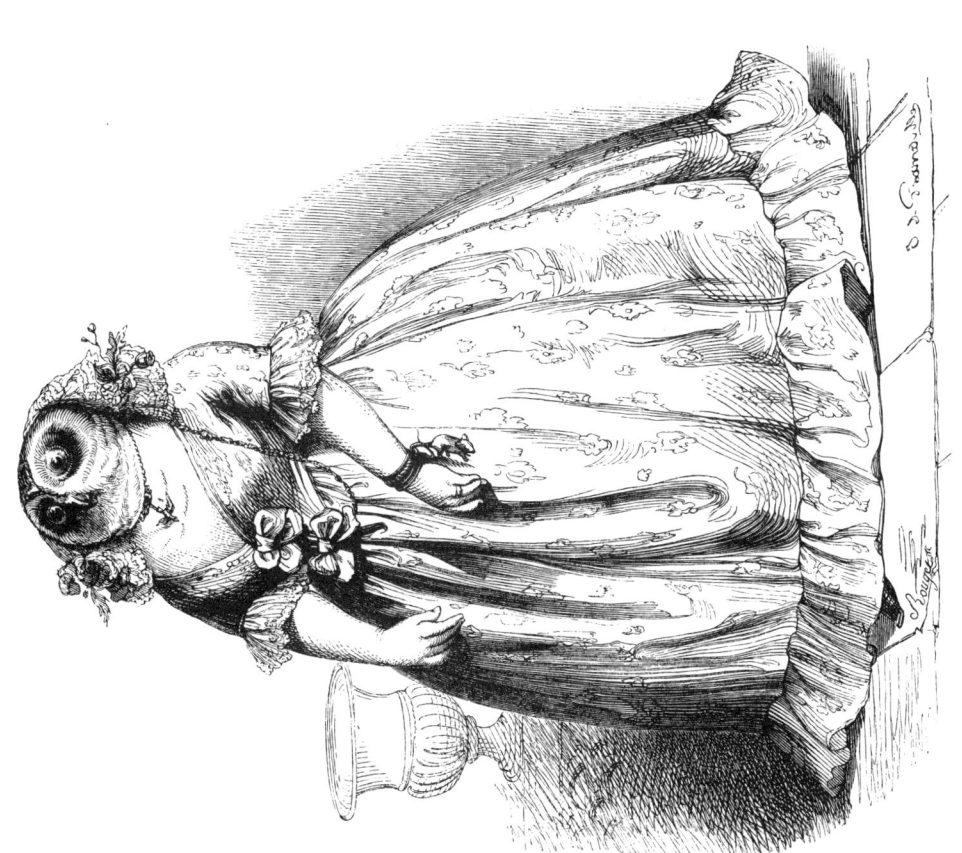

184. The ridiculous female owl who lived in the altered wing of the château.

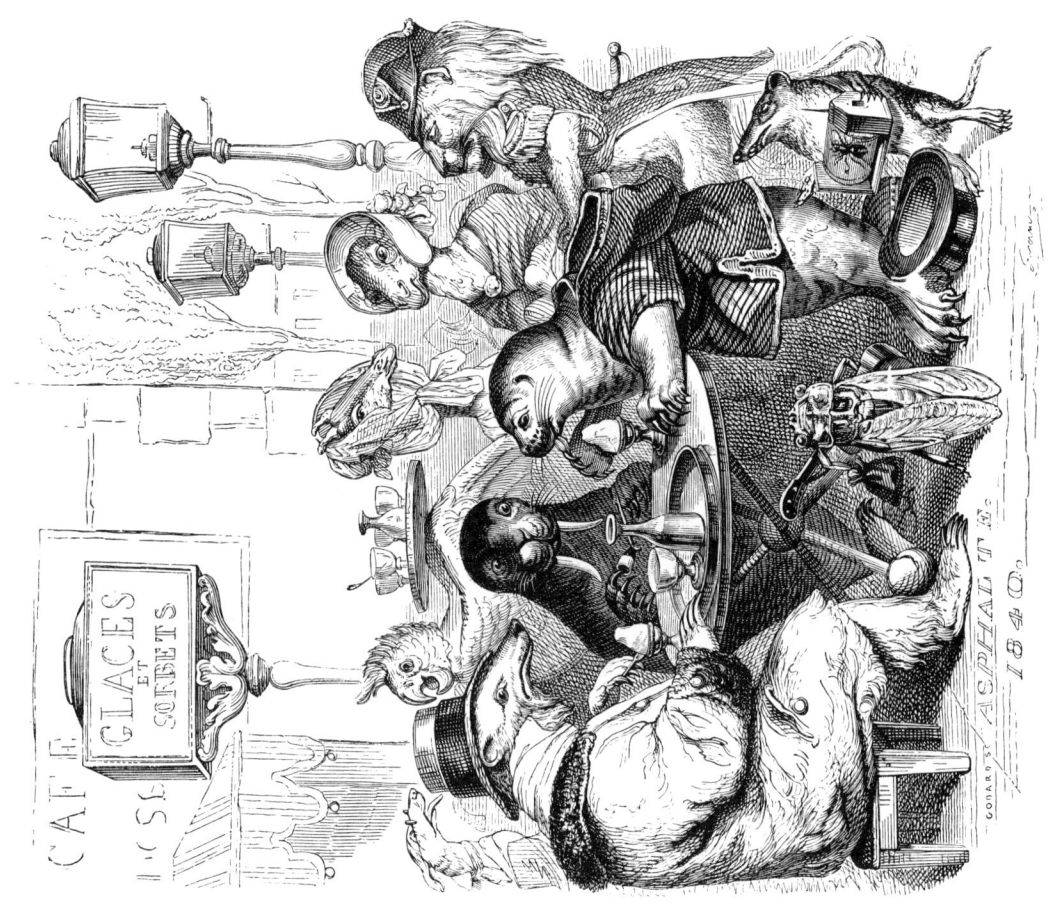

187. A café scene.

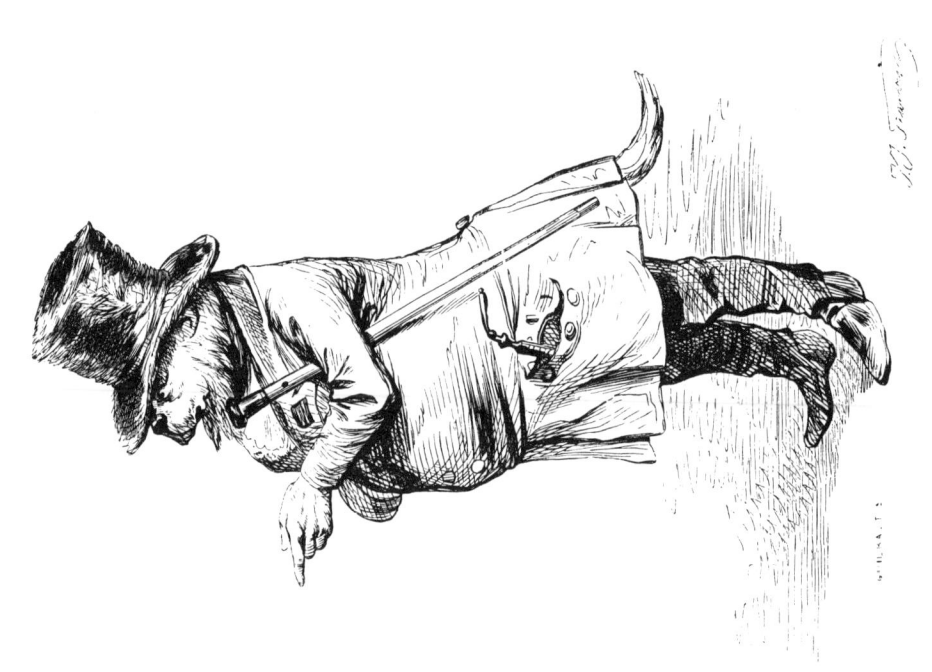

186. The dog who shows the lion around Paris.

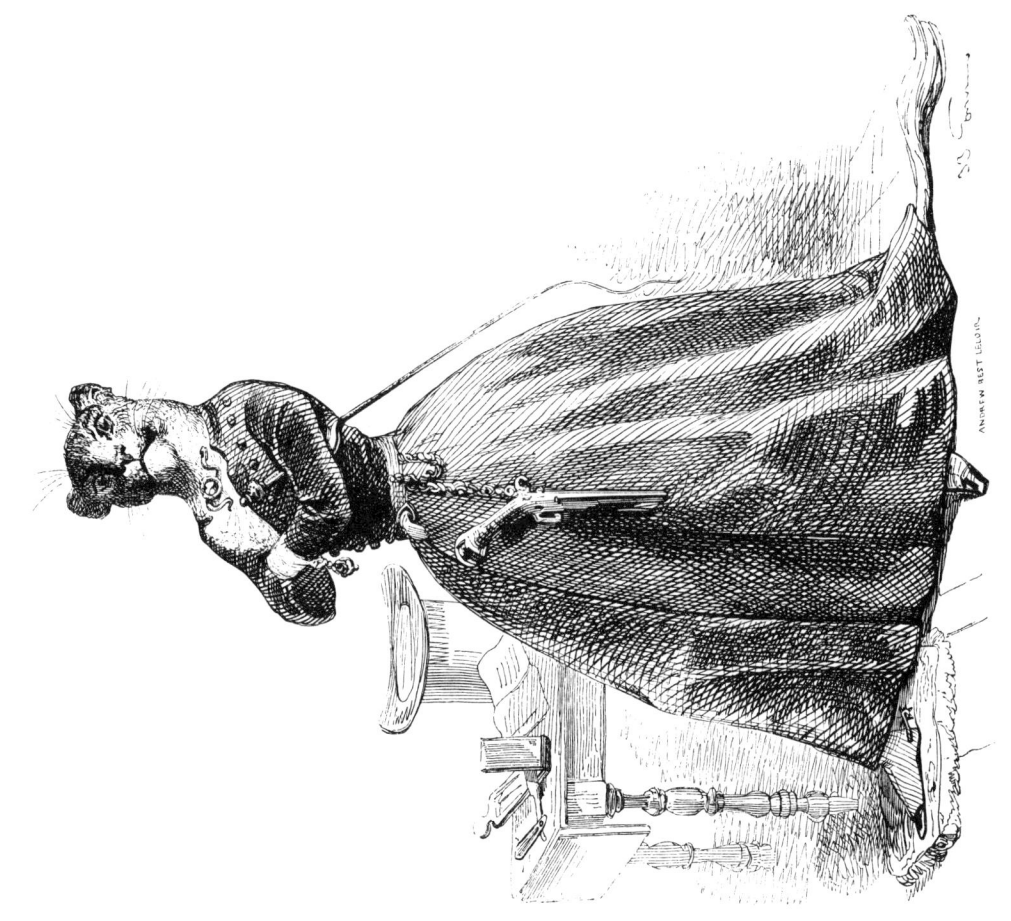

189. A *lionne* of Paris.

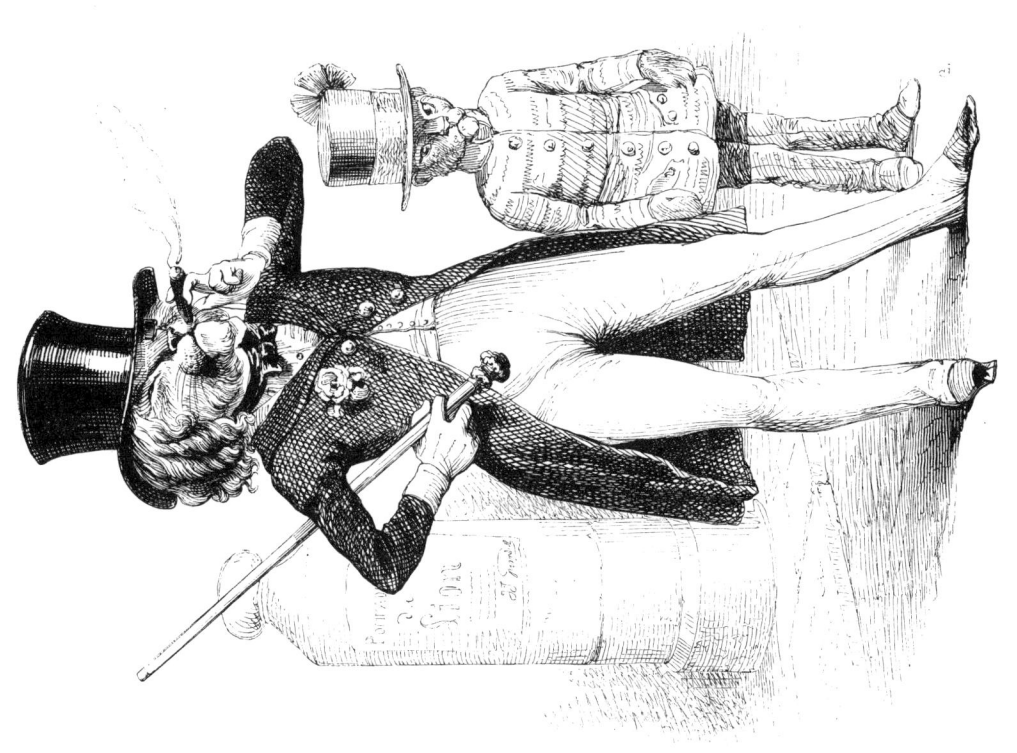

188. A lion (dandy) of Paris with his young page.

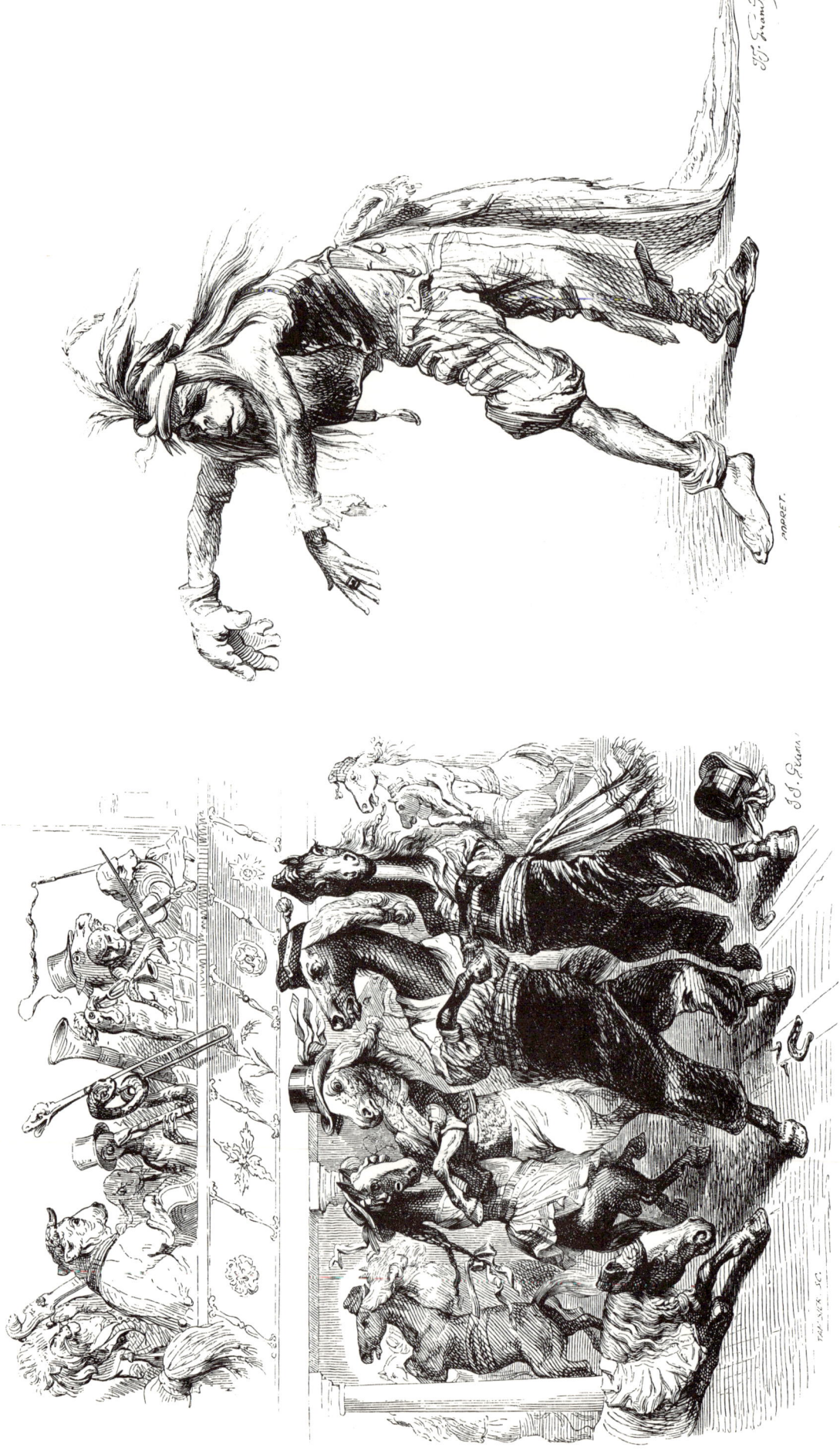

191. "Animal passions break out in man."

190. A scene at a Carnival ball.

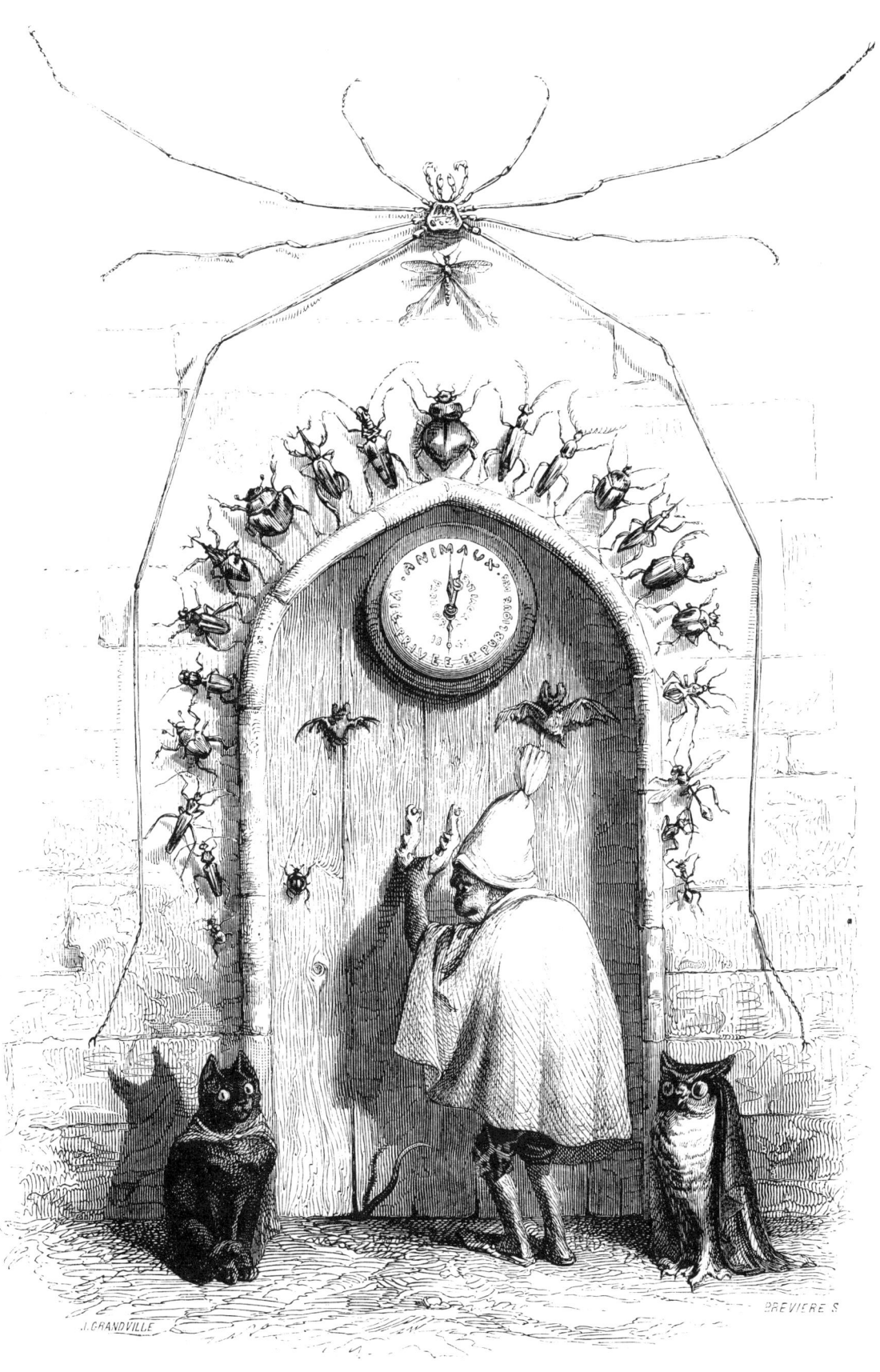

192. "Goodnight, then, dear reader. Go home, lock your cage well, sleep tight and have pleasant dreams. Until tomorrow."

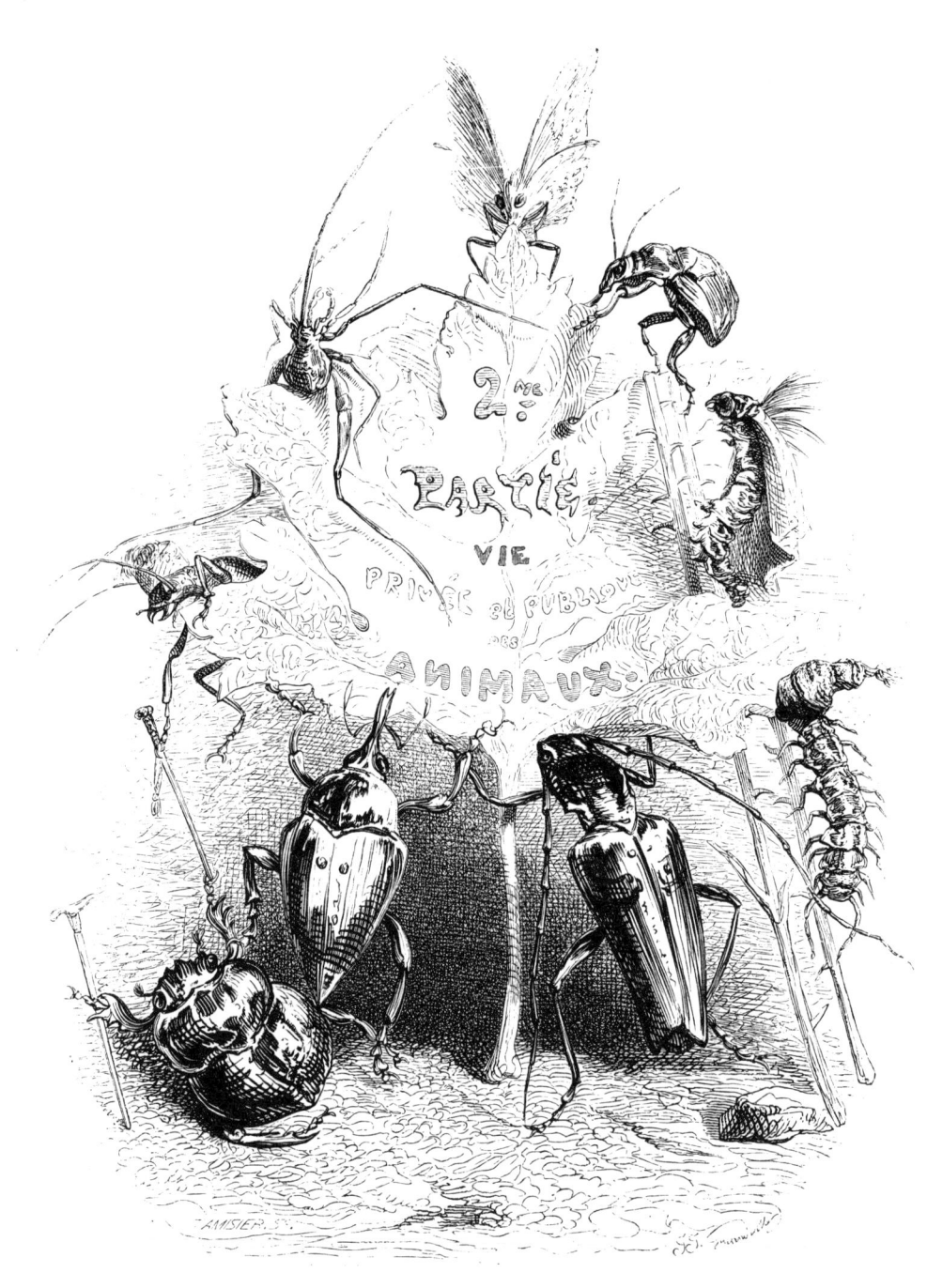

193. Part title to Volume II.

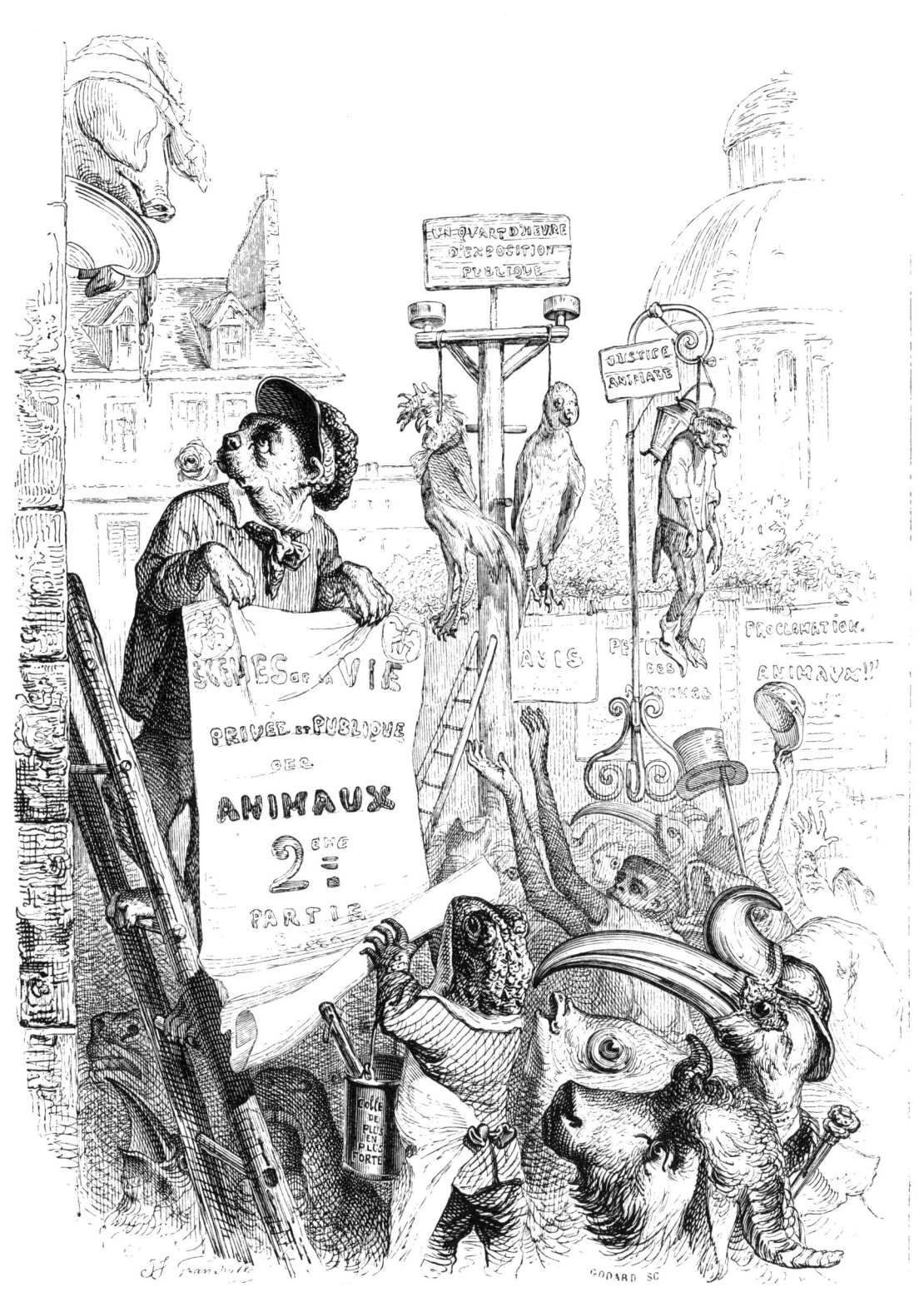

194. Second part title.

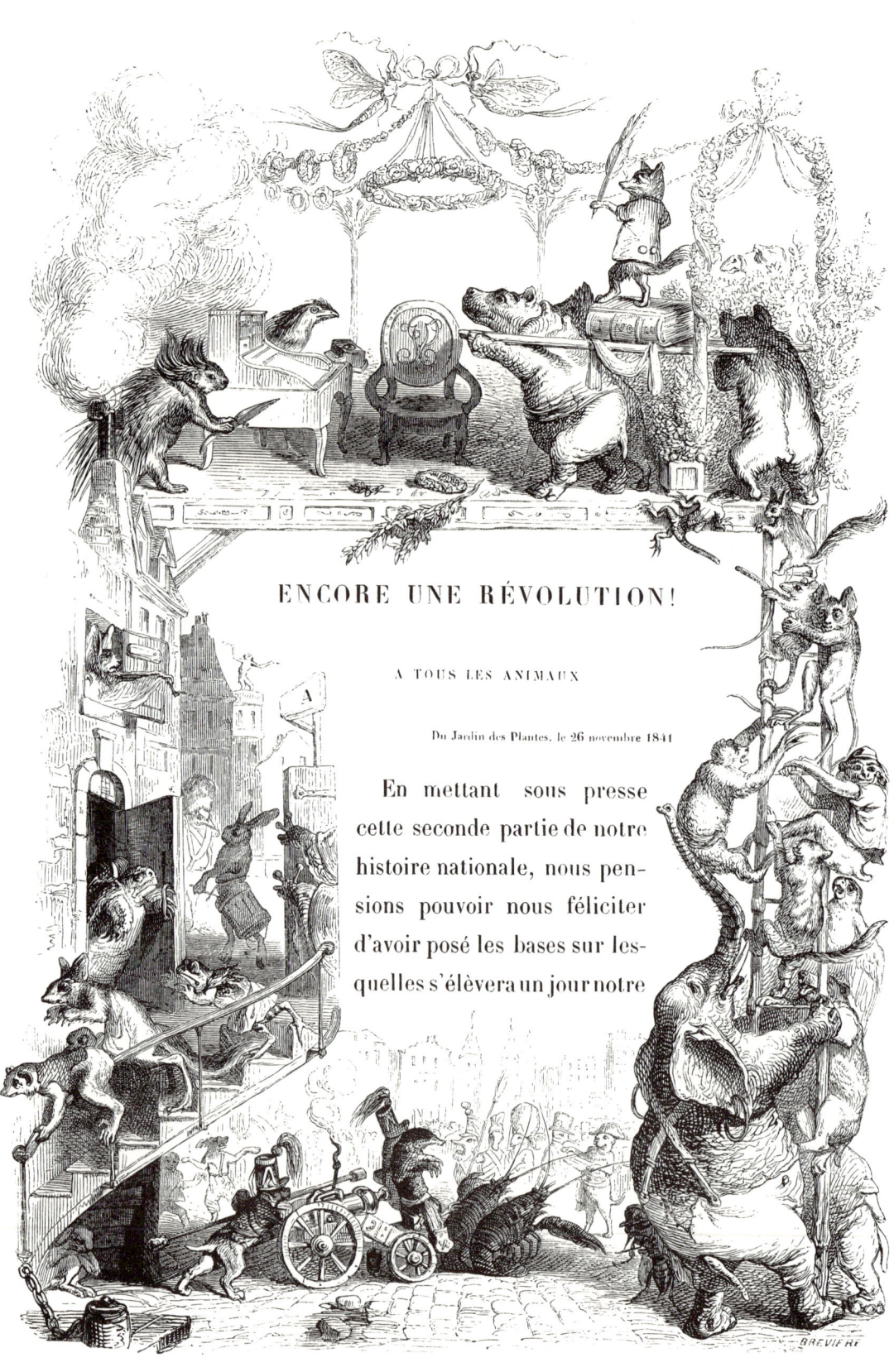

ENCORE UNE RÉVOLUTION!

A TOUS LES ANIMAUX

Du Jardin des Plantes, le 26 novembre 1841

En mettant sous presse cette seconde partie de notre histoire nationale, nous pensions pouvoir nous féliciter d'avoir posé les bases sur lesquelles s'élèvera un jour notre

195. Frame illustration for the first page of text: the fox becomes sole editor.

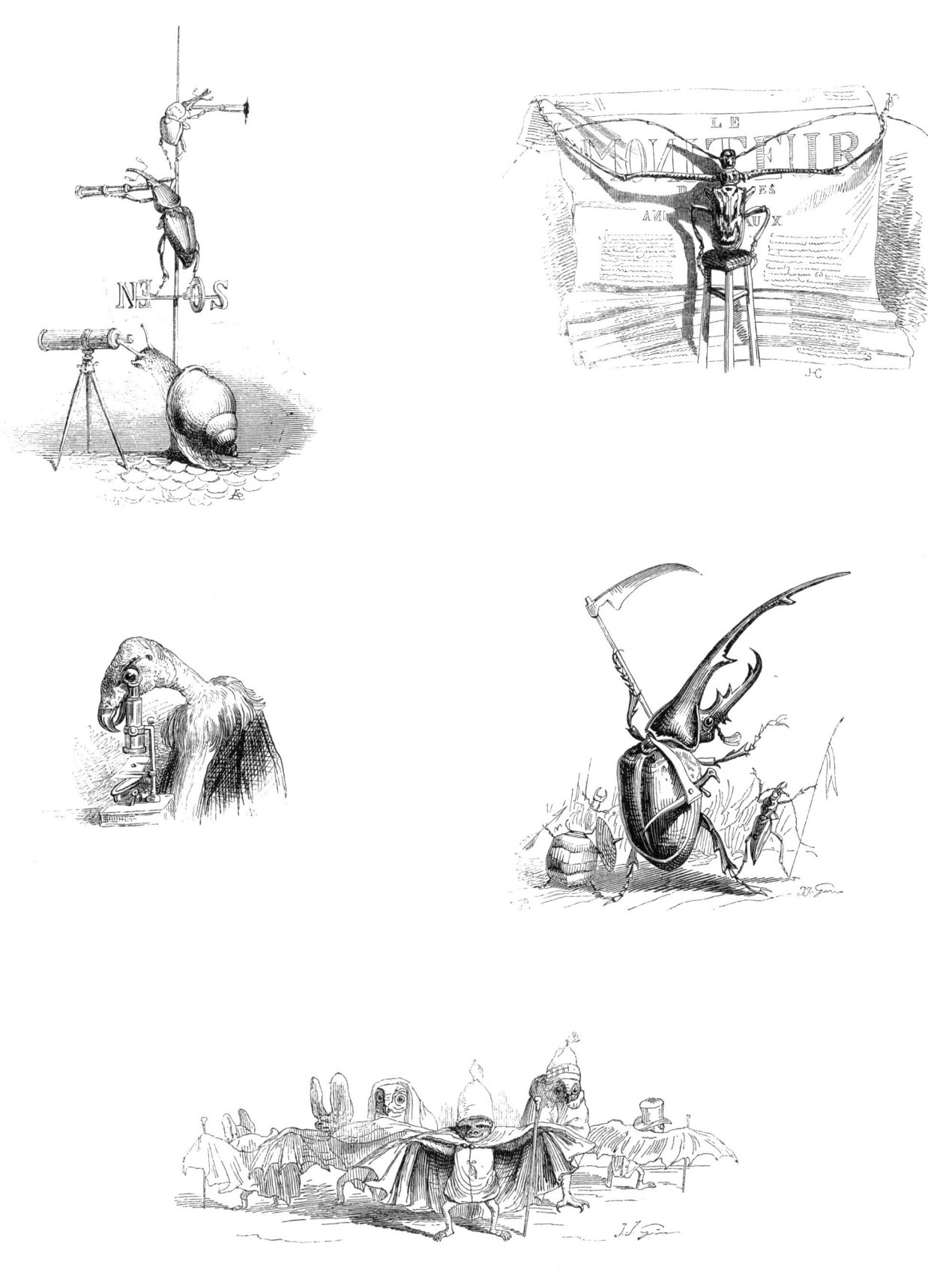

196–200. Assorted activities during the animal revolution.

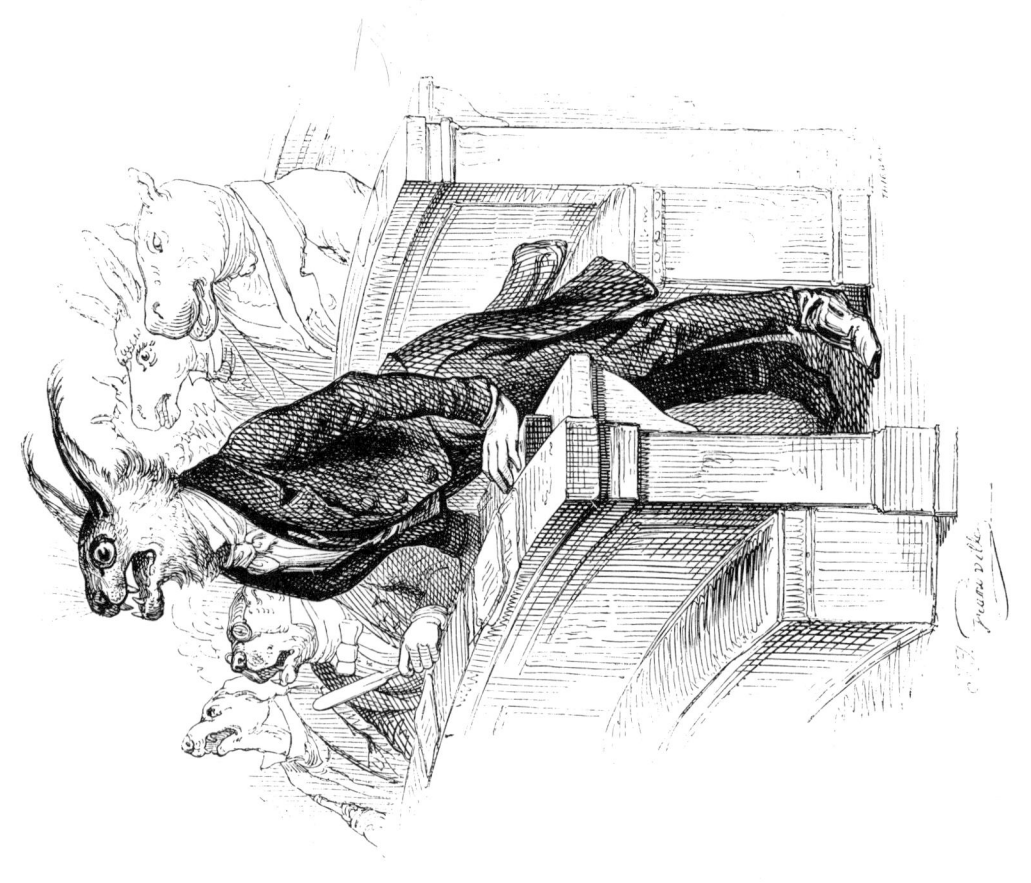

202. Another fiery orator demanding speedy action.

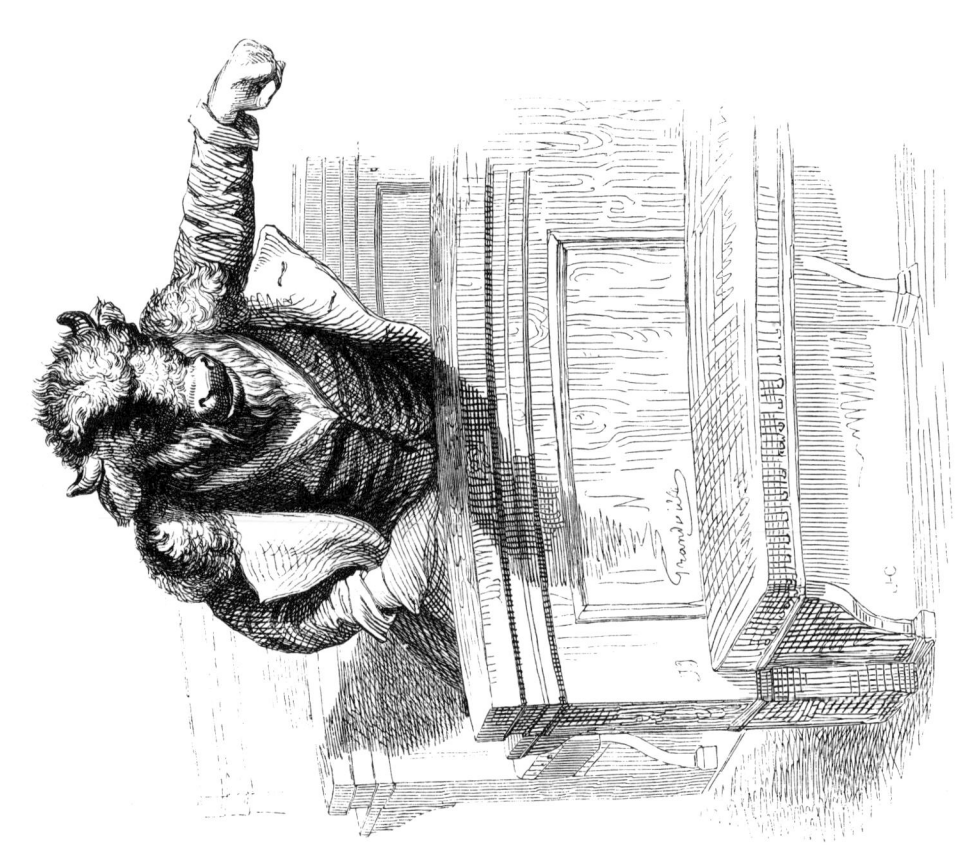

201. The bison speaks out at a meeting of the rebels.

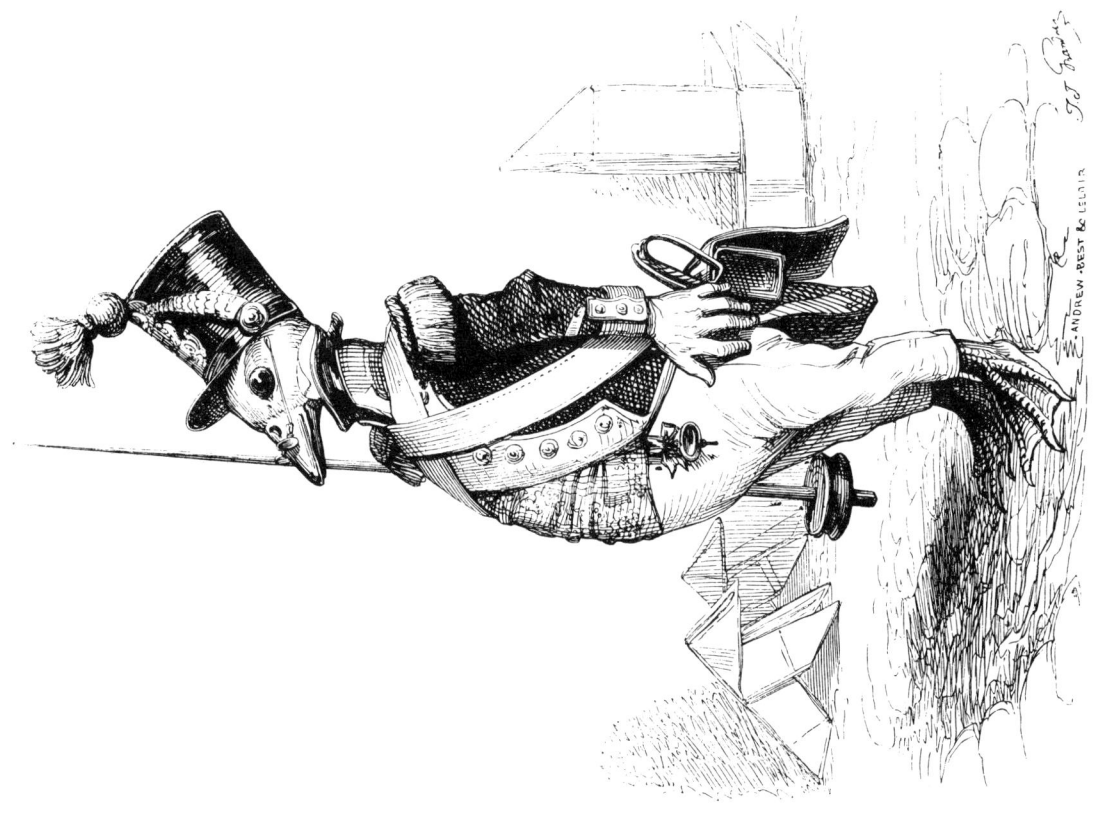

204. A loyal guardian of the old regime on sentry duty.

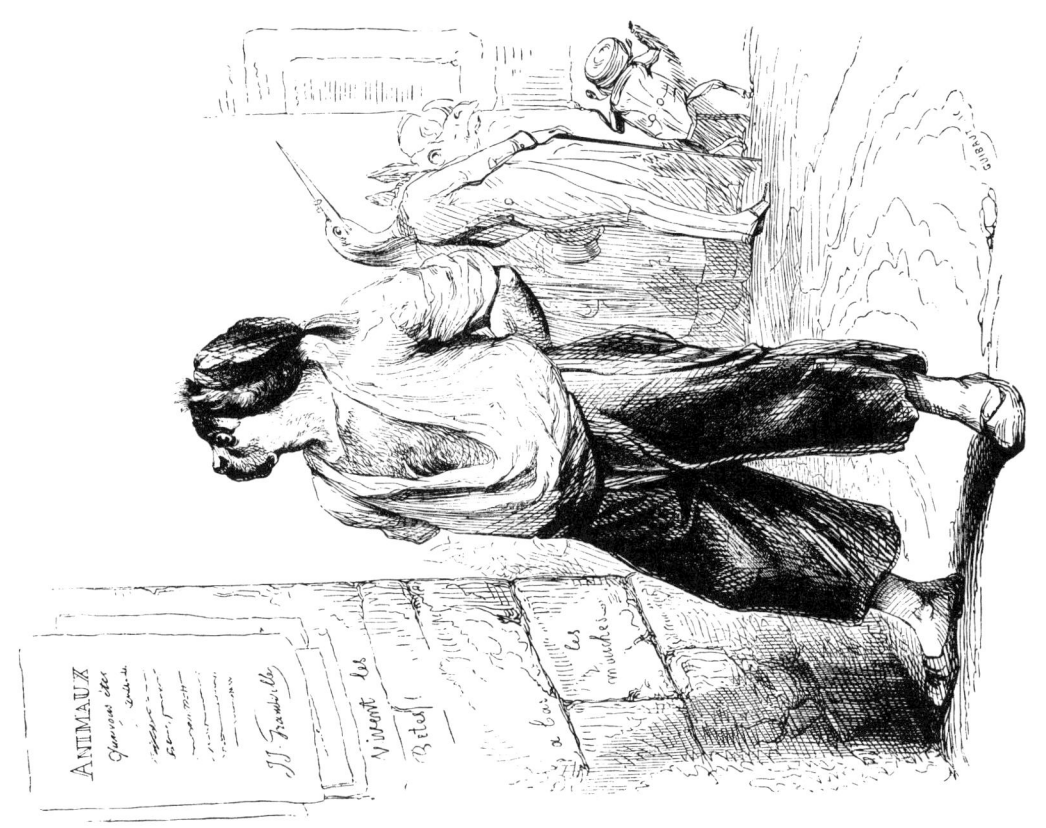

203. During the revolt, walls are covered with political manifestos.

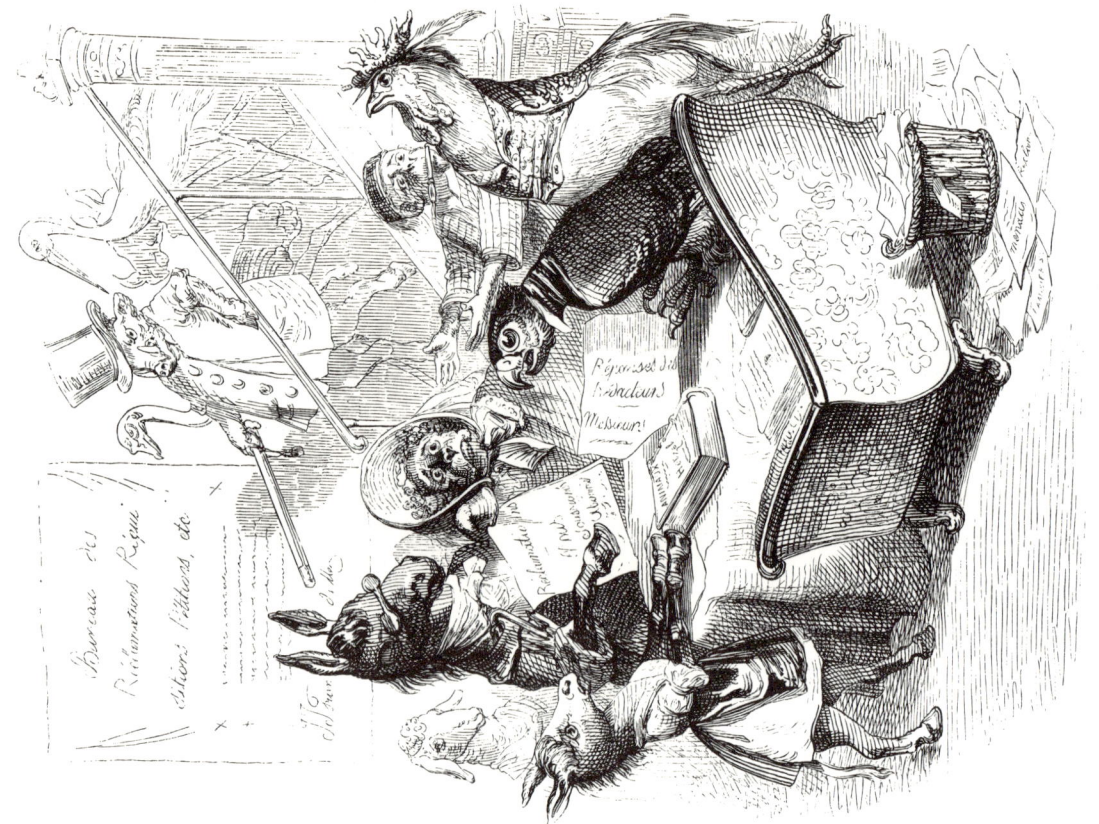

206. Animals bringing complaints to the old editors.

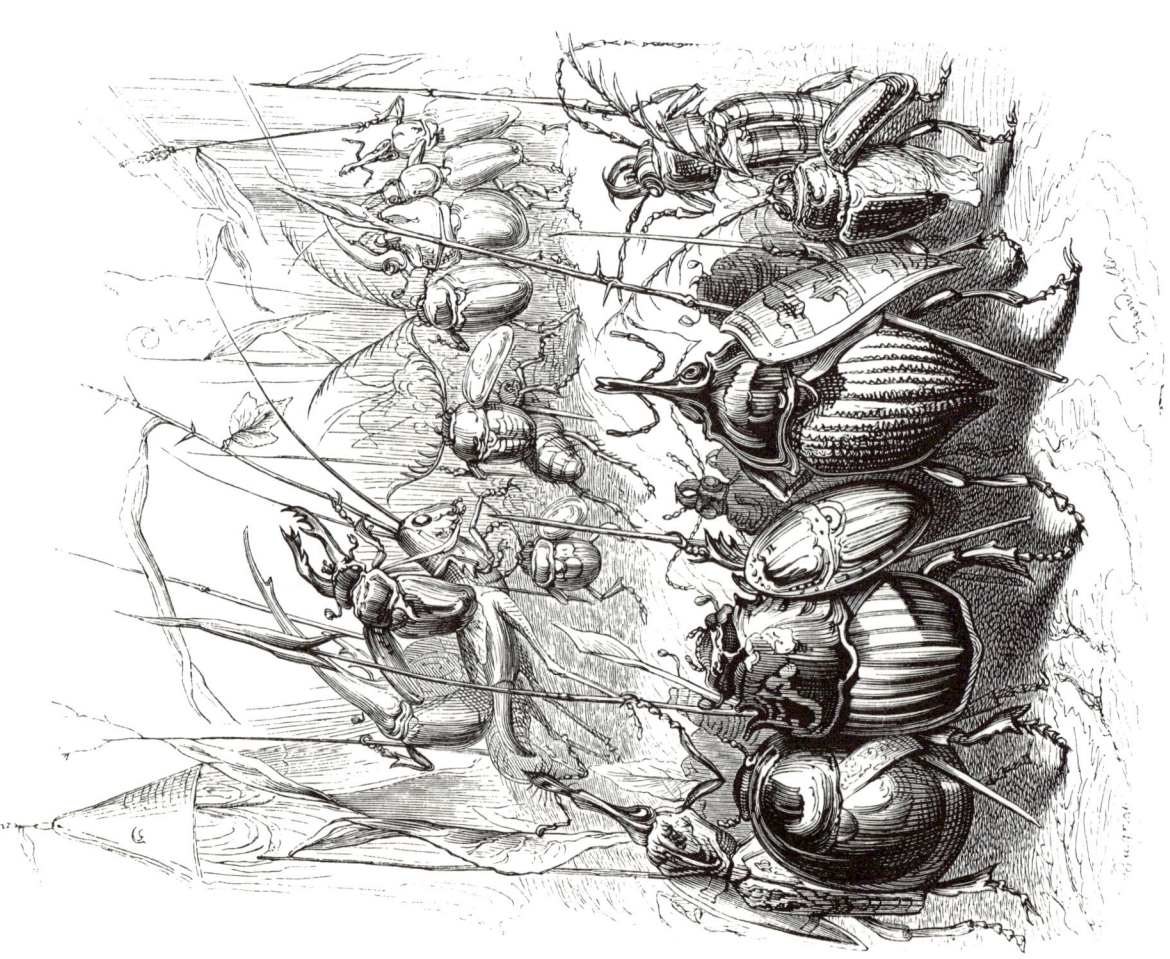

205. The heavy infantry of the rebellious insects.

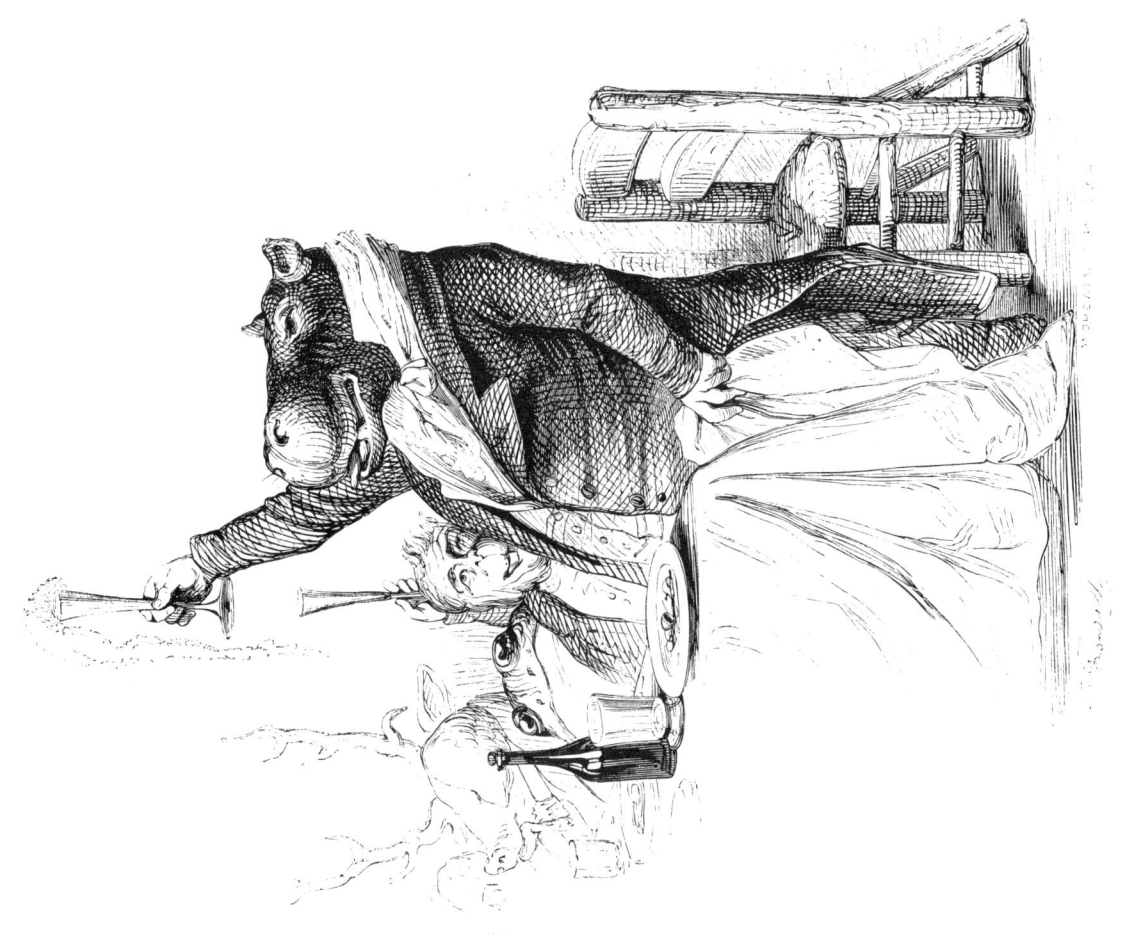

208. A gallant gentleman toasts the fair sex.

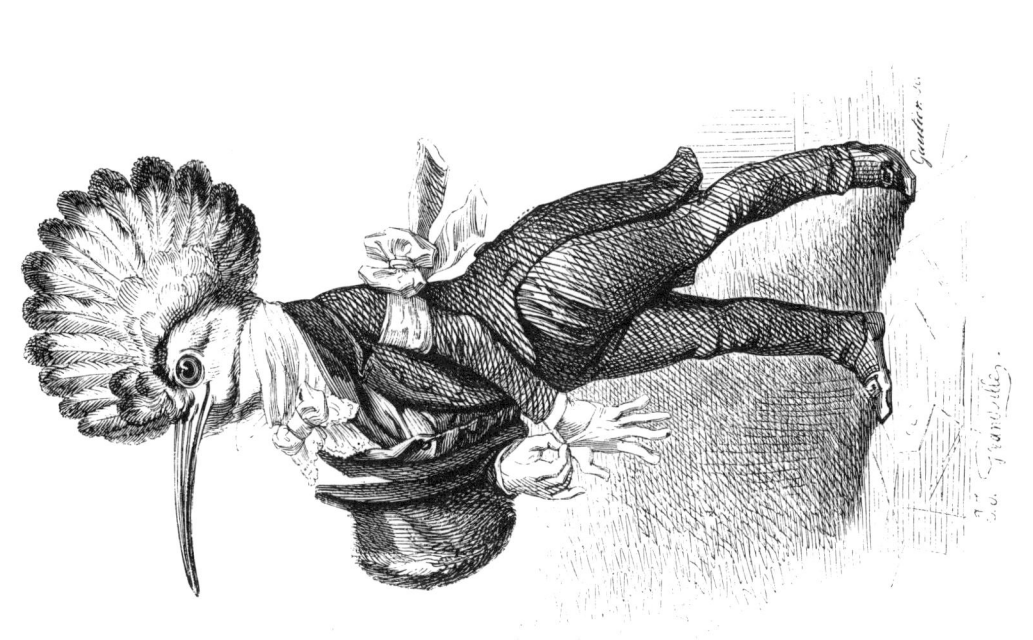

207. At the rebels' victory banquet, the showy hoopoe acts as steward.

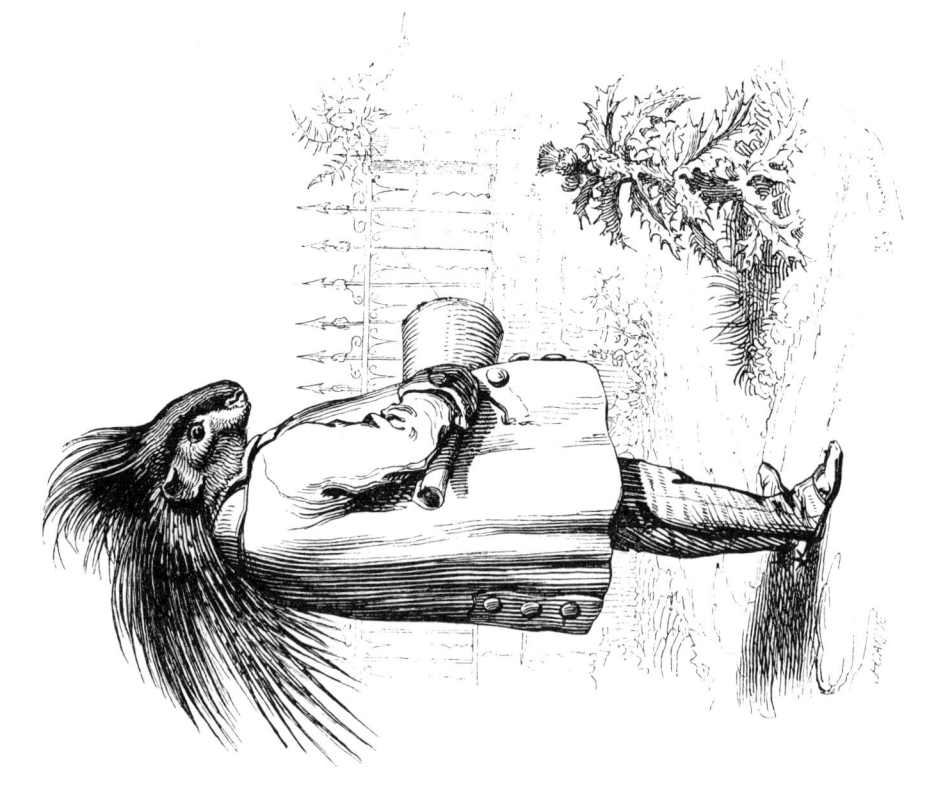

210. The hedgehog, a disagreeable neighbor of the toad.

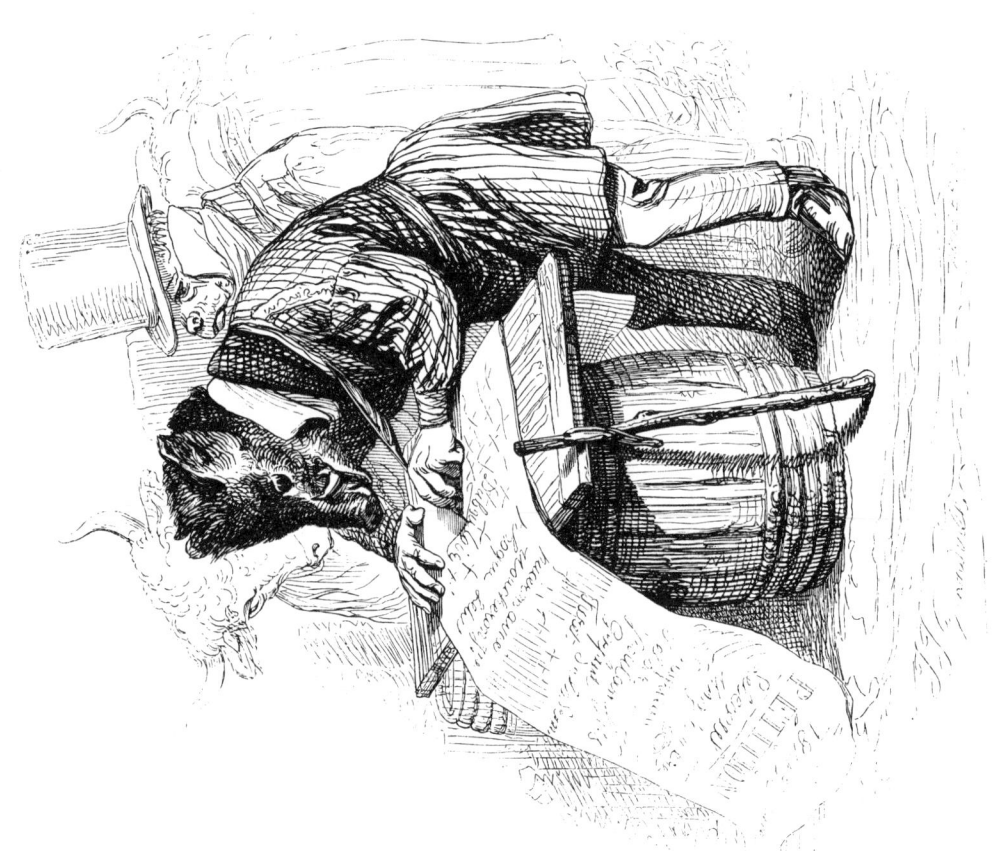

209. After the fox is in power, the animals continue to draw up many petitions, which are systematically ignored.

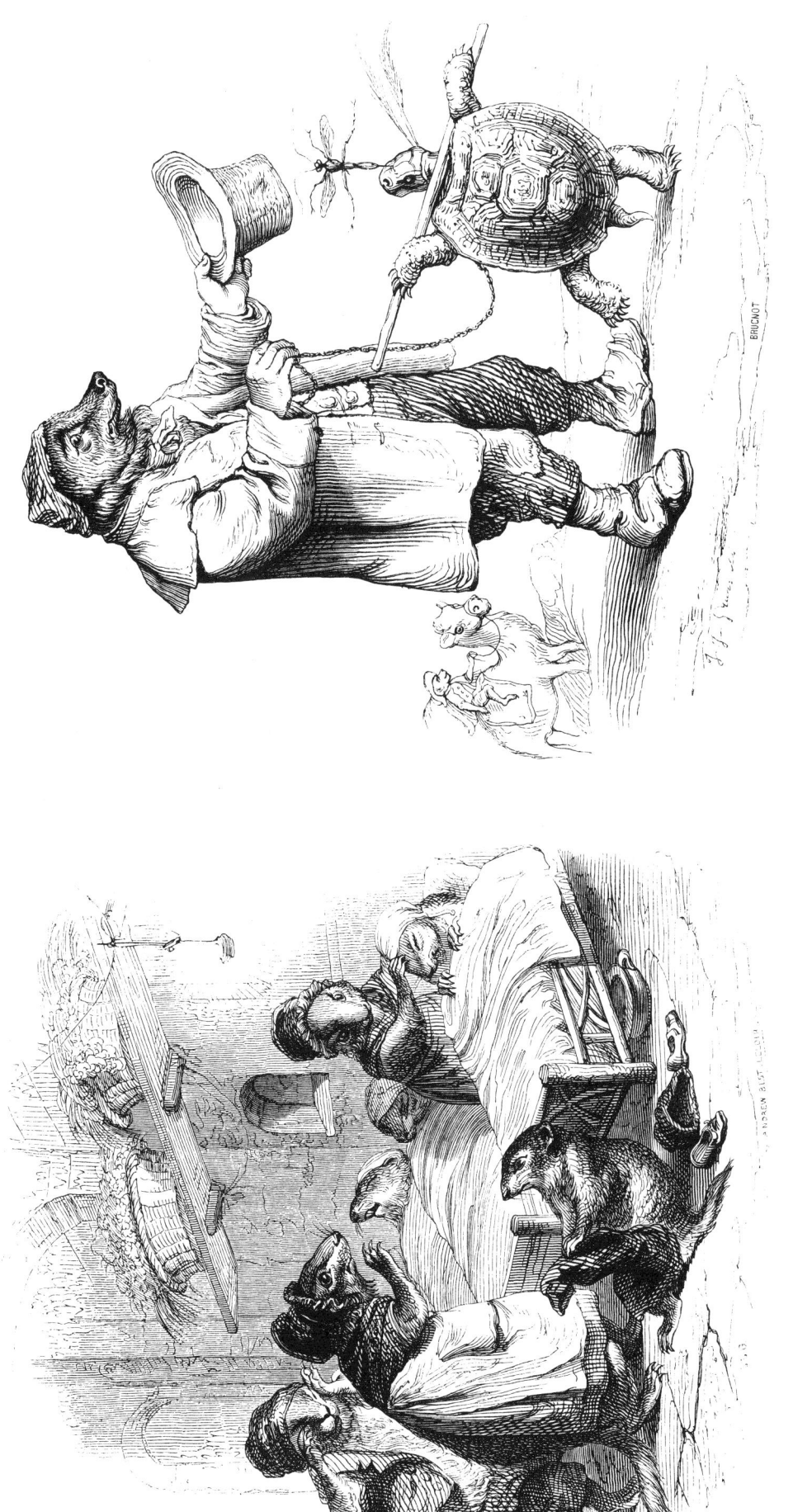

212. A performing tortoise in the marmot's troupe.

211. The marmot family preparing to hibernate.

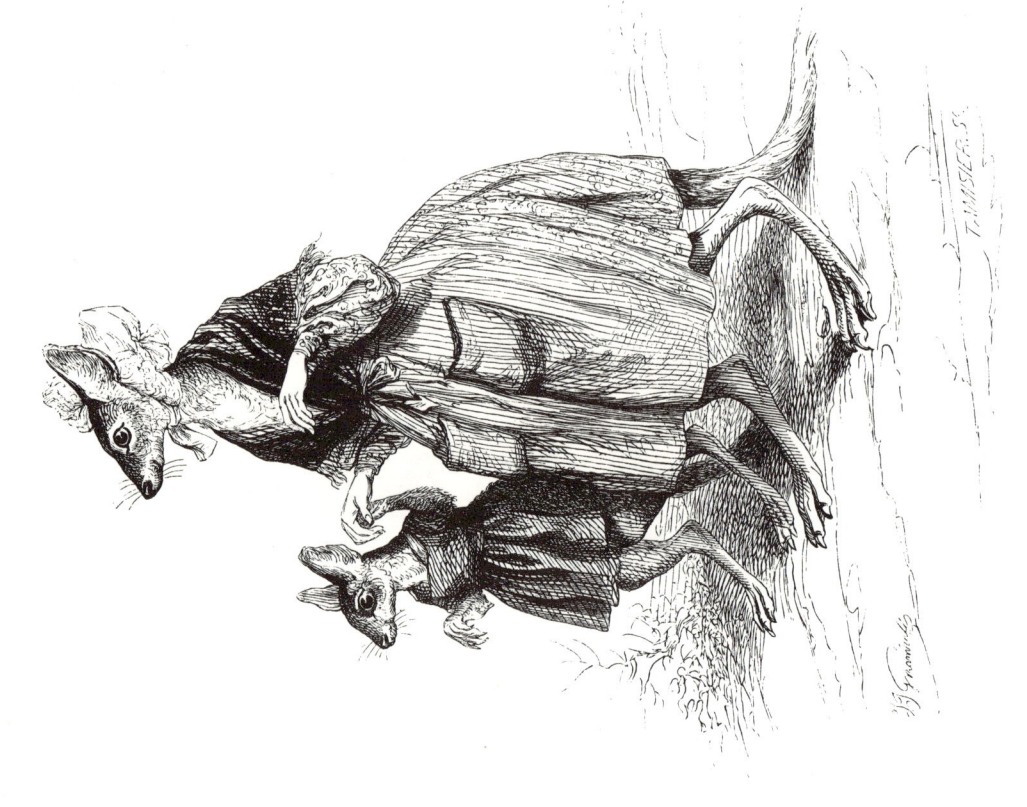

214. A mother kangaroo in the zoo.

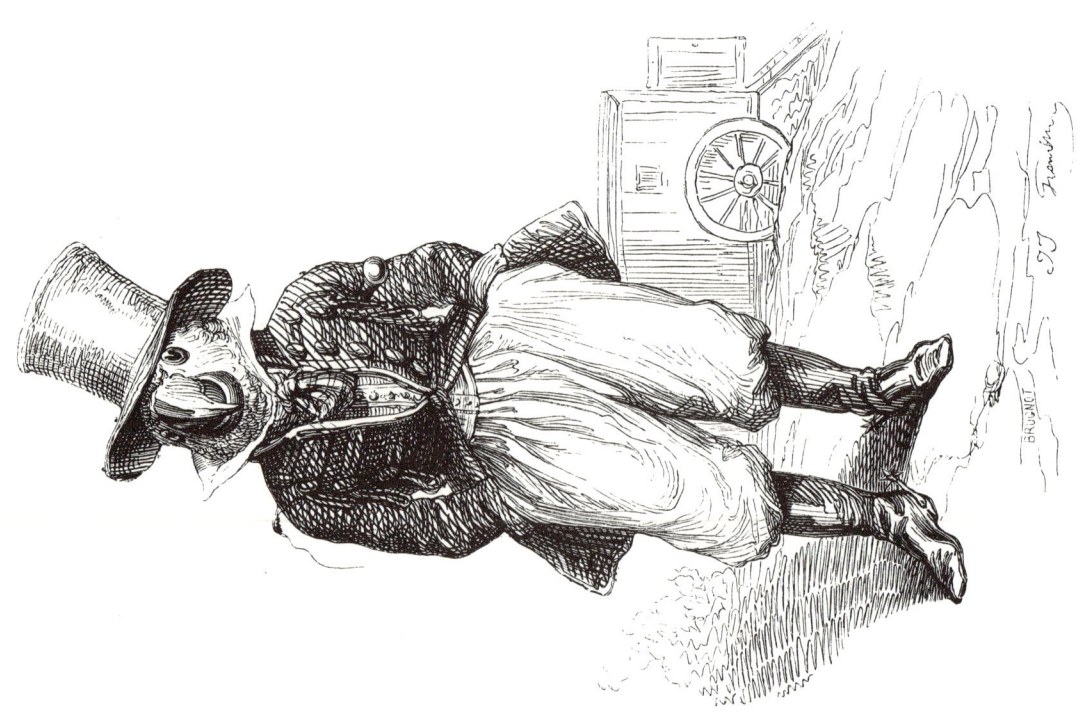

213. The brutal director of the troupe.

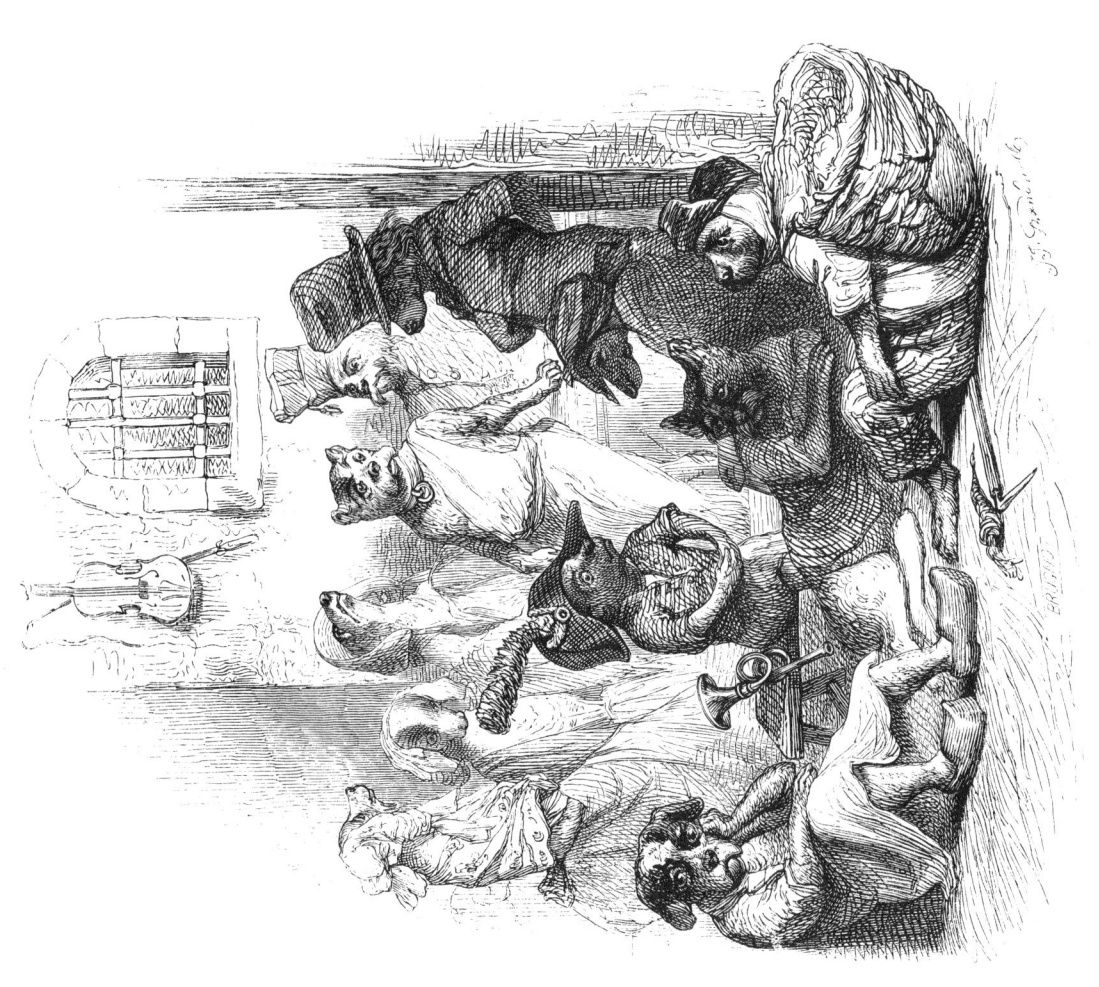

216. The dog pound.

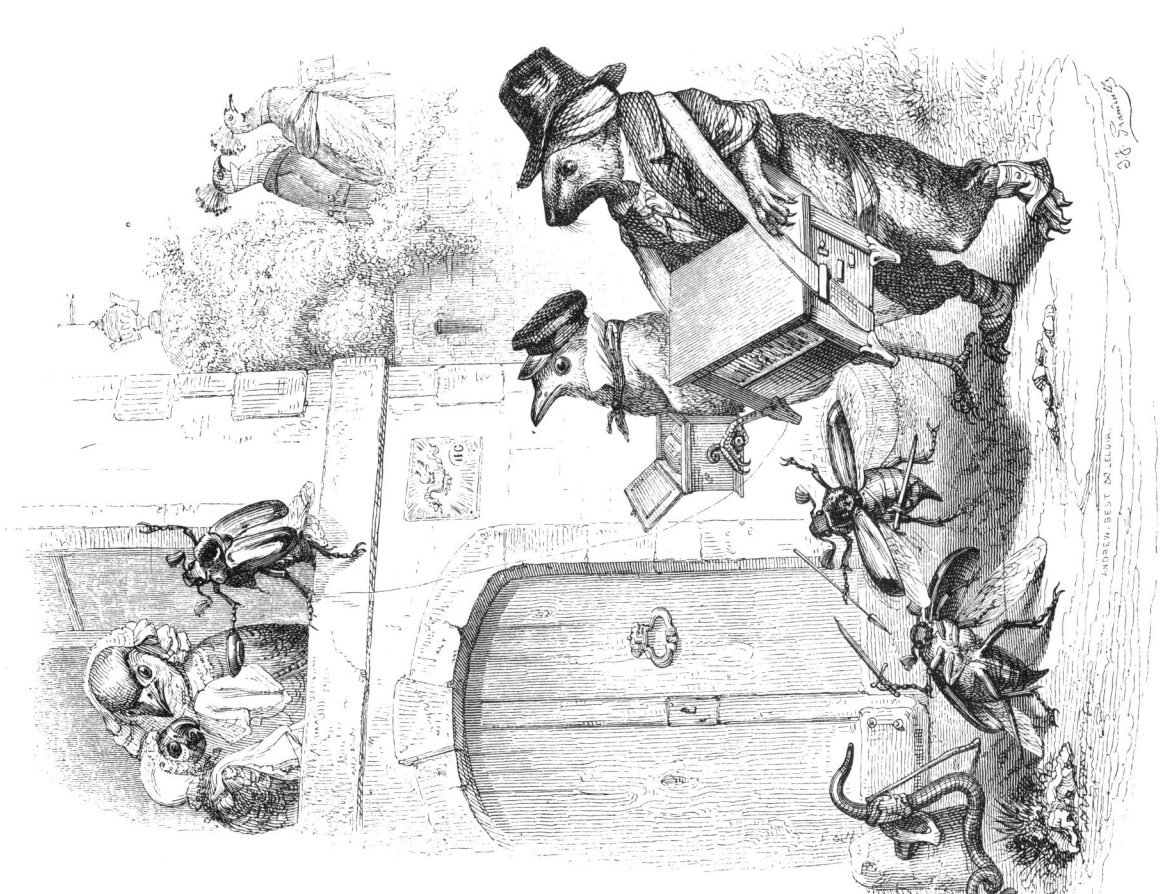

215. The marmot dreams that she is an independent exhibitor, owner of performing junebugs.

Les Animaux 139

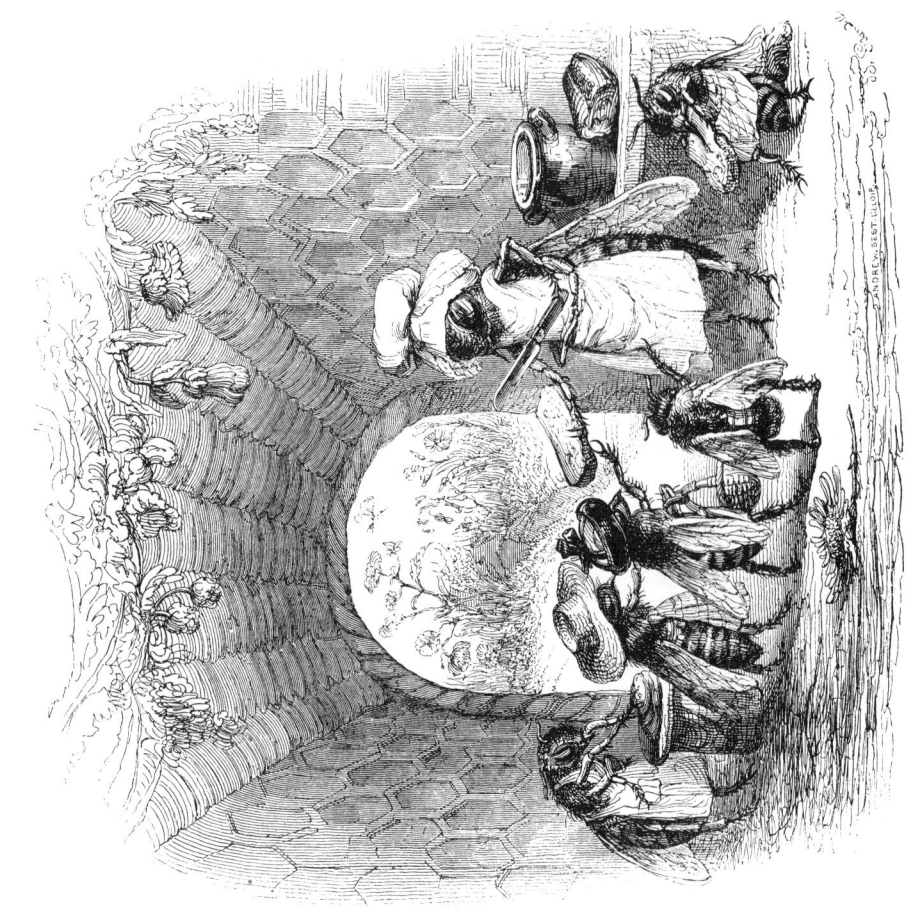

218. A bee-nursemaid in the hive giving her charges bread and honey.

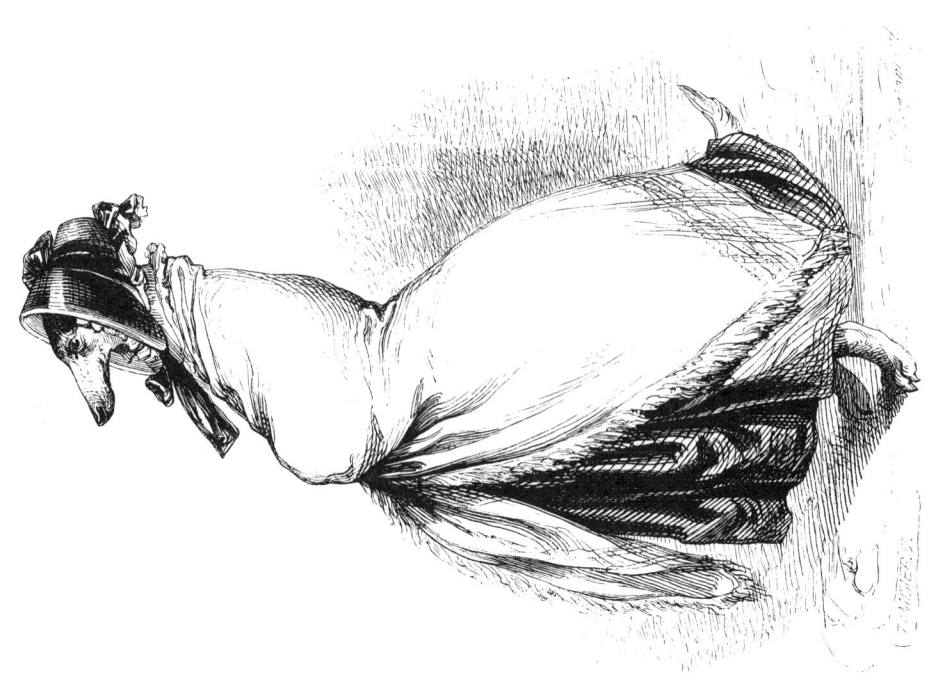

217. A female greyhound who got lost and was impounded.

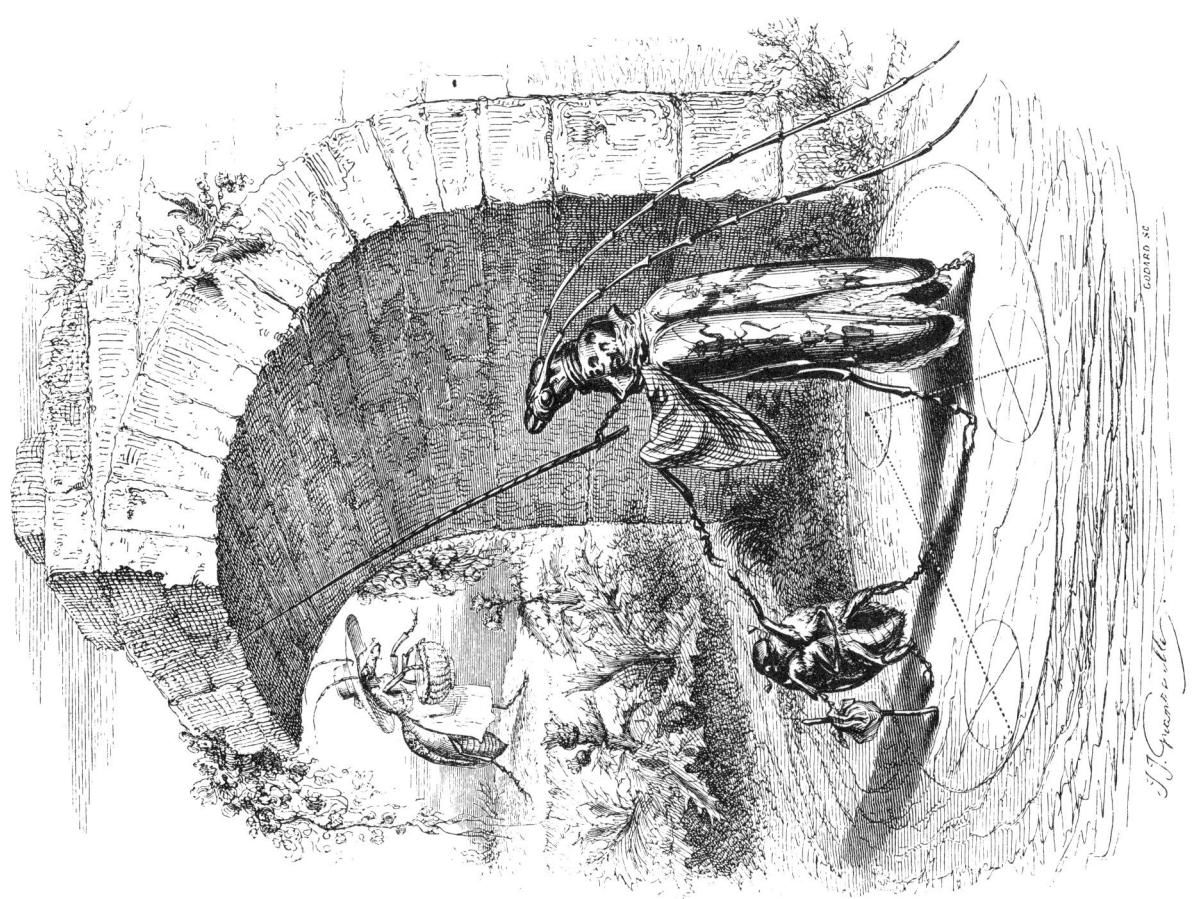

220. The capricorn beetle casting the click-beetle's horoscope.

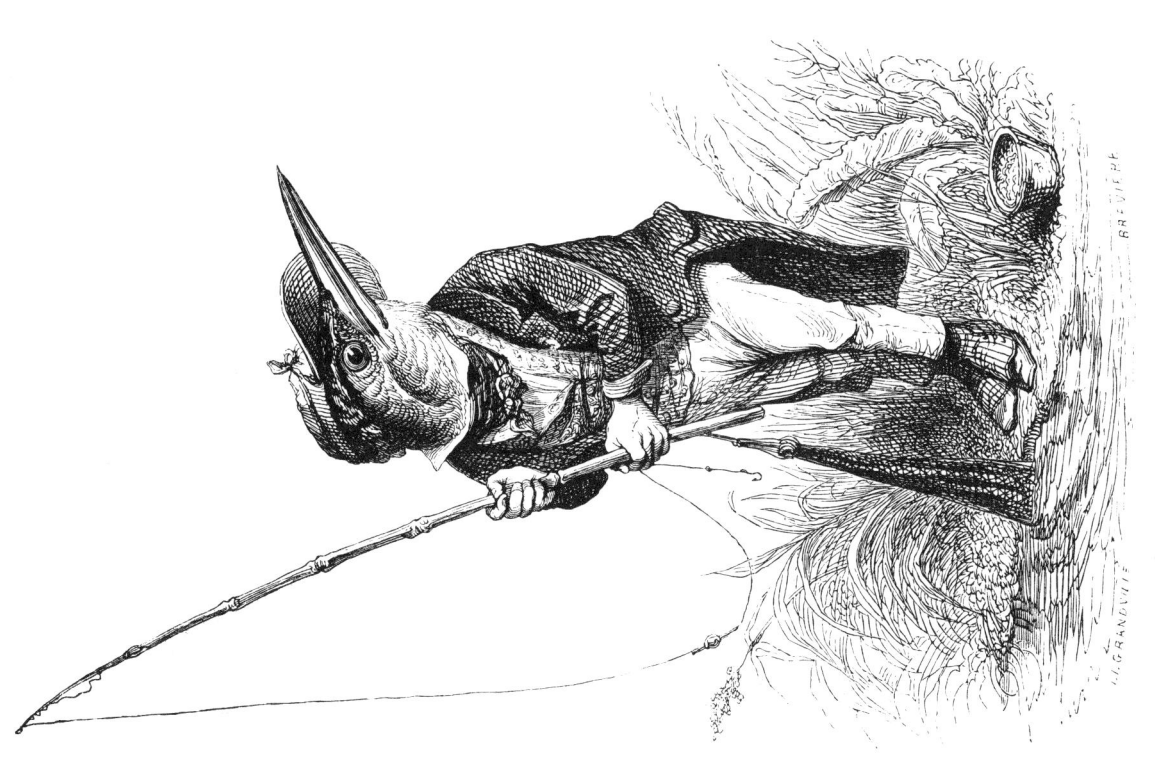

219. The kingfisher, a rival of the toad as a consumer of bees.

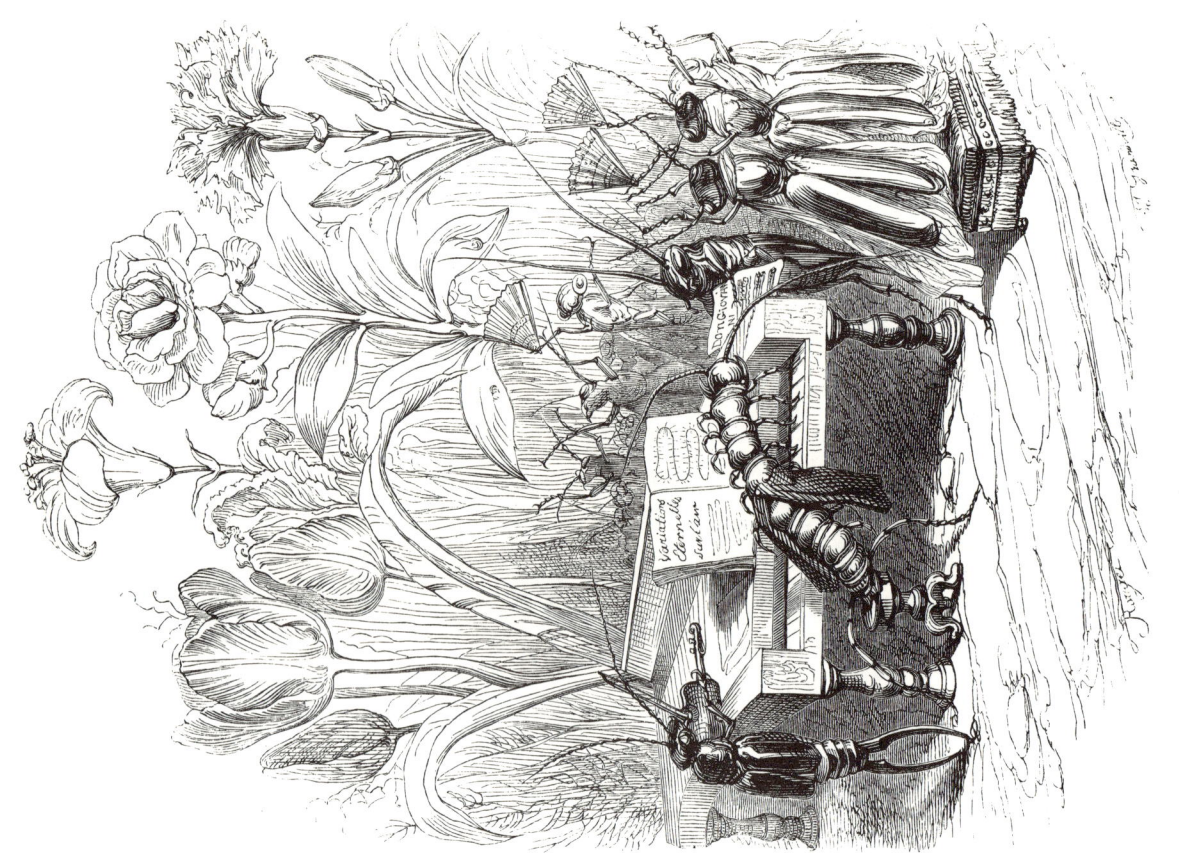

222. A grand concert, with a virtuoso pianist.

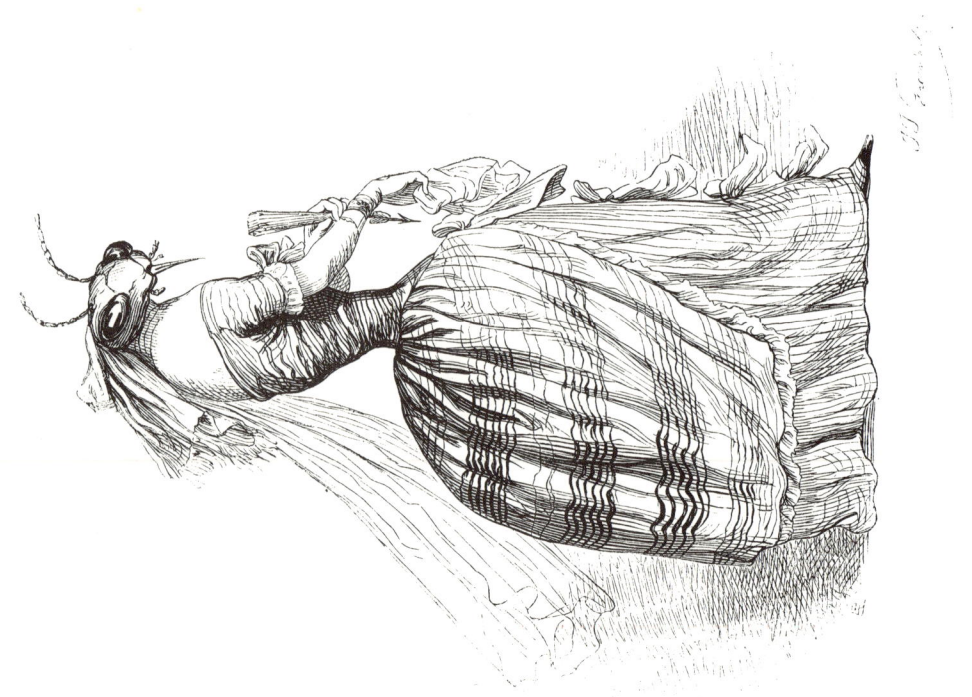

221. The elegantly narrow-waisted wasps one meets in society.

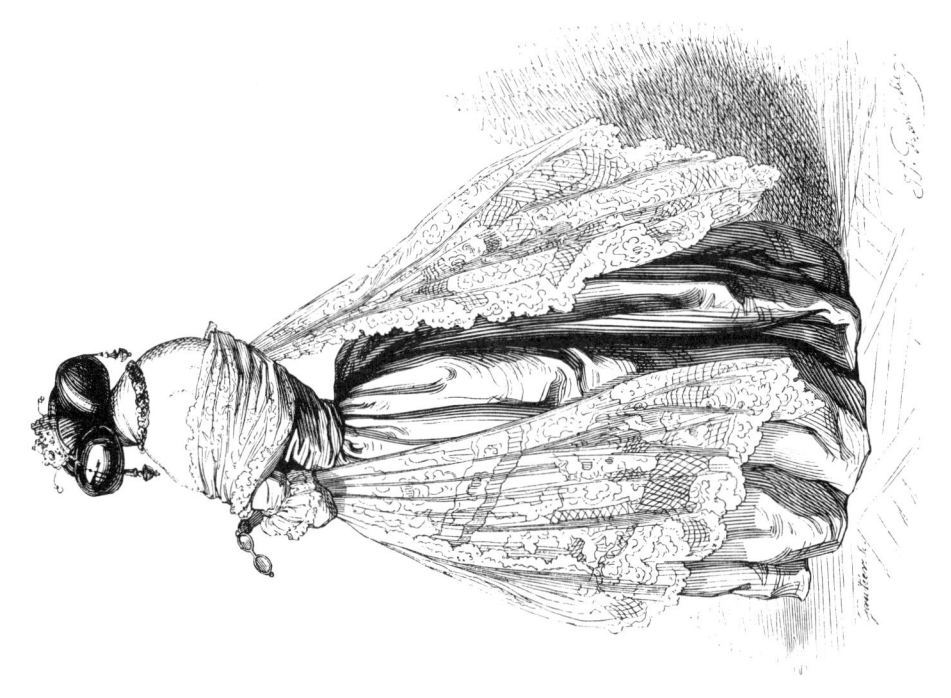

224. A painted-lady butterfly, a potential danger to young insects.

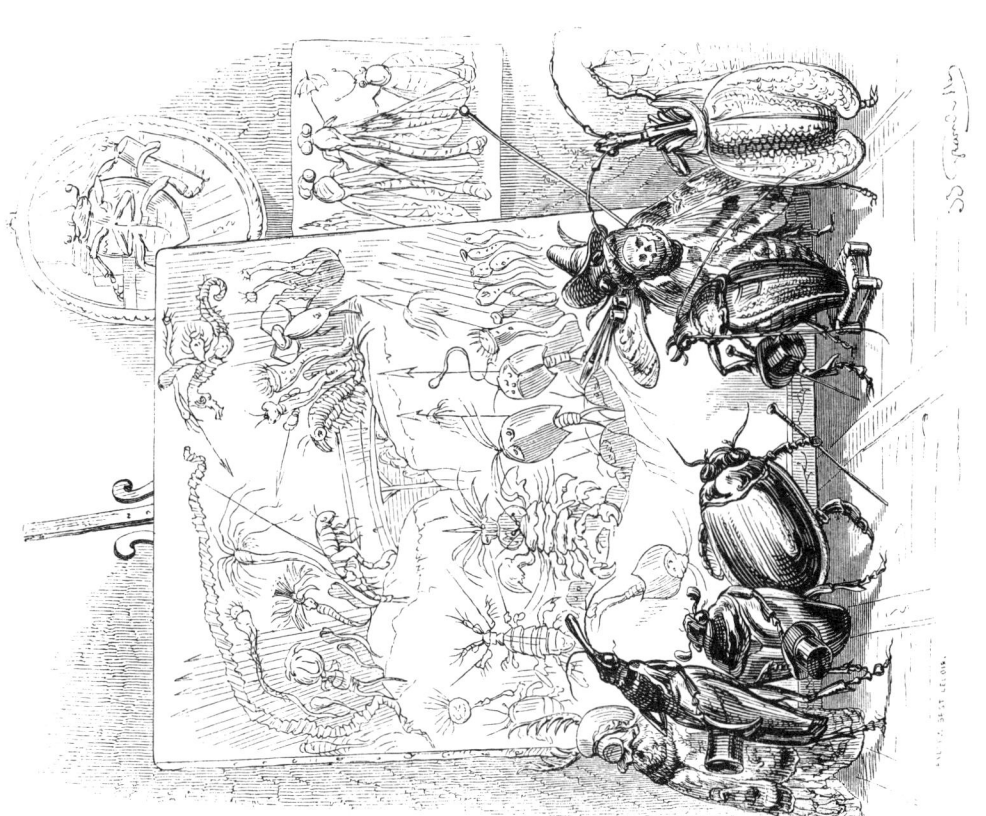

223. A painting of the animalcules that live in a drop of water.

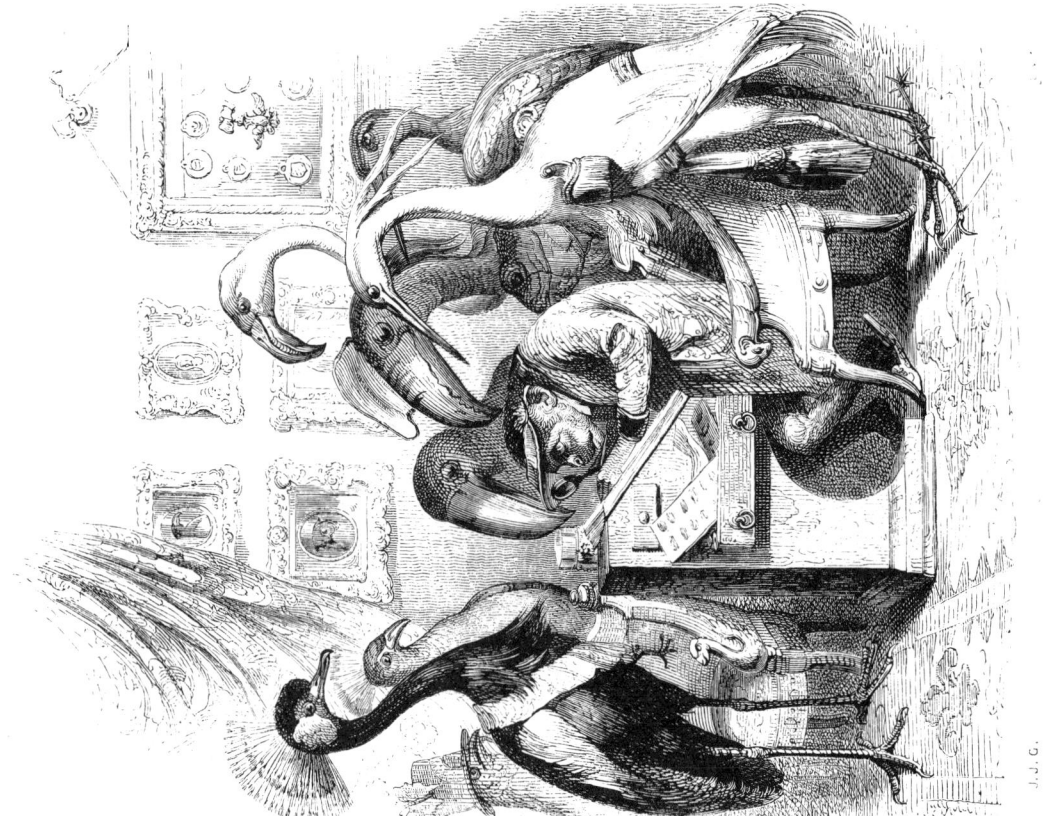

226. Topaz retouches a daguerreotype in his studio, to a chorus of comments by gawkers.

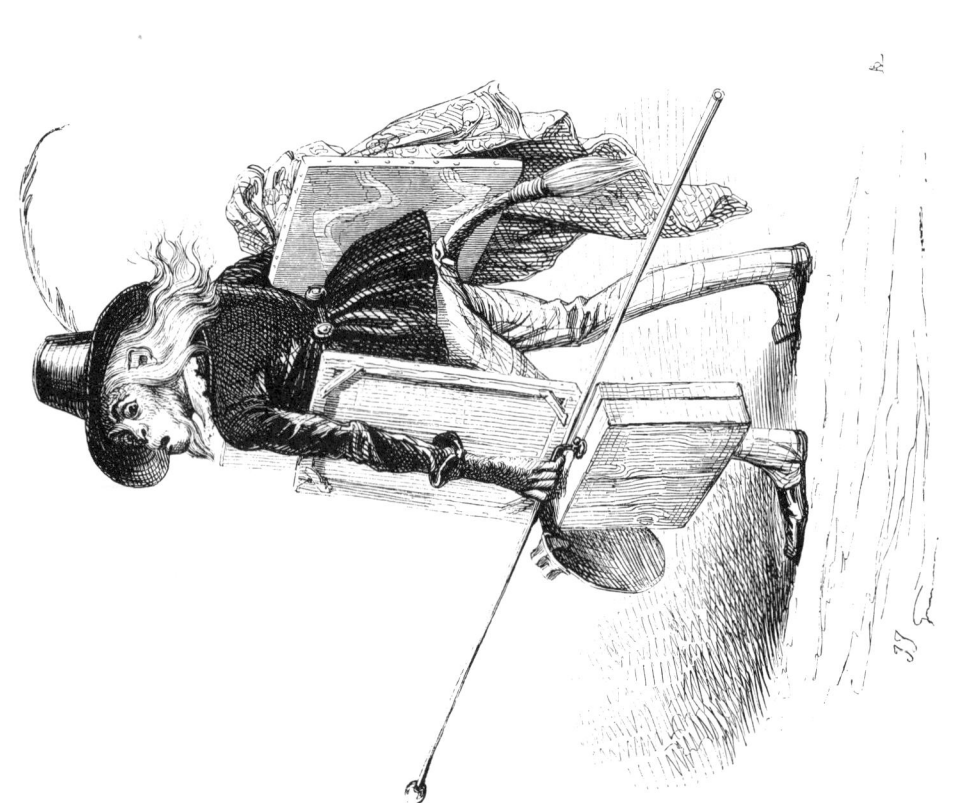

225. Topaz on his way to an art lesson.

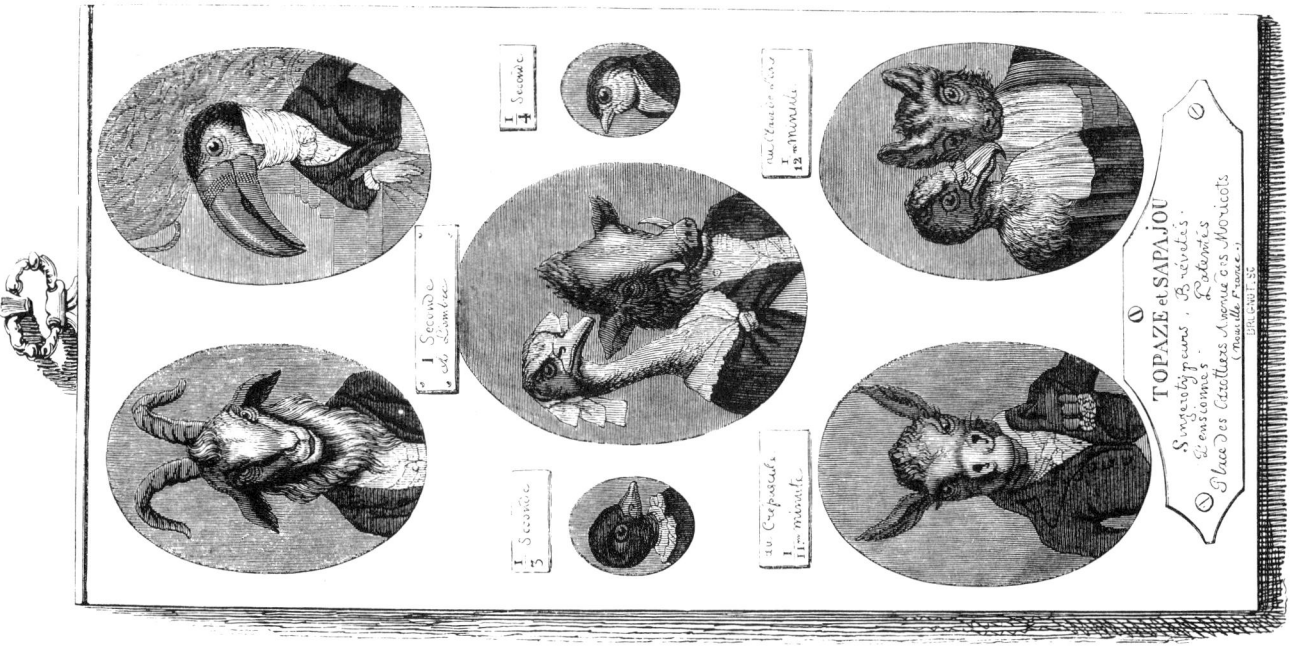

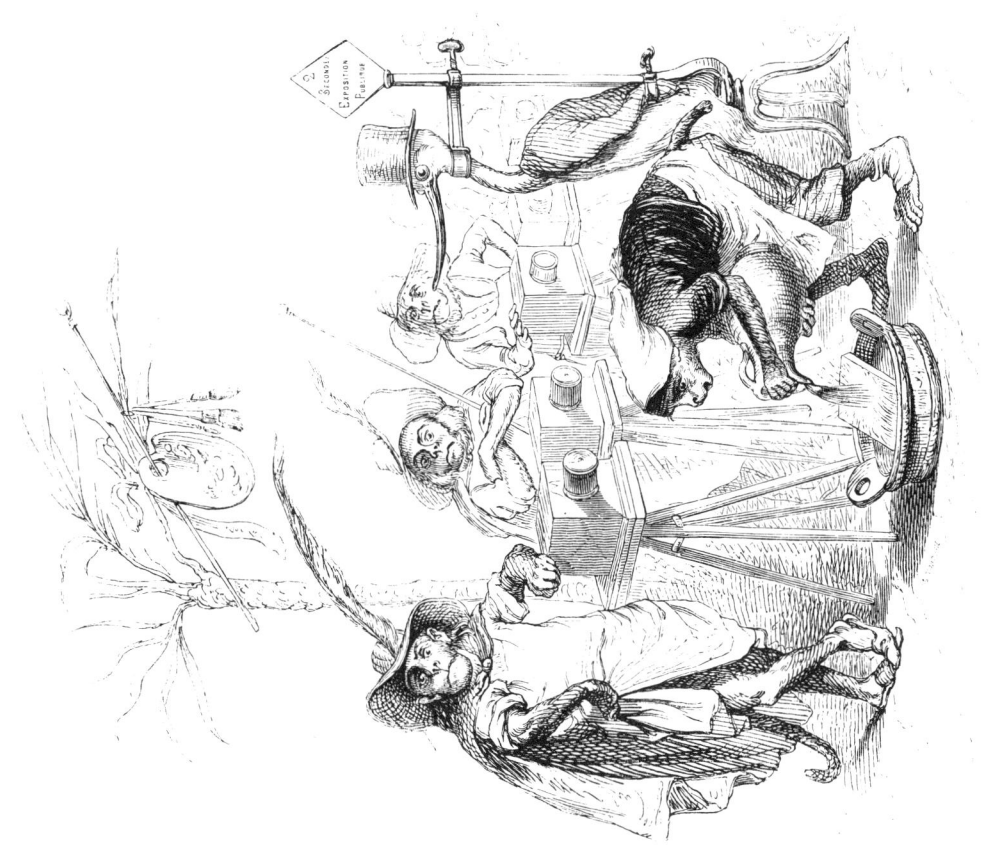

227. Topaz taking a picture.　**228.** Pictures of Topaz's customers.

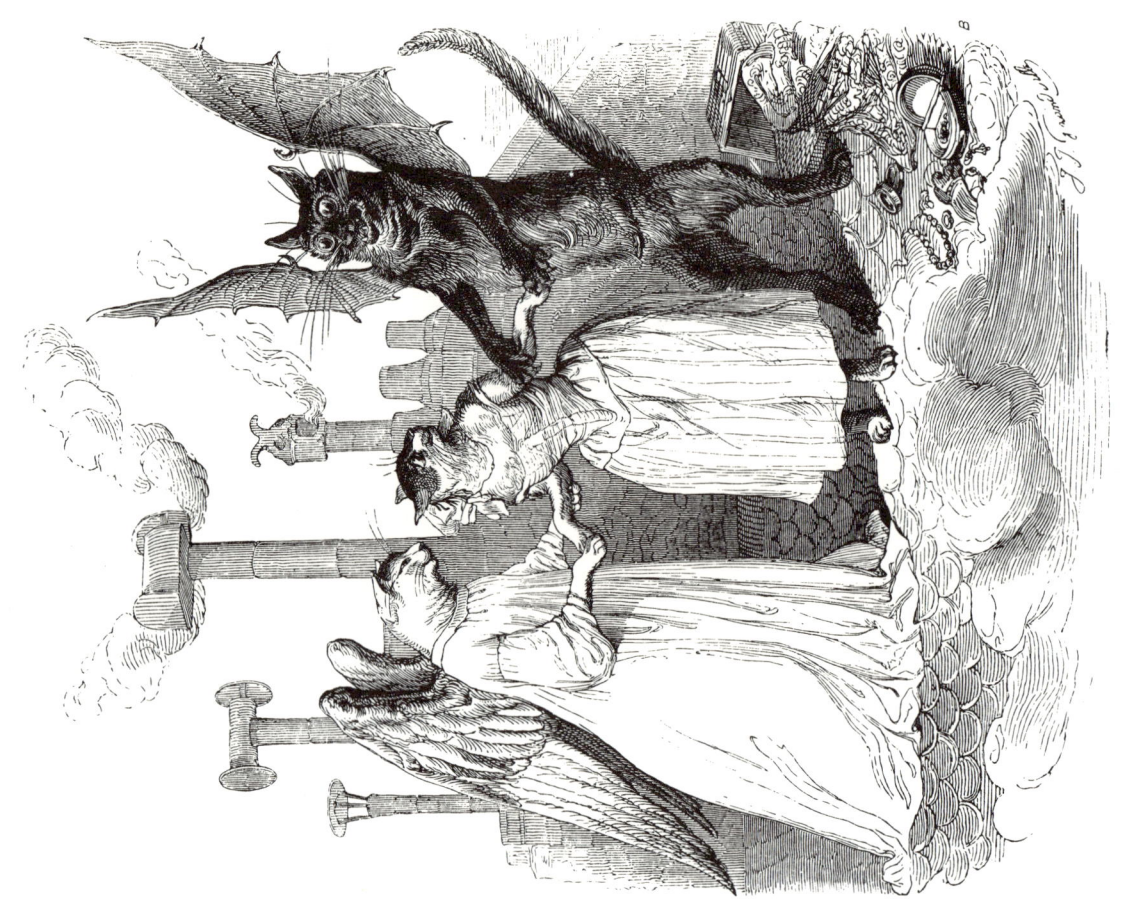

230. The heroine pays more attention to her evil genius, who promises wealth, than to her guardian angel.

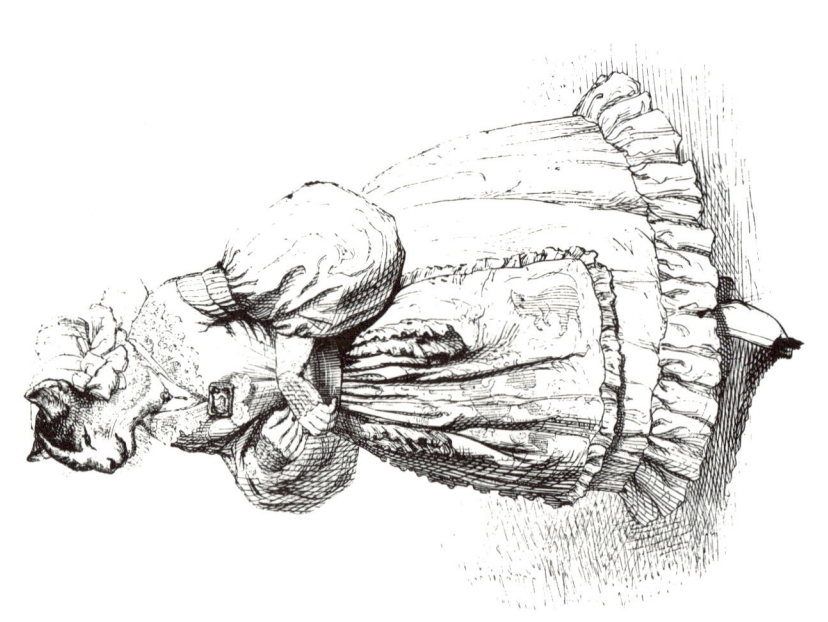

229. The poor mistress of the two sister cats, who lives by sewing.

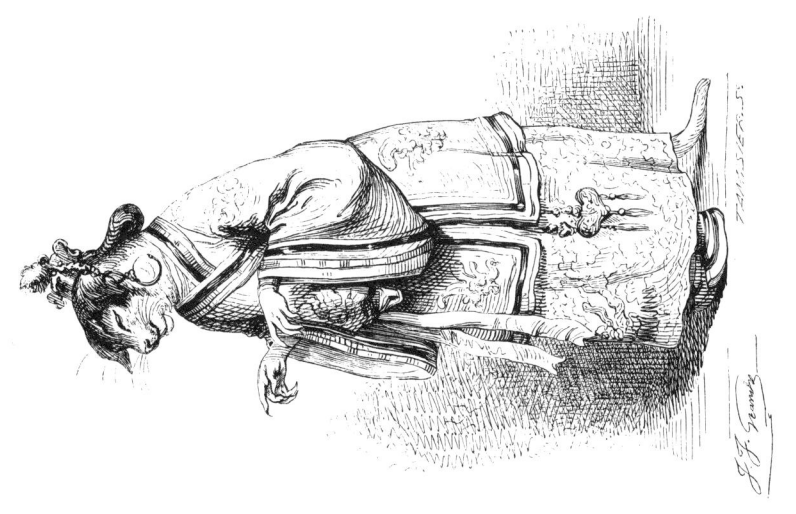

232. The Chinese beauty.

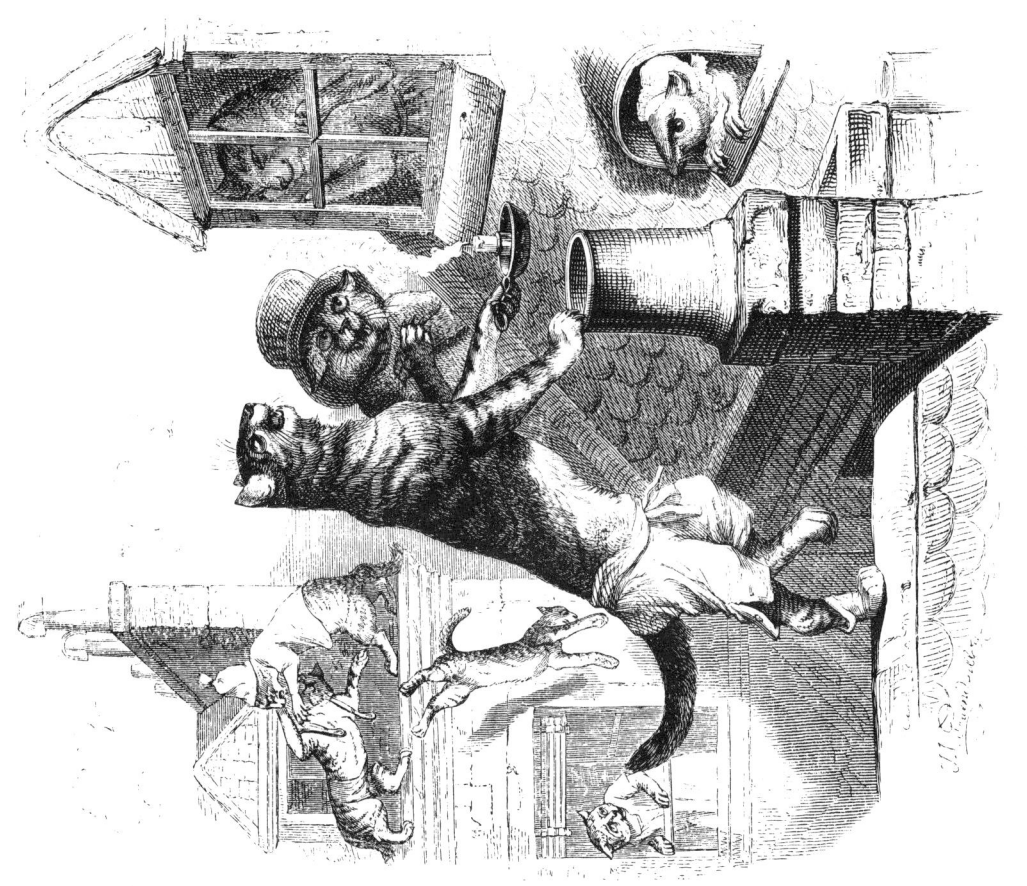

231. After her adventures, she turns a deaf ear to toms who come court-ing.

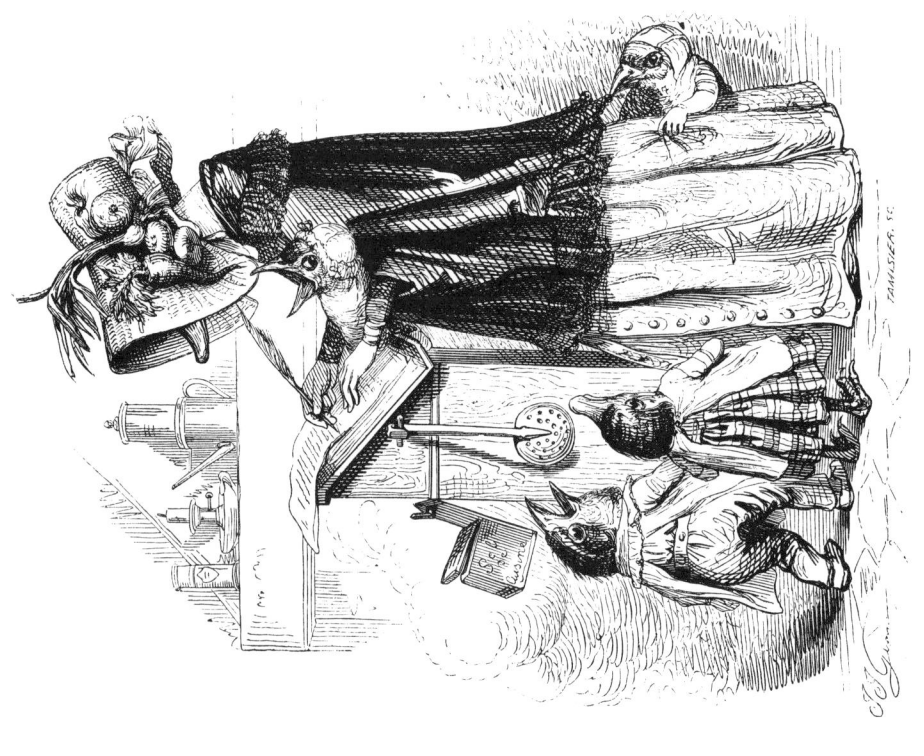

234. The problems of an authoress mother.

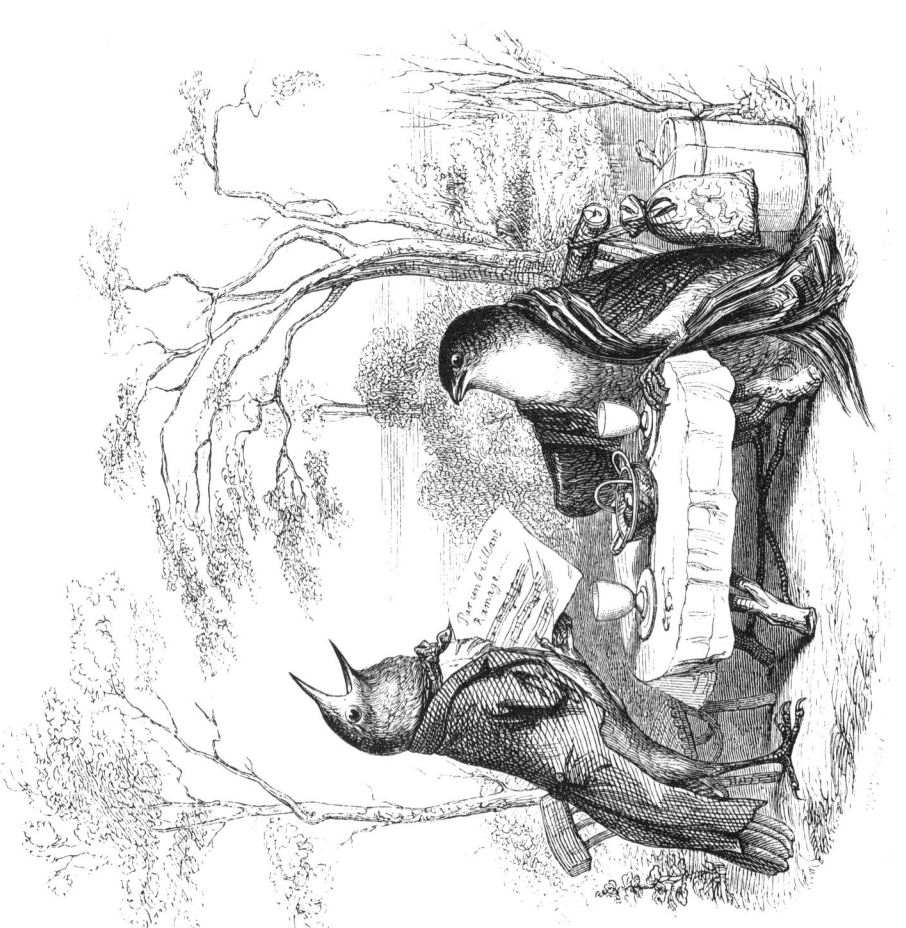

233. The swallow meets a nightingale tenor who advises her to live for pleasure.

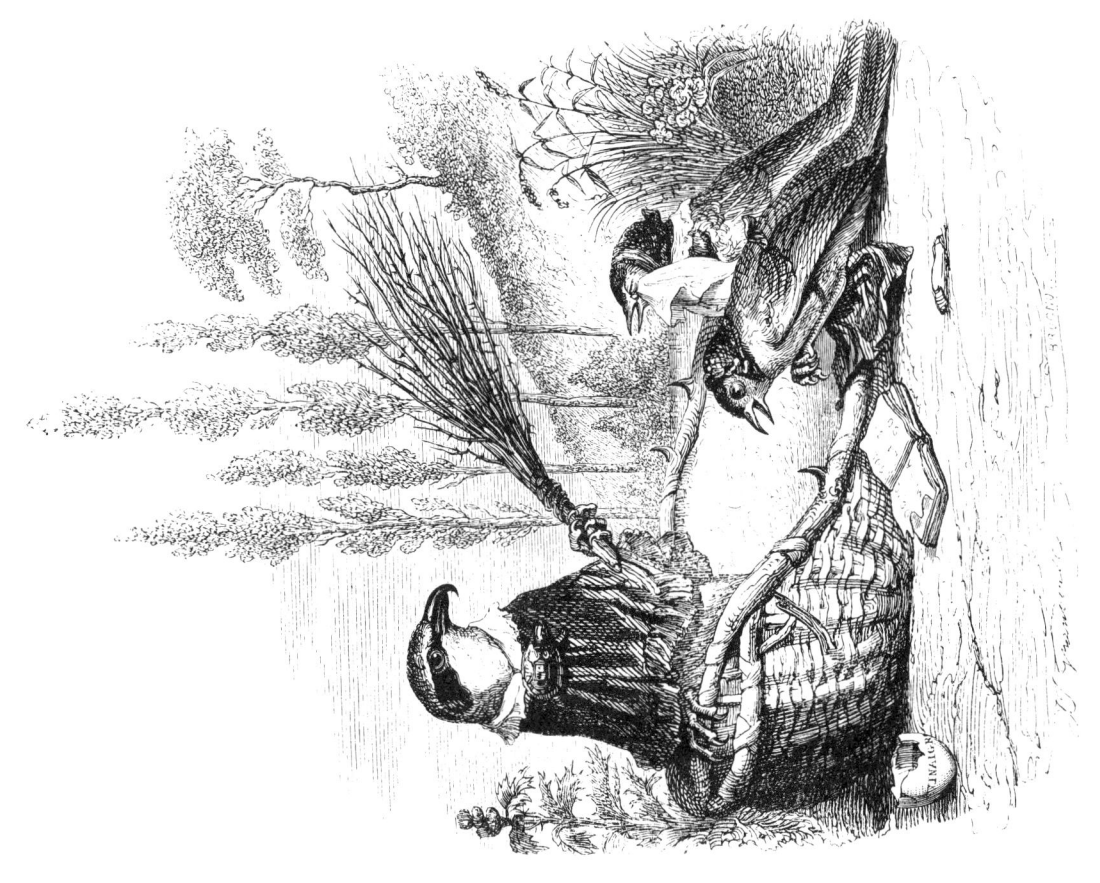

236. A shrike, stepmother of two warblers, makes their life miserable.

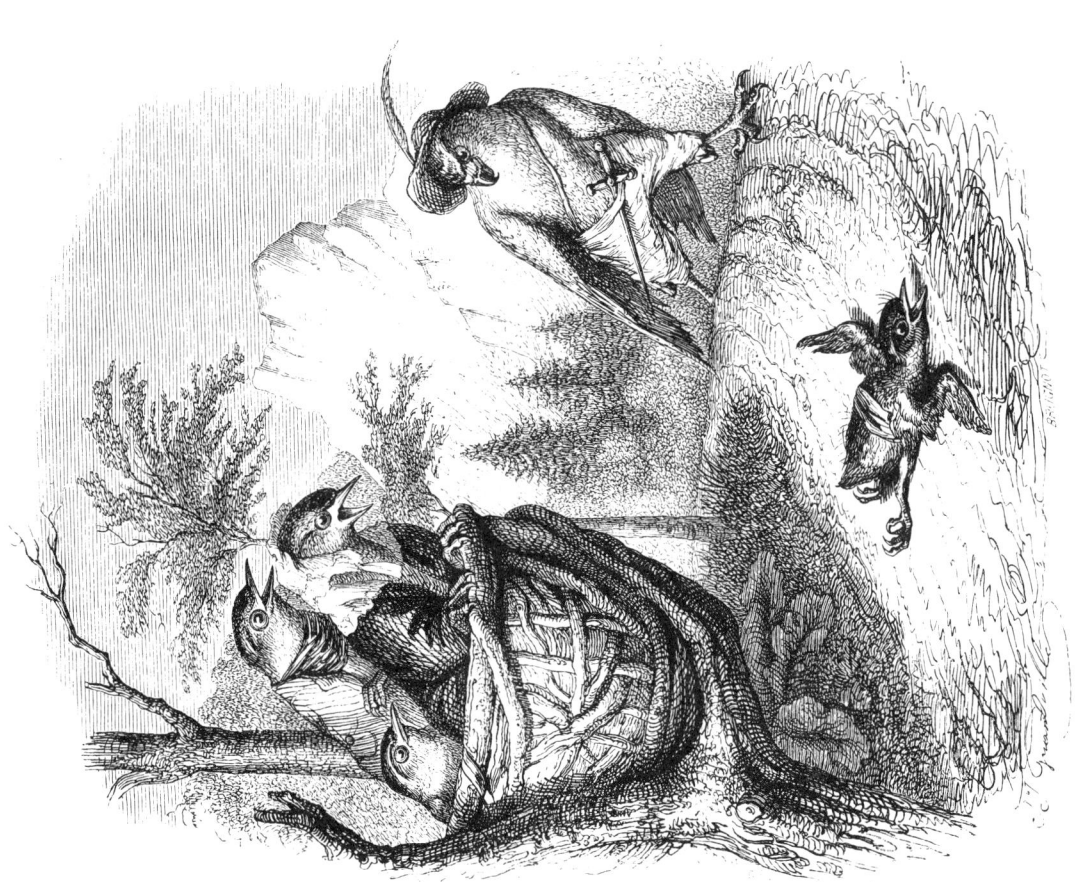

235. Tragedy in a robin family: a fledgling falls from the nest while a bird of prey is near.

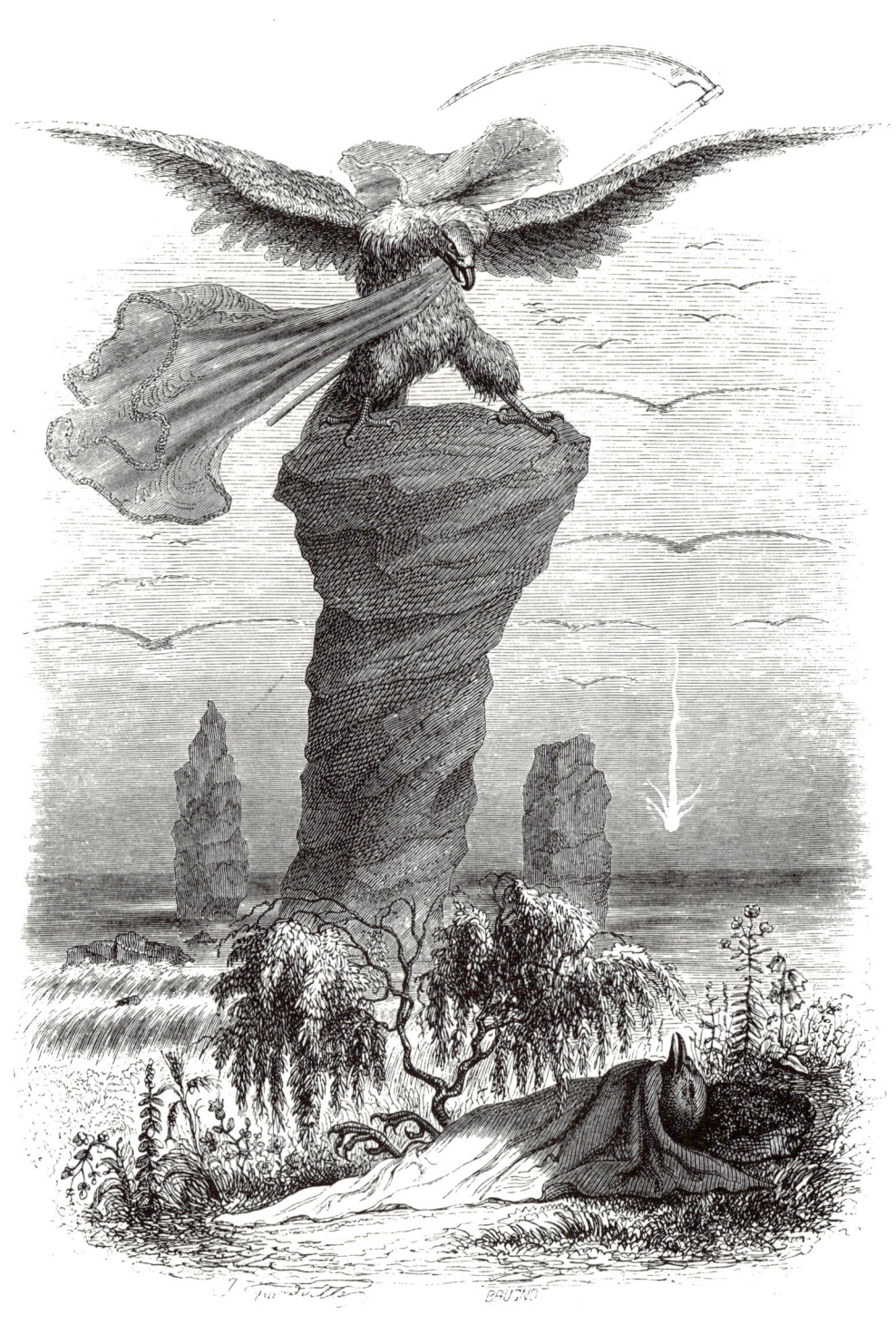

237. The moment of the turtledove's passing, as recounted in his poem.

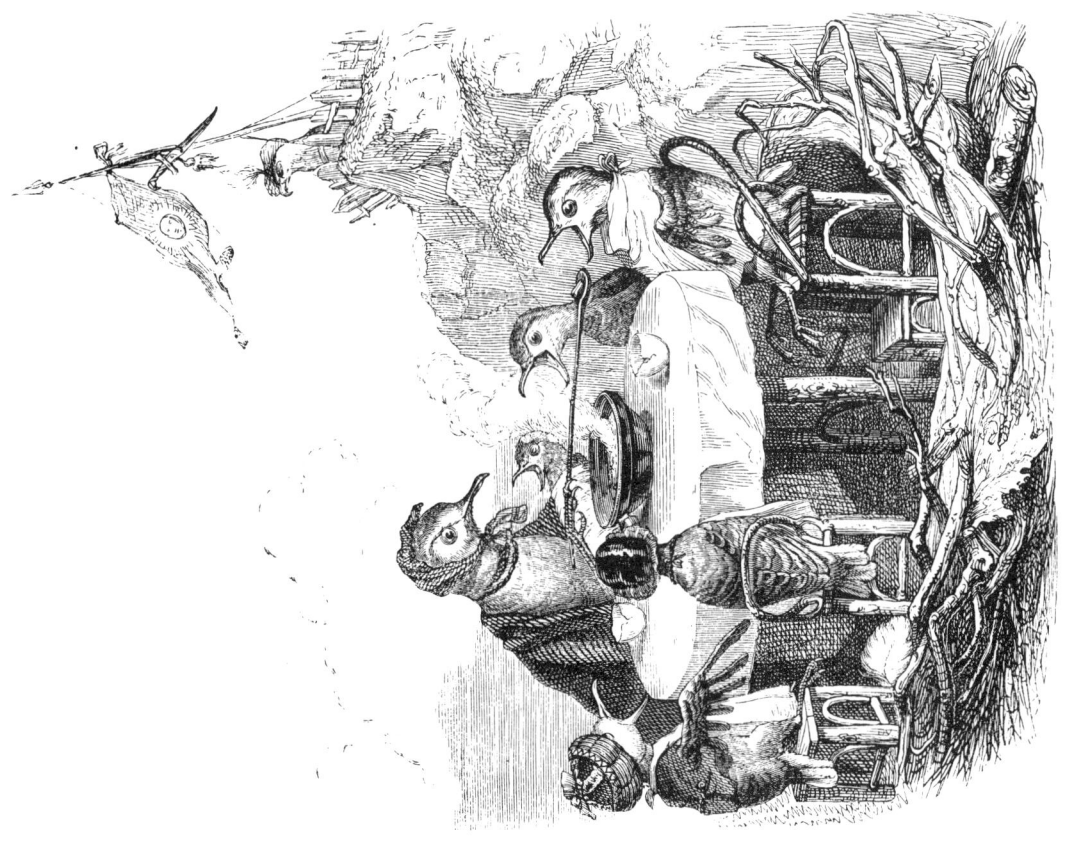

239. His sweetheart, now mother of a numerous brood.

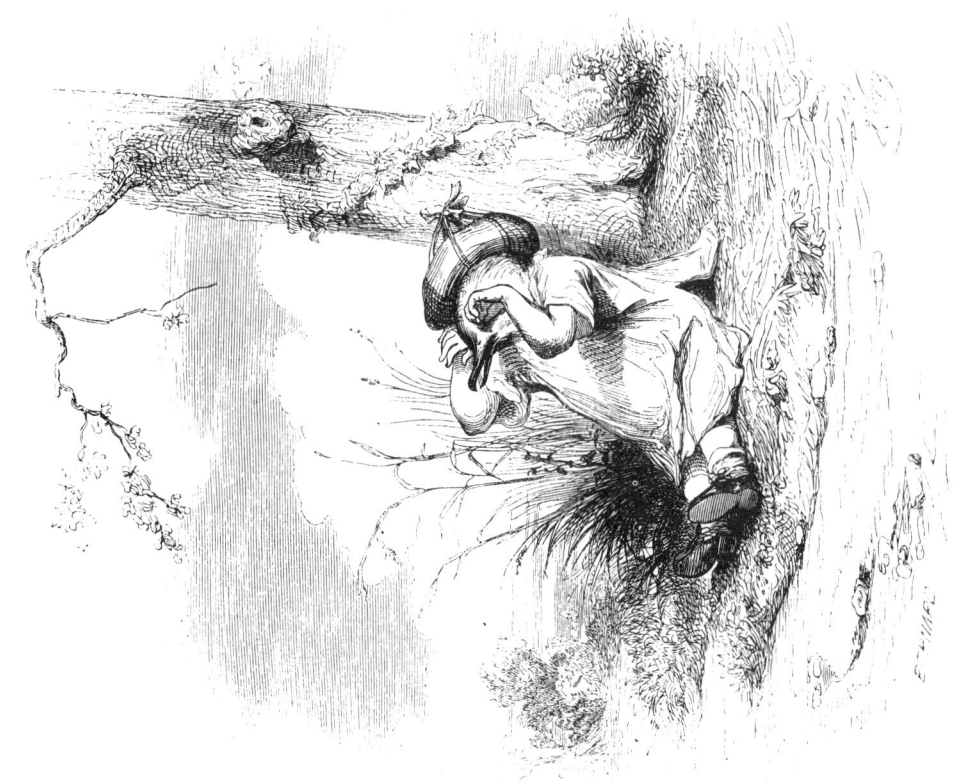

238. The turtledove loses his parents while still very young.

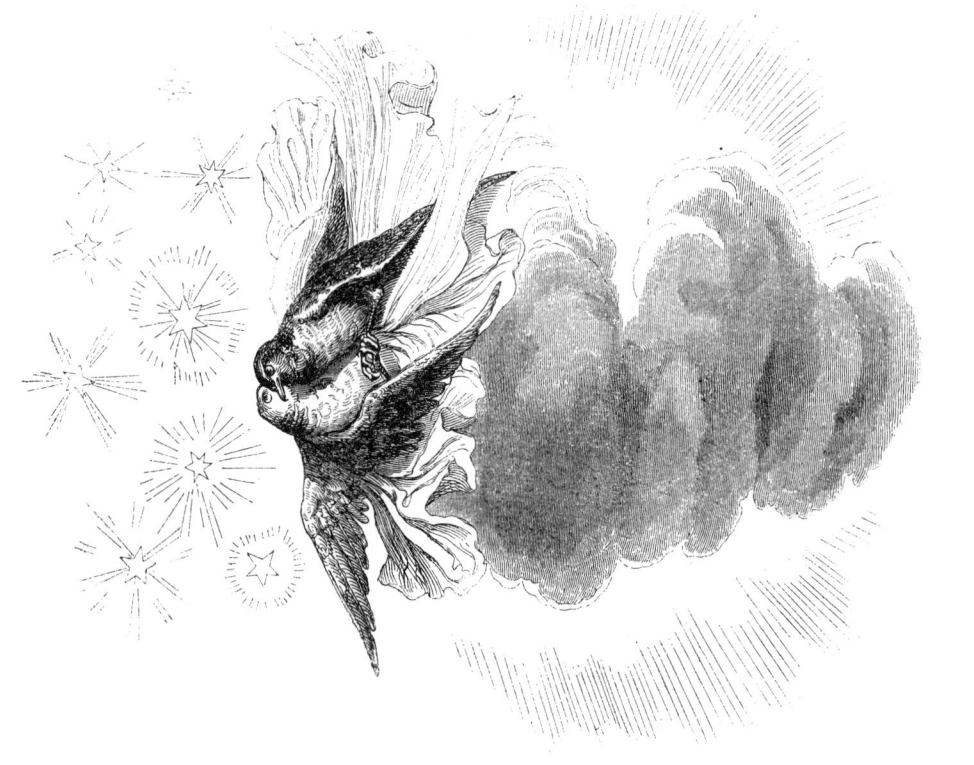

241. Vision of the lovers' souls reunited in the seventh heaven.

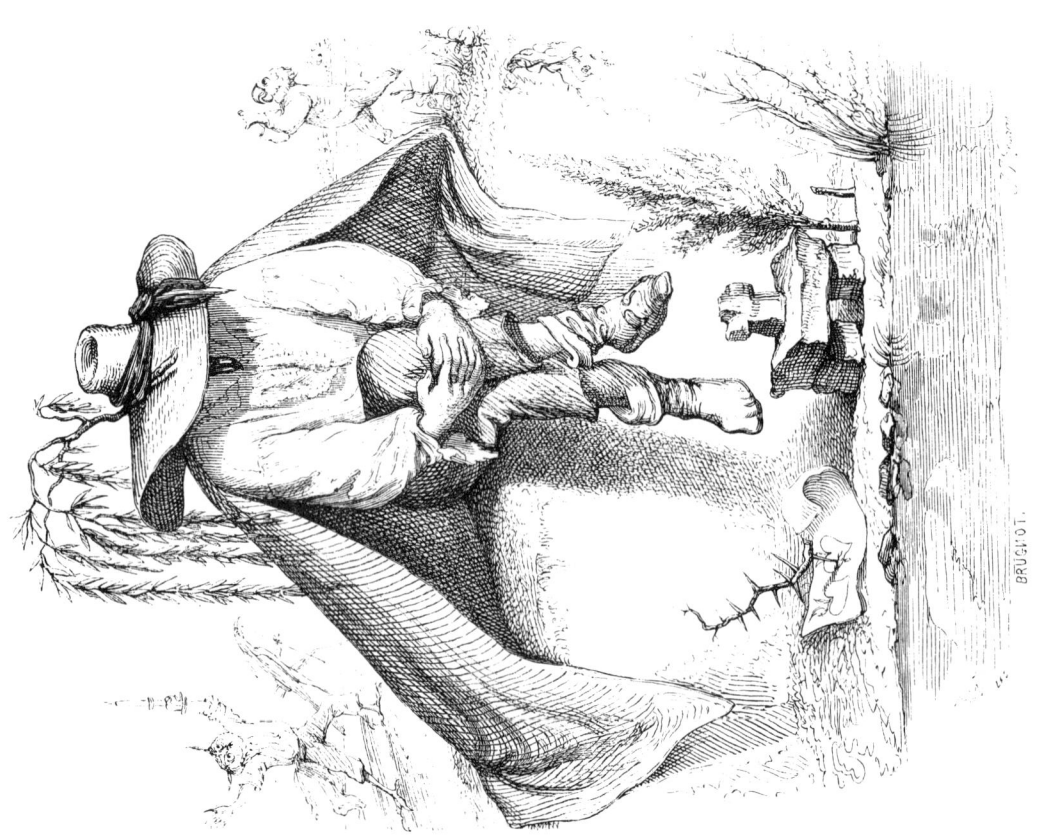

240. The turtledove becomes a solitary dreamer.

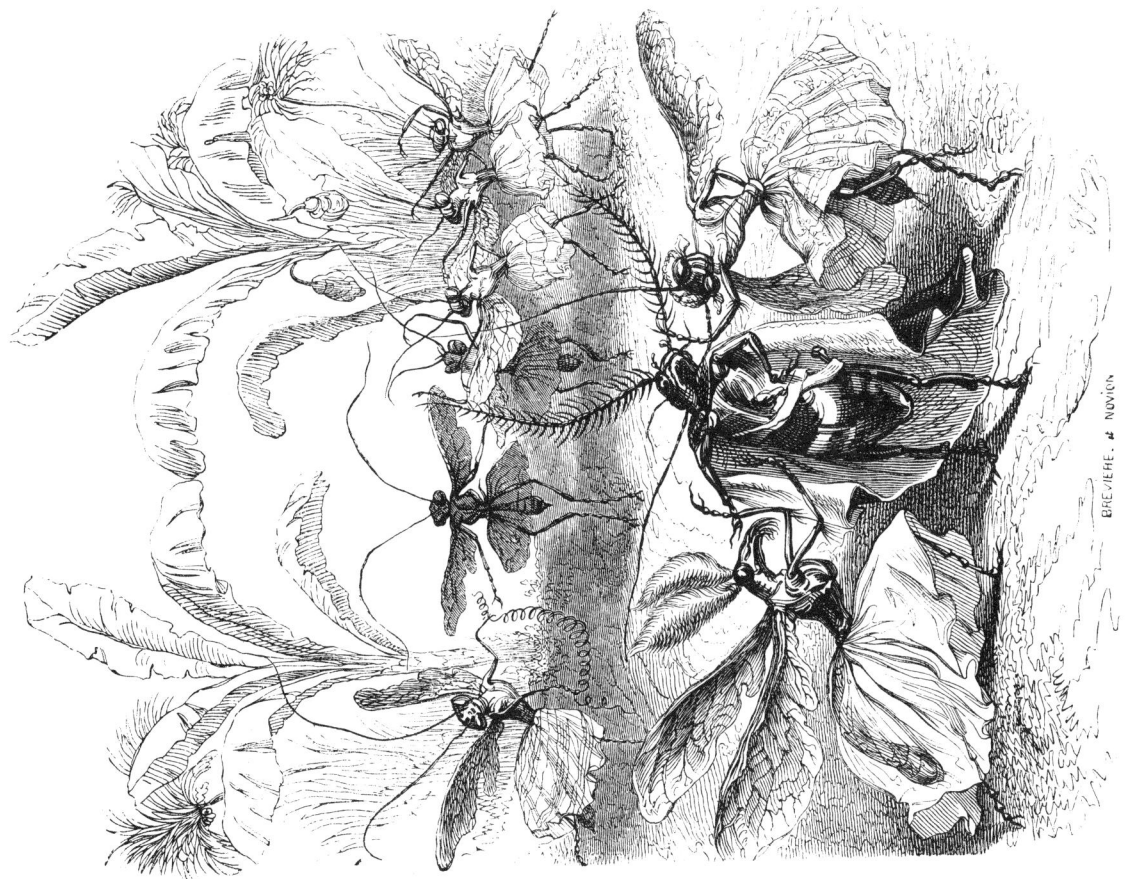

243. The male cochineal insect rejecting the advances of imperfect mates.

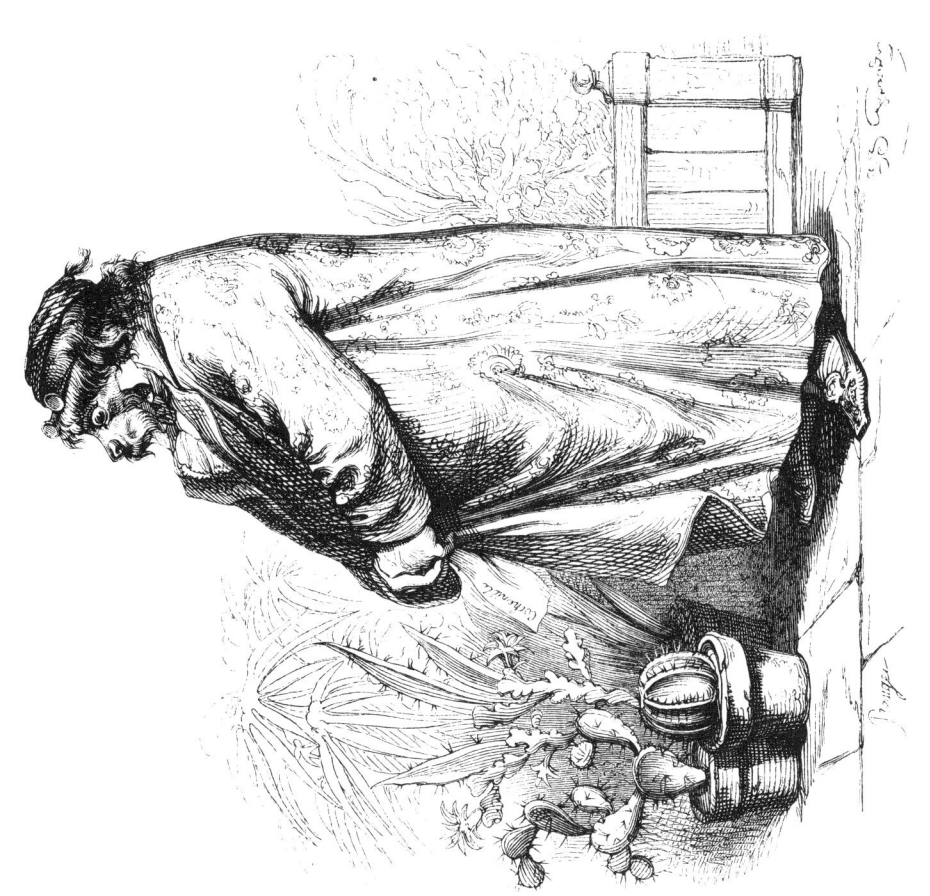

242. The professor with a paper container of scale insects which he will place on a cactus (they will colonize it as parasites).

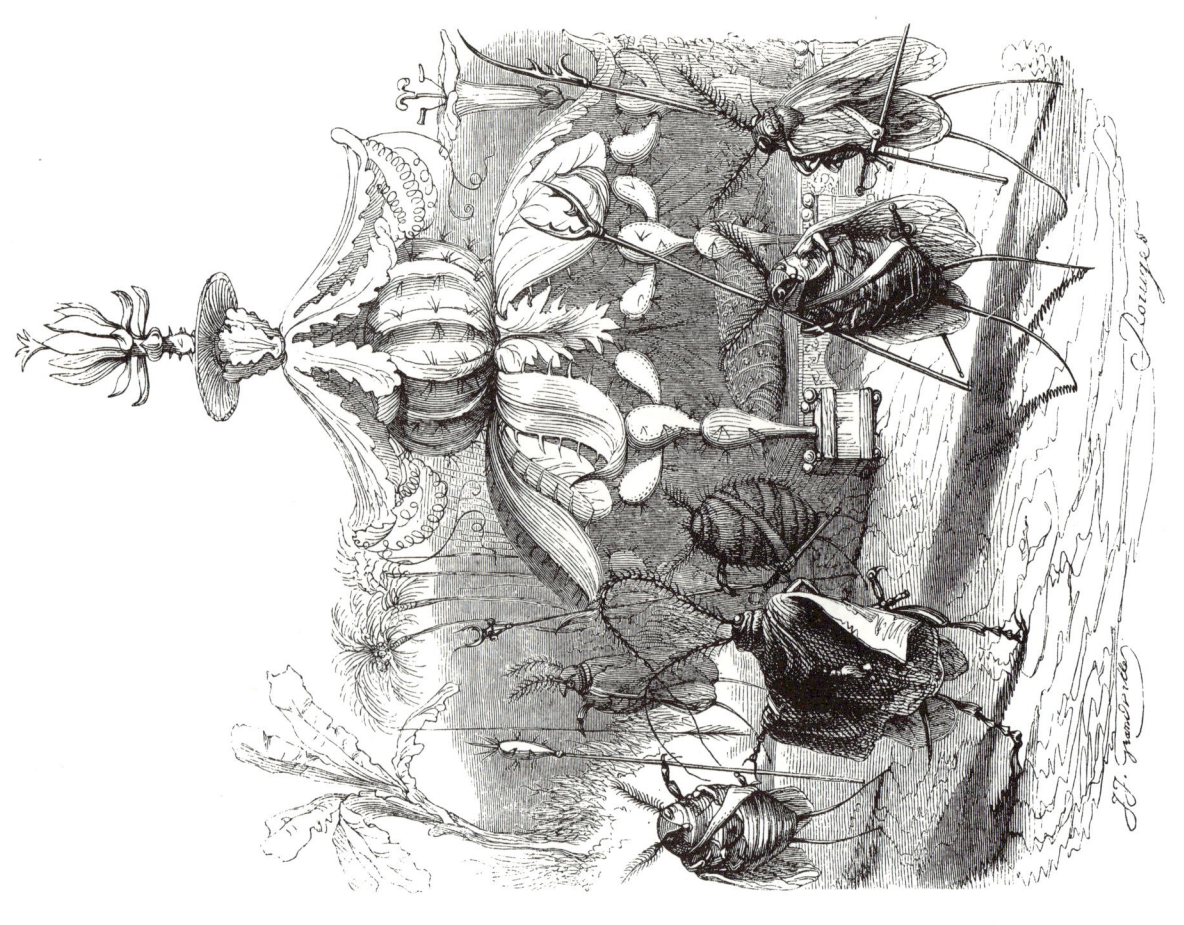

245. Guards encircle the ideal mate, who is still in the larval stage.

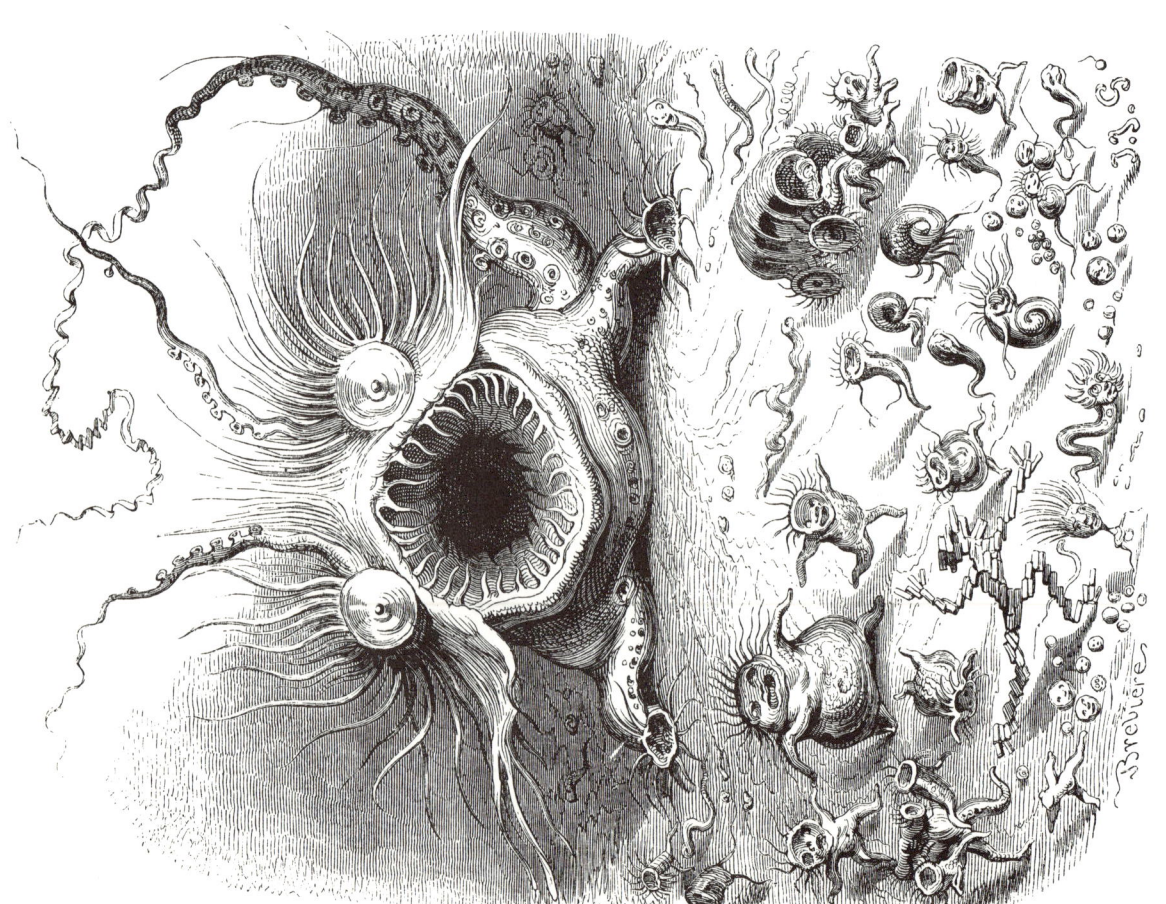

244. A volvox epidemic strikes the near-microscopic world of the scale insects.

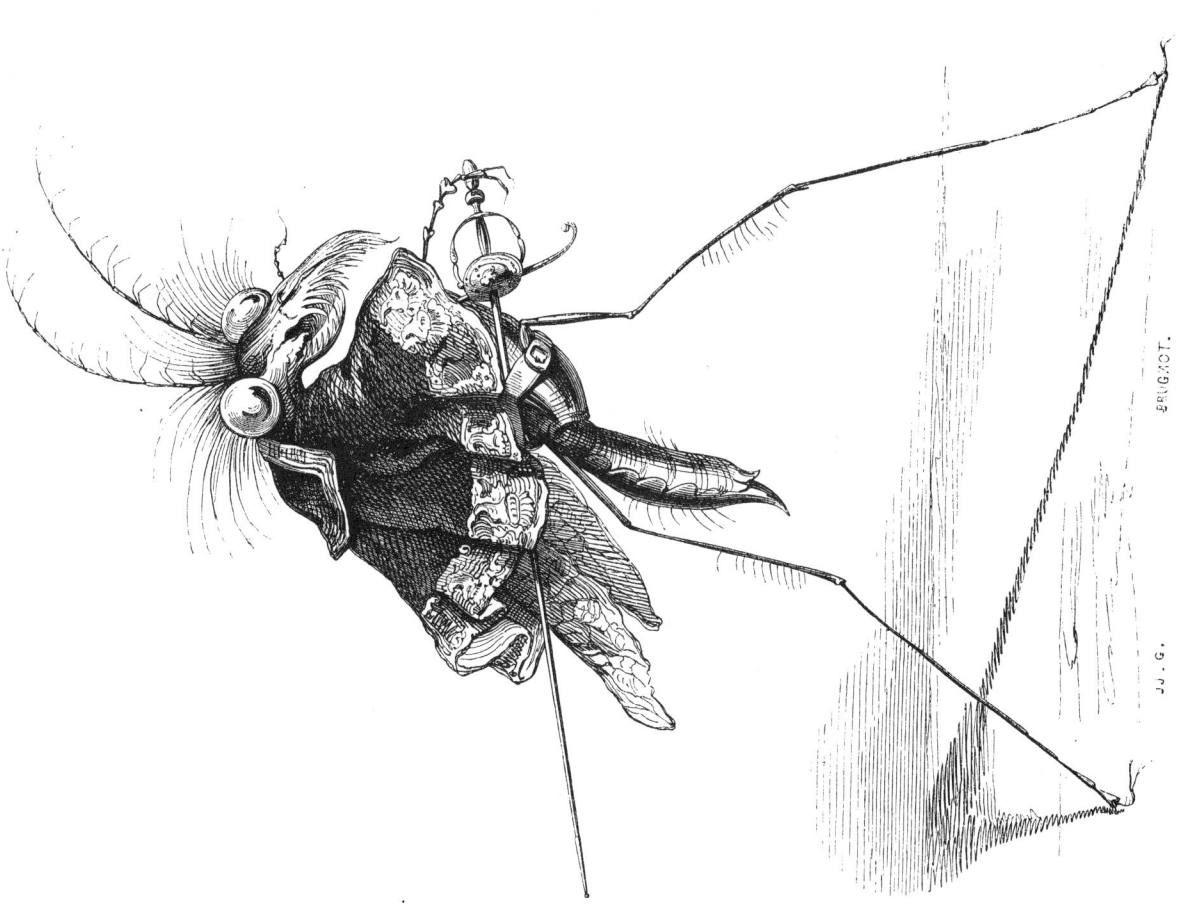

247. The courtship of the scale insects.

246. A strange insect called the "misocamp," fond of eating scale insects.

Les Animaux 155

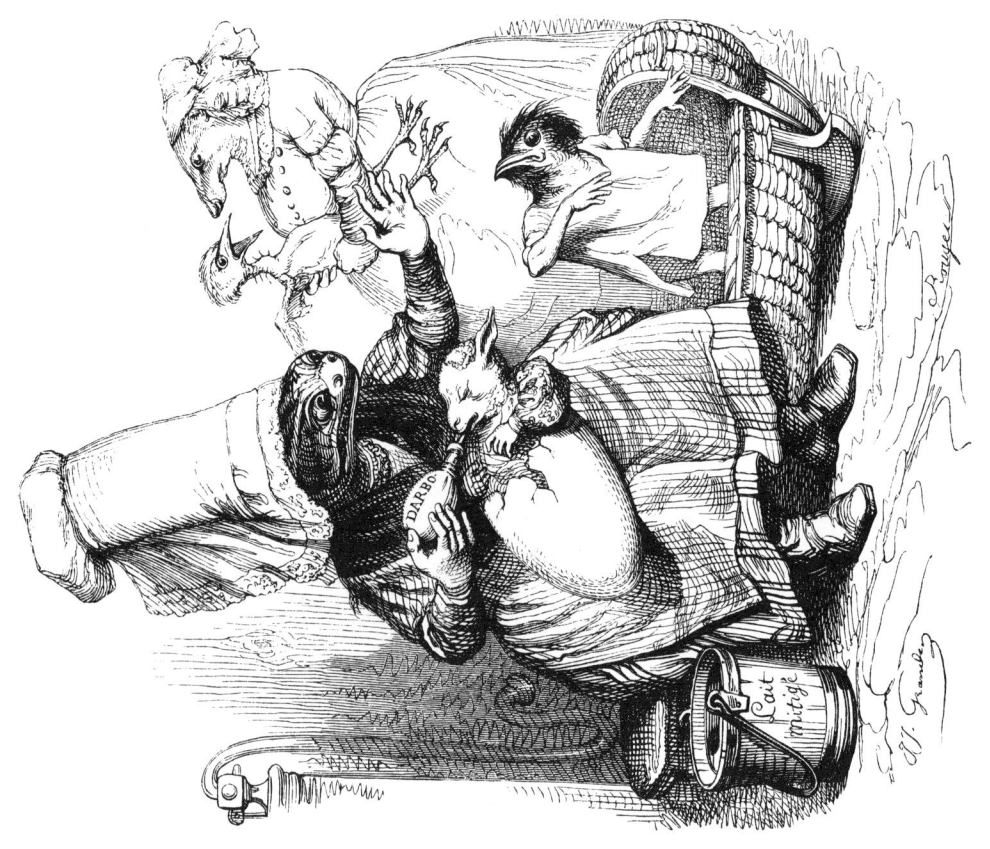

249. On Happy Island, all children are reared communally—by serpents and other dangerous animals.

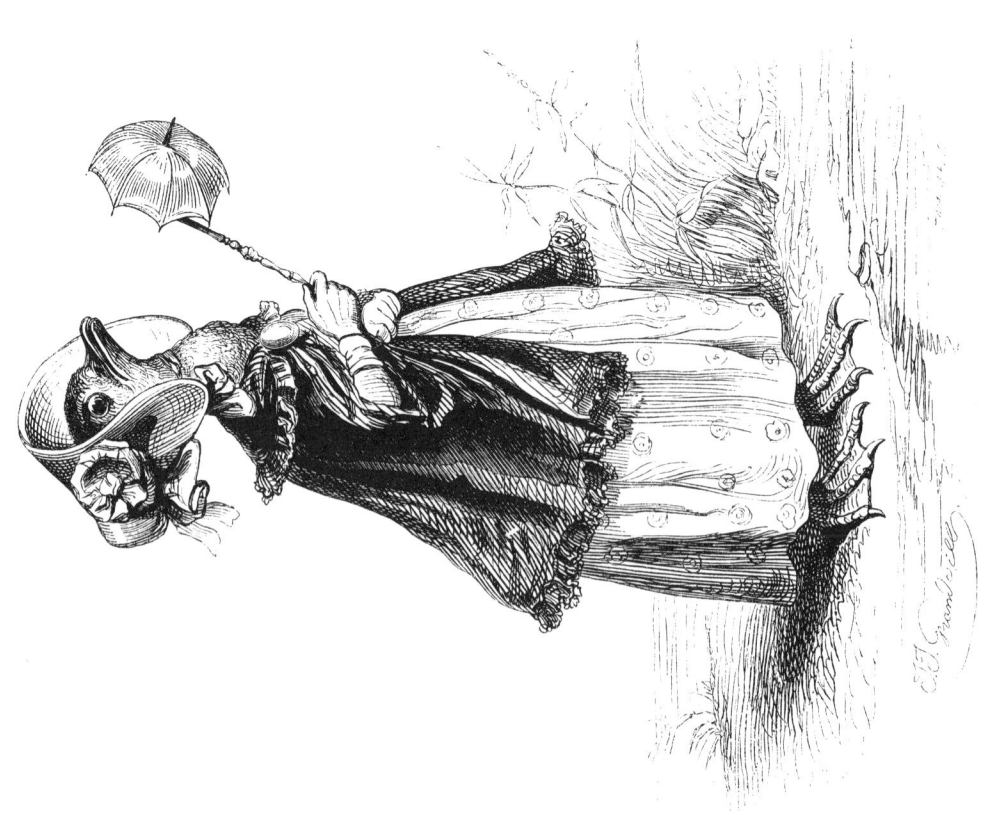

248. The ugly and silly heiress whom the young man marries.

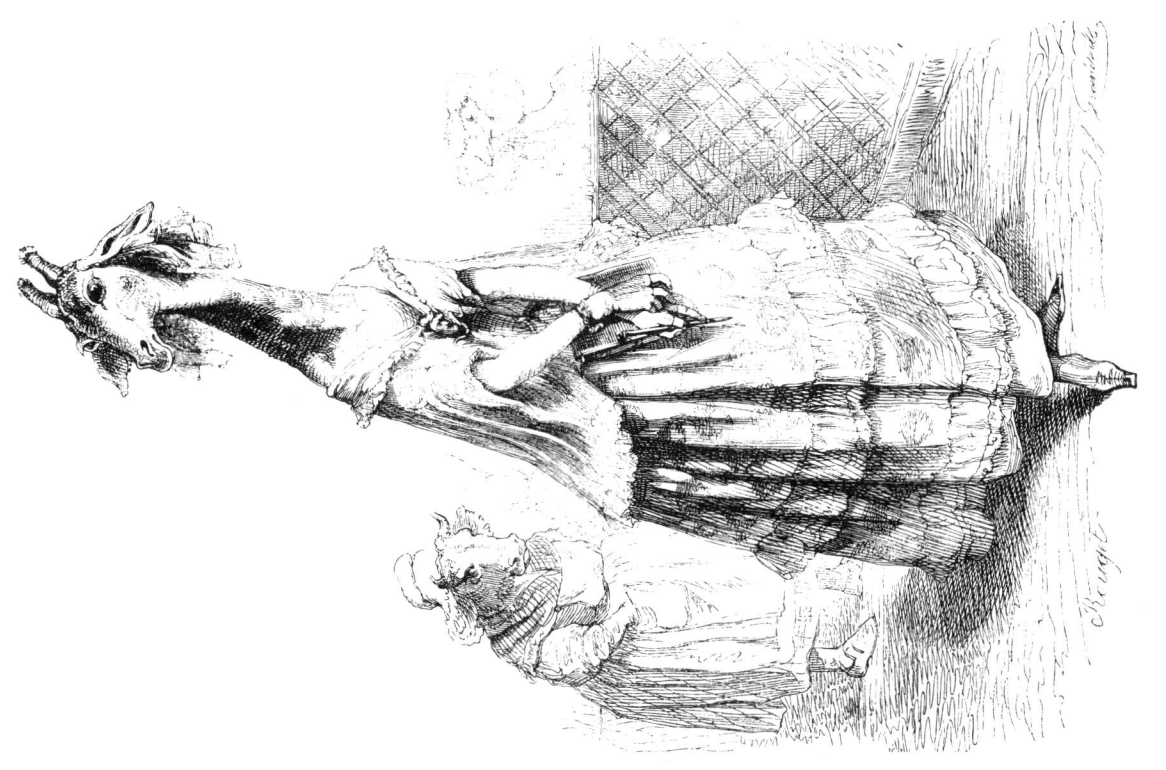

251. The giraffe of the Jardin des Plantes.

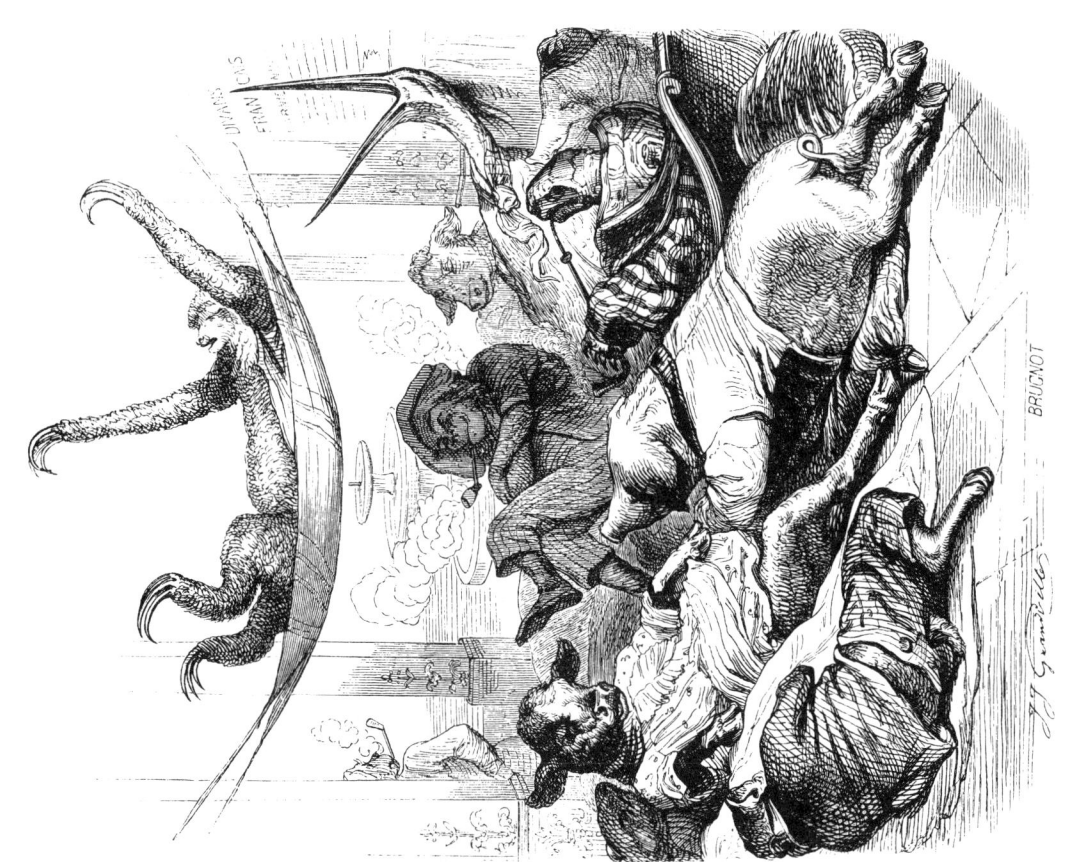

250. A study hall on Happy Island.

Les Animaux 157

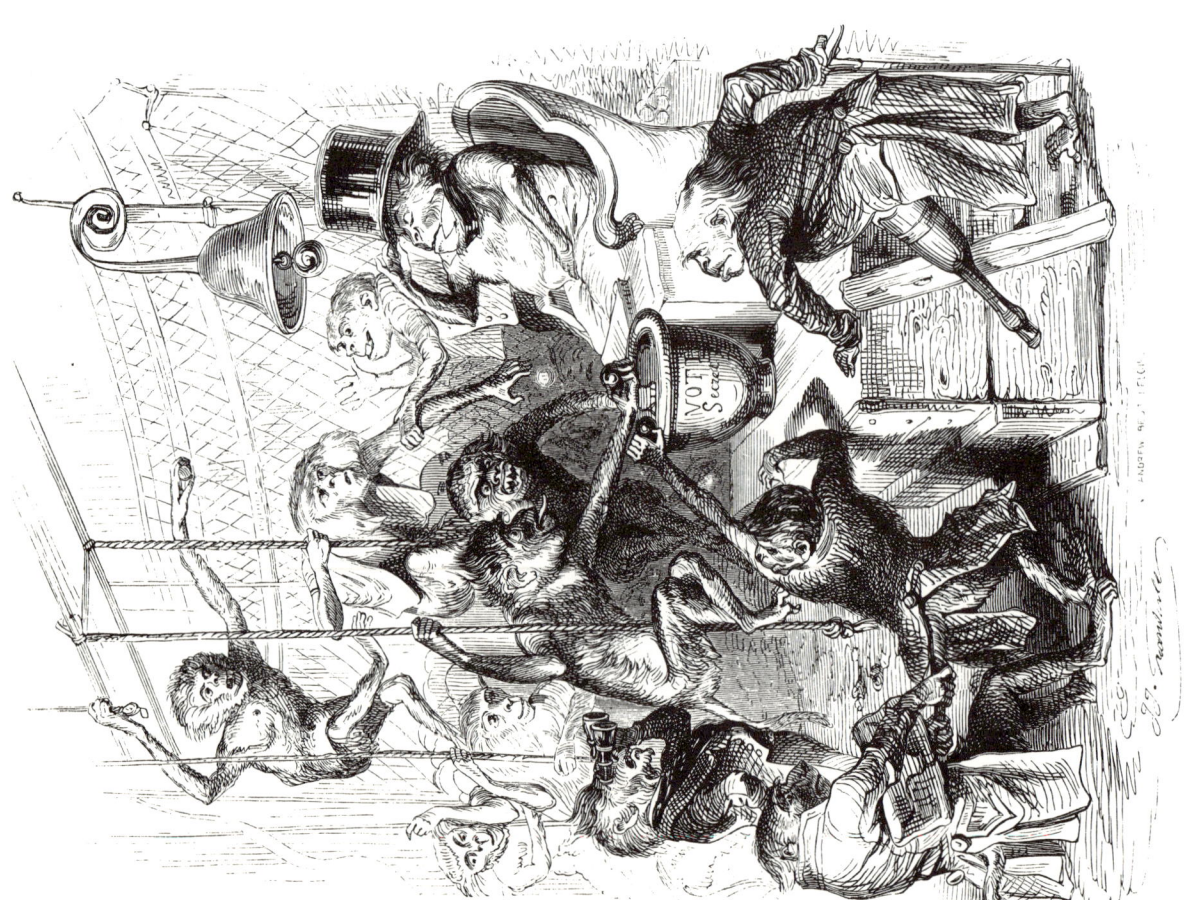

253. Two modern lovers in the zoo.

252. In her letter, the giraffe mistakes the monkey house in the zoo for the Chamber of Deputies in session.

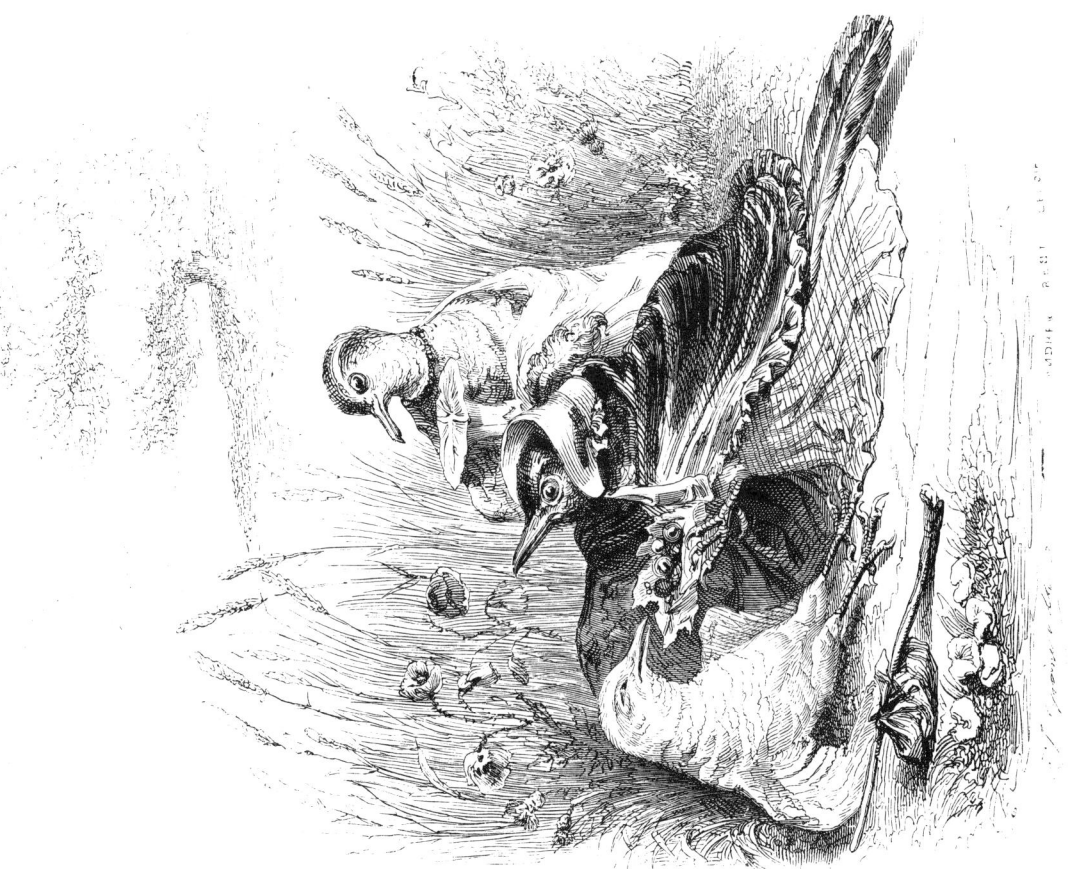

255. The magpie and the dove come to the aid of the exhausted white blackbird.

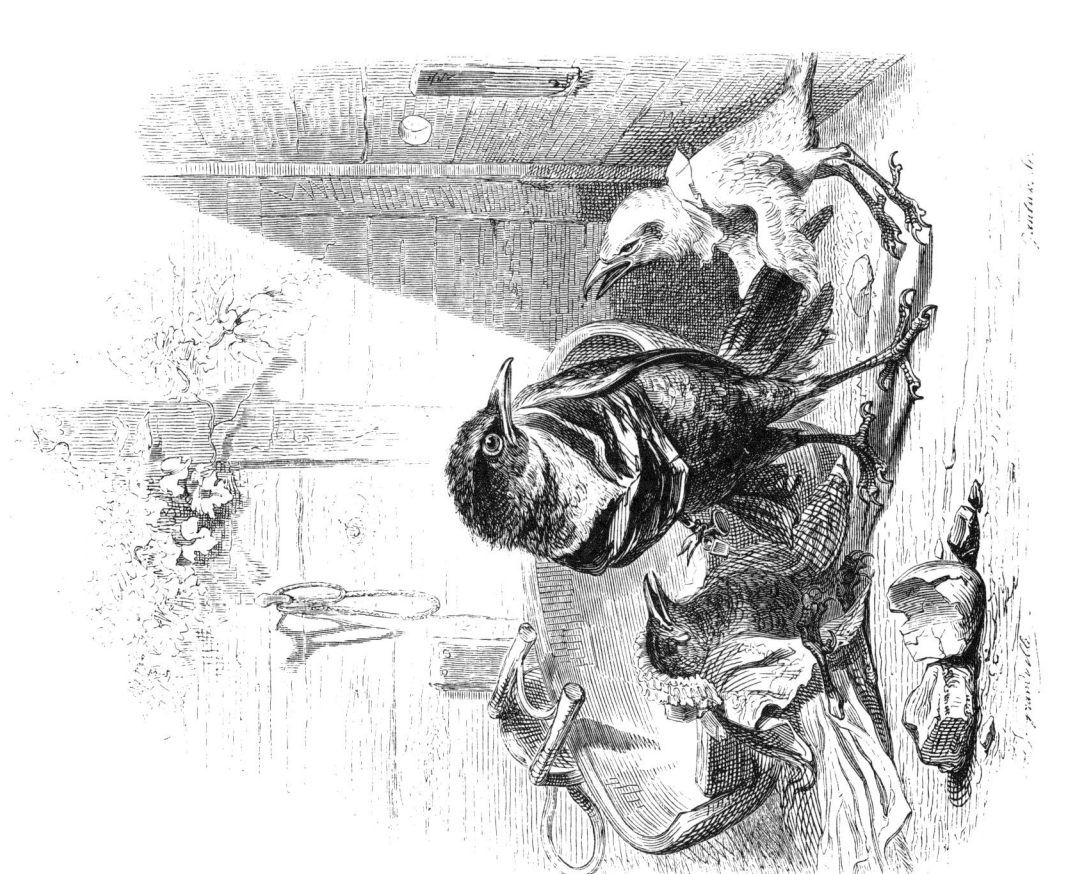

254. As his mother weeps, the young white blackbird is disowned by his father.

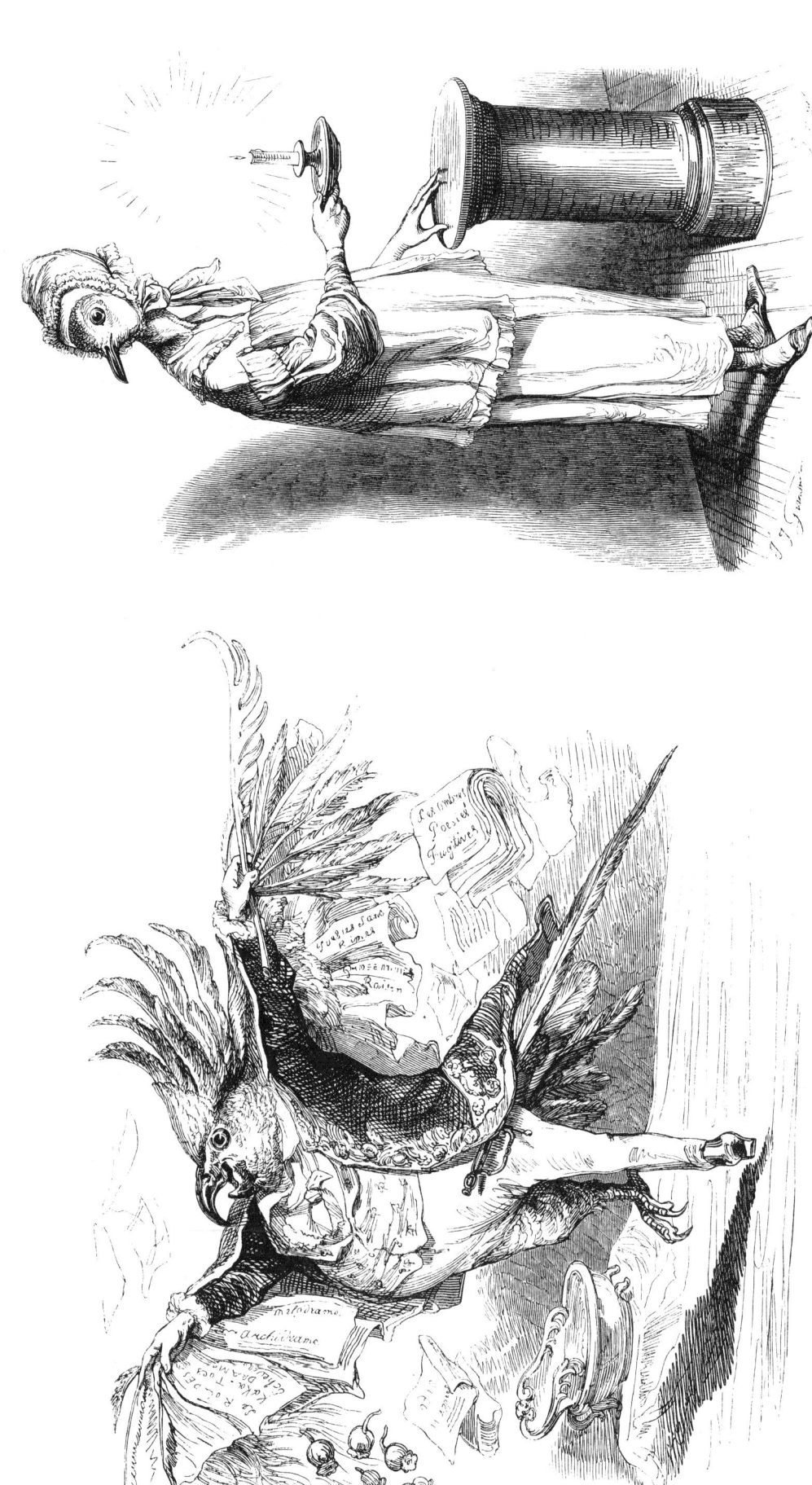

257. An unfriendly old dove, one of the birds encountered in the woods by the white blackbird.

256. The cockatoo-poet.

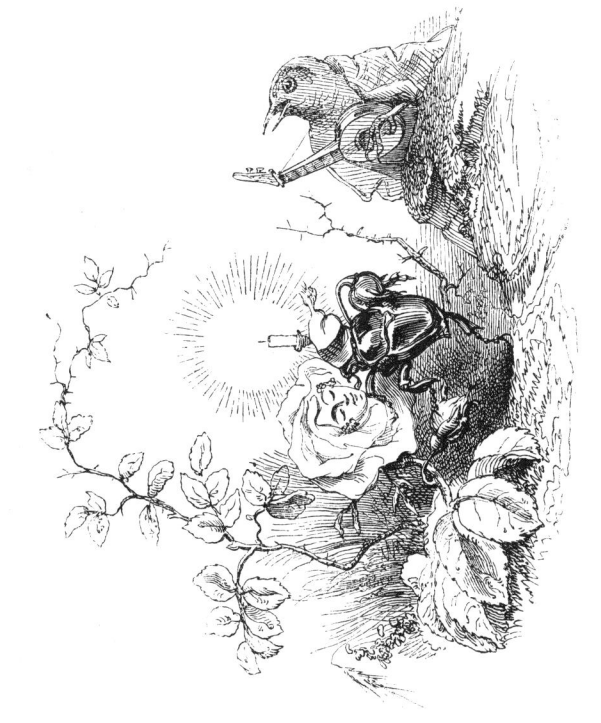

259. The nightingale and the rose.

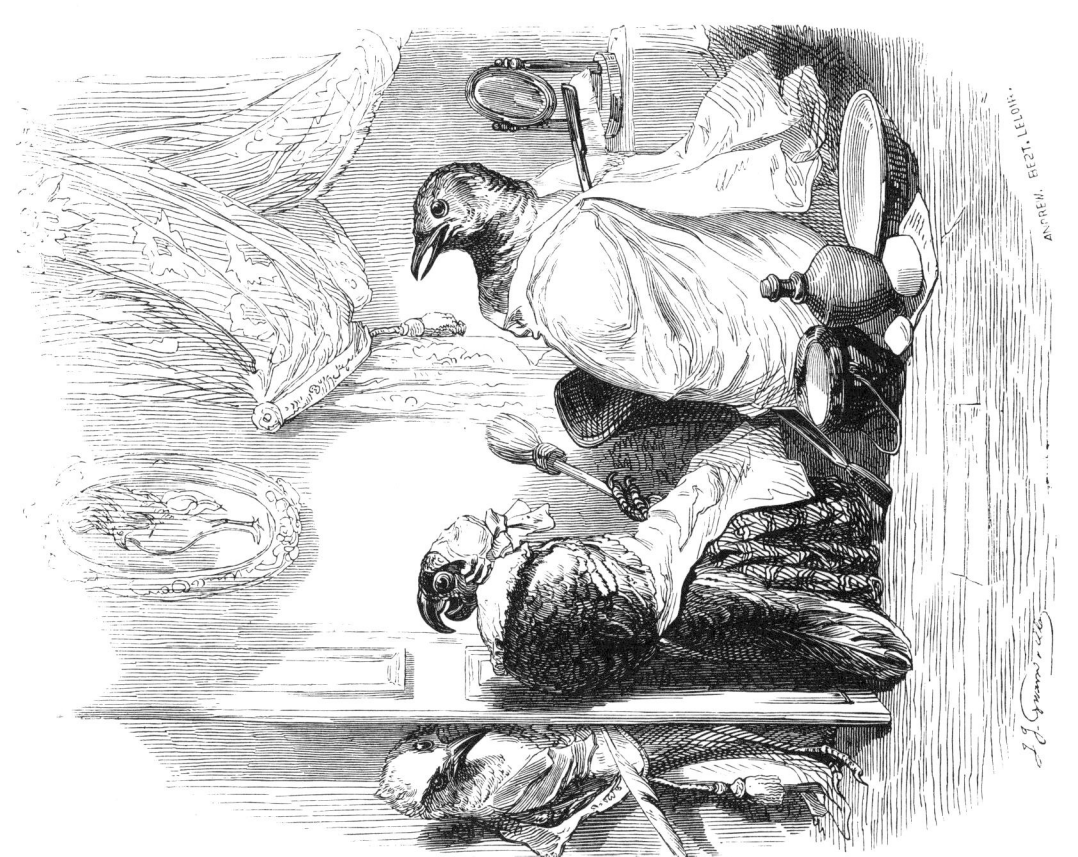

258. The blackbird discovers his wife's cosmetic secrets.

Les Animaux 161

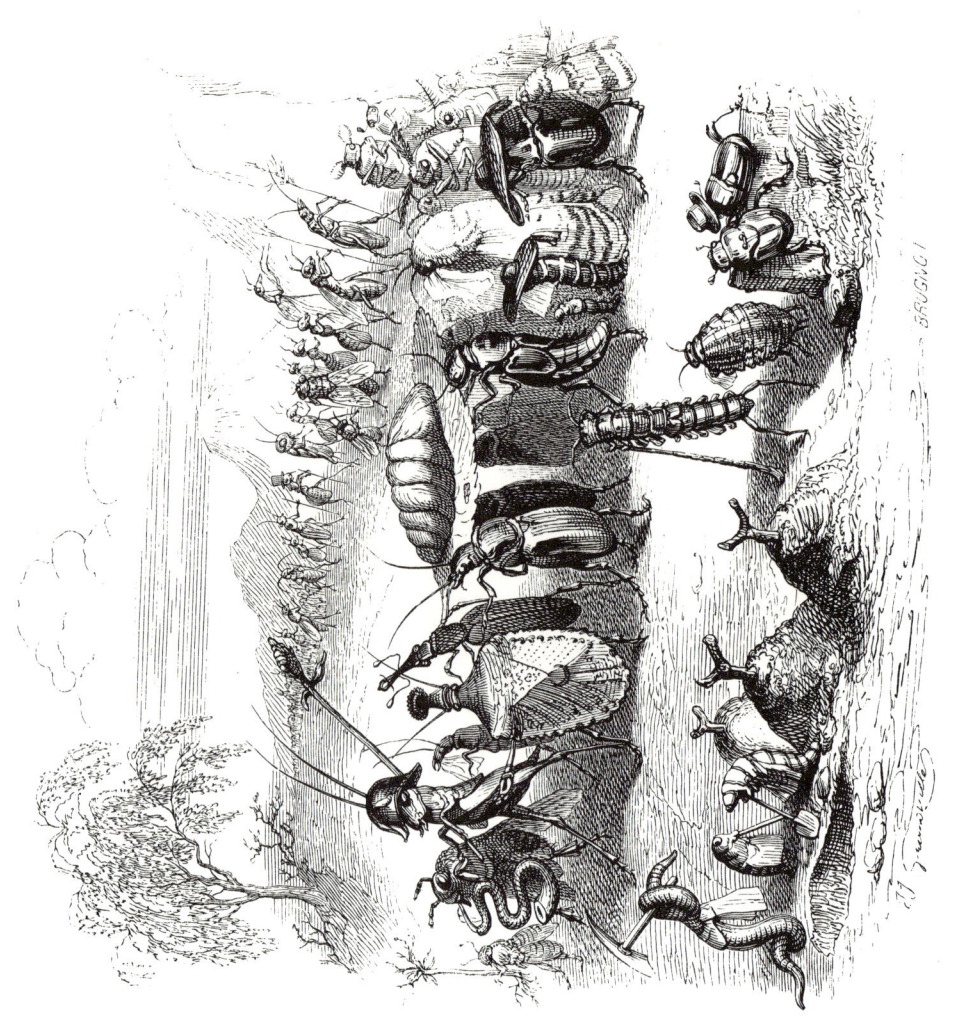

261. The silkworm's funeral procession.

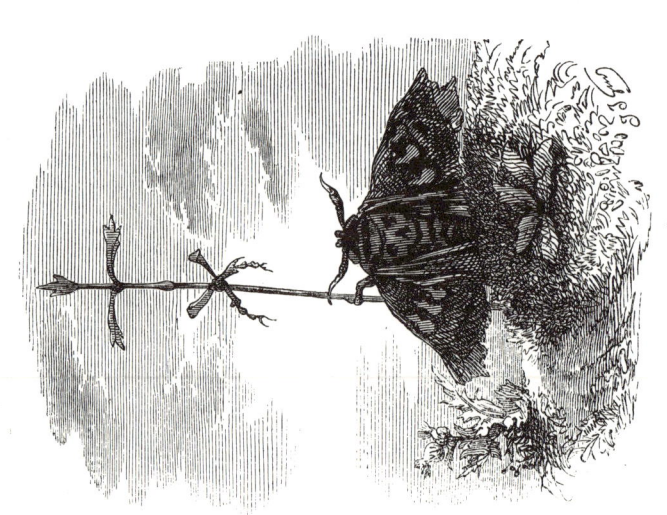

260. The death's-head moth gives the signal for the procession to begin.

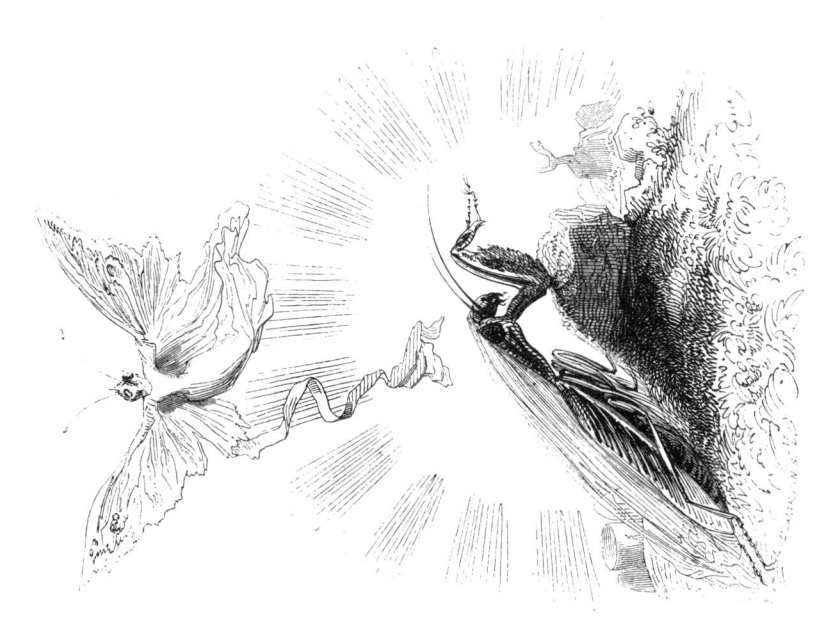

263. The praying mantis tells the insects: "To die is to be reborn into a better life."

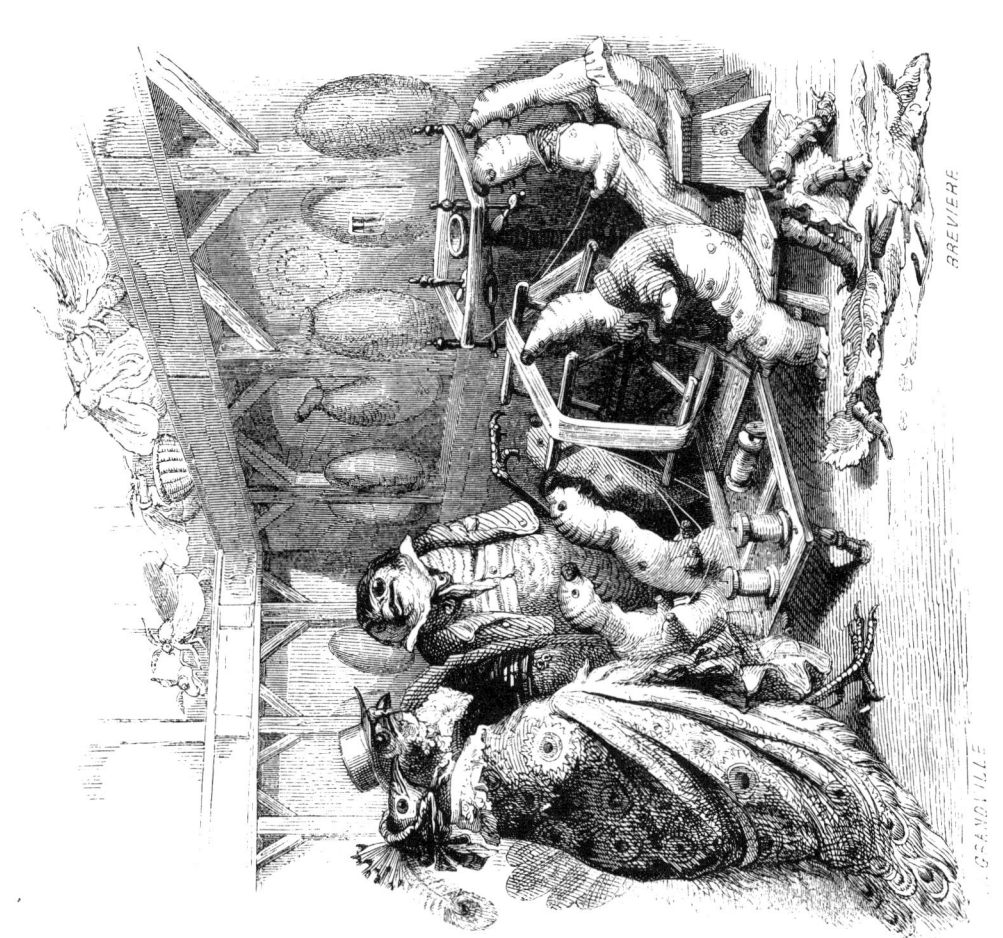

262. A silk mill.

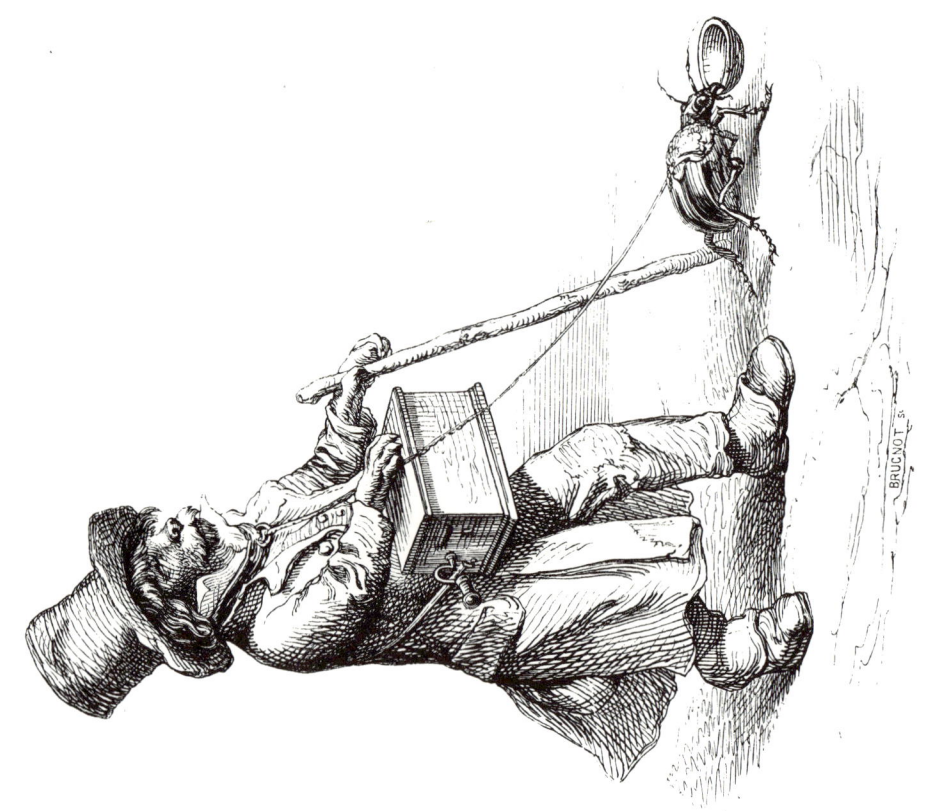

265. Another latecomer.

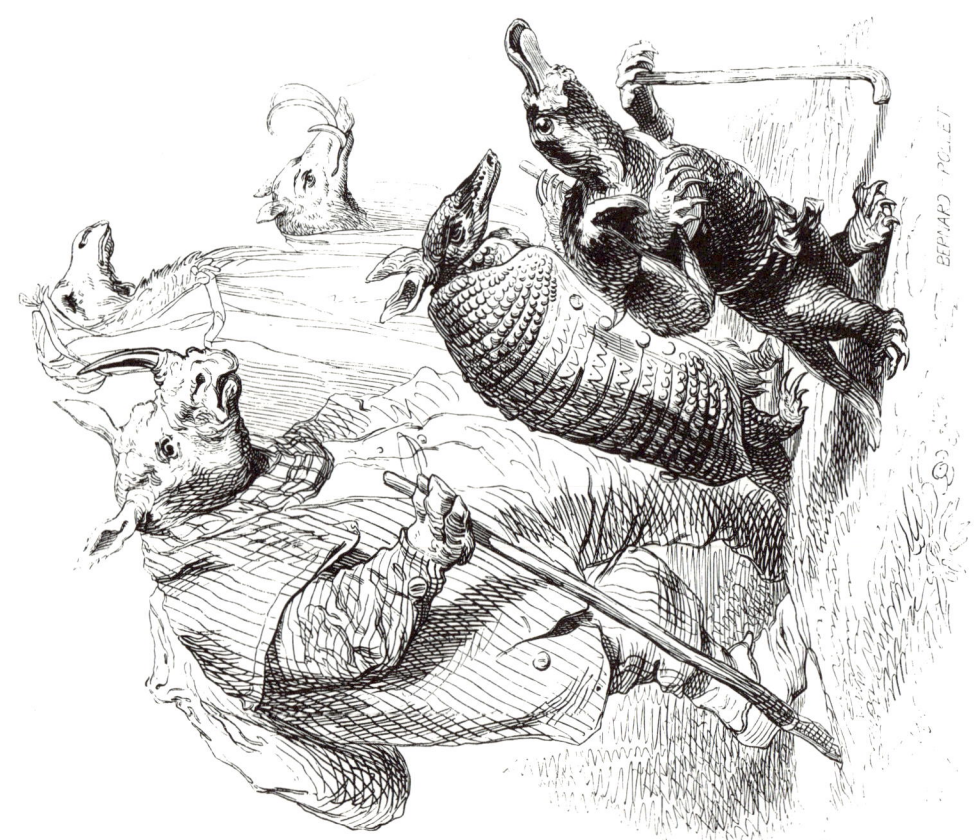

264. Animals from distant countries arriving too late to join in the rebellion.

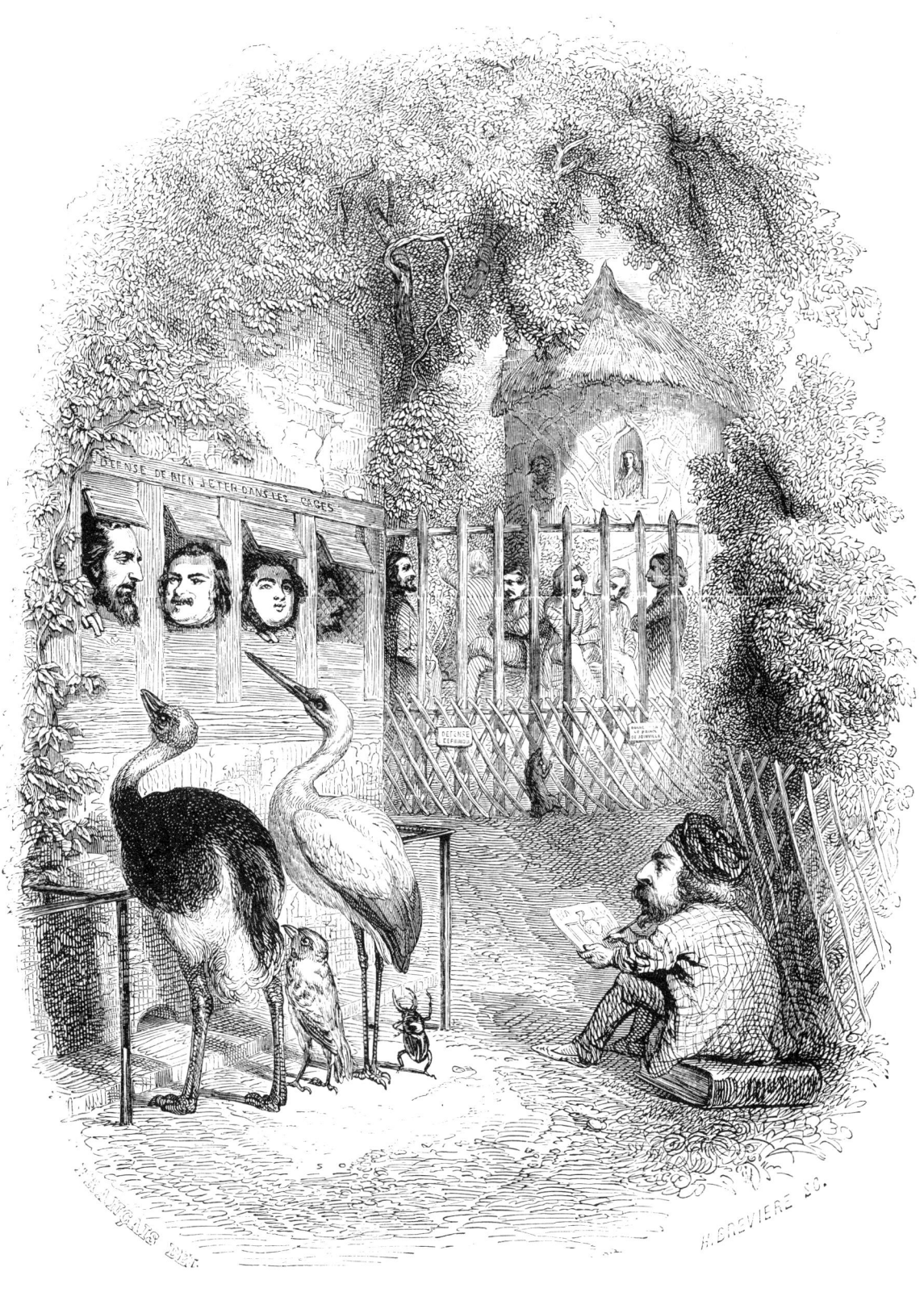

266. [Drawing by Français.] Grandville sketching Hetzel, Balzac and Janin, who are locked up in the zoo, along with other contributing writers.